Slow Journalism

Slow Journalism has emerged in recent years to enact a critique of the limitations and dangers of the speed of much mainstream contemporary journalistic practice. There have been types of journalism produced and consumed slowly for centuries, of course. What is new is the context of the hyper-acceleration and overproduction of journalism, where quality has suffered, ethics have been compromised and user attention has eroded. Many have been asking if there is another way to practice journalism. The emergence of Slow Journalism suggests that there is.

Many international scholars and practitioners have been thinking critically about the problems wrought by speed and are utilising the concept of "slow" to describe a new way of thinking about and producing journalism. This edited collection offers theoretical perspectives and case studies on the practice of Slow Journalism around the globe. Slow Journalism is a new practice for new times.

This book was originally published as two special issues, of *Journalism Practice* and *Digital Journalism*.

Megan Le Masurier is a Senior Lecturer in the Department of Media and Communications at the University of Sydney, Australia.

Journalism Studies: Theory and Practice
Series editor: Bob Franklin, Cardiff School of Journalism, Media and Cultural Studies, Cardiff University, UK

The journal *Journalism Studies* was established at the turn of the new millennium by Bob Franklin. It was launched in the context of a burgeoning interest in the scholarly study of journalism and an expansive global community of journalism scholars and researchers. The ambition was to provide a forum for the critical discussion and study of journalism as a subject of intellectual inquiry but also an arena of professional practice. Previously, the study of journalism in the UK and much of Europe was a fairly marginal branch of the larger disciplines of media, communication and cultural studies; only a handful of Universities offered degree programmes in the subject. *Journalism Studies* has flourished and succeeded in providing the intended public space for discussion of research on key issues within the field, to the point where in 2007 a sister journal, *Journalism Practice*, was launched to enable an enhanced focus on practice-based issues, as well as foregrounding studies of journalism education, training and professional concerns. Both journals are among the leading ranked journals within the field and publish six issues annually, in electronic and print formats. More recently, 2013 witnessed the launch of a further companion journal *Digital Journalism* to provide a site for scholarly discussion, analysis and responses to the wide ranging implications of digital technologies for the practice and study of journalism. From the outset, the publication of themed issues has been a commitment for all journals. Their purpose is first, to focus on highly significant or neglected areas of the field; second, to facilitate discussion and analysis of important and topical policy issues; and third, to offer readers an especially high quality and closely focused set of essays, analyses and discussions.

The *Journalism Studies: Theory and Practice* book series draws on a wide range of these themed issues from all journals and thereby extends the critical and public forum provided by them. The Editor of the journals works closely with guest editors to ensure that the books achieve relevance for readers and the highest standards of research rigour and academic excellence. The series makes a significant contribution to the field of journalism studies by inviting distinguished scholars, academics and journalism practitioners to discuss and debate the central concerns within the field. It also reaches a wider readership of scholars, students and practitioners across the social sciences, humanities and communication arts, encouraging them to engage critically with, but also to interrogate, the specialist scholarly studies of journalism which this series provides.

Recent titles in the series:

Slow Journalism
Edited by Megan Le Masurier

Writing the First World War after 1918
Edited by Adrian Bingham

The Future of Journalism
Risks, Threats and Opportunities
Edited by Stuart Allan, Cynthia Carter, Stephen Cushion, Lina Dencik, Iñaki Garcia-Blanco, Janet Harris, Richard Sambrook, Karin Wahl-Jorgensen and Andy Williams

For more information about this series, please visit: https://www.routledge.com/Journalism-Studies/book-series/JOURNALISM

Slow Journalism

Edited by
Megan Le Masurier

Routledge
Taylor & Francis Group

LONDON AND NEW YORK

First published 2019
by Routledge
2 Park Square, Milton Park, Abingdon, Oxon, OX14 4RN, UK

and by Routledge
52 Vanderbilt Avenue, New York, NY 10017

First issued in paperback 2020

Routledge is an imprint of the Taylor & Francis Group, an informa business

© 2019 Taylor & Francis

British Library Cataloguing-in-Publication Data
A catalogue record for this book is available from the British Library

ISBN 13: 978-0-367-58712-3 (pbk)
ISBN 13: 978-1-138-60217-5 (hbk)

Typeset in Myriad Pro
by codeMantra

Publisher's Note
The publisher accepts responsibility for any inconsistencies that may have arisen during the conversion of this book from journal articles to book chapters, namely the possible inclusion of journal terminology.

Disclaimer
Every effort has been made to contact copyright holders for their permission to reprint material in this book. The publishers would be grateful to hear from any copyright holder who is not here acknowledged and will undertake to rectify any errors or omissions in future editions of this book.

Contents

CONTENTS

Citation Information

The following chapters were originally published in *Journalism Practice*, volume 10, issue 4 (June 2016). When citing this material, please use the original page numbering for each article, as follows:

Chapter 6
Slow journalism in Spain: New magazine startups and the paradigmatic case of Jot Down
Alejandro Barranquero Carretero and Garbiñe Jaurrieta Bariain
Journalism Practice, volume 10, issue 4 (June 2016) pp. 521–538

Chapter 7
Is there a future for slow journalism? The perspective of younger users
Nico Drok and Liesbeth Hermans
Journalism Practice, volume 10, issue 4 (June 2016) pp. 539–554

Chapter 8
Editing, fast and slow
Susan L. Greenberg
Journalism Practice, volume 10, issue 4 (June 2016) pp. 555–567

The following chapters were originally published in *Digital Journalism*, volume 4, issue 4 (June 2016). When citing this material, please use the original page numbering for each article, as follows:

Chapter 9
Networked news time: How slow—or fast—do publics need news to be?
Mike Ananny
Digital Journalism, volume 4, issue 4 (June 2016) pp. 414–431

Chapter 10
Multimedia, slow journalism as process, and the possibility of proper time
Benjamin Ball
Digital Journalism, volume 4, issue 4 (June 2016) pp. 432–444

Chapter 11
The Sochi Project: Slow journalism within the transmedia space
Renira Rampazzo Gambarato
Digital Journalism, volume 4, issue 4 (June 2016) pp. 445–461

Chapter 12
Slowing down media coverage on the US–Mexico Border: News as sociological critique in Borderland
Stuart Davis
Digital Journalism, volume 4, issue 4 (June 2016) pp. 462–477

Chapter 13
Resiliency in Recovery: Slow journalism as public accountability in post-Katrina New Orleans
Jan Lauren Boyles
Digital Journalism, volume 4, issue 4 (June 2016) pp. 478–493

Chapter 14
Time to engage: De Correspondent's *redefinition of journalistic quality*
Frank Harbers
Digital Journalism, volume 4, issue 4 (June 2016) pp. 494–511

Chapter 15
"Make every frame count": The practice of slow photojournalism and the work of David Burnett
Andrew L. Mendelson and Brian Creech
Digital Journalism, volume 4, issue 4 (June 2016) pp. 512–529

Chapter 16
The business of slow journalism: Deep storytelling's alternative economies
David Dowling
Digital Journalism, volume 4, issue 4 (June 2016) pp. 530–546

Chapter 17
Slow journalism and the Out of Eden Walk
Don Belt and Jeff South
Digital Journalism, volume 4, issue 4 (June 2016) pp. 547–562

For any permission-related enquiries please visit:
http://www.tandfonline.com/page/help/permissions

Notes on Contributors

Mike Ananny is an Assistant Professor in the Annenberg School of Communication at the University of Southern California, Los Angeles, USA.

Benjamin Ball is a Lecturer in Law at the University of Wollongong, Australia.

Alejandro Barranquero Carretero is an Assistant Professor in the Department of Journalism and Audiovisual Communication at Universidad Carlos III de Madrid, Spain.

Don Belt is an Adjunct Professor of Journalism at the University of Richmond, USA.

Jan Lauren Boyles is an Assistant Professor of Journalism/Big Data at Iowa State University, Ames, USA.

Geoffrey Craig is a Professor and Head of Research in the School of Communication Studies at Auckland University of Technology, New Zealand.

Brian Creech is an Assistant Professor of Journalism in the School of Media and Communication at Temple University, Philadelphia, USA.

Stuart Davis is based in the Department of Communication Studies at Baruch College, New York, USA.

David Dowling is the Director of Undergraduate Studies in the School of Journalism and Mass Communication at the University of Iowa, Ames, USA.

Nico Drok is a Lecturer in Media and Civil Society at Windesheim University of Applied Sciences, Zwolle, The Netherlands.

Renira Rampazzo Gambarato is a Senior Lecturer in Media and Communication Studies at Jönköping University, Sweden.

Susan L. Greenberg is a Senior Lecturer in the Department of English and Creative Writing at the University of Roehampton, London, UK.

Frank Harbers is an Assistant Professor of Journalism at the University of Groningen, The Netherlands.

Anne Kirstine Hermann is a PhD Fellow in the Centre for Journalism at the University of Southern Denmark, Odense, Denmark.

Liesbeth Hermans is a Lecturer in Constructive Journalism at Windesheim University of Applied Sciences, Zwolle, The Netherlands.

Garbiñe Jaurrieta Bariain was previously based at Utrecht University, The Netherlands.

Megan Le Masurier is a Senior Lecturer in the Department of Media and Communications at the University of Sydney, Australia.

Andrew L. Mendelson is an Associate Dean in the Graduate School of Journalism at the City University of New York, USA.

Erik Neveu is a Professor of Political Science at Sciences Po, Rennes, France.

Matthew Ricketson is a Professor of Journalism at the University of Canberra, Australia.

Jeff South is an Associate Professor of Journalism and Director of Undergraduate Studies in the School of Media and Culture at Virginia Commonwealth University, Richmond, USA.

Helene Maree Thomas is an independent radio documentary producer, based in Tasmania. She previously taught at Macquarie University, Sydney, Australia.

SLOW JOURNALISM
An introduction to a new research paradigm

Megan Le Masurier

When Bob Franklin asked me whether I thought there was potential interest in the topic of slow journalism for a special issue of *Journalism Practice* I was keen to send out a call for papers to see what fish might be in that sea. But I was quietly sceptical that the haul could fill an issue. The response was surprising; a sizeable catch of enough quality abstracts, from scholars in many countries, to fill not just an issue of *Journalism Practice* but an issue of *Digital Journalism* as well. While "Slow Journalism" as a term has only had a sketchy existence over the past 10 years, and more so in media than in scholarship, it appears that the concept has traction. Many scholars and practitioners internationally have been thinking critically about the problems wrought by speed, and are utilising the concept of "slow" to explain a new way of thinking about and producing journalism.

My contribution to the development of the scholarly understanding of slow journalism was an article published in *Journalism Practice* in 2015, "What is Slow Journalism?" The title, a question, was perhaps misleading in suggesting there could be a firm answer. As I wrote, "this journalism does not require a checklist of key characteristics to qualify as Slow. The term, like the Slow movement itself, is more a critical orientation to the effects of speed on the practice of journalism" (Le Masurier 2015, 143). Slow Journalism is not prescriptive, but those practitioners who use the term to describe their work, and those journalists whose work embodies the spirit of the term, are all producing journalism that *enacts a critique* of the limitations and dangers of the speed of much of the mainstream contemporary journalistic environment. This is why the concept of Slow Journalism has emerged now, and seems to carry such appeal, even though there have been types of journalism produced and consumed slowly for centuries. What is new is the context of hyper-acceleration and over-production of journalism, where quality has suffered, ethics are compromised and user attention has eroded. The ethical problems that have surfaced in journalism across the past decade, with greater importance and urgency than ever, provide the context for the emergence of slow journalism as a consciously ethical practice. The need for speed and the capitalist news ethic of beating the competition have left many asking if there is another way to practise journalism. The emergence of Slow Journalism suggests that there is. Also new are the self-reflexivity of journalists and the emergence of new media outlets that are embracing slow, and experimenting with new business models to fund their practice. Slow Journalism is a new term for new times.

In the opening article of *Journalism Practice*, Erik Neveu (2016) explores the utility of the concept slow journalism "to work as a shorthand description of the variety of changes and alternatives which are simmering in the field" (*Journalism Practice* 10.4). He discusses the polysemy of the term, and whether its many levels of signification—slow as taking time; as investigative; as less; as longer-form narrative; as fair, transparent, ethical; as serving a community; as participatory; as telling untold stories—might work against its value for empirical use. By deploying Weber's concept of the "ideal type," the function of which is "to question reality, not to describe or summarise it," Neveu suggests that if we avoid trying to pin slow journalism down too closely, or viewing it as a simplistic binary opposition to hyper-modern fast practices, it can indeed be a "remarkably fruitful" concept to make sense of the current changes in journalism practice. He argues for a "softer mapping" of slow journalisms as "explanatory, non-fiction and mobilised." Journalism is a plural noun and the practices of slow journalism reflect this.

In his essay "Reclaiming Slowness in Journalism: Critique, Complexity and Difference," Geoffrey Craig (2015; *Journalism Practice* 10.4) builds on his seminal work on slow living (Parkins and Craig 2006), taking some of these insights to journalism. He argues that we need both fast and slow journalism, of course, but that a slower practice can reinforce key functions of journalism that are under challenge: the need for journalists to critique the society they report; to synthesise and thoroughly explain the informational complexities of contemporary life; and report knowledgeably about difference in an increasingly pluralist society. Craig writes:

> Fast forms of journalism must rely to a greater degree on the mobilization of political, social and cultural assumptions in reportage but this becomes increasingly problematic when so many expressions of identity and lifestyle challenge more traditional ways of life and understandings of community.

To respond thoughtfully to these social and cultural changes, journalists require time to explore other perspectives, to listen and to embrace an ethic of care.

In a hyper-mediated world, the politics of listening has become a subject for scholarly attention (see Couldry 2006; O'Donnell, Lloyd, and Dreher 2009). The synergies of this body of work with slow journalism are potentially strong. In her contribution, "Lessening the Construction of Otherness: A Slow Ethics of Journalism," radio journalist and scholar Helene Thomas (2016) is concerned with listening and how a slow approach to interviewing in a local Rwandan context leads to a quite different result for the journalist, one that tries to consciously avoid othering (*Journalism Practice* 10.4). The focus of her practice was to tell the story of the serial killing of 18 Rwandan women sex workers in 2012 and two murders in 2013, which resulted in a radio documentary *A Silent Tragedy*. Giving the "true storytellers" the time and space to tell the story on their own terms, and learning from them, Thomas developed a "slow ethics" of interviewing which offers a challenge to the traditional interview techniques of Western journalists, where time limits, control, interjection, direction and often an adversarial approach tend to dominate. The core principles involve reciprocity, responsibility, respectfulness, patience and hospitality, which, Thomas argues, "leads to ethical encounters with far-away Others and an ethical media process."

Mike Ananny (2016), in his essay "Networked News Time: How Slow—or Fast—Do Publics Need News to Be?," explores the concept of "the public right to hear" through an analysis of the temporal elements of the networked press, which he terms a "temporal assemblage" (*Digital Journalism* 4.4). In the context of contemporary news time, the challenge is to connect accounts of how press assemblages create journalistic rhythms with theories of what publics need from networked news time. He writes:

> If networked news rhythms are set by labor, platforms, algorithms, and laws, then forces with the power to do so might configure their relationships in ways that realize the time required for a public right to hear—pauses to reflect, hesitate, and doubt *and* make timely interventions into the inextricable consequences of shared social life.

Ananny adds a temporal dimension to Roger Silverstone's argument that the media can create "proper distance" (configurations of space and meaning that are "distinctive, correct, and ethically or socially appropriate;" Silverstone 2003, 473) with the idea of "proper time." Benjamin Ball (2016), in his contribution "Multimedia, Slow Journalism as Process and the Possibility of Proper Time," also builds on Silverstone (*Digital Journalism* 4.4). "Proper time" for Ball refers not to "perfect duration, pace, tempo or length, but— instead—it is about reflexive consideration, on the part of journalists, for how understanding can be achieved in, and through, journalism." Slow journalism describes the "moral tenor of the communicative process" rather than its duration, tempo or formal characteristics. While communication may be increasingly faster and easier, Ball argues "understanding one another in media is a task that requires time."

Slow journalism has actually been a term that anthropologists have used to describe their ethnographic work based on long-term immersion in communities. Anne Hermann (2015) uses this as a take-off point to elaborate a theory of slow ethnographic journalism, where time operates in a number of registers (*Journalism Practice* 10.4). Based on interviews with prominent ethnographic journalists such as Ted Conover, William Finnegan and Alex Kotlowitz, Hermann develops a tri-partite model of temporal practice, building on Ulf Hannerz' (2004) work on "writing time." To "regimentation" (where tight deadlines are abandoned in favour of time-consuming research and the writing of longer-form narratives) and "representation" (where slow ethnographic journalists report on the quotidian and non-urgent stories), she adds "reorientation" (a temporal tipping point, where, through the experience of immersion, the journalist abandons preconceptions and develops a situated point of view). In slow journalism, Hermann writes, "'wasting time' can, in fact, produce 'added value' by delivering something radically refined compared to the news products that flood the internet."

Matthew Ricketson (2015), in his essay "When Slow News is Good News," also explores the value of longer-form slow journalism, but here as book-length journalism about historic news events, the atomic bomb in Hiroshima in 1945 and the invasion of Iraq in 2003 (*Journalism Practice* 10.4). He draws on James Carey's (1986) argument that journalism needs to be understood as a corpus, rather than a set of isolated immediate stories. "The obsessive identification of journalism with a thirst to be first with the news has drastically narrowed public understanding of it as a democratic social practice," writes Ricketson. He explores how the immediate news, especially in the context of war, cannot provide the detail, depth and perspective that can turn limited pieces of information into understanding and knowledge.

As the skills required to create journalism across platforms proliferate, and the possibilities for more layered and complex journalism increase in response, the need for co-operation between once hermetically sealed organisations emerges. Teamwork and collaboration is a feature of the slow journalism of *Borderland: Dispatches from the US–Mexico Border*, a multimedia collaboration between National Public Radio's (NPR) *Morning Edition* and San Francisco's Center for Investigative Reporting (CIR). As Stuart Davis (2016) explores in his case study, this collaboration allows for in-depth and multi-layered reporting—the qualitative ethnographic approach of NPR and the quantitative data-driven approach of CIR—that challenges the often surface and sensationalised news coverage of the border, allowing for a far more complex story to be told about the political, economic and cultural life in the region (*Digital Journalism* 4.4). Davis notes, "the extensive degree of cooperation between these two organizations with different approaches to news production illustrates how common advocacy-related goals might create bridges between aesthetic styles or representational strategies."

Non-competition is a radical practice for traditional media organisations but as Jan Boyles' (2015) case study of the news media in post-Katrina New Orleans shows, a number of news organisations have been teaming up to produce the slower in-depth journalism that is needed for the local community, sharing the costs, the by-lines and branding (*Digital Journalism* 4.4). Based on in-depth fieldwork and interviews with major players in the ecological restructuring of journalistic practice in the Crescent City, Boyles maps three phases in the development of new "accountability reporting:" competitive chaos, territorial exclusivity and, finally, collaborative newswork. In the need for resilience and relevance after the crisis, New Orleans' news ecosystem "effectively stumbled into the practice of slow journalism, which reordered practitioner routines in the digital age."

A context of economic and media crisis in Spain provided the ground and motivation for journalists who lost their jobs to become entrepreneurs and start their own media outlets. This is the background of Alejandro Barranquero Carretero and Garbiñe Jaurrieta Bariain's (2016) case study of *Jot Down Culture Magazine*, "an ode to slow production," and one of a new network of slow journalism publications that have emerged in Spain since 2008 (*Journalism Practice* 10.4). Their analysis explores the innovative business model of *Jot Down* along with its collaboration and distribution experiments with these other start-ups, including a pooling of expertise to revive the historical Spanish newspaper *Heraldo de Madrid*, which had been closed since 1939.

Crisis of a different kind was the motivation behind the crowd-funded slow journalism start-up *De Correspondent* in the Netherlands, a perceived crisis of quality journalism under pressure not only from the demands of commerce and speed, but from the traditional norm of objectivity. In his case study analysis, Frank Harbers (2016) situates *De Correspondent*'s rejection of objectivity, and its embrace of a more personalised, engaged and transparent approach to "the news," in a broader context of postmodern ideas about the social construction of representation and knowledge (*Digital Journalism* 4.4). Its founder, Rob Wijnberg, has built *De Correspondent* around the principle that "the truth" can be constantly updated. He calls this slow journalism. Moreover, readers are part of the journey towards truth and its contestation, especially as *De Correspondent*'s journalists are encouraged to be open in the writing and research process about their passion, frustration and interpretation about the topic at hand.

It becomes clear in many of the contributions to this double special issue that slow journalism has been emerging in alternative spaces, away from the mainstream of big media. The question is how these new practices of slow journalism can be funded. David Dowling (2015) investigates "The Business of Slow Journalism" by examining the revenue models of a number of start-ups (*Digital Journalism* 4.4). There is no one business model that emerges, but a suite of creative and innovative for-profit approaches that often avoid display, banner or pop-up advertising, but utilise crowd-funding, brand sponsorship through events, creative agencies, native advertising, subscription and, for print, high cover price. Dowling writes: "In a news ecosystem increasingly dominated by advertisers who entice media organizations to provide free content, most Slow Journalism publishers instead believe readers would be willing to pay for stories written according to this higher journalistic standard."

Slow journalism is not just about words, be they print or digital. David Burnett is a photojournalist who, for the past decade, has been practising his craft using a 60-year-old Speed Graphic film camera to produce celebrated work of "a significantly different aesthetic" in an age where everyone is a photographer, and most professional photojournalists are expected to produce speedy digital photographs. Andrew Mendelson and Brian Creech (2016) explore the possibilities of slow photography for journalism in their study of Burnett's work about, for example, Hurricane Katrina, the Sochi Winter Olympic Games and the survivors of Pinochet's reign in Chile (*Digital Journalism* 4.4). "The use of film is more than just an aesthetic or technological choice," they write, "it is a philosophical one as well, as its permanence, scarcity, and finitude place more pressure on the photographer to think about every frame and make it count." The current conventions of photojournalism derive from a production routine that privileges standardisation. These conventions are critiqued in Burnett's "acts of slow photojournalism:"

> This is not the way news photographs are supposed to look. If conventional news photographs are declarative, stating definitively, "this is," Burnett's photographs force viewers to think beyond the "this is:" to wonder, question, and think about the subject. A slow and mindful approach to photography lends itself to a slow and mindful reception.

Slow photojournalism is just one element of the transmedia storytelling (TS) behind The Sochi Project, an ongoing multi-platform work of slow journalism that tells the hidden story behind the 2014 Winter Olympics, created by Dutch documentary photographer Rob Hornstra and journalist/filmmaker Arnold van Bruggen. In "The Sochi Project: Slow Journalism Within the Transmedia Space," Renira Rampazzo Gambarato (2015) uses the principles of slow journalism and her own analytic model of TS to explore this complex project (involving interactive documentary, print media, digital publications, photographic exhibitions) (*Digital Journalism* 4.4). The Sochi Project began shortly after the Winter Olympics were announced in 2007 and Hornstra and van Bruggen plan to continue their work. This commitment to a project for an extended period of time is another aspect of slow journalism, although not shared by all practitioners. Perhaps the most ambitious project so far is that of Paul Salopek who is mid-way through his Out of Eden Walk, travelling the world on foot from Ethiopia to the southernmost tip of South America, tracing the pathway of human migration out of Africa. The walk took two years in the planning and began in January 2013. Along the way Salopek has been reporting in a wide range of modes: long-form magazine articles for *National Geographic*, videos, photographs, sound files, interviews, social media posts and detailed Milestones ("the editorial equivalent of a geologist's core sample") which are embedded on the project's interactive map.

One aim of Salopek's project is educational, and it is this aspect that Don Belt and Jeff South (2015) explore in their contribution (*Digital Journalism* 4.4). The Out of Eden Walk became the basis for a course taught by Belt at Virginia Commonwealth University, where students have been encouraged to develop a slow journalism walk of their own using multimedia storytelling skills. The detailed explanation of this innovative approach to teaching slow journalism is inspiring for journalism educators, and Belt's course was the basis for a Pulitzer Center journalism education symposium in May 2015.

In pondering future research directions for slow journalism scholars, Erik Neveu wonders if slow journalisms are simply preaching to the converted, to a fractional public with high cultural (and economic) capital. It is a pertinent observation, and one often made about the slow food and slow living movements as well. Who has the time to slow their consumption of journalism and engage with longer, more complex narratives? And do consumers want to? Here, there is much work to be done. Nico Drok and Liesbeth

Hermans (2015) offer a beginning with their research into younger Dutch news consumers, presenting the results in their essay "Is There a Future for Slow Journalism? The Perspective of Younger Users" (*Journalism Practice* 10.4). They found that while younger users do want news to be available quickly, mobile and for free, they also found that one in three younger users were interested in slow journalism—in-depth stories that provided context, that offered a greater variety of sources and perspectives, that offered solutions and opportunities for public collaboration. The next step in this area of research would not just be what readers say they want, but finding out what slow journalism they engage with and what meanings they make from it.

Another fruitful line of enquiry for future research is offered by Susan Greenberg, who sparked the discussion of slow journalism with a piece of journalism she wrote in 2007 (Greenberg 2007). In her prescient way, Greenberg (2015) takes our thinking about slow and journalism in a new direction by looking at the history of editors and editing practices in her essay "Editing, Fast and Slow" (*Journalism Practice* 10.4). Those of us who have worked as editors, be that the fast pace of editing online breaking news or the slower editorial pace of magazines, books and scholarship, know how much work is involved and how integral editors are to the final product, yet little academic investigation into the editors and editing practices of journalism has been done. Quality slow journalism and the editing it requires are "labour-intensive luxuries," argues Greenberg.

> For both reporting and editing, the way to survive and even prosper is to make the case for value. But while good reporting comes with a ready-made set of arguments about an informed citizenry and the public good, the case for good editing has been, to date, more fragmentary. If anything, editing has seen a fall in its cultural capital; positioned as it is by some new media ideologies as an oppressive handmaid of the mainstream media. As a result, the motivation to make room for high-quality editing, in the face of financial pressures, cannot be taken for granted.

Many of the contributors draw on the potential connections between the slow food movement and slow journalism. While an overly literal mapping of one movement (food) on to another (journalism) is not wise, there are principles from slow food that do indeed seem to bear parallels with emerging practices of slow journalism. The core slow food principles of "good, clean and fair" were first imagined as applicable to journalism by Harold Gess (2012). Another principle of slow food that bears promise for slow journalism research is the idea of "co-production." For Carlo Petrini, the founder of the slow food movement, "co-production" involves a re-thinking of the role of the consumer in the production process. Petrini (2007, 165) argues against the very term "consumer" with its connotations of "wearing out, using up, destroying, progressively exhausting." Instead, he offers the term "co-production," where the "old consumer" is actually the final stage in a more sustainable production process. "The old consumer must begin to feel in some way part of the production process—getting to know it, influencing it with his preferences, supporting it if it is in difficulty, rejecting it if it is wrong or unsustainable" (165). For slow journalism, "co-production" requires a new level of responsibility for the consumer of journalism, a kind of ethical and critical consumption of not just the text, but of the producers and their media organisations. This would demand of the readers or users of journalism a different level of media literacy beyond interpretation, and a responsibility to learn *how* the journalism they consume is produced and financed. But there is another step, another responsibility for the co-producer of slow journalism; and that is the preparedness to become a green media citizen, as Richard Maxwell and Toby Miller (2012) so brilliantly explore in their field-shifting work *Greening the Media*. The slow green co-producer of media needs to learn about the environmental inputs and outputs of the media technologies they use.

> Green consumers will need to be familiar with processes that take place behind their screens yet at some distance from their media use, such as the environmental impact of prior inputs to media technologies from the Earth, extracted via mining, logging, and drilling; and subsequent outputs from technology into the Earth from emissions into air, land, and water whenever a media device is made. (Maxwell and Miller 2012, 26)

While Maxwell and Miller do not explicitly talk of the green media citizen as a slow media citizen, there are fruitful synergies in their work for future researchers of slow journalism to explore. Can the concept of slow journalism be useful in elaborating and propelling research and awareness around the issues of media-induced environmental damage?

In recent decades we have witnessed what could be called a proliferation of adjectival journalisms: public, civic, citizen, new new, wisdom, knowledge, ethnographic, etc. The adjectives in themselves suggest that if there ever was a dominant singular version of journalism (which historians of journalism clearly refute; see Conboy 2004), that is patently no longer the case. The study of journalism was for a long time fixated on journalism as news, an unmarked term that saw every other type of journalism as a deviation that required marking with an adjective. That time in the field has passed. All journalism requires an adjective now and journalisms, as Barbie Zelizer (2009, 1) argues, are multiple. Journalism practitioners and scholars have entered a period of high experimentation and theorisation. Whether slow journalism continues to be a useful way of conceptualising and gathering together many of the diverse experiments against and in response to fast journalism remains to be seen. A number of contributors have referred to slow journalism as a "movement." It is hoped that this double special issue will provoke journalism researchers and practitioners to further debate on this and other trajectories.

DISCLOSURE STATEMENT

No potential conflict of interest was reported by the author.

REFERENCES

Ananny, Mike. 2016. "Networked News Time: How Slow – or Fast – do Publics Need News to be?" *Digital Journalism* 4 (4). doi:10.1080/21670811.2015.1124728.

Ball, Benjamin. 2016. "Multimedia, Slow Journalism as Process, and the Possibility of Proper Time." *Digital Journalism* 4 (4). doi:10.1080/21670811.2015.1111768.

Barranquero Carretero, Alejandro, and Garbine Jaurietta Bariain. 2016. "Slow Journalism in Spain. An Overview of *Jot Down* and the New Slow Magazines." *Journalism Practice* 10 (4). doi:10.1080/17512786.2015.1124729.

Belt, Don, and Jeff South. 2015. "Slow Journalism and the Out of Eden Walk." *Digital Journalism* 4 (4). doi:10.1080/21670811.2015.1111768.

Boyles, Jan. 2015. "Resiliency in Recovery: Slow Journalism as Public Accountability in Post-Katrina New Orleans." *Digital Journalism* 4 (4). doi:10.1080/21670811.2015.1104256.

Carey, James. 1986. "The Dark Continent of American Journalism." In *Reading the News*, edited by Robert Manoff and Michael Schudson, 146–96. New York: Pantheon Books.

Conboy, Martin. 2004. *Journalism: A Critical History*. London: Sage.

Couldry, Nick. 2006. *Listening Beyond the Echoes. Media, Ethics, and Agency in an Uncertain World*. Boulder, Colarado: Paradigm.

Craig, Geoffrey. 2015. "Reclaiming Slowness in Journalism: Critique, Complexity and Difference." *Journalism Practice* 10 (4). doi:10.1080/17512786.2015.1100521.

Davis, Stuart. 2016. "Slowing Down Media Coverage on the US-Mexico Border: News as Sociological Critique in *Borderland*." *Digital Journalism* 4 (4). doi:10.1080/21670811.2015.1123101.

Dowling, David. 2015. "The Business of Slow Journalism: Deep Storytelling's Alternative Economies." *Digital Journalism* 4 (4). doi:10.1080/21670811.2015.1111769.

Drok, Nico, and Liesbeth Hermans. 2015. "Is There a Future for Slow Journalism? The Perspective of Younger Users." *Journalism Practice* 10 (4). doi:10.1080/17512786.2015.1102604.

Gambarato, Renira Rampazzo. 2015. "The Sochi Project: Slow Journalism Within the Transmedia Space." *Digital Journalism* 4 (4). doi:10.1080/21670811.2015.1096746.

Gess, Harold. 2012. "Climate Change and the Possibility of 'Slow Journalism'." *Equid Novi: African Journalism Studies* 33 (1): 54–65.

Greenberg, Susan. 2007. "Slow Journalism." *Prospect*, February 25. Accessed August 19, 2015. http://www.prospectmagazine.co.uk/magazine/slowjournalism/#.UzAX0F7j744.

Greenberg, Susan. 2015. "Editing, Fast and Slow." *Journalism Practice* 10 (4). doi:10.1080/17512786.2015.1114898.

Hannerz, Ulf. 2004. *Foreign News: Exploring the World of Foreign Correspondents*. Chicago: University of Chicago Press.

Harbers, Frank. 2016. "Time to Engage. *De Correspondent's* Redefinition of Journalistic Quality." *Digital Journalism* 4 (4). doi:10.1080/21670811.2015.1124726.

Hermann, Anne. 2015. "The Temporal Tipping Point. Regimentation, Representation and Reorientation in Ethnographic Journalism." *Journalism Practice* 10 (4). doi:10.1080/17512786.2015.1102605.

Le Masurier, Megan. 2015. "What is Slow Journalism?" *Journalism Practice* 9 (2): 138–152.

Maxwell, Richard and Toby Miller. 2012. *Greening the Media*. New York: Oxford University Press.

Mendelson, Andrew and Brian Creech. 2016. "'Make Every Frame Count:' The Practice of Slow Photojournalism in the Work of David Burnett." *Digital Journalism* 4 (4). doi:10.1080/21670811.2015.1124727.

Neveu, Erik. 2016. "On Not Going too Fast with Slow Journalism." *Journalism Practice* 10 (4). doi:10.1080/17512786.2015.1114897.

O'Donnell, Penny, Justine Lloyd, and Tania Dreher, eds. 2009. "Special Issue: Listening – New Ways of Engaging with Media and Culture." *Continuum* 23 (4).

Parkins, Wendy, and Geoffrey Craig. 2006. *Slow Living*. Oxford: Berg.

Petrini, Carlo. 2007. *Slow Food Nation*. New York: Rizzoli.

Ricketson, Matthew. 2015. "When Slow News is Good News: Book-length Journalism's Role in Extending and Enlarging Daily News." *Journalism Practice* 10 (4). doi:10.1080/17512786.2015.1111772.

Silverstone, Roger. 2003. "Proper Distance: Toward an Ethics for Cyberspace." In *New Media Revisited: Theoretical and Conceptual Innovation in Digital Domains*, edited by Gunnar Liestol, Andrew Morrison and Terje Rasmussen, 469–490. Cambridge and London: The MIT Press.

Thomas, Helene. 2016. "Lessening the Construction of Otherness: A Slow Ethics of Journalism." *Journalism Practice* 10 (4). doi:10.1080/17512786.2015.1120164.

Zelizer, Barbie. 2009. "Introduction: Why Journalism's Changing Faces Matter." In *The Changing Faces of Journalism; Tabloidization, Technology and Truthiness*, edited by Barbie Zelizer, 1–10. London: Routledge.

ON NOT GOING TOO FAST WITH SLOW JOURNALISM

Erik Neveu

The phrase "slow journalism" is (slowly) entering the dictionary of journalism scholars. Le Masurier's contribution in this journal in 2015 was a stimulating invitation to understand how "slowness" could summarise many current changes in journalistic practices, and to remind also that "Journalism is a plural noun." This article firstly questions the polysemy of "slow journalism." Slowness may wrap many layers of meaning. Slow means far from pack reporting, investigative, and more selective in its targets. But slow could as well suggest: narrative, fair (with its sources and readers), participative, community oriented, and finally, giving priority to untold stories. How can researchers deal with such a richness of meanings? The suggestion here would be double. Slow journalism should be considered as a Weberian ideal-type, questioning, not mirroring, the reality of journalism. A "soft" mapping could invite rethinking the space of slow journalisms in three (overlapping) subgroups: explanatory, narrative, and mobilised. But claiming the need for "soft" mapping also means paying attention to fuzziness in journalistic practices.

Introduction

New words and categories often mirror changes in practices and behaviours. Journalism, or more exactly journalisms in the plural, are changing and, in the newsroom as in the school of journalism, new words and adjectives are mobilised to coin changes, as is visible in the changing labels of the Pulitzer Prizes. There is no shortage of variations on the theme of the return of literary journalism. Newness can be so striking that it even suggests the existence of a "new-new" journalism (Boynton 2005). Some reporters are claiming the practice of "immersion" journalism, others speak of "empathy" journalism. Perhaps because it seems able to wrap more dimensions of changes, the category of "slow" journalism is gaining increasing currency amongst media commentators and practitioners. The first to use the phrase "slow journalism" was Susan Greenberg (2007), and since then the most developed theoretical reflection so far comes from Megan Le Masurier (2015). This article invites a discussion of this important and stimulating contribution, to challenge it too, exploring its contradictions and potential utility in making sense of the current changes and innovations within the journalistic field.

Le Masurier's work highlights significant changes among journalism practices. More and more editors and journalists are questioning the dominant trends of their activities. Which levels of fact-checking, of explanations and ethical standards remain possible when excellence in journalism is defined as being able to report events "live?" How is newsworthiness redefined when the logic of breaking news channels transforms the story of a woman fined because she was driving with a "Muslim veil" into the major event of the day, over-covered by press and television news bulletins as a new case of Islamic threat on

French identity? The *Charlie Hebdo* slaughter in Paris in January 2015 gave a pathetic illustration of such situations: the media-pack covered the tiniest and meaningless moves of police forces during the killers' hunt. A breaking-news channel was even clever enough to air the information that customers had been hidden by an employee in the Jewish supermarket's cold storage when the terrorist besieged there was still threatening to kill all hostages. Conversely, the experience of living in some of the French *"banlieues,"* the social-spatial and sometimes ethnic segregation, the feeling of "no future" experienced by part of the youth living there, remained under-reported; and when reporting does occur, it is usually heavily biased by prejudices and clichés (Sedel 2013).

Is transforming the press into a carbon copy of the screens of breaking-news channels a good plan to reconquer audiences or a suicidal spiral? Is it reasonable to consider that the most spectacular, shocking, or outrageous events are those which allow us to make sense of the world we live in? Should one identify news only with hot or moving events, at the risk of under-rating the impact of morphological changes and slow moves in social organisation? Should journalism highlight processes and causes or limit itself to stage the froth of spectacular or ritual events? May I add that, mobilising data and cases from various countries, Le Masurier's overview escapes from the Anglophone parochialism which too often limits the changes worth being studied to those visible in the United States and the United Kingdom. One can agree with Tunstall's provocative statement that the media "are American" (Tunstall 1992) (or "were American"; Tunstall 2007) and still pay attention to the innovations in the press and media visible in Amsterdam, Capetown, or Paris.

Le Masurier reminds us, too, that "journalism is a plural noun." Social scientists do know that history is always written from the winner's point of view, however they often fall victim to that fallacy. Journalism is a field (Benson and Neveu 2004). In a field of cultural production the most common situation is the existence of a "legitimate" type of product and skills. One can agree with Schudson (1978) when he describes the triumph of a professional orthodoxy in the history of the American press, or with Chalaby (1996) when he argues that an Anglo-American style of news-gathering and processing was established at the international level as Journalism with a capital J, against the more literary, more politically committed styles of journalism visible in Italy and France. But the existence of legitimate or dominant patterns of journalism should not prevent researchers paying attention to the fact that the journalistic field is a space of competition and permanent innovations. This is visible in the mosaic of "alternative," "muckracking," or "intimate" journalisms, in the variety of magazines produced or the endlessly replayed battles of the newcomers versus the established, so visible in Tom Wolfe's (1973) manifesto of the "New Journalism." As journalism and the press are currently facing the challenge of extraordinary changes in technologies, audiences' behaviours, and literacy, such attention to journalism as something plural is more needed than ever. Change is both an opportunity and an imperative for the survival of something called journalism, whatever its future definition between being a compass for citizens in a public sphere and a provider of advice and services for consumers (Brin, Charron, and de Bonville, 2005).

Finally—and ambiguity may start here—the interest of the notion of "slow journalism" comes from its power to work as a shorthand description of the variety of changes and alternatives which are simmering in the field. Born in Italy, the slow food movement mentioned by Le Masurier suggests a fruitful comparison. Slow food is not simply the claim that subtle and tasty cooking requires time. Its Manifesto "Che cos'é Slow Food" values "sensual pleasure and slow, long-lasting enjoyment."[1] It also pleads for "the respect of the product, of environment and taste," for an education about the variety and pleasures of food, for a sustainable agriculture. Slow journalism too, combines a great variety of significations. It is what makes the label so attractive and stimulating. But this very variety of meanings may also be what threatens its value in replacing the impoverishing vision of journalism as an homogenous activity by a couplet fast/slow which would, too, over-simplify our vision of the mediascape.

Accordingly, this article will be structured around two major developments from the observations above. The first one explores the polysemy of "slow" journalism. It will also suggest from this starting point the possible contradictions of a concept whose multiple levels of signification may challenge its value for empirical use. The second part of this paper suggests why we should keep "slow journalism" as a useful shorthand to make sense of convergent reactions to the current crisis of journalism. It will conclude by developing some critical suggestions to prevent "slow journalism" becoming a soft or catch-all label.

A Polysemic Category

In his exciting contribution to the epistemology of social sciences, the French sociologist Jean-Claude Passeron highlights a major challenge for any conceptual work. He writes: "Two obstacles, which seem reverse at first sight, are preventing the production and articulation of definitions in social sciences" (Passeron 2006, 97). On the one hand, when researchers are looking for clear analytical categories, they may invent concepts cleverly indexed on the factual relations that they summarise, but at the risk of being so specific to the research in progress that they could never be articulated to other theoretical notions. On the other hand, when using more classical, more long-range theories, the use of such concepts may work as the Trojan horse of a huge and sometimes embarrassing legacy of uses, meanings, and debates. One can think here of notions such as "literary journalism" or "newsgathering" that combine an enormous variety of texts and practices, depending on their time-space location. Passeron concludes about such difficulties in the use and invention of concepts:

> Few sociological concepts escape this dilemma: whether being too theoretical (lacking in univocal meaning for having been used to deal with questions both different and close, none of these questions having made the others obsolete) or being not theoretical enough (which means too specific to supply a usable power of analogy or generalisation beyond the specific data whose relation they express as a shorthand). Sociological concepts are "polymorphous" or "stenographic" … they combine the too much and the not enough degrees of abstraction. (Passeron 2006, 97–98)

The notion of slow journalism typically faces such a strain. Looking at first sight as a "stenographic" notion, compressing in a phrase the peculiarity of current changes, its explanatory ambition makes it "polymorphous," bringing back, as one explores its levels of meaning, many debates as old as journalism.

The more empirical facts a concept is able to grasp, the bigger the risk that it would lack a very precise meaning. One can think here of the endlessly expanding uses of "populism" or "Islamism" in some quarters of academia, politics, and journalism. If slow journalism could be found in "essay," "muckraking," "long-form narrative journalism," "creative non-fiction," "New journalism," and "literary journalism," there is no doubt that common denominators could also be found in these varied genres. But it would also be easy to argue that significant differences question the utility of a common label. Muckraking has always been linked to a critical and political commitment which is not shared by all the "new" or "new-new" (Boynton 2005) journalists. Literary styles of journalism could be used not only for more slow-moving subjects, but also to report "hot" events followed by "herds" of journalists: one could think here of the astounding sketches of the Kuwaiti highways to Iraq covered by scores of burnt cars and trucks and their exhibition of charred and torn corpses in Michael Kelly's (1993) *Martyr's Day*. On the other hand, one could argue that the very polysemy of "slow journalism" is a strength which allows the concept to be tested. In his *Logic of Scientific Discovery*, Karl Popper ([1934] 2002) argues the more precise a theory, the more it faces the risk of empirical denials. Conversely, the more a complex theory faces victoriously the challenge of empirical testing, the more scientific it is. Let us follow this track.

Listing Meanings

The more I read and re-read Le Masurier's paper, the more I had the feeling of discovering new dimensions and stakes suggested by the two words "slow journalism." Reception theory has shown how texts are re-interpreted, re-written by their readers. With the hope of being faithful to the author's analysis, I would argue that her paper suggests seven elements of definition, and questions one more.

A first meaning of slow is linked to the criticism of the cult of speed and live reporting. Here slow means … slow. Journalism needs time to check facts, to gather and process data. Some social groups or activities are resistant to investigation. Such mistrust can be triggered by the fear of being stigmatised or simply by the social distance between reporters and their targets. It can also be explained by the nature of some activities because they are illegal or need secrecy to develop. Slowness may also be the price of gaining a proper understanding of complicated processes or of activities mobilising technical devices or scientific knowledge. The difficulty of reporting financial activities (Davies 2007) is a good illustration of the inescapable slowness of some reporting. Such activities are developing in a close world of insiders and they require the understanding of highly complex dealings. This dimension of slowness should also be understood as a reaction to the "informational whirlwind" (Klinenberg 2000) experienced in newsrooms in the age of "convergence." Here the idea of deadline has no more meaning, the website or the 24-hours-a-day channel needing its constant information fodder.

A second meaning of slowness could be linked to "investigative," to the rehabilitation of time-consuming legwork and investigations. One of the most unpleasant experiences of many newcomers in journalism is the discovery that they will be trapped in the space of the newsroom, being connected to the real world by the twin prostheses of a computer screen and a cell-phone. Escaping from the packaged news of the PRs requires time to structure one's network of sources, to check facts. Wasting time in cultivating contacts and playing the game of the gift and counter-gift of attention and coverage is also the price of good journalism. The stake here is to think of journalism as a practice of gathering and producing news, not of recycling or commenting on it.

In a third layer of definition slow means less. Slow journalism expresses a reaction to the overdose of "news" streaming from breaking news channels, cell-phone screens, radios, and magazines. The criticism also targets the triviality of what is labelled as news, with the emphasis on celebrities and sensational situations, the fascination for artificial dramatisation that transforms micro-events (a prostate check-up by the French president) into a dramatised rollercoaster of narratives on his health. "Better less but better" could be the motto. Slow journalism is selective, explanatory. The choice of some websites to develop only one long story a day is typical of this strategy.

In a fourth dimension slow suggests narrative, and often longer-form writing. If slow journalism can be found in varied styles of reporting, it fits especially well with narrative journalism reaching the size of a short story. Also more length means more time: for the journalist who builds a structured and data-rich article for the viewer-reader. Reading the 160 pages of the French quarterly *XXI* requires more time than browsing the compact articles of the free daily *20 Minutes* whose very title is a time-management programme.

Le Masurier suggests a fifth dimension which could be linked to the idea of fairness. The aim of the slow-food movement is also to institutionalise fair relations with producers —who would be better paid, and invited to pay attention to quality and to the treatment of animals and the earth—and consumers who should have access to healthy and tasty meals for a fair price. In the same logic, slow journalism works to structure a new ecology of information production. It reclaims autonomy in front of the army of PR enlisted by powerful sources. It pleads for more empathy and responsibility with its rank and file informants among community leaders and laypersons. It promotes—and the comparison with food makes sense again—a traceability of news, a more transparent explanation of the source of information, of its possible biases.

This dimension of fairness leads to two other elements of definition, which appear more as variants than as compulsory elements in Le Masurier's conceptualisation. Slow journalism could include an element of commensality or community. It claims then to serve a community, to feed its forum and public sphere. The emphasis on community bridges towards a last element of definition which is participation. The community ("imagined," or "real" if it is a local newspaper) would thus be invited to bring its contribution, posting its comments, reports, and videos, taking a stand in a forum. Slow journalism transforms its audiences into partners.

Exploring the definition of slow journalism could even suggest one more dimension and question. Is it possible to practise slow journalism on any issue or event, or does the definition exclude some topics? Le Masurier suggests that it "avoids sensationalism and herd reporting" as well as (quoting here Mark Berkey-Gerard) "celebrity," to leave space for "untold stories." Agreeing on the fact that slow journalism would hardly fit with the usual media dedicated to celebrities in glossy gossip magazines, or with the hollow live covering of dramas (like the Boston marathon bombing or the repetition of shark attacks in La Réunion's island) does not allow us to conclude that it could not have such targets. The famous long-form profile from Gay Talese ([1966] 2003) "Frank Sinatra has a Cold," speaks of a celebrity. But wasn't it slowly produced, significantly different from the flow of celebrities' portrayals? The reports of Kelly (1993), Anderson (2004), or Langewiesche (2006) on the wars in Iraq deal with events covered by "herds" of journalists. Nevertheless, they supply a vision, an understanding of the context, of the subjective experience on both sides of the event which is completely different from the contribution of dispatches or reports focusing on cruise missile launchings or statesmen's statements. Slow may thus have an eighth meaning which could be "deep," "untold," or "backstage." It would once again mobilise the opposition between the froth—and explosions—of the hot event and the depths of social life, something like an ethnographic, bottom-up vision of society.

Cumulative Criteria?

This multi-layered definition shows the richness of the concept. It challenges it too. The "Popperian" objection would be that if all the dimensions of the definition are needed to identify slow journalism, few empirical cases would fit with the complete check-list of the concept. This is crystal clear with variables six and seven, community and participation. The British *Granta*, the French *Feuilleton*, and the American *New Yorker* are publishing a style of reports sharing many elements of slow journalism (few but long narrative papers, systematic fact-checking and intensive legwork, focus on "untold" stories more than on breaking events, etc.). But their readers are not the co-producers of the magazines. Created in 2003, the French monthly *So Foot* successfully invented a surprising style of soccer magazine, almost completely disconnected from the coverage of the hot events of European (Champion's League) and French football, mostly made of para-sociological reports on clubs and fans, of long biographical interviews, and tongue-in-cheek evocations of football events. It does not mobilise any significant participation from its readership. Also—apart from their lack of passion for the deferential, sometimes jingoist style of reporting of the established football magazines—describing the magazine's readership as a community is probably worth debating. Focusing the definition on four of its five first elements would probably make it stronger. But problems would remain. Even without any suspicion on their true quest of "fairness," many among the media who are developing slow journalisms have in common the position of outsiders, lacking in financial resources. One of the answers to this situation could be participative crowd-funding … but it can also involve an intensive use of students from journalism schools, working as interns and poorly paid, when they are paid. Mobilising another French case, the website *Mediapart*, the flagship of investigative journalism in France, certainly takes part in the slow journalism logic if one considers the quality of its reportings, the limited amount of papers that it puts on-line, and its reluctance for anything linked to the topics producing "buzz." But *Mediapart* can post short papers, and one can question the narrative and literary qualities of some of the contributions that are produced by the academics co-operating with the website. One can also wonder if fairness fits with the style of investigations made by *Mediapart*. One of the website's most famous scoops was the revelation, in 2012, that the French minister of finance, Jerome Cahuzac, who was crusading against tax fraud, had a secret and illegal bank account in Switzerland. Thinking that such investigations could be developed in full transparency or by absolutely fair or unambiguous relations with sources is probably wishful thinking. Journalism here needs secrecy and must use cunning to face the hidden agendas of some if its sources and the resistance of its targets.

To put it in a nutshell, I would argue that the situations in which the eight possible criteria ("slow" as taking the time of gathering and processing news, as serious investigation, as limiting the information flow, as narrative, as fair, as community-serving, as participatory, as valuing "untold" stories) are cumulative and are rare. A solid core definition could probably focus on criteria one to four, or even extend this list to criterion eight. But this abridged definition would then just as readily fit with New Journalism 50 years ago, the "intimate" (Harrington 1997) journalism or the "new-new" journalism of the past 20 years. Should we then suspect that slow journalism is just a new label on old practices? Should we—following Feldstein's (2006) model that explains the rises and falls of muckracking in the United States—use the idea of cycles of critical reaction among journalists? Like the interpretive reporting of the 1920s (Schudson 1978) or the new journalism of the

1960s (Pauly 2014), would slow journalism then be nothing more or nothing less than a renewal of the endless quest for answers in front of the double challenge of technological change and professionalisation of sources (Schlesinger 1990)?

Paying attention to the existence of cycles of re-institutionalisation of critical styles of journalism is worth thinking about. But the repetition of these critical reinventions should not prevent us from questioning their variety and differences. I would thus argue that if researchers could reach a clear consensus on its status and uses, "slow journalism" will be an important tool to make sense of the peculiarities of the current changes in journalism practice.

A Thought-provoking Category

How can we mobilise the concept of slow journalism? What uses could be made of a notion of such complex and multi-layered significance? And what is a category which appears both as strongly illuminating but often as revealing a big gap between its definition and the variety of empirical situations? The answer is simple in the sociological tradition. The only fruitful use of the concept is to consider it as a Weberian "ideal-type." Weber (1922) defines "ideal-type" as the construction of concepts whose function is to question reality, not to describe or summarise it. Weber explains the building of a type ideal as based on two operations: "emphasising" some features of a social fact which seem strongly peculiar, and "linking a multitude of phenomenon … that could be found sometimes in great number, sometimes in smaller number, sometimes not at all" (1922, 172). He writes, "One would never find empirically such description in its conceptual purity: it is an utopy" (1922, 173). The best summary of the ideal-type comes from Aron:

> A mental image which is not produced by a generalisation of the features common to all cases but by utopian rationalisation. We gather features which are more or less present here and there, we highlight, we suppress, we overstate: finally we are substituting a coherent and rational whole to the confusion and incoherence of reality. (Aron [1935] 1981, 86)

Using "slow journalism" as an ideal-type which questions changes in journalism but does not claim to identify a coherent and clear new practice brings two advantages at least. It prevents any essentialism. It rules out the problem of purity as the question of checking the complete list of definitional elements loses its centrality. It invites us conversely to pay attention and to explore the differences, the sub-categories in the practice of slow journalisms. This is what this second part of this article will do, sketching a map of these varieties of slow journalism, which will itself suggest new questions on the hybridisations, ambivalences, and mediums of these practices.

Mapping the Space of Slow Journalisms

Slow journalism must be understood as plural. But this approach re-opens the definition trap. Should we replace the anxious checking of the presence of the seven or eight elements of definition by the invention of a sophisticated typology? Should we fall into a classifying frenzy and coin each of the possible combinations of the elements of definition by a name? Let us suggest a softer mapping which could be threefold: explanatory, non-fiction, and mobilised.

A first space of slow journalism could be linked to the idea of "explanatory journalism" which appeared in 1984—and became "explanatory reporting" in 1998—as one of the areas for the Pulitzer Prizes. The Pulitzer website mentions a style of "reporting that illuminates a significant and complex subject, demonstrating mastery of the subject, lucid writing and clear presentation, using any available journalistic tool." The peculiarities of these varieties of slow journalism could be linked to the emphasis on long and complex fieldwork. Its foci are very selective, mostly targeting significant social stakes. (The Prize was created in 1984 to make a distinction between these kinds of reporting and the lighter, more entertaining, genre of feature journalism.) "Untold" questions are connected here to the hidden sides of intensively reported events (e.g. tax avoidance by major companies, threats to public health), or to the understanding of slow social, environmental, and technological changes.

A second sub-space, "non-fiction narratives," could be linked to the narrative dimension, with long articles (and even books) making a sophisticated use of writing techniques borrowed from literature. A significant number of the US "new-new" journalists could be ascribed to this space. But the same could be said of Kapuscinsky's (2011) depiction of the fall of the Negus regime in Ethiopia. Some reports of the Columbian novelist and journalist Garcia-Marquez (1999, 2013) on the adventures of a castaway from the local military fleet or on the abductions of journalists by the narcos also belong to this family. Here the core ingredients of slow journalism—deep and long investigation, selective attention to "untold" stories—are visible, as is the absence of any "participatory" dimension, or even of any explicit reference to a target "community." But the peculiar identity of this sub-genre comes from the centrality of narrative skills, longer forms, and style.

Finally, a third sub-category could be coined as a "mobilised" slow journalism, linked to an idea of commitment. The report on the mobilisation of Naxalite peasants in the Indian forests by the Booker Prize-winning novelist Arundhati Roy (2011) could illustrate this sub-genre. The elements of definition "fair," "community-oriented," "participatory" are here the DNA of these slow journalisms. We would locate here the experiences based on the mobilisation of audiences, of the "community" (defined by a territory, a hobby, a commitment) that journalists claim to support or express. "Mobilised" could go beyond the idea of participatory, and suggest a more activist style of reporting, defending groups and causes, combining thus the notions of slow and alternative journalisms. Some parts of the "indie" magazines and news websites could be linked to this style of news coverage (Le Masurier 2012).

A possible objection to this sketch could be that the three categories suggested here overlap. And they do. Many among the reports of new-new journalism would be hard to ascribe to only one of our two first categories. Leon Dash's Pulitzer Prize-winning eight-part series "Rosa Lee' Story" for *The Washington Post* in 1994 and the book *Rosa Lee: A Mother and Her Family in Urban America* (Dash 1998) is a biographical report on a poor Afro-American woman, trafficking drugs to survive and support her family. It is both a masterpiece of interpretive reporting and a great non-fiction narrative. Roy's reports among the villagers in the Indian forest are both narrative journalism and a plea for resistance to the oppression of poor peasants. When the *Guardian* (Rusbridger 2009) mobilised internauts to open the thousands of files of the British Members of Parliament's expenses bills to search for illegal uses of public money, it developed simultaneously a style of mobilised reporting and an in-depth and explanatory investigation on the morality of elected representatives. One could even argue, to challenge this mapping, that all the reports rewarded by the "explanatory reporting" of the Pulitzer Prize cannot be identified as slow journalism. Among the papers of Boxall and Cart—the *Los Angeles Times* journalists who won in 2009 for reporting on the menace of wildfires—some are short, directly based on breaking events, closer to the best of traditional journalism than to its "slow" expressions. The only possible answer to such objections would be that the subtlest or most sophisticated of typologies would always be challenged by the creativity of journalists and the hybridisations between genres. But if "there are no true or wrong definitions, just more or less fruitful" (Aron [1935] 1981, 88), the three sub-categories suggested here remain useful. They help identify practices of slow journalism whose expressions—whatever the uncertainty of their frontiers —are significantly different in their ambitions, forms, and medium.

The Strength of Fuzziness

Thinking about slow journalism as an ideal-type rather than a coherent and close category helps us to question the changes in journalistic practice and also invites stimulating explorations.

The first one could be identified as the scattering power of this style of reporting. To explain it simply, our first reflex as researchers is often to look for the existence of specific magazines or websites that could be identified as the focus or flagships of these new styles of journalism; and they do exist and are well visible in the examples given by Le Masurier. But the point is also that, facing the combined challenges or technological changes, increased competition and audiences' changing habits, even the most traditional actors of the press and media are paying attention to the possible contribution of slow journalisms. In the French case, this is clearly visible in the changes of the national press, desperately struggling against the loss of readers and financial resources. One of its answers to the crisis has been the growing space dedicated to reports and sections which are borrowing the style of slow journalism. If one considers the changes in *Le Monde*, it is worth mentioning the growing space dedicated to long reports (one, sometimes two full pages), valuing a bottom-up approach to hot events. As the terrifying series of shipwrecks killing thousands of immigrants in the Mediterranean Sea was occupying the headlines, *Le Monde* published several reports by Maryline Baumard, a journalist specialising in immigration. Going from Libya to the Greek Islands and from Macedonia to the night train crossing the Italian–French border, she gave an illuminating description of the dangers and violence of the immigrants' experiences.[2] Her long narrative of this exodus gave space to the testimonies of people trapped between European law enforcement institutions and local mafias. One could also mention the importance taken by full-page profiles (in *Libération*) or the renewal of obituaries as a genre allowing long stories which are also alibis to explore the past, to highlight changes in professions or social relations. The suggestion here is that slow journalism does not work according to the binary logic of an alternative, of something replacing more traditional, condensed hard news. Slow journalism works as a resource, a family of "approaches" and "genres" which can combine with the most classical styles of journalism (interview, short reports, news-analysis). Benson's (2014) recent comparison of the coverage of immigration news in the French and US press shows with great strength how this combination of very different genres and styles of reporting— but also of interviews and computer graphics—supplies a more comprehensive approach in the French press. This style of coverage, close to Gans' (1979) vision of multi-perspectival journalism, is not produced by slow journalism replacing older styles of reporting, but by the polyphony and combination of different styles of journalism in the same pages.

The combination of slow journalism with the most classical styles of news reporting expresses the challenge of thinking about it as both a real change in journalistic practices and as something capable of hybridisation. More than a binary divide, a clear border between slow and traditional or "live" styles of reporting, the image of a moving frontier, of fuzzy combinations could make sense of the current changes in journalistic practice.

The metaphor of fuzziness can also be illuminating to identify the locations of slow journalism. Common sense would suggest that daily newspapers, magazines, and websites are the logical places to monitor these innovations. But slow journalism can also colonise movies or television programmes. The success of Morgan Spurlock's film *Supersize Me* on fast food is a good illustration of the presence of this style of reporting in documentary movies. Spurlock is also the host of the US reality television show *Thirty Days* (Baym and Gottert 2013), a case which reveals another surprising location of this new style of reporting. An episode of the show featured an anti-illegal immigration activist sharing the life and home of a family of illegal Mexican immigrants in California over several weeks, producing for the audience—and the activist—an illuminating understanding of the experience and motivations of these immigrants. Books are not usually considered as the major medium of journalism. Such a classification may be challenged too. One of the peculiarities of the recent take-off of magazines typical of the French style of slow journalism (*XXI, Feuilleton, Muse*, and *6 mois* for photo-reporting) is the invention of a mixed genre between magazine and book, all those titles being mostly sold in bookshops rather than in newsstands. Lacking a tradition of literary magazines such as the American *New Yorker, Vanity Fair*, or *Esquire*, the French practitioners of slow journalism are mainly using books to publish their reports; and this move from press to book is often a success. Jean Hatzfeld's (2014) extraordinary trilogy on the genocide in Rwanda was rewarded by literary prizes. Florence Aubenas' (2011) report on the work of night cleaners and maids (a book comparable to Barbara Ehrenreich's [2001] *Nickel and Dimed*) became a best-seller. Jean-Baptiste Malet's (2013) undercover report on the working conditions in the warehouses of Amazon triggered a public debate on the giant company's job policy. The practice of slow journalism invites us also to question the traditional couple of the newsroom and the press or media company. Slow journalism can be found beyond the traditional sites of information production: on websites, in books and talk-shows, even in graphic novels if one thinks of Joe Sacco's stories.

The concept of slow journalism can be a most useful tool for reflection. But its users should not be tempted by the analytical shortcut of an essentialist vision of something homogenous which could be defined by a sophisticated combination of criteria, or in the vision of a discrete category working in a binary opposition with traditional or hyper-modern practices of journalism. Conversely, if used as an ideal-type whose aim is to question the practice of journalism and not as a straitjacket trussing it up in a close definition, the concept of slow journalism could be remarkably fruitful. Combining in fact rather different parameters, it invites us to pay attention to all the dimensions of the current changes. It invites us to escape from the routinised vision of journalism as something existing only in newspapers, magazines, and websites. It can make sense of many of the current innovations developed by journalists, press, and media companies. Using the plural, slow journalisms give keys to re-map the space of practices, to explore the invention of multi-perspectival styles of reporting. The "old" tool of Jakobson's (1960) language functions could be useful here. The "explanatory" style of slow journalism could be described as focusing more on the referential and metalingual functions; the "non-fiction" type combines high attention to the referential and poetic functions; the "mobilised" one focuses on the expressive and conative[3] functions to maximise the effect on its audiences. That is not to say that all the functions of language are not used in each type of journalism, but that the specific tune of each one may be highlighted by the hierarchy and focus on such or such function.

Let us also suggest an open question for future exploration: who are the audiences and readerships of this new space of reporting? Are slow journalisms simply preaching to the converted, rallying the fractions of the public with high cultural capital (and wealthy enough to subscribe to expensive magazines or documentary channels)? Or are they able to channel back into news consumption, into a critical and citizen use of information, the working-class audiences? Could slow journalisms invent a way of "talking about society" (Becker 2007) that is simultaneously illuminating and entertaining? Could they be able to combine the comprehension of subjective experiences and the production of causal explanations (Neveu 2014)? Here is probably the major challenge of the promising innovations of slow journalism and its research.

DISCLOSURE STATEMENT

No potential conflict of interest was reported by the author.

NOTES

1. See http://www.slowfood.com/about_us/eng/manifesto.lasso.
2. See, for instance, "Subotica, nouvelle porte d'entrée dans Schengen," *Le Monde*, March 20, 2015; "Kosovo; l'appel de l'ouest", *Le Monde*, March 26, 2015; "Caché dans les bagages du 'train des migrants", *Le Monde*, May 26, 2015.
3. Jakobson defines the "conative" function of language as the dimensions of a message which are targeting and engaging the addressee/receiver. This dimension would be especially important if one of the message's aims is to mobilise, to move the audience.

REFERENCES

Anderson, John Lee. 2004. *The Fall of Bagdad*. London: Penguin.

Aron, Raymond. [1935] 1981. *La sociologie allemande contemporaine*. Paris: PUF.

Aubenas, Florence. 2011. *The Night Cleaner*. London: Polity.

Baym, Geoffrey, and Colby Gottert. 2013. "30 Days: Social Engagement." In *How to Watch Television*, edited by Ethan Thompson and Jason Mittel, 159–167. New York: New York University Press.

Becker, Howard. 2007. *Talking About Society*. Chicago: Chicago University Press.

Benson, Rod. 2014. *Shaping Immigration News. A French-American Comparison*. Cambridge: Cambridge University Press.

Benson, Rod, and Erik Neveu. 2004. *Bourdieu and the Journalistic Field*. London: Polity.

Boynton, Robert. 2005. *The New New Journalism*. New-York: Vintage.

Brin, Colette, Jean Charron, and Jean de Bonville. 2005. *Nature et transformations du journalisme : théorie et recherches empiriques*. Quebec: Presses de l'Université Laval.

Chalaby, Jean. 1996. "Journalism as an Anglo-American Invention: A Comparison of the Development of French and Anglo-American Journalism, 1830s-1920s." *European Journal of Communication* 11 (3): 303–326.

Dash, Leon. 1998. *Rosa Lee: A Mother and Her Family in Urban America*. New York: Profile Books.

Davies, Aeron. 2007. *The Mediation of Power: An Introduction*. London: Routledge.

Ehrenreich, Barbara. 2001. *Nickel and Dimed. On (not) Getting by in America*. New York: Metropolitan Books.

Feldstein, Mark. 2006. "A Muckracking Model. Investigative Reporting Cycles in American History." *Press/Politics* 11 (2): 105–120.

Gans, Herbert. 1979. *Deciding What's News*. New York: Pantheon Books.

Garcia-Marques, Gabriel. 1999. *Journal d'un enlèvement*. Paris : Le livre de poche.

Garcia-Marques, Gabriel. 2013. *Relato de un naufrago*. Madrid: Debolsillo.

Greenberg, Susan. 2007. "Slow Journalism." *Prospect*, February 26. http://www.prospectmagazine.co.uk/magazine/slowjournalism/#.UiahWuDtKfR.

Harrington, Walt. 1997. *Intimate Journalism. The Art and Craft or Reporting Everyday Life*. London: Sage.

Hatzfeld, Jean. 2014. *Récits des marais rwandais*. Paris: Seuil.

Jakobson, Roman. 1960. *Closing Statements: Linguistics and Poetics, Style in Language*. New York: T.A. Sebeok.

Kapuscinsky, Riszard. 2011. *Le Négus*. Paris: Flammarion.

Kelly, Michael. 1993. *Martyr's Day: Chronicles of a Small War*. New-York: Random House.

Klinenberg, Eric. 2000. "Information et production numérique." *Actes de la recherche en Sciences Sociales* 134: 66–75.

Langewiesche, William. 2006. *Rules of Engagement*, http://www.vanityfair.com/news/2006/11/haditha200611

Le Masurier, Megan. 2012. "Independent Magazines and the Rejuvenation of Print." *International Journal of Cultural Studies* 15 (4): 383–398.

Le Masurier, Megan. 2015. "What is slow journalism?." *Journalism Practice* 9 (2): 138–152.

Malet, Jean-Baptiste. 2013. *En Amazonie : Infiltré dans le 'meilleur des mondes'*. Paris: Fayard.

Neveu, Erik. 2014. "Revisiting Narrative Journalism as One of the Futures of Journalism." *Journalism Studies* 15 (5): 533–542.

Passeron, Jean Claude. 2006. *Le raisonnement sociologique*. Paris: Albin-Michel.

Pauly, John. 2014. "The New Journalism and the Struggle for Interpretation." *Journalism* 15 (3): 589–604.

Popper, Karl. [1934] 2002. *The Logic of Scientific Discovery*. London: Routledge.

Roy, Ahrundati. 2011. *Walking with the Comrades*. New-Delhi: Penguin.

Rusbridger, Alan. 2009. "I've seen the future and it's mutual." *British Journalism Review* 20 (3): 19–26.

Schlesinger, Philip. 1990. "Rethinking the Sociology of Journalism: Source Strategies and the Limits of Media Centrism." In *Public Communication: The New Imperatives*, edited by Marjorie Ferguson, 61–83. London: Sage.

Schudson, Michael. 1978. *Discovering the News. A Social History of American Newspapers*. New York: Basic Books.

Sedel, Julie. 2013. *Les médias et la banlieue*. Lormont: Le bord de l'eau.

Talese, Gay. 2003. *The Gay Talese Reader*. New York: Walker and Cy.

Tunstall, Jeremy. 1992. *The Media are American*. London: Constable.

Tunstall, Jeremy. 2007. *The Media were American*. Oxford: Oxford University Press.

Weber, Max. 1992. *Essais sur la théorie de la science*. Paris: Presses Pocket.

Wolfe, Tom. 1973. *The New Journalism*. London: Picador.

RECLAIMING SLOWNESS IN JOURNALISM
Critique, complexity and difference

Geoffrey Craig

This article outlines an argument for the value of slowness in journalism. It makes an initial argument that our experiences of modernity are not singular experiences of speed and geographical dislocation but increasingly complex negotiations of different temporalities and spatial contexts and given this we also require different forms of fast and slow journalism. The article explores how journalism operates at particular speeds because of the comparative advantage of timeliness and also because there is a need for journalism to align itself with the temporalities of the institutional fields on which it reports. It discusses how various types of slow journalism act as interventions in the field of journalism, highlighting the political economy of fast journalism, and providing an alternative to dominant forms of contemporary journalistic practice. The article then focuses on the necessity and importance of slowness within contemporary journalism through a discussion of the concepts of critique, complexity and difference. It is argued that slowness is required for the journalistic task of critiquing power relations that are increasingly manifested in the mastery of the speed of public life. It is also argued that slowness in journalistic practice helps in offering effective scrutiny of public issues that are characterized by informational and conceptual complexity. Finally, it is argued that contemporary democracies involve growing levels of pluralism and proliferations of difference and that slowness is necessary in the representations and understandings of diverse identities, value systems and cultural practices.

Introduction

When Wendy Parkins and I first expounded on the concept of slow living (Parkins and Craig 2006), we wanted to demonstrate the virtues and usefulness of slowness in a globalized environment increasingly characterized by speed. Our subject of analysis, the Slow Food movement, was also a vehicle to more broadly explore the philosophy and politics of slowness. Our study noted the provocative character of slow living: to promote and adopt slowness across our personal lives, our working lives and public life is to set oneself at odds with dominant societal rhythms and values. We also noted that slow living did not involve a disengagement from the dilemmas and "realities" of contemporary existence; rather it is a means of critique of those dilemmas, and also that it offers the possibility of managing, in a deliberate and conscious way, the non-synchronous character of modern everyday life. Finally, and importantly, we noted that slow living involves the reclamation of time in order to be able to devote care and attention to practices, and that such "mindfulness" facilitates not only the cultivation of a particular self but also an ethical orientation to other people, places and times. Slow living was not a "self-help" exercise and it did not offer a prescriptive list of practices or activities; rather, it was a way of illustrating how the contexts of globalization have rendered the dynamics of everyday life less self-evident, providing many stresses and challenges but also providing means for self-reflexive subjects to variously negotiate those stresses and challenges and also forge new ways of living. This was often captured in engagements with forces of globalization at the level of the local, expressed as a kind of "ethical glocalism" (Tomlinson 1999, 195–196), and for Slow Food followers this could range from critiques of the global agri-food industry and the development of alternative food networks through to the considered pleasures of food and conviviality around a shared table. Slow living was also not just an individual response to such contexts of globalization; we also explored, for example, how the concept of slow living was manifested at the level of governance through the *Città Slow* (Slow Cities) movement where municipalities initiated a raft of public policy measures relating to transport, health, agriculture, tourism and business in order to enhance the quality of life. Slow living can be understood as a form of "lifestyle politics" that gives expression to the trend that Jonathan Rutherford has previously identified:

> A new relationship between the individual, the local and the global is emerging, and it is here, not in the public realm of governance, that there is a re-evaluation of what an ethics of living might be ... [that] is not simply an aesthetic of lifestyle, but the necessary emotional work of everyday life. (Rutherford 2000, 66)

I am pleased that the philosophy of the Slow Food movement has permeated other areas of life (Honoré 2004) and, in particular, that it has been adopted in more recent years in the practices and study of media and journalism. In this article, I want to extrapolate from the ideas of slow living that we previously articulated and suggest their relevance in the practices of contemporary journalism.

In the early working through of the philosophy of the Slow Food organization, the historian Massimo Montanari (1996; see also Parkins and Craig 2006, 58–59) noted in the second issue of the movement's *Slow* magazine that slowness should not be valued for its own sake but for what it enabled, and for Montanari this was encapsulated in the simple idea of "care." Slow Food was about caring for and about those who provide food, how it is grown, the selection of ingredients, the cooking, the sensory pleasures of food, and the conviviality associated with its consumption. More recently, Lavis, Abbots and Attala (2015) have also explored the complex relationships between eating and caring. This invoking of "care" has parallels with the idea of an "ethic of care" that has been outlined in feminist theory. Joan Tronto (1993, 1995), for example, outlines how this normative ethical theory is in contrast to universalistic theories of justice and how it privileges a view that sees people "as constantly enmeshed in relationships of care" (1995, 142) rather than as independent actors who achieve autonomy through the rational pursuit of self-interest. Such an ethic of care is crucially concerned with an examination of the positive and deleterious ways that different institutions facilitate relationships of care. As Lavis, Abbots and Attala (2015, 6) are keen to stress, caring is a complex, hybrid phenomenon that does not have a necessarily benign character and it also works crucially as "a biopolitical force that governs and disciplines." A comprehensive investigation of the idea of "care" is beyond the scope of this study but nonetheless I believe that it can be suggestive of how care can be important in our understandings of slow journalism. To promote the values of slow journalism is to care about those who practice the craft and to recognize the value of what the practice provides, to care about how journalists interact with others, and it is motivated by the recognition that care is required in the practice as it explores, critiques and communicates what is happening in the world.

I hope to contribute to the understanding of slow journalism here by locating such forms of journalism within the contexts of the broader journalistic field (Benson and Neveu 2005) and exploring how reportage is influenced by the degree of temporal alignment between the journalistic field and the fields that are the object of reportage. This will not produce an argument that slow journalism is "better" than more mainstream, everyday journalism, but it is a means by which we can ask why contemporary journalism operates according to particular social speeds and whether journalism can also be well served through a *disjuncture* between its temporality and the speed of the fields which are the object of scrutiny. This discussion will be preceded by a more general re-appraisal of the conventional narrative that modernity is only characterized by greater speed and geographical dislocation, and also a brief historical overview of the development of the speed of journalism within that tale of modernity. Finally, the article will elaborate on the possible contributions that forms of slow journalism can offer through the perspectives of critique, complexity and difference. It will be argued that slowness can be a valuable feature of reportage given the journalistic task of critiquing power relations that are increasingly manifested in the mastery of the speed of public life. It will be argued that forms of slow journalism can be useful in making sense of a public life that is characterized by growing informational and conceptual complexity. In addition, it will be argued that an understanding of the growing levels of pluralism and proliferations of differences that give shape to modern democratic life can also be facilitated by a slow and more reflective journalism.

Speed and Time in Modernity and Journalism

It is something of a conventional narrative that the history of modernity and contemporary existence is marked by ever-increasing speed. Historical accounts of industrialization, from the introduction of the railways through to the instantaneous communicative networks of the internet, reveal the extent to which human experience has undergone profound transformative change during this period as a result of technological innovation. This "exponential acceleration" thesis (Ross 1995, 10) has been expressed by a number of theorists (Berman 1983; Virilio 1986) and such changes have also been said to alter temporal *and* spatial relations: David Harvey's now famous "time-space compression" (Harvey 1989) thesis—noting how geographic space has been condensed or elided by faster forms of communication and travel with accompanying impacts on identity and social relations—develops Karl Marx's earlier observation of the "annihilation of space by time" (Marx [1939–41] 1993).

While such observations speak to obvious historical developments, the singularity of the narrative needs to be countered by recognition of the *differential* temporalities of modernity (Osborne 1992; Ross 1995; Williams 1973). Doreen Massey (1994, 149), for example, has noted the "power-geometry of time-space compression" whereby different groups of people variously experience speed and mobility in modernity with different degrees of control over such movements. We have different conceptualizations of time, making distinctions between natural time and the social time of industrial capitalism. Barbara Adam has argued for a distinction between "non-temporal" time, which is measurable and repeatable, and "temporal" time, which is the experience of the flow of time which has a constitutive capacity but which cannot be captured (Adam 1995; see also Parkins and Craig 2006, 40). There is also a necessarily comparative understanding and lived experience of speed in modernity. The increased speed of many of our lived experiences also highlights the relative *slowness* of other experiences. The historical basis of this point has been made with regard to the way that the introduction of the railways accentuated the virtues of the slowness of alternative forms of transport (May and Thrift 2001, 19; Nowotny 1994; Parkins and Craig 2006, 41–42).

We need, then, to posit an understanding of modernity that recognizes that we do not encounter singular experiences of speed and geographical dislocation but rather complex negotiations of different temporalities and spatial contexts. Here, my argument draws on May and Thrift's (2001) account of *timespace* that emphasizes the heterogeneity of social time and spatial engagements. As they state:

> the picture is less of any simple acceleration in the pace of life or the experiences of spatial "collapse" than of a far more complex restructuring in the nature and experience of time and space … With these changes space is seen to both expand and to contract, time horizons to both foreshorten but also to extend, time itself to both speed up but also slow down and even to move in different directions. (May and Thrift 2001, 10)

We also need to do more than simply acknowledge such a reality; we also need to promote the *desirability* of being able to move at different speeds through our everyday lives and to engage with various kinds of social spaces. Slowness provides us with respite from the pressures of "fast life," offering us opportunities for revival and critique, but slowness can be also at times frustrating and counterproductive. Equally, greater speed in many contexts is desirable and efficient, in turn providing the possibility of slowness at other times. The value of being able to manage multiplicities of slowness and speed in a harmonious and productive way is recognized in areas such as town planning (Ambroise 1997) and it is suggested that we can extend this insight into other areas, including our engagements with the mediated contexts of public life.

Modernity is marked by not only the greater speed of social life but it also ushered in new understandings of time, and journalism was central to such change. Benedict Anderson's ([1983] 1991) famous work on the rise of "imagined communities" discusses how early forms of journalism and the novel enabled a regularizing of time and an idea of simultaneity which the medieval mind would not have recognized. Imagined communities came about through what Anderson calls "print-capitalism" and the formation of a new modern subject—"a sociological organism moving calendrically through homogeneous, empty time" (26)—enabled not only a collective, political identity and modern democratic impulses but also a more disciplined and regularized subject that could serve a burgeoning capitalist order and growing administrative powers of emerging nation-states. Journalism is still a central means by which this understanding of time is reproduced and the daily and ongoing reproduction of news production, the regular replenishment of "new" information that helps propel us ever forward in time, is also a means by which journalism is commodified.

Of course, the history of speed in journalism is also folded into the broader account of speed in modernity. As Matthew Rubery (2009, 160) has noted, the propensity of Victorian newspapers to use the term "Express" in their title "registered the public's fascination with the rapid transmission of news that seemed to embody the experience of modernity." Although, even in the midst of this transformative time, there arose a "slow print culture" within radical political circles that responded to concerns about the emerging commercial press, the creation of a mass, consuming public, and the dissolution of crafts associated with printing (Miller 2013). Indeed, it was the speed of journalism—through its adoption and use of new forms of technology and its status as a means of communication —that facilitated both economic and political developments in modernity. Reuters, the international news agency and financial data company, for example, was initially integral to flourishing trade flows through its exploitation of the speed of the transmission of information via the telegraph cable in the mid-nineteenth century (Read 1994) and it was subsequently central to the establishment of the "electronic age" (Parsons 1989) of computer-based trading in the 1970s and 1980s, enabling live trading through their monitors. As Read (1994, 310) notes: "Only through Reuters could dealers communicate with each others at high speed to buy, sell, or lend money through the same screen, taking hard copies of transactions from an associated teleprinter." More generally, we have observed the increased speed of news cycles with innovations in media technologies: the introduction of rolling 24-hour news services in the 1980s and 1990s meant that: "news on 'real-time' satellite and cable became a *flow* medium ... a turbulent river of journalistic data" (McNair 2006, 109). The culture of spin in an age of social media has more recently given rise to highly integrated, complex and quickly evolving "political information cycles" (Chadwick 2013) and it has been observed that the 24-hour news cycle has now been cut to the 21-minute news cycle following the 2012 US Presidential campaign (Mills 2012).

We now live in an *instantaneous* online news culture that incorporates not only the instantaneous dissemination of news but also immediate reactions to, and commentary on, that news (Karlsson 2011). When breaking news occurs, we now have "a visceral need for instantaneity," as writer James Gleick has observed (Dowd 2013). The information environment of breaking news has been changed in particular by mobile social media that allow continuous and contemporaneous streaming of interactive news from a range of journalistic and citizen sources that contribute to the phenomenon of what Mimi Sheller (2015) has called "news now." Indeed, in such situations the traditional sequential relationship between events and reportage is overturned: "Reporting on the event no longer follows the event, but is contemporaneous and in some ways may even precede the full unfolding of 'the news'" (20).

In response to such developments, the concept of slowness has also been promoted and applied across a range of communicative practices and media in recent years—slow communication, slow reading, slow blogging, slow television, slow news, slow media and slow journalism. Cumulatively, these burgeoning communicative commitments and practices are responding to a digital media environment that is characterized by informational ubiquity, the increased velocity of circulation of that information, and growing expectations that citizens and consumers will align themselves with the temporality of such a digital media environment. In response, it has been asked what is lost with such fast communication and media, and what do we gain in those instances where we communicate slowly. Such questions have been taken up by the Slow Media movement (http://slowmedia.typepad.com/slow-media/), outlined in the Slow Media manifesto (http://en.slow-media.net/manifesto) and explored by a number of slow media practitioners across a range of types of media. Outlets such as *Delayed Gratification* (http://www.slow-journalism.com/delayed-gratification-magazine), *Narratively* (http://narrative.ly), *Aeon* (http://aeon.co/magazine/) and *Long Play* (http://longplay.fi/), for example, have been flagged as publications where there is a commitment to a slower form of journalism which is attuned to different rhythms of news production and reception, and the possible coverage of subjects not normally scrutinized by mainstream journalism. Academic research has started to give voice to the idea of slow journalism (Gess 2012; Greenberg 2012; Le Masurier 2015; Rauch 2011), sometimes attempting to translate the philosophical basis of the Slow Food movement—captured in its principles of "Good, Clean and Fair"—to the craft of journalism. Gess (2012, 60), for example, suggests that: "Good" could be manifested in quality journalism, "a measured and well-researched journalism that is more than just a gathering of 'facts'"; "Clean" could be applied to the production and consumption of a journalism "which is not corrupt or abusive of the communities in which it is practiced"; and "Fair" could be journalism that is "accessible to a community" and where "conditions of employment and remuneration … are not exploitative."

The Temporality of the Journalistic Field

If we are to understand and locate the value of slowness in journalism we must appreciate the various and complex contributions that journalism has made in the development of modernity. As John Hartley has noted:

> journalism is *the* sense-making practice of modernity … [it] is caught up in all the institutions, struggles and practices of modernity … to such an extent that in the end it is difficult to decide whether journalism is a product of modernity, or modernity a product of journalism. (Hartley 1996, 33–34, author's italics)

I have argued that journalism has contributed to both the disciplinary and emancipatory impulses of modernity (Craig 2000, 2004): it has been and is implicated in the ongoing growth and logics of the capitalist order and the governance of populations while it also animates a fundamental political indeterminacy whereby society is perpetually problematized and critiqued. It is too simple to necessarily align forms of fast journalism with the former impulse but the argument is made here that slowness is a temporal feature that enables the latter function of critique. Journalism has thus always had a dual character: both deeply implicated in the production and rhythms of the culture in which it operates while also fundamentally and importantly distanced or "estranged" from such culture, always calling it to account.

Why does journalism operate at particular speeds? Firstly, journalism champions speed and timeliness because it yields the value of comparative advantage: just as one financial markets trader has an advantage over another if they have earlier access to information, so a journalistic outlet has an advantage if they are able to break news stories before their competitors. In this instance, the speed of reportage can be presented as a marker of quality journalistic practice—good journalism is timely journalism, presenting people with information as soon as possible—but this is allied with the material benefit the journalistic outlet receives from its capacity to be faster than others. Over many years I have told my journalism students the story of the day my Reuters bureau chief reprimanded me because my story on the release of the latest financial data was mere seconds behind our competitors. On a day when the financial figures moved the market that was nonetheless enough time for traders to exploit the temporal advantage.

This, in turn, suggests the second reason why journalism operates at particular speeds: journalism must to some degree be aligned with the temporality of the domains of public life that are the object of reportage. As Pierre Bourdieu (1991, 2005) outlined, journalism is a particular "field": an institutional site that polices the conditions of entry to the field and manages its skills, competencies and bodies of knowledge. Fields govern the actions and discourse of practitioners while also endowing them with power and authority. Professional fields, such as the legal field or the political field, are thus structured in a way that generates an internal consistency and logic but equally fields are partly defined by, and generate power through, their particular relationships with other social fields. Journalism, unlike other fields such as higher education, is a field that is particularly defined through its regular and highly public engagements with other fields as it participates in the sense-making processes and play of power that give shape to public life. The meanings of actions and speech within particular fields is partly determined by the temporal contexts in which they occur and journalism in some ways must operate according to the same temporality in order to make sense of what is happening—the maneuvering that might occur over a bill before a vote, or the fluctuating share price of a company after a profit announcement. Timeliness, or speed of reportage, in this sense does not have an inherent quality or value in itself—it is linked to the procedures and operations of other institutional fields. Such temporal unfolding of public events is nonetheless determined through a dialectical relationship between journalism and other fields: journalism not only responds to the rhythms of other institutions but it in turn can also influence the timing and speed of actions and speech. We are well aware, for example, that politicians may time the release of information in accord with news program scheduling and that they will structure their discourse into sound bites that can be harmoniously incorporated into the narrative of short news stories.

As we have noted with regard to speed in modernity, journalism and the fields that are the object of reportage do not operate at a singular, ever-increasing speed even though public life can be characterized generally by greater velocity. Different journalistic rounds attune themselves to the respective temporalities of their areas of reportage but also each individual field must negotiate different temporalities, managing the relationship between short-term and long-term perspectives. Political leaders, for example, have to move between the fast pace of daily politicking and the slow rhythms of international diplomacy. Journalists must also have a temporal flexibility to make sense of different phenomena. Reporting on climate change, for example, requires that journalists have ways of covering its different manifestations and representations, ranging from the sudden collapse of an Artic ice shelf to the measurement of quite literally glacial time, from the frenetic negotiations of a climate change summit to the *longueurs* of painstaking scientific research.

What ramifications does such discussion have for any positioning and valuing of slow journalism in the journalistic field? The journalistic field, like all fields, is characterized by a reputational hierarchy where the range of quality of particular news media outlets is proclaimed and perpetually policed, and where there is a wide range in the political economy of labour that spans high-profile journalistic entrepreneurs and celebrities and a journalistic proletariat (Bourdieu 1998, 5–6). The very provocative assignation of slowness to journalism is suggestive of its marginalized status within the journalistic field, challenging as it does conventional wisdom about the merits of fast, timely journalism that is synchronous with the rhythms of other powerful social fields. Most of the emerging slow journalism outlets have consciously adopted an "alternative" journalism status, seeking to avoid competitive pressures, taking time and staff resources to thoroughly investigate a more focused range of issues, and using long-form, narrative-driven modes of storytelling (Le Masurier 2015). As Le Masurier (2015, 143) states: "Effectively this means such journalism has to be produced in an independent or alternative space, probably small-scale, where such values can be realized." Of course, within the multiplicity of journalisms (Zelizer 2009) different types of journalism operate across a range of news cycles: news magazines and book-length journalism, for example, not only function at different speeds from more daily forms of journalism but they can also claim authority and prestige within the journalistic field *because* of their slower, more analytical approaches. While it occurs less frequently, slow and fast journalism could also co-exist within the one publication: *The Guardian*'s recent introduction of "in-depth reporting, essays and profiles" under the section of "The Long Read" is one example of a commitment by a major, mainstream news company to cater to different temporalities of news production and consumption. Indeed, given my earlier observation about the desirability of being able to move between different speeds, such a feature of journalistic reportage could be encouraged further with the more explicit conjunction of immediate, short-form reportage and slower, more detailed and contextual stories across individual journalistic rounds. But as Le Masurier (2015, 141) has noted, slow journalism is about much more than temporality in production. It encompasses a broader orientation towards journalism and the production of public knowledge that we can now investigate in more detail.

Critique, Complexity and Difference

We need forms of fast journalism that are attuned to the speed of modern life and which can inform us in an appropriately "timely" manner but nonetheless there are also many well-documented concerns about the contemporary state of fast journalism. The crisis in the profitability of the journalism industry due to the collapse of advertising revenue has resulted in job losses, and for those fortunate enough to retain employment, employers have demanded greater productivity levels. Journalists must not only produce more copy but also work across platforms and continually update stories. As a result of these kinds of pressures, the incidences of "churnalism" have grown (Davies 2009). It is increasingly difficult for journalists to fulfill important political and social functions given this journalistic landscape: less time for the fundamental tasks of reporting and checking facts means it is harder for journalism to perform its vital watchdog role. These concerns are underlined when the changing nature of modern life is considered. We need a journalism that is able to engage with: global economic uncertainty and the influence of neoliberal thought; necessary political and social structural changes in response to climate change; the growth of technological change and online culture; and increased global flows of people and political struggles over identity and lifestyle. The disjuncture between the state of the journalism industry and this political and social complexity only highlights the importance and value of time and slowness in journalism. The following discussion will unpack this significance through reference to the ability of journalism to offer critique, explain complexity, and investigate pluralism and difference.

In recent years there has been something of a recasting of journalism and journalistic authority in response to the contexts of online news, social media, and the mobile modes of news consumption. In his discussion of the changing spaces of news consumption, Peters (2012) notes that journalism is now produced in accord with the speed of the information age, the increasingly mobile spaces of consumption, and it now provides and interacts with multiple channels of access for news consumers (699–700). He declares that "the emerging technologies and increasingly mobile spatialities of journalism do more than just replicate news content—by changing the public's experience of journalistic consumption, they change what news *is*" (701, author's emphasis). More particularly, with regard to the immediacy and speed of online news, it has been noted how the ability to master the accelerated speed of news production informs self-perceptions and normative evaluations of journalistic practice amongst online journalists (O'Sullivan and Heinonen 2008; Robinson 2007). These changing dynamics of journalistic production and practice have thus triggered challenges to understandings about the nature of truth production in journalism and journalistic authority. Journalists' traditional authority stemmed from their ability to gather information and engage in processes of verification in order to present a finished authoritative product to news consumers. Now, the fast and perpetual dissemination of news alters its truth-value and knowledge claims: "Immediacy means that different provisory, incomplete and sometimes dubious news drafts are published" (Karlsson 2011, 279). Truthfulness is therefore rendered more problematic and determined more through modes of public reception and journalistic authority is generated through a strategy of transparency where it is demonstrated there has been a fulsome and fluid dissemination of information (283).

As already flagged, there are significant expressions of concern and challenges to such processes and value positions. It could be argued that the long-standing tension within journalism to be both accurate and timely has been stretched to breaking point with the sacrifice of the former, and that there has been subsequent declines in the quality of journalism. The speed of access to news is said to alter the nature of public comprehension of the news: "The public's right to know has been supplanted by the public's right to know everything, however fanciful and even erroneous, as fast as technology allows" (Rosenberg and Feldman 2008, 17). Even if one acknowledges that the more problematic nature of truth production and its more public, contested character in fast journalism may be more desirable than its pre-determined and singular presentation in traditional journalism, we are still left with the problem of the public contexts within which such judgments are made. The fast pace of public life and the necessity of quick evaluations means that public understanding may be more likely to rely on the mobilization of pre-existing and often stereotypical frameworks and value systems.

In response to these outlined trends in contemporary journalism, we need to reassert the fundamental importance of critique for journalistic practice. Reportage that is primarily informed by the need to quickly transmit information can sacrifice the ability to apply a critical perspective to the subject of reportage. Critique, crucially, takes time. Agger (2004, 132–133) reminds us that Adorno and his Frankfurt School colleagues bemoaned that critical consciousness was eroding in fast capitalist culture and observes the "bigger picture, like a complicated jigsaw puzzle or mosaic, can only be grasped from the vantage of distance [and that] … social critics must slow down their worlds in order to grasp and then reorder them." Critique requires a thoughtful, considered response that involves the comparative evaluation of other, competing viewpoints. Critique has value because it can undermine or strengthen the validity of information and contentions, and it can also generate new understandings. Such an argument should not be seen as a romantic valorization of earlier journalistic times, nor should we establish a binary that denies contemporary journalists engage in the professional treatment of source material, but we do need to defend the value of time, indeed slowness, as a means for journalists to be able to exercise an essential function of their craft. It is true that social media such as Twitter can enable quick "fact checking," although research suggests that political journalists are primarily using the technology to quickly transmit statements and opinions rather than engage in verification of detail (Coddington, Molyneux, and Lawrence 2014). In addition, while such fact checking is an important function of journalism, it does not replicate the more substantive process of critique that has been outlined here.

The fourth estate role of journalism is predicated on the ability of journalism to critique the institutions of the state to ensure they are accountable and answerable to a well-informed public (Hampton 2010). While the intermediary value of journalists to facilitate dialogue between the governors and the governed may be evolving given the rise of social media and online contexts, journalists are still crucial as sense-making agents and their professionalism is based upon having "as full an awareness of the issues they are reporting on as possible" and that they are able "to bring considerable intellectual power and broad awareness to the issues they are investigating" (Economou and Tanner 2008, 12). In addition, as I have previously argued (Craig 2004, 19–20), journalism is more than a simple observer, providing notification when the democratic process goes awry: it fundamentally animates and extends democracy through its unending process of challenge and critique. The fourth estate function of journalism is also predicated on the separation and independence of journalism from those powerful institutions that are the subject of critique. I have already discussed the need for many forms of journalism to be synchronous with the fields on which they report but equally it is argued that the important need for journalism to be also independent from these powerful institutions can be partly facilitated by forms of slow journalism. Slowness provides journalism with the distance from the rhythms and "logics" of other fields that can enable critique. Of course, different forms of reportage within a particular round—ranging from breaking news to features—provides journalism with the flexibility to be both synchronous and more asynchronous with the temporality of the reported field, offering varying types and levels of critique, but the underlying point here is the value of slowness in the critique of fields that are increasingly governed by and valorize speed.

The complexity and simultaneity of contemporary public life demands not only immediate reportage but also forms of slow journalism. The development of modernity and the more recent emergence of digital culture have not only facilitated the greater speed of information transmission and pace of life but also an exponential increase in informational complexity. Such informational complexity offers great emancipatory potential and means of knowledge production but it also can give rise to information overload, cognitive dissonance, disorientation and risk. Finding times and spaces where one can disengage from and assess such complex information flows is an increasingly necessary feature in the management of everyday life and it is argued here that forms of slow journalism are also valuable means by which such informational complexity can be thoroughly explored and appropriately synthesized for public understanding. Of course, investigative journalism has long been a way of responding to the complexity of modernity. There have been many famous examples—such as the *Sunday Times* investigation of the Thalidomide scandal in the 1960s and 1970s—where journalists have slowly and painstakingly enquired into complex institutional contexts to reveal wrongdoing and injustices. Such journalism has helped reveal the contours of the risk society (Beck 1992) where we attempt to negotiate the hazards and insecurities that have been generated by the complexities of the modernization process.

Journalism has responded to the growing complexity of modernity through innovative forms of reportage, most recently through forms of data journalism. Here journalism is able to access available online data and use open-source tools to analyze the information

(Gynnild 2013). Major newspapers, such as *The Guardian* and *The New York Times*, have engaged in various data journalism projects which are valuable means by which journalism can use and assess government databases, build their own databases, receive public input and improve democratic transparency (Flew et al. 2012; Stray 2010). Sheller (2015) also tells of the ways that reportage of disaster zones has been assisted by the sharing through social media of various forms of geo-tagging and open-source news maps that provide information about the movements of people, the scale of infrastructure damage in particular areas and the distribution of relief supplies. Such forms of reportage are innovative uses of online media and technological innovations to match the growing speed and complexity of public life while also allowing reporters to continue to fulfill journalistic ideals. Such reportage, however, also takes time. Gynnild (2013) recalls the award-winning investigative project of Charles Duhigg and his team from *The New York Times* that used data journalism to unearth the scale of toxic water across the United States. She notes the resources and time required for such a project: the newspaper invested in 10 experts over a period of several months in order to complete the project. Complexity is also not only encapsulated synchronically in the form of a single mass of information but it is also manifested diachronically. The meaning of large, complex events, such as the disaster reportage that Sheller (2015) discusses, for example, is not only captured in their immediate occurrence but in their long and complicated unfolding, and slow journalism is able to capture the full, comprehensive effects of such events.

The complexity of modern democratic life is also expressed through the erosion of traditional value systems, increased pluralism and the more public circulation of expressions of difference. We have seen the universal, homogeneous nature of citizenship challenged by the particularities of identity politics (Plummer 2003; Young 1989). Fast forms of journalism must rely to a greater degree on the mobilization of political, social and cultural assumptions in reportage, but this becomes increasingly problematic when so many expressions of identity and lifestyle challenge more traditional ways of life and understandings of community. Of course, proliferating expressions of difference are now for many at least a taken-for-granted background of the mosaic of public life, but more substantively the value systems and identities of societies are increasingly challenged by processes of globalization and multiculturalism as we see, for example, in political and journalistic reactions to a whole raft of issues relating to identity, such as LGBT, indigenous and refugee rights, and political issues more broadly, such as terrorism, financial austerity and climate change.

Journalism has long had difficulties reporting on marginalized communities (Awad 2011; Bullock, Wyche, and Williams 2001; Mickler 1998; Sonwalkar 2005) and it has been well noted how the tenets of objective, balanced journalism and reliance on "authoritative," bureaucratic sources not only facilitate efficient forms of reportage and quick processes of news production but they also can serve to reinforce ideological bias (Bennett 2005). Journalists have been portrayed as "acultural" in that they "subscribe to the dominant culture's claims of 'cultural invisibility' and treat people 'with culture' ... as objectified others" (Awad 2011, 528; citing Rosaldo 1993, 197). Some have considered how journalism should respond to the contexts of increasingly complex and diverse societies. Glasser, Awad, and Kim (2009, 63), for example, observe that "rather than conceptualizing journalism in relation to a unitary public sphere, ... a multi-cultural conception of journalism [could] posit ... a range of publics whose discursive needs define the division of labor among newsrooms."

The importance of slowness in journalism in the reportage of difference can also be gleaned from work that highlights the importance of "listening" in journalism (O'Donnell

2009). The importance of listening has been recognized recently across a broader range of cultural and communicative processes (see *Continuum* special issue, Vol. 23, No. 4, 2009) and in journalism in particular it can be a useful corrective to the belief that the interests and well-being of particular communities can be resolved merely by the provision of a "voice" through a diversity of communicative channels in a culture of online media and social networking sites. Instead, as O'Donnell observes (2009, 505), "the redistribution of communication resources needed for community development begins with the issue of listening." Slow journalism is necessary in a world characterized by the increasingly close conjunction of expressions of difference. Quality reportage of difference requires journalists to take the time to explore the perspectives of others and to listen to such sources in a way that not only enables the reportage of what is said but also enables greater understanding of different perspectives. Importantly, such work does not leave the journalist unchanged but it requires the reporter to be self-reflexive, open to the unsettling of pre-established value positions. As O'Donnell (2009, 510) notes, "journalism-related listening practices … seek more than 'empathy' by foregrounding interactions outside individual/group comfort zones, that acknowledge and negotiate power differentials, and engage unfamiliar and/or hostile perspectives."

Conclusion

To declare the importance of slow journalism, as with declarations about the importance of slow food, is to leave one open to charges of being unrealistic about the "realities" of the subject at best and at worse subject to accusations of being reactionary, outdated, and irrelevant! In response, I have tried to show that the idea of slow journalism forces us to think through the issue of the speed and temporality of journalism and to ask ourselves what is lost and gained with forms of fast and slow reportage. I have sought to demonstrate that modernity is characterized by different temporalities—all of us have to negotiate the different speeds of experiences in our everyday lives, and some have more resources than others in that time management. That said, I have also argued that it is desirable that we manage multiplicities of speed and slowness and this extends to different kinds of journalism: at times we require journalism that is synchronous with the speeds of modern existence and at other times we require journalism that is able to distance itself from such requirements and is able to offer more contemplative and critical perspectives. I have briefly identified some of the news media outlets that are emblematic of the emerging "slow journalism" movement but my focus here has been more on reclaiming the importance of slowness in journalistic practice more generally, noting how it facilitates important functions of critique, the management of complexity and the comprehensive reportage of difference. I argued that the increased speed of public life and journalistic production makes it more difficult for journalists to engage in the substantive process of critique that is fundamental to the craft and that such critique requires time, and indeed slowness. Similarly, I have argued that slowness helps journalists respond adequately to the complexity of modern public life, even where reportage is facilitated by the use of new online resources, such as with forms of data journalism. Finally, it was argued that slowness could assist journalists engaging with expressions of cultural difference, allowing them time to understand alternative arguments and value systems, and also to reflect upon their own assumptions that they bring to their reportage.

ACKNOWLEDGEMENTS

The author wishes to thank Wendy Parkins for her work and assistance with references.

DISCLOSURE STATEMENT

No potential conflict of interest was reported by the author.

FUNDING

This work has not received any funding or grant support.

REFERENCES

Adam, Barbara. 1995. *Timewatch: The Social Analysis of Time*. Cambridge: Polity.

Agger, Ben. 2004. *Speeding Up Fast Capitalism*. Boulder: Paradigm.

Ambroise, S. 1997. "Fast but Slow." *Slow* 4: 83–55.

Anderson, Benedict. [1983] 1991. *Imagined Communities: Reflections on the Origin and Spread of Nationalism*. London: Routledge.

Awad, Isabel. 2011. "Latinas/os and the Mainstream Press: The Exclusions of Professional Diversity." *Journalism* 12 (5): 515–532.

Beck, Ulrich. 1992. *Risk Society: Towards a New Modernity*. London: Sage.

Bennett, W. Lance. 2005. *News: The Politics of Illusion*. 6th ed. New York: Pearson.

Benson, Rodney, and Erik Neveu, eds. 2005. *Bourdieu and the Journalistic Field*. Malden, MA: Polity.

Berman, Marshall. 1983. *All That is Solid Melts into Air: The Experience of Modernity*. London: Verso.

Bourdieu, Pierre. 1991. *Language and Symbolic Power*. Oxford: Polity.

Bourdieu, Pierre. 1998. *On Television*. New York: New Press.

Bourdieu, Pierre. 2005. "The Political Field, the Social Science Field and the Journalistic Field." In *Bourdieu and the Journalistic Field*, edited by Rodney Benson and Erik Neveu, 29–47. Malden, MA: Polity.

Bullock, Heather E., Karen Wyche, and Wendy Williams. 2001. "Media Images of the Poor." *Journal of Social Issues* 57 (2): 229–246.

Chadwick, Andrew. 2013. *The Hybrid Media System: Politics and Power*. Oxford: Oxford University Press.

Coddington, Mark, Logan Molyneux, and Regina G. Lawrence. 2014. "Fact Checking the Campaign: How Political Reporters use Twitter to set the Record Straight (or not)." *The International Journal of Press/Politics* 19 (4): 391–409.

Craig, Geoffrey. 2000. "The Australian Way of Life: Journalism, Citizenship and the Constitutional Convention." *Journalism Studies* 1 (3): 485–497.

Craig, Geoffrey. 2004. *The Media, Politics and Public Life*. Sydney: Allen & Unwin.

Davies, Nick. 2009. *Flat Earth News: An Award-winning Reporter exposes Falsehood, Distortion and Propaganda in the Global Media*. London: Vintage.

Dowd, Maureen. 2013. "Lost in Space." *The New York Times*, April 23. http://www.nytimes.com/2013/04/24/opinion/dowd-lost-in-space.html?_r=0.

Economou, Nick and Stephen Tanner. 2008. *Media, Power and Politics in Australia*. Frenchs Forest, Sydney: Pearson.

Flew, Terry, Christina Spurgeon, Anna Daniel, and Adam Swift. 2012. "The Promise of Computational Journalism." *Journalism Practice* 6 (2): 157–171.

Gess, Harold. 2012. "Climate Change and the Possibility of 'Slow Journalism'." *Ecquid Novi: African Journalism Studies* 33 (1): 54–65.

Glasser, Theodore L., Isabel Awad, and John W. Kim. 2009. "The Claims of Multiculturalism and Journalism's Promise of Diversity." *Journal of Communication* 59: 57–78.

Greenberg, Susan. 2012. "Slow Journalism in the Digital Fast Lane." In *Global Literary Journalism: Exploring the Journalistic Imagination*, edited by Richard Lance Keeble and John Tulloch, 381–393. New York: Peter Lang.

Gynnild, Astrid. 2013. "Journalism Innovation Leads to Innovation Journalism: The Impact of Computational Exploration on Changing Mindsets." *Journalism* 15 (6): 713–730.

Hampton, Mark. 2010. "The Fourth Estate Ideal in Journalism History." In *The Routledge Companion to News and Journalism*, edited by Stuart Allan, 3–12. London: Routledge.

Hartley, John. 1996. *Popular Reality: Journalism, Modernity, Popular Culture*. London: Arnold.

Harvey, David. 1989. *The Condition of Postmodernity: An Enquiry into the Origins of Cultural Change*. Oxford: Blackwell.

Honoré, Carl. 2004. *In Praise of Slow: How a Worldwide Movement is Challenging the Cult of Speed*. London: Orion.

Karlsson, Michael. 2011. "The Immediacy of Online News, the Visibility of Journalistic Processes and a Restructuring of Journalistic Authority." *Journalism*. 12 (3): 279–295.

Lavis, Anna, Emma-Jayne Abbots, and Luci Attala. 2015. "Introduction: Reflecting on the Embodied Intersections of Eating and Caring." In *Careful Eating: Bodies, Food and Care*, edited by Emma-Jayne Abbots, Anna Lavis, and Luci Attala, 1–21. Farnham: Ashgate.

Le Masurier, Megan. 2015. "What is Slow Journalism?" *Journalism Practice* 9 (2): 138–152.

Marx, Karl. [1939–41] 1993. *Grundisse*. Translated by Martin Nicolaus. London: Penguin/New Left Review.

Massey, Doreen. 1994. *Space, Place and Gender*. Cambridge: Polity.

May, Jon, and Thrift, Nigel, eds. 2001. *Timespace: Geographies of Temporality*. New York: Routledge.

McNair, Brian. 2006. *Cultural Chaos: Journalism, News and Power in a Globalized World*. London: Routledge.

Mickler, Steve. 1998. *The Myth of Privilege: Aboriginal Status, Media Visions, Public Ideas*. Fremantle: Fremantle Arts Centre Press.

Miller, Elizabeth Carolyn. 2013. *Slow Print: Literary Radicalism and Late Victorian Print Culture*. Stanford: Stanford University Press.

Mills, Stephen. 2012. "How Twitter is Winning the 2012 US Election." *The Guardian*, 16 October. http://www.theguardian.com/commentisfree/2012/oct/16/twitter-winning-2012-us-election.

Montanari, Massimo. 1996. "Beware!" *Slow* 2: 56–59.

Nowotny, Helga. 1994. *Time: The Modern and Postmodern Experience*. Translated by Neville Plaice. Cambridge: Polity.

O'Donnell, Penny. 2009. "Journalism, Change and Listening Practices." *Continuum: Journal of Media & Cultural Studies* 23 (4): 503–517.

O'Sullivan, John and Ari Heinonen. 2008. "Old Values, New Media." *Journalism Practice* 2 (3): 357–371.

Osborne, Peter. 1992. "Modernity is a Qualitative, Not a Chronological Category." *New Left Review* 192: 65–84.

Parkins, Wendy, and Geoffrey Craig. 2006. *Slow Living*. Oxford: Berg.

Parsons, Wayne. 1989. *The Power of the Financial Press: Journalism and Economic Opinion in Britain and America*. Aldershot: Edward Elgar.

Peters, Chris. 2012. "Journalism To Go: The Changing Spaces of News Consumption." *Journalism Studies* 13 (5–6): 695–705.

Plummer, Ken. 2003. *Intimate Citizenship: Private Decisions and Public Dialogues*. Seattle: University of Washington Press.

Rauch, Jennifer. 2011. "The Origin of Slow Media: Early Diffusion of a Cultural Innovation through Popular and Press Discourse, 2002–2010." *Transformations* 20. http://www.transformationsjournal.org/journal/issue_20/article_01.shtml.

Read, Donald. 1994. *The Power of News: The History of Reuters. 1849–1989*. Oxford: Oxford University Press.

Robinson, Sue. 2007. "'Someone's Gotta be in Control Here.' The Institutionalization of Online News and the Creation of a Shared Journalistic Authority." *Journalism Practice* 1 (3): 305–321.

Rosaldo, Renato. 1993. *Culture and Truth*. Boston: Beacon Press.

Rosenberg, Howard and Charles S. Feldman. 2008. *No Time to Think: The Menace of Media Speed and the 24-hour News Cycle*. New York: Continuum.

Ross, Kristen. 1995. *Fast Cars, Clean Bodies: Decolonization and Reordering of French Culture*. Cambridge: MIT Press.

Rubery, Matthew. 2009. *The Novelty of Newspapers: Victorian Fiction after the Invention of News*. Oxford: Oxford University Press.

Rutherford, Jonathan, ed. 2000. *The Art of Life: On Living, Loving and Dying*. London: Lawrence and Wishart.

Sheller, Mimi. 2015. "News Now." *Journalism Studies*. 16 (1): 12–26.

Sonwalkar, Prasun. 2005. "Banal Journalism: The Centrality of the 'Us-Them' Binary in News Discourse." In *Journalism: Critical Issues*, edited by Stuart Allan, 262–273. Maidenhead: Open University Press.

Stray, Jonathan. 2010. "How *The Guardian* is Pioneering Data Journalism with Free Tools." *Nieman Lab*, August 5. http://www.niemanlab.org/2010/08/how-the-guardian-is-pioneering-data-journalism-withfree-tools/.

Tomlinson, John. 1999. *Globalization and Culture*. Cambridge: Polity.

Tronto, Joan. 1993. *Moral Boundaries: A Political Argument for an Ethic of Care*. New York: Routledge.

Tronto, Joan. 1995. "Care as a Basis for Radical Political Judgments." *Hypatia*. 10 (2): 141–149.

Virilio, Paul. 1986. *Speed and Politics*. Translated by Marc Polizzotti. New York: Semiotext(e).

Williams, Raymond. 1973. *The Country and the City*. Oxford: Oxford University Press.

Young, Iris Marion. 1989. "Polity and Group Difference: A Critique of the Ideal of Universal Citizenship." *Ethics* 99: 250–274.

Zelizer, Barbie. 2009. "Introduction: Why Journalism's Changing Faces Matter." In *The Changing Faces of Journalism: Tabloidization, Technology and Truthiness*, edited by Barbie Zelizer, 1–10. London: Routledge.

LESSENING THE CONSTRUCTION OF OTHERNESS
A slow ethics of journalism

Helene Maree Thomas

Foreign reporting plays a significant role in shining a light on stories of conflict and hardship that would potentially remain untold, but a reoccurring problem in this practice, particularly when the reportage is about non-Western countries, is the construction of otherness. In the case of Africa, Western reportage has perpetuated particular ideas about racial difference. According to Stuart Hall, this "racialized regime of representation" persisted into the late twentieth century, and while racial stereotypes have been and always are being contested, there is extensive evidence that points to a particular rhetoric when writing about Africa. Focusing on this issue of represen-tation, as well as the role of the individual media practitioner in telling the stories of distant Others, this paper examines the extent to which a methodology involving deeper engagement may provide an effective strategy for subverting negative and dehumanising representations. Specifically, it examines a set of principles for the practice of slow journalism derived from an action research project carried out by the author in Rwanda from 2012 to 2014. The results demon-strate how by taking the time to engage and collaborate with local communities, a richer, more nuanced, and ultimately more culturally responsive form of journalism is possible.

Introduction

The journalist's mission to document human life, particularly the lives of distant Others, presents a range of challenges, responsibilities, and potential pitfalls. Among them are duty of care, in the process of story gathering, and representation. Some media critics argue that it is the fast pace of the modern media environment that leads to simplistic and distorted reportage (Franks 2010; Said, as quoted in Bhabha 2005). In speaking about the Western reporting of Africa, Suzanne Franks (2010, 72) argues that the speed-driven news media place almost unrealistic expectations on journalists to "perform quickly," resulting in reporting that is "superficial and frequently full of stereo-types," stigmatising those it represents. The nature of the correspondent's work has been described as a "treadmill;" the deadline-driven culture resulting in "less time to find things out" (Williams 2011, 107); the 24-hour news cycle giving journalists "No Time to Think" (Rosenberg and Feldman 2008). Edward Said was vehemently opposed to the rapid-ity of the media as he believed it rendered the world "one-dimensional and homogeneous" (as quoted in Bhabha 2005, 375).

Despite these drawbacks, foreign reporting plays a significant role in shining a light on stories of conflict and hardship that would potentially remain untold. A reoccurring problem though, particularly when the reportage is about non-Western countries, is the construction of otherness. Through different practices of representation, the European/ Western image of Africa has tended to perpetuate particular ideas about racial difference (Karnik 1998; Watney 1989). Stuart Hall (1997, 245) noted the "racialized regime of representation" in the late twentieth century, and while racial stereotypes have been and always are being contested, there is extensive evidence that points to a particular rhetoric that still applies in foreign reportage about Africa (Franks 2013; Härting 2008; Ibelema 2014; Mamdani 2010; Ndangam 2002).

It is important to note, however, that a recent scoping review of empirical research into US and UK media representations of Africa published between 1990 and 2014 concluded there was not sufficient existing evidence to draw any firm conclusions about the nature of media coverage of Africa (Scott 2015, 3). Martin Scott contends that it is a "myth that we know how Africa is covered in the US and UK media," and no less a myth, therefore, that Africa is predominantly represented as the "hopeless continent" (3). While this is an important critique of the research into US and UK representations of Africa, Scott's focus is on perceived levels of Afro-pessimism, but the focus for this paper is rather the journalistic method itself and the constant struggle over meaning when journalists attempt to tell stories about Africa.

This paper begins with a discussion of the difficulties involved in reporting on the Other. The author conducts a close reading of a *Time* online magazine story and identifies this process of "other-ing" (Ong 2014, 181), and draws attention to the perils journalists face in foreign reporting. The article then goes on to explore a slow ethics of journalism that may subvert negative and dehumanising representations.

"A 'Spectacle' of Otherness"

Constructing a "coherent representation" out of "incomprehensible realities" is one of the greatest challenges for journalists (Spurr 1993, 3), a challenge that becomes even more difficult when the Western journalist confronts such realities in the non-Western world. How to tell a story that shows "a suffering that is outrageous, unjust, and that should be repaired," but that does not also come across as confirming that "this is the sort of thing which happens in that place" (Sontag 2003, 71) is a challenge.

In 2010, the *Time* online magazine featured a five-minute video clip and a series of photographs recounting the dying moments of an 18-year-old Sierra Leone woman as she was giving birth to her second twin (Addario 2010a). Produced by freelance photographer Lynsey Addario, the images capture Mamma Sessay's "slow and painful death" during her birth to twins in a rural clinic in Sierra Leone (Warah 2010). The story's title "Dying to Give Birth: One Woman's Tale of Maternal Mortality" suggests that Mamma Sessay will speak and tell her own tale, but it is the photographer who speaks on her behalf. Denied her own voice, Mamma Sessay is rendered a "speechless subaltern stereotype" (Christians et al. 2008, 163).

Time online magazine offers another option to view Mamma Sessay's birthing ordeal and her death. This is presented as a slideshow (12 images in total). This is called, "Maternal Mortality in Sierra Leone: The Story of Mamma" (Addario 2010b). A smaller sub-heading reads, "One woman's journey from pregnancy to death." One image shows Mamma Sessay's face contorted and her body writhing in pain. The young woman's private nakedness is made public by another image which shows her sitting up on the birthing bed supported by a nurse, unclothed, staring into the distance with a large pool of blood beneath the bed. Each photograph has a caption offering an explanation of the image.

The story attracted considerable critical attention. While it is clear that Mamma Sessay is engaged in a natural and universal human (female) experience, she is symbolically fixed as Other because hers is a birthing practice that, according to Western values, is not "acceptable" or "normal." Hers is "different," inhumane and undignified: something to fear, to be repelled by.

The media operate within a culture that, according to Stuart Hall, depends on giving things meaning and establishing social and symbolic order. It does this by marking "difference" (Hall 1997, 237). According to this theory, the order relies on a symbolic frontier between the "normal" and the "deviant," the "normal" and the "pathological," the "acceptable" and the "unacceptable" (258). There are those who belong and those who do not, and the latter are deemed as Other. In the representation of Mamma Sessay, she is symbolically fixed in the category of the "abnormal":

> It facilitates the "binding" or bonding together of all of Us who are "normal" into one "imagined community"; and it sends into symbolic exile all of Them—"the Others"—who are in some way different—"beyond the pale." (Hall 1997, 258)

Daniel Waweru, commenting on the images, argues that the young woman captured by the photographer in "her moment of deadly suffering, is a thing, not a person." What is depicted, he declares, is a moment of "hideous dehumanisation" (Waweru 2010). Scholars of textual ethics argue that portrayals of sufferers without agency reduce the capacity for audiences to identify with the sufferers and reduce their humanity and dignity (Chouliaraki 2006). According to discourse analysis, rhetorical strategies such as giving a name to the sufferer and applying visual techniques of both long shots and close-ups are assumed to confer agency and humanise the sufferer (Ong 2014, 182). Both this strategy and technique were used in this case, so why does Waweru's reading of the text lead him to claim that the photographs dehumanise Mamma Sessay?

According to Brand and Pinchevski (2013, 118), when the face of the Other is used and reduced to "a marker of pain and suffering" it is dehumanising because it strips the person of the "possibility of an autonomous address." Mamma Sessay's ordeal is therefore rendered into "a 'spectacle' of otherness" (Hall 1997, 231–232). For Härting (2008, 63), this "full frontal view" of pain and death is typical of "hegemonic journalistic practices of representing African suffering," and "typical of the reportage of postcolonial Africa that has the effect of dramatising the African corpse as a sublime spectacle of empathy" (71). The "too real, too shocking or too mesmerizing" images are both captivating and crippling (Brand and Pinchevski 2013, 118). Mamma Sessay is both reduced and magnified into the equivalent of misery and abjection: "visualized as the picture of suffering" (118).

Addario's portrayal of Mamma Sessay exemplifies the process of othering in Western journalism and shows that the situation has not altered much since Hall (1997, 225) posed his question, "have the repertoires of representation around 'difference' and 'otherness' changed or do earlier traces remain intact in contemporary society?" Subverting dominant discourses that lead to constructions of otherness is a difficult challenge for Western journalism to overcome.

A recent study examining US press coverage of Africa from 2000 to 2012 found that the "element of otherness" is persistent, leaving sub-Saharan Africa as "the ultimate 'other'" (Ibelema 2014, 173). While Ibelema's study demonstrates that there is a more nuanced coverage of Africa emerging, with media coverage of Africa's conflicts less likely to be "unduly fixated on the ethnic and primordial tendencies," the study shows that the "dimension of otherness" is still strongly evident and that "Africa and Africans largely remain a remote 'other'" (198–200). In this article, and drawing on the work of media scholars, the concept of slow journalism is explored as a counter-strategy to othering.

How to Write About Africa

South African poet and writer Breyten Breytenbach states that "writing about Africa has historically been treacherously difficult," and poses the question: *"How* to write about Africa? Can it be done?" (as quoted in Alessandrini 2012). It is this question that I take as the starting point to explore this dilemma further. If "speed, fast decision-making, hastiness, and working in accelerated real-time" (Deuze 2005, 449) are not conducive to a considered, nuanced, contextualised journalism practice, would a more measured and contemplative journalism assist Western journalists to come to grips with the specific challenges of reporting on Africa?

In writing about how journalism needed to respond to the targeted killings of journalists at *Charlie Hebdo*, Aidan White, from the Ethical Journalism Network (EJN), insisted that the story needed to be handled with sensitivity and care. "This is a time for slow journalism," he wrote, and explained that slow journalism is "when everyone in media and even those would-be journalists outside the newsroom need to think carefully about the consequences of what they write and the images they show" (White 2015).

It is these and other kinds of ethical dilemmas within "this 'fast media' world" that have allowed the idea of slow journalism to crystallise (Gess 2012, 55). Some media scholars hold concerns that conventional reporting (mainly due to the 24/7 news cycle and its reliance on speed) does not have the capacity to adequately address and comprehensively represent some of the world's most pressing issues such as climate change (Gess 2012) and regional instability (Hargreaves 2005). A slow journalism has been put forward as a viable alternative.

But the concept of "slow" varies among scholars. Susan Greenberg who coined the term in 2007, places slow journalism at the other end of the spectrum of "basic news that comes cheap (on air and online)" and the traditional print journalism that is struggling to survive. "At the luxury end," she suggests, "there should be a growing market for essays, reportage and non-fiction writing that takes its time to find things out, notices stories that others miss, and communicates it all to the highest standards: 'slow journalism'" (Greenberg 2007). However, for Harold Gess (2012, 57), more value can be found in translating the philosophical ideas from the slow food movement to journalism, namely the ideas about society and sustainability, and the principles of "Good, Clean and Fair." In other words, reporting stories that require a connection to communities on a more local level and over a sustained period (54). At the very core of these connections, Gess argues, is "respect":

> If a true "slow journalism" is to develop, it needs to ground itself in the concept of "respect," as this is core to the concept of "slow": respect for its producers, respect for its consumers, respect for the crafts that make up journalism, and respect for the communities in which the journalists work. These ideas of respect are not new, but in a world of "fast journalism" little attention is seemingly paid to them. (Gess 2012, 60)

Taking the issue of representation as I have discussed earlier, and Gess's point here about respect, whereby the individual media practitioner carefully manages the treatment of story subjects and the communities in which they work and represents them in particular ways, I argue that an effective strategy for subverting negative and dehumanising representations can be found in a journalism practice that carefully tends to these concerns.

Philosopher Isabelle Stengers describes slowing down as being about "giving chance to the event, to the encounters which have you feeling and thinking" (as quoted in Zournazi 2002, 252). A slow ethics of journalism can improve or reform the fly-in fly-out appproach where the talent is briefly taken up and discarded after they have served the journalist's purpose. The slow journalism approach ensures that journalism is "Good, Clean and Fair," and that livelihoods are supported and sustained rather than stripped of their dignity and meaning.

Based on findings from an action research project carried out in Rwanda from 2012 to 2014 as part of a PhD study, I demonstrate through my own practice as a radio documentary maker how a more patient journalism, imbued with slow qualities, was an effective strategy for lessening the construction of otherness, avoiding media harm, and creating empathic connections with distant sufferers. Influenced by the local social practices I observed during my extended residency in the slums of Kigali, I now describe how collaboration with the community came to influence my own journalistic practice.

Looking Towards Non-Western Lifeways for a Counter-strategy

The aim of my PhD study was to look towards Rwandan local social practices and to examine the effect of applying them to Western journalism. I chose Rwanda because of my previous and ongoing work there as a radio documentary maker and the connections I had established with local people.

Two parallel and interdependent action research studies were set up, each with its own distinct methodology.[1] The first study focused on the research question: What lessons can be drawn from local social practices for reducing the potential for media harm and avoiding constructions of otherness? This involved setting up a participatory media project in Rwanda to observe how local people, without any formal journalism training, approached journalistic storytelling and the localised/culturally informed methods and techniques they employed in their practice. The second action research study applied these lessons and insights to my own journalism practice as an Australian freelance radio documentary maker. I examined the effects, both on the media process and the outcome on my own practice as I told the story of a serial killing of 18 Rwandan women sex workers in 2012 and two murders in 2013. *A Silent Tragedy*, a 51-minute radio documentary, was commissioned and broadcast on the Australian Broadcasting Corporation (ABC) on 30 March 2014 (Santi 2014).[2]

The media project was set up in an inner-city slum or akajagari[3] in Rwanda's capital, Kigali, where I had spent a considerable amount of time in previous years making radio documentaries for ABC. There were four participants in total. They were drawn from an existing unaffiliated group that met regularly to discuss potential projects such as film and music collaborations. The participants were equipped with the tools and technical skills necessary for the production of radio content. The participant storytellers[4] combined their own knowledge and skills, along with the technical know-how to facilitate their own storytelling.

As a foreign journalist, the second study allowed me to deal specifically with the "important ethical issues that arise in the *process* of media production," in particular, the interactions between the story subjects and myself as the media producer (Ong 2014, 180, original emphasis). Through my own practice I tracked this media process and reflected on the interactions during production, the textual strategies used to tell the story, and finally listener responses. By developing the two parallel and interdependent action research studies I was able to examine the problem with and alongside others and then apply those insights to my own practice and account for the ways in which I practise as a journalist in a culturally different context.

Lessons for Western Journalism Practice

Through my interactions with "the true storytellers" I learned some valuable lessons about the process of collecting stories, which I could then adapt to my own practice. This required relinquishing control and questioning some of the rigid Western journalism methods and styles in order to learn from observing the group members. This helped me to develop an awareness of how people approach a variety of situations, including and especially their encounter with others for the purposes of telling their stories.

The paradigm shift, or the "epistemological break," in this specific context came through adopting a "truly social approach" to the storytelling process in order to make the framework for the inquiry ethically responsive to the local situation and to people's needs, and to protect the story subjects in a more holistic way (Schmid 2001, 230). Respecting the sense of community and spirit of collectivism meant changing the way I would normally approach people for interviews and the methods I would use for interviewing. It required acting from the epistemological standpoint that *"we are wrapped up together in this bundle of life"* (Kaunda, 1966, 32, original emphasis). The ethical base therefore was built on the notion that there is a collective good, not an individual gain (Gyekye 2010); that there is "hospitality and connection" (Murithi, as quoted in Jovanovic 2012, 51); and that there is a departure from "me first" thinking to prioritising "concern for others" (51). Core values such as reciprocity, responsibility, respectfulness, patience, and hospitality were demonstrated through the journalistic interactions between "the true storytellers" and their story subjects.

I will now illustrate in more detail the key lessons I learned from the group work of the first study, and how these insights were applied to my own practice. I will demonstrate the impact on the production and outcome of the radio documentary, and on the way my relationship developed with the main story subjects in *A Silent Tragedy*, a group of women sex workers who knew the murder victims. The three practices I will highlight here are communal interviews, listening over asking, and being emotionally invested.

Communal Interviewing

The true storytellers.   As part of the first study, Storyteller 4 chose to do a story about heroin addiction in Kigali. Storyteller 4 had set up the interview by phone, but prior to this he had met with one of the heroin addicts face to face and explained his intention was to give them a voice and put a human face to a problem that had remained invisible in the local Rwandan media. The interview was to take place at a location determined by the addicts. Storyteller 4 had asked his first source to invite others to participate in the interview. His decision to do a group interview rather than one-on-one was based purely on intuition, knowing that the men would feel more comfortable and at ease in the presence of each other. They accepted him into their space because they trusted him; they were assured that he would do them no harm. When we arrived Storyteller 4 sat himself on the floor where most of the interviewees were seated.

Lessons for the Western journalist.   Storyteller 4 had challenged the "hierarchical conventions" of the conventional interview, where, as Keeble (2014, 552) notes, there is "the unspoken power-play" where "the journalist normally attempts (however subtly) to 'control' the dialogue."

I had observed in the first study how the group interview approach lessened the problematic power dynamics between the interviewer and subject. The interview with the heroin addicts was more collaborative. The story subjects were open and candid. One of the other storytellers commented that the interview session sounded like it was a therapy session for the addicts.

In the encounter between Storyteller 4 and his story subjects there was a great amount of consideration shown towards the heroin addicts. Along with empathy, Storyteller 4 felt a degree of responsibility for those lives he had entered as a guest. For Trautmann Banks (2002, 221) it is empathy and responsibility that make up the "ethical component of narrative."

For the interviews with the women sex workers, I borrowed the method employed by Storyteller 4 and conducted a group interview. Through my translator I asked one of the women sex workers if it was possible to arrange a group of women for an interview in a location where they all felt comfortable. Prior to the interview, the translator met with the women and explained the story proposal to each of them clearly. Before starting the interview and reading the consent forms, I spent time talking with the women to establish a rapport. The interview became an informal conversation even though there was, to a certain degree, the question and answer format. It was less rigid and more emphasis was placed on listening rather than controlling the dialogue.

Not in a Hurry

The true storytellers.   Storyteller 2 chose to do a story about a young man's recovery from alcoholism and drug addiction. She arranged a time to interview the story subject. At the beginning of the interview Storyteller 2 explained to "Jacques" (not his real name) why she was interested in his story and, without any prompting, Jacques began to tell his story. He proceeded to speak for nearly an hour and a half before Storyteller 2 asked any questions. Storyteller 2 listened intently, maintaining eye contact, making head-nodding gestures and displaying empathy at appropriate times. By not interrupting him she allowed Jacques the time to tell his story and to tell it on his terms.

Lessons for the Western journalist.   Observing this interview with Jacques revealed some important elements regarding the encounter between the journalist and story subject. Reflecting on the interview afterwards I wondered whether, if it had been my interview, I would have interjected and taken back control of the interview, adhering to Western journalism practice, and if so, what difference it would have made to the way Jacques told the story. During this encounter the controlled method of interviewing was turned on its head as Storyteller 2 granted Jacques the time and space to tell his story on his terms. Approaching the interview in this way, the journalist lets go of control of the situation so that the interview process can unfold more authentically; the journalist surrenders and listens intently to her story subject. This approach echoes Francis Nyamnjoh's sentiments on the journalistic interview:

> the quality of journalism should be: if you really want to understand the story, let me not rush. Let me sit down so I can tell you the story with all its nuances … Journalism should be storytelling, but not in a hurry. (Nyamnjoh, as quoted in Wasserman 2009, 292)

Uzodinma Iweala explains that allowing his interviewees to speak for "long periods of time" and to effectively "narrate and construct their own stories" had a positive experience on those he interviewed, and was more "fundamentally humanizing":

> just allow them to construct a story I think, allows you deeper into the way they see themselves … When someone is allowed to construct their own story they become a real person as opposed to just a face that you map to a statistic. (Iweala 2008)

Upon hearing his story played back to him once it had been edited, Jacques experienced strong emotions that brought him to tears. He made it clear that it was not from sadness but "an edifying emotion" (personal communication, February 8, 2013). The willingness of Storyteller 2 to listen to Jacques' story "with all its nuances" was imbued with respectfulness and patience.

The insights I gained from this encounter influenced the subsequent encounters that I shared with the women sex workers in the second study. I did not set a time limit on the group interview with the women, nor did I hurry the process. The interview lasted two and a half hours, and just as Storyteller 2 had done with Jacques, I stayed around after the interview. I showed human emotions such as empathy and compassion towards the women as they shared their stories with me. This approach to journalism makes space for the "common people" to articulate their own needs and possible solutions to their own problems (Christians 2004, 250). It requires the journalist to relinquish control, and again places more importance on listening over asking.

Emotional Investment

The true storytellers. Storyteller 2's impressions of the interview with Jacques revealed that listening to his story had a transformative effect on her. She considered the experience as life changing. She referred to her meeting with Jacques as "destiny" (personal communication, February 11, 2013). The interview marked a personal transformation—an epiphany —for her and she recognised her powerful position as intermediary. On reflecting about retelling Jacques' story, Storyteller 2 made it clear that she wanted to do his story justice and how she wanted to make the audience, "my audience," feel the emotions, and even have the experience that she had.

Lessons for the Western journalist. In conventional journalistic practice there is a certain professional distancing from the story subjects/sources. This kind of stand-offish persona, or aloofness, is anathema to the personable, hospitable, brother/sisterhood relationality that is inherent in the Rwandan cultural context. Drawing on inspiration from Storyteller 2, I used "intimacy" as part of my approach. In other words, I became emotionally invested.

When journalists partake in an experience; or put another way, when they take the time to feel into someone else's experience, the stories they tell become imbued with human qualities so that audiences partake in the experience also (Couldry 2006, 6). They are not just events "devoid of shared experience" but intimate accounts of a meaningful interaction that takes place between human beings (Carpignano, as quoted in Morley and Robins 1995, 144).

Like Storyteller 2, my encounter with the women went above and beyond simply retrieving their stories. Seeing them let their guard down, I reciprocated and let down mine, and during moments of emotional outpouring, I did not hold back from showing concern by reaching out and offering reassurance. The time spent engaging in conversation and hearing their testimonies moved the translator and me deeply. I walked away from the experience changed in some way, just as Storyteller 2 was after her encounter with Jacques. The professional distance that Western reporters are supposed to have with their subjects is to some extent antithetical to the core values of many African societies. As Kaunda (1966, 32) argues, "even amongst strangers there is an inherent bond."

This approach required spending time immersing myself in the place and getting to know the people. On previous reporting visits I had rented houses in the same neighbourhood so I was already a familiar figure. Dwight Conquergood (2013, 11) notes that the field experience is essential to "encounter the context—the smells, sounds, sights, emotional tensions, feel—of the culture." Likewise, Nyamnjoh notes the benefits to storytelling when journalists stay "long enough to create a relationship that brings out the issues with the necessary nuances and contradictions" (as quoted in Wasserman 2009, 292). Taking this approach required becoming a member of the community; it meant no longer being a "spectator of the process," but to have "a personal stake" in the process (Blankenberg 1999, 49–50). It is a kind of journalistic practice that aligns itself with "the interpretations and epistemologies of the 'common people' in order to tell the stories that accurately reflect, and reflect on, their concrete experiences and spiritualities" (59).

The impact of a slow and patient journalism practice can be, as Jacques explained, "edifying" for the story subject, and "life-changing" for the journalist, as experienced by Storyteller 2. In this sense, the storytelling process is mutually beneficial for both parties. In other words, it is collaborative, and not exploitative. It empowers both the story subject and the journalist, thus it is reciprocal.

Witnesses to the Representation

I will now consider the effect the radio documentary had on listeners. This comprises an analysis of the listener responses following the broadcast of *A Silent Tragedy* on ABC Radio National. The responses included comments on the website, a phone message left on the station's feedback line, and one hand-written letter addressed to myself.

I also include here responses from two sessions that were set up to gather feedback from specific audiences. There were two groups set up for this purpose. One group consisted of three females (35+, middle class, European Australian). The second group comprised five Rwandan male journalists (30+, middle class). Both groups listened to the documentary and then engaged in an open discussion. The participants engaged with questions of representation, such as whether the story subjects are portrayed with humanity and agency and whether applying local social practices resulted in a practice that lessened the construction of otherness, reduced the potential for media harm, and gave greater consideration for the story subjects. This feedback was recorded and transcribed.

Listener Responses Following Broadcast

After hearing the documentary four female listeners contacted the station. Two of these women felt compelled to "do something." One of the women was moved by the programme and was particularly concerned by Julienne's story (one of the murder victims) and the fate of her surviving children:

Listener 1

19 May 2014 7:05:27 am

… congratulations on a powerful, moving program which was so respectful of the women and their families and explored the utter helplessness of their situations with such clarity. I would like to do something to assist Julienne's family if possible. With the view of then doing something for the bereaved families of other murdered women, and the women currently working in such a dangerous occupation.

Another woman also said the documentary moved her deeply. She posted a comment on the programme website:

Listener 2

4 April 2014 3:15:15 pm

This is a beginning, to speak the truth.

Now.

What can we do to help these women?

Seriously, what can I do to help? Can I petition someone?

Can a fund be started for the children of these murdered women? Is there a charity that is seeking to empower these women like Opportunity Australia?

Can you post what we can do from here?

Thank you.

Another listener expressed a similar response:

Listener 3

31 March 2014

I was very moved by this story and wondered what I could do to give these women and their children hope, dignity and an escape from their situation … I would happily lend these ladies some money to start their own business to get a new start on life.

Another comment emphasised the "dignity and courage" portrayed in the documentary:

Listener 4

6 April 2014 3:18:30 pm

In my 60's now and this has got to be one of the best documentaries I've ever heard! Story is terrible, wonderful to hear, extremely sensitive. It's about dignity and courage in the extreme. One's quality of life is deepened immeasurably by being edified by this one! Thank you ABC!

The first three of these responses suggest that the women felt a sense of responsibility to the women, those who had suffered, and who were still suffering, which led to a desire to take action (Listener 1 fundraised for six months post-broadcast and raised over A$10,000). The listeners expressed discourses of compassion. These women were able to locate the "distant sufferers" inside their own community of belonging and deemed the suffering relevant; they were able to empathise with the women and their situations (Chouliaraki 2008, 7). These responses illustrate that these listeners were able to approach the "distant sufferers" with a "degree of comprehension and sensibility" (Silverstone 2002, 770).

Feedback Sessions

There were similar sentiments expressed in the feedback sessions. Journalist 1 commented that the documentary had not reduced the humanity or dignity of the story subjects and had instead portrayed the women sex workers in a "positive" way:

In terms of how you have portrayed an African story I think for that you are very successful in that you don't portray any condescending attitude towards Africans. Your story gives the subjects the equal human dignity you would give an Australian citizen if they were facing a similar problem which is a credit to you. For me as a Rwandan I don't have any complaint with that portrayal, even for the listeners in Australia they would connect with the women as equal people who facing a problem, some of who are being murdered but it does not portray Africans as wretched, that attitude does not appear there.

Other comments such as "there's no power imbalance;" "there's an equality;" "there's a reverence for their stories;" "you told such a depressing story with such beauty and dignity … you gave a depressing story a real sense of power" demonstrate that for these listeners the documentary succeeded in humanising the women story subjects.

And it feels like the story has so beautifully given us an experience into their life, and it's through having the empathy or that connection with these women that we can take that into our hearts and then we can feel we have that connection. (Woman 2)

While the small sample has no statistical validity, the responses do provide some insight into the impact of the documentary format on listeners. The women, for example, reacted differently to the men, supporting Martin Scott's findings that older and female participants are more likely to have emotional responses to distant suffering. The longer storytelling format also provoked emotional and empathic responses, again reflecting Scott's observation that

Compared to talk and comment about news texts, participants' responses to documentaries and current affairs television programming had significantly greater association with multiple forms of emotion and action, with suffering others occupying space–times of greater complexity and with humanised distant others. (Scott 2014, 18)

Drawing on the insights and values from the first action research study resulted in a practice that presented the distant Other with human qualities, and therefore lessened the construction of otherness. It was an invitation for the listener to enter a "lived felt experience" (Holman Jones, as quoted in Mason 2012, 139). In many ways it conflicts with the norms of Western journalism such as independence and detachment but it is more in tune with the "specificities of the locale" (Nyamnjoh, as quoted in Wasserman 2009, 281). To use Nyamnjoh's words, doing journalism that is "not in a hurry," and that "dig[s] at the roots of issues," means that a story can never be summarised, and can never produce any straightforward answers (292–293).

Conclusion

The aim of this study was to overcome perceived shortfalls of Western journalism and to address the political and ethical dilemmas that Western journalists face in attempting to tell Africa's stories. The first study provided the opportunity for me to watch and learn from those with local knowledge. "The true storytellers" used methods informed by their own cultural values, beliefs, paradigms, social practices, and ethical protocols: methods that are more compatible with their local contexts and social fabrics (Muwanga-Zake 2010, 69–70). Through them I gained new insights about practice. I became witness to a more patient journalism, imbued with "slow" qualities.

During his encounter with the heroin addicts, Storyteller 4 extended the normative African ethic of brotherhood, which incorporates social and moral virtues such as hospitality and responsibility (Gyekye 2010). Likewise, the willingness of Storyteller 2 to listen to Jacques' story "with all its nuances" was imbued with respectfulness, patience, and reciprocity; qualities that reflect a slow storytelling practice. Based on these observations and application to my own practice, I have established a set of principles that are applicable for a slow ethics of journalism:

- *Reciprocity*: mutually beneficial; the journalistic encounter is empowering and transformative to both story subject and journalist.
- *Responsibility*: due consideration given to story subjects: collective responsibility (responsibility to oneself and to others).
- *Respectfulness*: respectful relationships with story subjects.
- *Patience*: a slowly evolving storytelling practice; allowing interviewees to speak for long periods of time; letting go of control.
- *Hospitality*: concern for others (attending to the stranger as an equal); communal feeling; hospitality towards the stranger, the different, the Other.

Applying these principles, I contend, leads to ethical encounters with far-away Others and an ethical media process. The importance of immersion and slowing down is emphasised; a slowing down that allows the story to emerge and develop, relationships to deepen, and trust to build. Slowing down and taking time is a somewhat daunting idea in light of the media blitz of fast and furious news and endless streams of up-to-the-minute headlines and sound bites which attempt to capture the world's events as they are unfolding. Slowing down means bucking the current media system. In many ways, it is an anti-capitalist idea because it refuses to "grab" and "react," instead it wants to "feel the possibility of new creations, new connections" (Stengers, as quoted in Zournazi 2002, 250).

In the age of rationalisation of resources where journalists have less time for developing rapport with story subjects and allowing trust to develop, merely suggesting a more patient journalism that allows for longer, drawn out interviews, emotional investment, and spending long periods of time getting to know the people and the place could easily be scoffed at by time-poor journalists as well as harried editors and producers. But with an increasing number of voices demanding more ethical encounters between journalists and their subjects, and the creation of narratives that preserve their worthiness and dignity, it may be time to seriously question the efficacy of an "instant" or fast journalism (Hargreaves 2005, 2), especially when it results in abuse, stereotyping, and injustice within the communities in which it is practised.

ACKNOWLEDGEMENTS

In developing the ideas presented here, I have received helpful input from Dr Gail Phillips. This study was conducted with an ethical clearance from the Human Research Ethics Committee of Murdoch University, Western Australia.

DISCLOSURE STATEMENT

No potential conflict of interest was reported by the author.

NOTES

1. For a full explanation of the methodology, see Thomas (2015).
2. I used a pseudonym to protect the identity of the story subjects who were granted anonymity in the radio documentary.
3. In the Kinyarwanda language, highly populated low-income communities with many small houses intermingled together are called *akajagari* (the word literally translated means disorder).
4. The participants of the first study gave themselves the title, "the true storytellers." It is for this reason that I refer to the participants cited later in this article as Storytellers 2 and 4.

REFERENCES

Addario, Lynsey. 2010a. "Dying to Give Birth: One Woman's Tale of Maternal Mortality." *TIME*. June 14. http://content.time.com/time/video/player/0,32068,89844377001_1994479,00. html.

Addario, Lynsey. 2010b. "Maternal Mortality in Sierra Leone: The Story of Mamma." *TIME*. June 14. http://content.time.com/time/photogallery/0,29307,1993805,00.

Alessandrini, Anthony. 2012. "Imagine Africa." *Jadaliyya* January 31. Accessed November 27, 2014. http://www.jadaliyya.com/pages/index/4208/maghreb.jadaliyya.com/ [27 November 2014].

Bhabha, K. Homi. 2005. "Adagio." *Critical Inquiry* 31 (2): 371–380.

Blankenberg, Ngaire. 1999. "In Search of Real Freedom: *Ubuntu* and the Media." *Critical Arts* 13 (2): 42–65.

Brand, Roy, and Amit Pinchevski. 2013. "Towards an Ethics of Seeing." In *Ethics of Media*, edited by Nick Couldry, Mirca Madianou, and Amit Pinchevski, 39–56. London: Palgrave Macmillan.

Chouliaraki, Lilie. 2006. *The Spectatorship of Suffering*. London: Sage.

Chouliaraki, Lilie. 2008. "Distant Suffering in the Media: Professor Lilie Chouliaraki Inaugural Public Lecture." February 27. LSE (unpublished). http://eprints.lse.ac.uk/21453/.

Christians, G. Clifford. 2004. "Ubuntu and Communitarianism in Media Ethics." *Ecquid Novi: African Journalism Studies* 25 (2): 235–256.

Christians, G. Clifford, Shakuntala Rao, Stephen J. A. Ward, and Herman Wasserman. 2008. "Toward a Global Media Ethics: Theoretical Perspectives." *Ecquid Novi: African Journalism Studies* 29: 135–172.

Conquergood, Dwight. 2013. *Cultural Struggles: Performance, Ethnography, Praxis*. Ann Arbor: The University of Michigan Press.

Couldry, Nick. 2006. *Listening Beyond the Echoes: Media, Ethics and Agency in an Uncertain World*. Boulder: Paradigm Publishers.

Deuze, Mark. 2005. "What is Journalism?: Professional Identity and Ideology of Journalists Reconsidered." *Journalism* 6: 442–464.

Franks, Suzanne. 2010. "The Neglect of Africa and the Power of Aid." *The International Communication Gazette* 72 (1): 71–84.

Franks, Suzanne. 2013. *Reporting Disasters: Famine, Aid, Politics and the Media*. London: Hurst.

Gess, Harold. 2012. "Climate Change and the Possibility of 'Slow Journalism'." *Ecquid Novi: African Journalism Studies* 33 (1): 54–65.

Greenberg, Susan. 2007. "Slow Journalism." *Prospect*, February 26. http://www.prospectmagazine.co.uk/magazine/slowjournalism/#.UiahWuDtKfR.

Gyekye, Kwame. 2010. "African Ethics." *Stanford Encyclopedia of Philosophy*. September 9. http://plato.stanford.edu/entries/african-ethics/.

Hall, Stuart. 1997. *Representation and Signifying Practice*. London: Sage.

Hargreaves, Ian. [2003]2005. *Journalism: A Very Short Introduction*. New York: Oxford University Press.

Härting, Hieke. 2008. "Global Humanitarianism, Race, and the Spectacle of the African Corpse in Current Western Representations of the Rwandan Genocide." *Comparative Studies of South Asia, Africa and the Middle East* 28 (1): 61–77.

Ibelema, Minabere. 2014. "'Tribal Fixation' and Africa's Otherness: Changes and Resilience in News Coverage." *Journalism & Communication Monographs* 16 (3): 162–217.

Iweala, Uzodinma. 2008. *A New Way to Speak About HIV/AIDS. The Big Think*. http://bigthink.com/videos/a-new-way-to-speak-about-hivaids.

Jovanovic, Spoma. 2012. *Democracy, Dialogue, and Community Action: Truth and Reconciliation in Greensboro*. Fayetteville: The University of Arkansas Press.

Karnik, Niranjan. 1998. "Rwanda & the Media: Imagery, War & Refuge." *Review of African Political Economy* 25 (78): 611–623.

Kaunda, D. Kenneth. 1966. *A Humanist in Africa*. London: Longmans.

Keeble, L. Richard. 2014. "Intimate Portraits: The Profiles of Kenneth Tynan." *Journalism* 15 (5): 548–560.

Mamdani, Mahmood. 2010. *Saviours and Survivors: Darfur, Politics, and the War on Terror*. New York: Three Rivers Press.

Mason, Bonita. 2012. "A Death in Custody Story: Critical Reflexivity in Journalism and Writing." PhD diss., Edith Cowan University. http://trove.nla.gov.au/work/180938533?q=+&version Id=197072002.

Morley, David, and Kevin Robins. 1995. *Spaces of Identity: Global Media, Electronic Landscapes and Cultural Boundaries*. New York: Routledge.

Muwanga-Zake, W. F. Johnnie. 2010. "Narrative Research across Cultures: Epistemological Concerns in Africa." *Current Narratives* 1 (2): 68–83.

Ndangam, N. Lilian. 2002. "'Heart of Darkness'—Western Media Rhetoric on Africa: Constructing and Associating Meaning Over Time." Paper Presented at 23rd Conference and General Assembly of the International Association for Mass Media Research, Barcelona July 21–26.

Ong, C. Jonathan. 2014. "'Witnessing' or 'Mediating' Distant Suffering? Ethical Questions across Moments of Text, Production, and Reception." *Television New Media* 15 (3): 179–196.

Rosenberg, Howard, and Charles S. Feldman. 2008. *No Time To Think*. New York: Continuum.

Santi, Ziyah. 2014. *A Silent Tragedy. 360Documentaries, Radio National*. Australia: ABC. March 30. http://www.abc.net.au/radionational/programs/360/a-silent-tragedy/5338592.

Schmid, F. Peter. 2001. "Authenticity: The Person as His or Her Own Author. Dialogical and Ethical Perspectives on Therapy as an Encounter Relationship. And Beyond." In *Congruence*, edited by G. Wyatt, 217–232. Ross-on-Wye: PCCS Books.

Scott, Martin. 2014. "The Mediation of Distant Suffering: An Empirical Contribution Beyond Television News Texts." *Media, Culture & Society* 36 (1): 3–19.

Scott, Martin. 2015. "The Myth of Representations of Africa." *Journalism Studies*. doi:10.1080/1461670X.2015.104457.

Silverstone, Roger. 2002. "Complicity and Collusion in the Mediation of Everyday Life." *New Literary History* 33 (4): 761–780.

Sontag, Susan. 2003. *Regarding the Pain of Others*. New York: Farrar, Strauss, and Giroux.

Spurr, David. 1993. *The Rhetoric of Empire: Colonial Discourse in Journalism, Travel Writing, and Imperial Administration*. Durham & London: Duke University Press.

Thomas, Helene. 2015. "Lessening Africa's Otherness in the Western Media: Towards a Culturally Responsive Journalism." PhD. diss., Murdoch University. http://trove.nla.gov.au/work/193319028?q&versionId=211686119

Trautmann Banks, Joanne. 2002. "The Story Inside." In *Stories Matter: The Role of Narrative in Medical Ethics*, edited by Rita Charon and Martha Montello, 219–226. New York: Routledge.

Warah, Resna. 2010. "Images of the 'Dying African' Border on Pornography." *Daily Nation*, July 4. http://allafrica.com/stories/201007050357.html.

Wasserman, Herman. 2009. "Extending the Theoretical Cloth to Make Room for the African Experience." *Journalism Studies* 10 (2): 281–293.

Watney, Simon. 1989. "Missionary Positions: AIDS, 'Africa' and race." *Critical Quarterly* 31 (3): 45–62.

Waweru, Daniel. 2010. "Dehumanised Africa." *The Guardian*, Opinion, June 30. http://www.theguardian.com/commentisfree/2010/jun/30/recognising-africas-humanity.

White, Aidan. 2015. "Charlie Hebdo: How Journalism Needs to Respond to this Unconscionable Attack." *Ethical Journalism Network*, 7 January. http://ethicaljournalismnetwork.org/en/contents/charlie-hebdo-how-journalism-needs-to-respond-to-this-unconscionable-attack

Williams, Kevin. 2011. *International Journalism*. London: Sage.

Zournazi, Mary. 2002. "A 'Cosmo-Politics'—Risk, Hope, Change: A Conversation with Isabelle Stengers." In *Hope: New Philosophies for Change*, 245–272. Annandale: Pluto Press Australia.

THE TEMPORAL TIPPING POINT
Regimentation, representation and reorientation in ethnographic journalism

Anne Kirstine Hermann

"Slow journalism" is a term anthropologist and sociologists sometimes use to describe their empirical work, ethnography. To journalists and media observers, meanwhile, "slow journalism" signifies a newfound dedication to serious long-form journalism. Not surprisingly, thus, "ethnographic journalism"—a genre where reporters adopt research strategies from social science—takes "slow" to the extreme. Immersing themselves in communities for weeks, months and years, ethnographic journalists seek to gain what anthropologists call "the native's point of view". Based on in-depth interviews with practitioners and analyses of their journalistic works, this paper offers a study of ethnographic journalism suggesting that slow time operates in at least three separate registers. First, in terms of regimentation, ethnographic journalism is mostly long-form pieces that demand time-consuming research and careful writing and editing. Second, in terms of representation, practitioners report on the quotidian rather than urgent events. Third, deceleration is an essential tool for acquiring an insider's perspective. Ethnographic journalists describe a point during reporting at which their attitudes begin to change and they start to understand how things make sense to their sources. Their accounts reveal processes of "reorientation"—an added aspect of deceleration that must be included in the debate on "slow journalism".

Introduction

"Slow journalism" is a term with which anthropologists and sociologists have, sometimes jokingly, described their work—ethnography (Pedelty 2010; Spickard 2003). Indeed, the essential difference between ethnography and journalism was imagined as a temporal one (Marcus 2003). This no longer holds true. Today, "slow journalism" is shorthand for serious narrative journalism (Greenberg 2007; Le Masurier 2015). Adopted into journalism from a general "slow movement" at a moment in time where the internet affords media an ability to publish constantly and instantaneously, the term "slow journalism" promises more informed, interpretive and explanatory reporting "with a good dose of pleasurable narrative style" (Le Masurier 2015, 149). One genre within this realm of journalism combines the original and the novel notions of "slow journalism". So-called ethnographic journalism takes "slow" to the extreme by adopting immersion strategies from social science in order to penetrate cultures and communities foreign to reporters and their readers. Based on in-depth interviews with prominent ethnographic journalists and analysis of their works, this paper presents a study of ethnographic journalism focused on the temporal dimensions of the practice. It argues that time operates in at least three separate registers.

First, ethnographic journalism abandons the traditional *regimentation* in journalism (Hannerz 2004), i.e. tight deadlines, since it is mostly long-form pieces that demand time-consuming research and carefully crafted narratives. Second, in terms of temporal *representation* (Hannerz 2004), ethnographic journalists report on not the urgent and immediate but the quotidian. Third, deceleration is an essential tool that reporters use to acquire what anthropologists call the "native's point of view". Ethnographic journalists describe a tipping point at which they begin to abandon their assumptions and adopt the outlook of their sources. Accordingly, this research suggests a third temporal dimension that I call *reorientation*: a changed set of attitudes and beliefs borne out of prolonged immersive experiences. Crossing this temporal tipping point, thus, is key to their ethnographically informed accounts from the margins. In other words, this third and hitherto neglected temporal dimension contributes another layer to our understanding of the "slow movement's" potential for journalism.

Journalistic Tempi

Since the invention of the telegraph in the early nineteenth century, the role of time in journalism has become increasingly significant. Michael Schudson (1986) attributes the very conventions of modern journalism to the industrialization of the American society, generally, and of the press, specifically. Industrialization changed the pre-industrial conception of time as cyclical—following the rural calendar—to linear—resembling the course of the assembly line: the passing of time, now, meant progress. Anthropologist David Harvey observes:

> Before the industrial revolution, time had simply "passed"; it had ebbed and flowed with the tides and the seasons, with night and day. Time was cyclical, not linear, its measurements imprecise. Few people had watches, and so they had to rely upon the church bells or the sun-dial. In the industrial revolution, time "became" money; it was to be "spent" assiduously (not "wasted") on the owner's behalf; it was recorded meticulously on time-sheets. (Harvey 2012, 11)

Schudson, in his analysis of the press' preoccupation with timeliness, argues that as news became a "constant commodity", the press developed a "fetishism of the present" (Schudson 1986, 80–81). This, he argues, resulted in time taking charge in a dual sense: on one hand, discontinuity and news pegs became a "straitjacket" for journalists, keeping them from reporting on context rather than sensation. On the other hand, "News reporters place greatest emphasis on what may often be the least publicly vital feature of media work—getting out the story on the most recent events" (Schudson 1986, 104, 108). While speed was always a factor in journalism, whether it involved rushing to meet a deadline or breaking the news before a competitor, the increasing speed of news is enabled, if not driven, by technological changes brought about by the development of 24-hour news channels, the internet and, most recently, social media (Hermida 2012, 314). Transporting Schudson's original analysis to present-day journalists, anthropologist Ulf Hannerz argues that they are "writing time" on two separate levels:

> On the one hand, it can refer to the practical, urgent fact of deadlines: It is time to write, to get your stuff ready for delivery. On the other hand, there is the sometimes more,

sometimes less obvious understanding that something about temporality is said, or implied, or assumed, in just about anything you offer your audience. (Hannerz 2004, 209)

According to Hannerz (2004, 209), these two types of temporality are matters of *regimentation* and *representation*, respectively. In other words, temporality matters in journalism in both its production—the tight organization of reporting—and its products—the temporal implications contained in its text. Scholars have engaged with the temporal aspects of journalism practices in several ways. One strand of literature is concerned with the constraints of deadlines in journalism including loss of accuracy and decontextualization of events and policy (e.g. Gitlin 1980; Reich and Godler 2014; Schlesinger 1978). Another strand of the literature is concerned with the changing chronological focus of journalism exhibiting how it not only reports on past and present events but also speculates about the future and manipulates time in the service of immediacy (e.g. Hyde 2006; Neiger 2007; Jaworski, Fitzgerald, and Morris 2003). These aspects of journalistic tempi can be indexed within existing frameworks of temporality in journalism as matters of regimentation and representation, respectively.

While news tends to dominate discussions in and on journalism, there is a long tradition, particularly in the United States, for slow-paced literary journalism. Boynton (2005, xxiii) attributes the development of long-form non-fiction to the "penny press", an inexpensive form of tabloid-style newspapers produced in the United States from the 1830s in the wake of the invention of the steam-powered press. According to Boynton, this medium gave rise to the "human interest story", i.e. information ordered in a narrative structure about "other people". Literary forms of journalism continued to emerge in American media during the twentieth century. One of the most well-known genres, "new journalism", was codified in Tom Wolfe's (1973) manifesto. Wolfe objected to the conventions of modern journalism like objectivity, news structure and speed. New journalism required immersion—or what Wolfe called "saturation reporting" (Hartsock 2000, 256). While slow forms of journalism like this have existed for decades if not centuries, "slow journalism" is a novel concept describing a contemporary response to problems caused by the acceleration of journalism, in both its production and consumption. Coined by Susan Greenberg in 2007, the term has been taken up by journalists, media commentators and a few scholars to refer to reportage, long-form nonfiction and investigative journalism that takes its time in research and production resulting in high-quality work. In the scarce academic literature on slow journalism, the main focus has been on slowness as an approach to production (decelerating the reporting process to "a human pace"), publication (e.g. launching of a quarterly news magazine) and consumption (engaging people's attention for a meaningful period of time) (Le Masurier 2015). These temporal dimensions of "slow journalism" can also be indexed within Schudson and Hannerz' distinction between regimentation (decelerated reporting, slower publication) and representation (decelerated, long narratives).

Ethnographic journalism is a domain within the field of slow journalism, which has grown into an explicit genre in the United States over the past three decades (Hermann 2014). Ethnography, in the most basic sense, comprises two interconnected activities: first-hand participation in an unfamiliar social world and the production of accounts of that social world, which draw upon the participatory experience (Emerson, Fretz, and Shaw [1995] 2001, 1). Like journalism, ethnography is thus the process and product of describing and interpreting social and cultural behavior (Barnard 2000, 4; Schwandt 2007, 96). Anthropology's ethnographic tradition is commonly attributed to Bronislaw Malinowski ([1922]

1961, 25), who described the essential task of the ethnographer as gaining "the native's point of view", i.e. learning to make sense of cultural practices from an insider's perspective. This modern ethnographic posture was later challenged by the "crisis of representation" in anthropology, propelled by the so-called "Writing Culture" movement (Clifford and Marcus 1986). This post-modern anthropology rejected the paternalistic attitude of earlier anthropologists and, inspired by philosophers like Michel Foucault, felt uneasy with the idea of "giving voice" to "subalterns" and the relationship between knowledge and power that such endeavors implied. Moreover, post-modern anthropologists critiqued the strategy of modernist ethnography of defining itself by contrast to adjacent discourses like journalism. For instance, Mary Louise Pratt (1986, 27) challenged Malinowski's writing as "symptomatic of a well-established habit among ethnographers of defining ethnographic writing over and against older, less specialized genres, such as travel books, personal memoirs, journalism, and accounts by missionaries, settlers, colonial officials, and the like".

Nonetheless, the basic tasks of ethnographers are observing, interviewing and writing, and several anthropologists have noted their inherent kinship with journalists (see e.g. Boyer 2010; Hannerz 2004; Pedelty 2010; Singer 2009). Generally, Bird (2005) observes, news journalists tend to "know the story" before even beginning reporting. In contrast to this, ethnographic journalists immerse themselves in communities without an "angle" and they also pose very different questions to very different people (Bird 2005; Cramer and McDevitt 2003). As ethnographic journalist William Finnegan told me during an interview in 2014, "This is like deep news about the country." Simply put, he and his colleagues look for meaning rather than facts, examine the ordinary rather than the extraordinary and talk to "regular", often marginalized, people rather than relying upon official sources. They have to negotiate the norms of journalism and ethnography, for instance, that of loyalty. Whereas journalists are traditionally loyal to the Public, ethnographers have to protect the people they write about (Singer 2009). Finnegan said, comparing ethnographic to traditional reporting, "my job changes". Powerful people—the traditional sources in journalism—should be held accountable, whereas "writing about somebody who's working in McDonald's I'm not there to study hard, did she cook that burger exactly as it should have been cooked. It's just completely different. I'm there to understand how she gets by". Consequently, the skeptical posture of traditional journalism is replaced with a more empathetic one. In fact, Alex Kotlowitz and Ted Conover both describe their work as "journalism of empathy". Reporting on original subjects, ethnographic journalists immerse themselves for weeks, months and years with the communities they seek to portray. The results are magazine and book-length writings and feature documentaries for film and radio.

As an emergent genre developing in the United States, I recruited interlocutors[1] among influential ethnographic journalists, whose work set the standard of excellence in their field by winning the most prominent American journalist awards. Accordingly, they were winners of the Pulitzer Prize, National Book Critics Circle Award, Robert F. Kennedy Journalism Award, American Society of Magazine Editors' National Magazine Award and Peabody Awards, in addition to one Academy Award nominee for best documentary. In order to gain the most valid insights possible, I sought to recruit interlocutors who worked on diverse subject areas like health, immigration, sports, foreign affairs, national affairs, crime and justice. I also sought, though with little success, to balance interlocutors in terms of race and gender. This proved difficult, however, since—as with many elites— white males dominate the field. Also, three women turned down my interview requests.

Consequently, I conducted semi-structured interviews with nine ethnographic journalists of which seven are men. Apart from one interview, which was conducted over the phone, I met with each interlocutor in different parts of the United States, including Chicago, Los Angeles and New York, during 2014 and 2015. Moreover, I was able to follow some interlocutors more closely and recurrently learn about their practices. Since these journalists work independently outside of newsrooms, this approach sought to replace conventional newsroom ethnography yet pursue a situated account. As we shall see, in addition to regimentation and representation, the empirical material revealed a third temporal dimension, which I call *reorientation*. Together, these three dimensions structure the following account.

Regimentation

Ethnographic journalism, being mostly book-length and magazine pieces about complex phenomena, demands time-consuming research and careful writing. For instance, my interlocutor Anne Fadiman spent several years interviewing Hmong refugees and medical staff in California to understand cultural conflicts within the American healthcare system and, in turn, the scientific paradigm of health and illness. Her book, *The Spirit Catches You and You Fall Down* (Fadiman [1997] 2012), ultimately took her nine years to report and write. Alex Kotlowitz, who wrote *There Are No Children Here* (Kotlowitz 1992), spent three years in a Chicago ghetto to gather the material he needed. More recently, he spent five months "embedded" at the notorious Harper High School in Chicago, where 29 current or recent students were shot in the span of a single year, to make a two-part episode for National Public Radio's *This American Life* (2013a, 2013b). Leon Dash spent four years with a drug-selling grandmother and her family to portray the life of America's "underclass" in *Rosa Lee*, an eight-part series in the *Washington Post*. Mike Sager spent weeks with a crack gang in Venice Beach, wounded veterans (Sager 2008) and a morbidly obese gentleman to provide perspectives from America's margins in *Esquire* and *Rolling Stone*. Nicholas Dawidoff put similar techniques to use in sports reporting when he spend a season with the New York Jets to get a view inside the mysterious world of NFL football in *Collision Low Crossers* (Dawidoff 2013). For a year, Sebastian Junger lived with US troops in Afghanistan on and off in order to understand the phenomena of bravery and brotherhood in a marine platoon. He described his experiences in articles for *Vanity Fair*, the book *War* (Junger 2010) and the feature length documentary film *Restrepo*. Sonia Nazario spent nearly five years reporting her series for the *Los Angeles Times* and subsequent book *Enrique's Journey* (Nazario [2007] 2014). Determined to go through the exact same journey thousands of Latin American minors embark upon every year to enter the United States, Nazario made the trip from Honduras to Texas riding on top of trains and crossing the Rio Grande. Reporting "Newjack", Ted Conover, spent a year working inside New York's Sing Sing prison to examine why violent dynamics between inmates and guards persist (Conover [2001] 2002). More recently, he became a certified federal meat inspector and spent months on the job in order to describe industrialized meat production closely in an article for *Harper's* (Conover 2013). William Finnegan, for his book *A Complicated War* (Finnegan 1993), spent two months in Mozambique trying to decipher the civil war. Recently, for *The New Yorker*, he spent five months with fast-food workers in New York City to learn about the people affected by the national debate over minimum wages (Finnegan 2014).

Common to these journalists, all of whom I interviewed, is that they rely on something similar to what anthropologist Clifford Geertz (1998) called "deep hanging out". Alex Kotlowitz, talking about his reporting from Harper High School, said,

> I embedded myself in this small social worker office in the middle of the school, and over the course of five months would visit there regularly and essentially listen in on the conversations in that room. I'd of course follow-up with loads of questions. So there's that part of my reporting—a kind of hanging out.

Evidently, gaining access and immersing oneself in a variety of communities and foreign territory, in one form or the other, takes time. Navigating new communities requires that reporters learn the ways of their subjects. For instance, Nicholas Dawidoff had to "learn to speak football" before he could report on life inside the New York Jets: "I mainly listened for a long time because football has its own language and it took me a long time, frankly, to understand what was going on." Others, like William Finnegan, like to let their stories "mature" before beginning the actual reporting. Moreover, to accumulate enough information to describe the everyday life of their subjects and their routines, ethnographic journalists must observe similar events over and over. Hence, apart from doing actual interviews, they spend much of their time with subjects "just socializing. You know, it's all part of developing a relationship—that they're comfortable with me, I'm comfortable with them", Leon Dash explained. Said Alex Kotlowitz, "you've got to recognize that much of your time is not terribly productive. In some ways, it is kind of wasted. But you spend all this time with people to capture those moments that do matter". This is why they can confidently give illuminating details of the mundane. Why Kotlowitz could confidently describe an ordinary shopping list of a single mother in Chicago's Henry Horner Homes. Why Sebastian Junger could account for the immense boredom in between firefights in the Korengal Valley. And why Leon Dash could tell order from chaos in the constant crisis of a heroin-addicted family:

> Her routine is the same: she orders Cheerios or the breakfast special of pancakes, sausage, and scrambled eggs. This particular morning, she settles on Cheerios. She tears open seven packages of sugar, dumps them in her coffee, then rips open several more and empties them onto her cereal. She can't stand to eat anything until she drinks her methadone, so this is her first food of the day. (Dash 1997, 101)

In addition to gaining insights as to the everyday life of their subjects, this informal time spent also helps ethnographic journalists cultivate relationships with and thus gain the trust of their subjects. Sonia Nazario said,

> The best stuff I get—if I'm reporting for six months—it's usually in the fifth and sixth month and that's when I really have to decide: am I going to stop reporting now—you have 110 notebooks, it's time to stop. Or do you keep going because that's when your subjects have really let down their guard. They're being more honest, they're being more open, they're doing what they normally do; they're not trying to keep certain things from you.

Similarly, William Finnegan had worked for several months on a story about fast-food workers, getting only "superficial" (factual) stuff like "wages and living conditions" and not the "inner life" of his subjects. Then, he decided to go with a source on a bus to Chicago for a national meeting in the movement for higher minimum wages:

We'd been there cramped together in this little seat for 18 hours and I felt like "now she trusts me". She felt physically close to me. I'm not just some reporter that she's not too sure about. I'm her buddy from the bus. From then on my reporting with her went much better and she really let me inside to learn a lot about how she felt and how she really lived, which made the piece work to me.

Naturally, the more material the reporter gathers and the longer texts he or she writes, the longer time the process of writing itself requires. Nicholas Dawidoff explained that once the compiling of information—the reporting phase—is over, the assembling of a narrative can be an overwhelming and time-consuming endeavor. Once he returned to his desk from the Jets, he went through all his 8000 pages of notes and created two outlines. One was thematic ("Pain", "Race", "Fear", etc). The other was a chronological record of events. These outlines, Dawidoff said, "were carefully braided into one. My notebooks were catalogued and cross-referenced through both outlines so I could easily find whatever information was relevant to whatever section of the book I was writing". Evidently, ethnographic journalism abandons the traditional temporal regimentation in journalism—the order and discipline imposed by the "urgent fact of deadlines" (Hannerz 2004, 213). This suggests a different journalistic regimen, a way of organizing or managing reporting and writing, which runs counter to conventional conceptions in most journalism scholarship.

Representation

As we know from earlier scholarship, temporality is a question of representation in addition to regimentation. In ethnographic journalism, this temporal representation has at least four separate aspects: something about temporality is implied in the themes and in descriptions of subjects, authors and of the reporting process itself. In terms of themes, ethnographic journalists focus not on immediate events but everyday reoccurring ones. They report not on what has just happened but on a phenomenon that is ongoing. Sometimes, they reconstruct past events to put the present situation into context. In other words, this journalism operates with different "slices of temporality" than ordinary news (Hannerz 2004, 214). In terms of authors, all interlocutors in this project took an "endpoint" position in the narrative, meaning that they made full use of what they ultimately came to know during fieldwork. Obviously, writing a narrative like this entails a measure of retroactive reinterpretation of events. Further, it lends an air of omniscience to the narrator when the journalist speaks from a temporal vantage point. A brief example is Sebastian Junger's narration of a combat event in Afghanistan:

> Unknown to Winn and his men, three enemy fighters are arrayed across the chest of the ridge below them, waiting them with AK-47s. Parallel to the trail are ten more fighters with belt-fed machine guns and RPSs. In the U.S. military, this is known as an "L-shaped ambush". (Junger 2010, 117)

Moreover, most of these writers do not distinguish between observed and reconstructed events in their narratives, although several accounts in their works are reiterations of past events presented smoothly as part of the chain of events observed in the field. In contrast to the end-point narration in journalistic ethnographies, real-time descriptions of events allow for a methodological self-consciousness through which the author can identify and explicate their own processes for discovering or attributing meaning

(Emerson, Fretz, and Shaw [1995] 2001, 107). Similarly, the use of omniscient narrators produce realist tales with an objective tone that obscures how activities and meanings unfolded for sources and how the journalist came to understand them (100).

As for reporting, its length and character is often designed in service of narrative and consummated endings. For instance, the reason Leon Dash' stories about Rosa Lee ended up taking four years was the fact that her daughter, Patty, got involved in a murder. Dash agreed with his editor to stick around and follow the trial: "The whole thing was held up a year and a half by her getting involved in the murder." Similarly, Ted Conover explained, following a conversation with his literary agent, he decided to continue in his job into the new year, in part so that he could work a shift on New Year's Eve: he had heard that the stroke of midnight was perennially chaotic, with inmates setting fire to magazines, toilet paper and other things that could burn. He wanted to see how other officers managed this, and also wanted to understand the unsettling symbolism of "setting your own house on fire". Also, this enabled Conover to describe the different seasons inside prison and the changing of the calendar, observing up-close regularly occurring events like fights, suicides, prisoners ejaculating on guards and the like. This idea is not unlike the classical anthropological trope of spending one year in the field to observe all seasons of the rural calendar, but it was, at least in part, designed to make a compelling ending to the book. Similarly, Sebastian Junger, in his account from Afghanistan, refers to "my year" (Junger 2010, 132). He explained, "the deployment was a little bit more than a year. I wanted to spend as much time as possible with them but within the constraints of my personal life and the army had rules". In the same vein, Alex Kotlowitz decided to delineate his immersion at Harper High School to a whole semester. Nicholas Dawidoff, whose book bears the subtitle "A Year Inside the turbulent World of NFL Football", "wanted to see how it worked, start to finish". As Robert Boynton told me in a conversation on September 23, 2014, this conceit, "a year of", communicating a sense of wholeness to the reader, is becoming more popular in literary journalism. As in traditional anthropology, such slowness, seemingly, serves to validate the journalistic account. According to anthropologist George Marcus, "all of the performative elements of demonstrating ethnographic authority—have depended on the valorization of a temporality of slowness" (Marcus 2003, 10). In other words, slowness itself is what validates an ethnographic account. What is time consuming in the description of certain sites and actors is not the kind of descriptive thickness that influential anthropologist Clifford Geertz (1973) promoted, but rather, Marcus (2003, 5) argues, "attention to extra dimensions of situations and sites brought into analytic relation so as to demonstrate the symbolic, real, and imaginary relations existing among them, justifying the particular assemblages of objects, subjects, and situations that the ethnography describes".

As for subjects, ethnographic journalism disposes of routine reliance on official sources and ideological elites, which is a trademark of traditional journalism (Cramer and McDevitt 2003, 131–132). Often, though not always, this journalism concerns marginalized or "subaltern" groups in society: residents in social housing, refugees, drug addicts, gang members, the underprivileged youths, immigrants, prisoners, the morbidly obese, HIV patients, minimum wage workers. Groups that are not so much part of the traditional journalistic "Public" as they are "subaltern counterpublics", i.e. members of subordinated social groups—women, workers, peoples of color, and gays and lesbians—who constitute parallel discursive arenas to mainstream public discourse (Fraser 1990, 67). However, as Johannes Fabian (1983) has pointed out, ethnographers risk representing other cultures as both exotic and simple to grasp by denying (implicitly) temporal "coevalness", i.e. the fact that "the other" and the ethnographer are contemporaries. Identifying a divergence in use of time in anthropological writing and research (fieldwork), respectively, Fabian emphasized how spatialized time distances the observer from the observed, which, in turn, removes coevalness between subject and ethnographer once the latter returns to his desk. Several of my interlocutors described how they sought to "compensate" for the close personal relationships they cultivated during reporting by distancing themselves, physically and mentally, during the writing process. Alex Kotlowitz described this process of detachment:

> When I sit down to write, I need to put some distance between myself and my subject as in the end I'm not writing for them but that rather I'm writing for my readers. That tension of loyalty is one that I think every writer of non-fiction narrative faces. In the end, your loyalty must be to your reader.

Evidently, the dual loyalty of the ethnographic journalist to subjects (the ethnographer's obligation) and to readers (the journalist's obligation) creates a certain tension in practice.

Reorientation

Thus far, we have seen how slowness affects both the regimentation and representations of journalism. But in addition to this, the analysis of ethnographic journalism reveals that temporality is also often a matter of *reorientation* in the sense that prolonged reporting time helps journalists reevaluate and abandon their expectations in favor of locally situated perspectives. In other words, deceleration is an essential tool that reporters use to acquire something similar to what an anthropologist would call "the native's point of view". My interlocutors described a sort of tipping point at which they began to identify with their sources. "Killing begins to make sense to me", Sebastian Junger stated in his writing, and in our interview he described how this reorientation took place after his second trip to Afghanistan, where he was immersed with the same platoon of US troops:

> You know, I'm a child of the 60s, I grew up in Cambridge, Massachusetts, during Vietnam. All that war and killing stuff was absolutely taboo. For me it was quite a long journey from that to being in a place out there long enough to understand even some pretty unseemly displays of enthusiasm for killing and the way I understood it ultimately was: I really care about these guys. At that point I was fully affiliating myself with them and was allowing myself to be subject to anything that they would be subject to. Whether that be physical danger or moral danger. You know, the moral danger of normalizing killing.

Nicholas Dawidoff explained how, during his immersion with the Jets, "I felt like I was in a foreign country". But after spending months on end with the team, he was "completely orientated":

> You know, there's a tension when you're doing this sort of work because you're doing the work for your reader but it was essential—when you're writing about a group—that, in one way or another, you become part of the group. If I didn't become part of the group it would have been impossible to do the job.

Ted Conover experienced growing sympathy with prison guard brutality due to the amount of time spent in Sing Sing. Similarly, he adapted over time to the mentality of a federal meat inspector while reporting *The Way of All Flesh*:

Both after working in the prison a couple months and working in the meat factory, I started saying "we" when I referred to my co-workers because you're in it together with them even if part of your brain takes note at night and thinks, "what a strange world this is". And I've often thought—after each of these experiences—that I'm not quite the same as when I began. My identity has changed a little bit, usually in a way I like but not always. With each immersion my sense of my own identity expands a little—I think of it as a rubber band. It gets pulled. It contracts again when I'm finished but never goes back to the original shape. And it's the difference between the original shape and the new that I find so significant, and am always trying to understand.

Anne Fadiman, who was effectively immersing herself in two communities—the Hmong community and the medical community in Merced, California—explained how her perception of these communities changed over time:

> Over the years, Hmong culture began to seem less strange to me and medical culture began to seem more strange. Actually, I started off not realizing medicine *was* a culture. I thought, "Oh, that's just the place I'm standing myself"—as if medicine were America and America were the default center of the universe. It took a long time for it to dawn on me: "Hmm, medicine is a culture too: it has its own vocabulary and special clothes and mores and taboos." I didn't think of that at the beginning. But once I did, understanding both cultures as cultures became very, very important.

Evidently, the "cultural apprenticeship" of these journalists enable them to exchange the "neutral" journalistic "view from nowhere" (Rosen 2010) with a situated insider's perspective or "native's point of view". In fact, there appears to be a critical point in the reporting process beyond which significant changes take place. We might think of this as a temporal tipping point: the critical point in an evolving reporting situation that leads to a new and irreversible development. For some, as seen above, this tipping point is a moment at which things that seemed strange begin to make sense. But for others, like William Finnegan, the tipping point is not a "eureka moment" but a moment of utter—but ultimately productive—confusion. As an example, he described his experiences reporting from the Mozambiquean civil war:

> I had a very firm understanding of the war because I'd never been there and didn't actually know anything. Then I went there and I reported from the countryside for a couple of months and was completely disoriented. I mean, I heard many, many, many things that overturned my idea of the war: who was who; who did what; who's responsible for which massacres and atrocities, and so on. And I eventually was just completely … I felt like I was having a nervous breakdown. For a variety of reasons I couldn't believe my own material. So that for me is more frequent. It's not that I suddenly say: "Oh, I see!" It's that I don't see and I can't see and I'm losing my grip on what I thought was true.

The experience ultimately led to his book on *A Complicated War* (Finnegan 1993) . It resembles a classic case of ethnographer's confusion, displayed as early as Malinowski's own field diaries (Blommaert and Jie 2010, 37). These accounts from practitioners—whether they are of identity changes, full affiliation, "orientation", abandoning ones "default center" or simply loosing grip—display some revelatory experiences that take place when journalists take their time. Such examples overturn established ideas not only *within* journalism but also *about* journalism.

Secondary Effects of Deceleration

With the ever-increasing swiftness of journalism, reports become equally brief—what my interlocutor Mike Sager called "the Packman of journalism". Observers have warned that "speed kills" accuracy (Campbell 2012, 4). But according to Rosenberg and Feldman (2008, 8), speedy journalism also results in "cognitive cherry-picking". By selecting only "symptoms" (information) that confirm their original hypothesis (angle), journalists content themselves with the easiest obtainable answers and are thus subject to a "bias of convenience". As Angela Phillips (2009, 99) observes, some reporters barely leave the newsroom. In fact, the democratic potential of the internet is crushed by the speed of online news, which compels journalists to prioritize "safe", well-known sources and, thus, reestablish the traditional source hierarchies of the press (100). But as this study of ethnographic journalism shows, slowness has the potential of producing revelatory experiences, which overturn the commonsense of reporters—what I call *reorientation*. This speaks to both the problems of "cognitive cherry-picking" and source hierarchies. Instead of relying upon "safe" sources, ethnographic journalists seek out untraditional ones, i.e. "ordinary" or marginalized people, and rather than confirming their "hypothesis", they invest time with their sources in order to adopt a new perspective, i.e. undergo *reorientation*. Further, such a process involves reducing the distance between subject and observer, overturning the traditional adversarial posture and "objectivity" of a news reporter. Often, my interlocutors developed friendships with their subjects. In fact, several ethnographic journalists spoke of *intentionally* subjective journalism: not commentary but journalism in which reporters invest enough time to deliver a situated analysis of events, structures and relationships. Junger said,

> My goal is to be as factually truthful as I possibly can be. And part of being truthful is acknowledging that I'm not objective. I was trying to communicate the human experience of being a soldier in a platoon in combat and by definition that human experience is a subjective one. So for me to understand that human experience, I myself have to understand the subjectivity that they're experiencing. I can't be objective and experience that subjectivity. And, you know, these are obviously delicate matters for journalists.

According to Gaye Tuchman's (1972, 662) seminal observations concerning journalistic objectivity, it is invoked, ritually, by journalists in part to make up for the fact that time pressures of news writing prohibit them from determining what is "true or false" in a given issue. Similarly, Michael Schudson (2001, 155) argues that the growing commercialism of journalism in the nineteenth century, during which speed became an essential factor in competition, was an important precondition for modern notions of objectivity. In other words, what we recognize as journalistic objectivity is tied to the urgency with which traditional journalism is produced. Over the years, however, this strategy seems to have defeated its purpose. According to Rosen (2010), the "objective" perspective—the "view from nowhere"—discourages journalists from educating their readers about what they have learned from their research: "A major reason we have a practice less intelligent than its practitioners is the prestige that the View from Nowhere still claims in American newsrooms." But not only is this kind of journalism "dumber" than it ought to be, it also does a disservice to democracy. As James Carey (1997, 139–140) observed, one can be content with "giving the facts" only where there are generally accepted rules for interpreting the facts, whether those rules rest upon cultural, political or economical values. Such conditions are certainly nonexistent when it comes to structural, economical and cultural differences like those between Hmong refugees and American doctors as portrayed by Anne Fadiman. For ethnographic journalists, having intimate knowledge of a subject enabled by time spent with sources seemingly prompts nuanced accounts, evaluations of evidence and autonomous interpretations. Fadiman explained,

> Again, time is helpful. It's helpful for years to go by because I'd go through phases in which I felt frustrated first by one side, then by the other, but time let it all come out in the wash. Eventually, I ended up with a more appropriate view of the characters on each side as flawed but basically very, very good people. That assessment is subjective in that it's how I feel about people who have become my friends, but I think it's also accurate in that I believe it to be the truth.

Investing sufficient time to (partly) abandon their own cultural commonsense, seemingly, affords ethnographic journalists with the kind of "valorization of a temporality of slowness" that anthropological authority arguably rests upon (Marcus 2003, 10). According to Mitchell Stephens (2009), the acceleration of news and abundance of information compel journalists to sell something else. That, he argues, should be "wisdom journalism": "an amalgam of the more rarified forms of reporting—exclusive, investigative—with more informed, more interpretive, more explanatory, even more impressionistic or opinionated takes on current events" (Stephens 2009, 4). This, he states, is a means of "adding value" to journalism and, in turn, making quality journalism competitive with the "hordes of Internet entrepreneurs" (13). Similarly, Neveu (2014, 539) argues that mobilizing the competitive advantages of investigative and narrative journalism by adopting tools from social science and literature can help journalism in its struggle against bloggers, aggregators and short-format news sources. This echoes the experiences of my interlocutors. Said Sonia Nazario of her journalistic niche, "I think that's what brings a value added to newspapers that people can't get anywhere else." If so, we might recast the industrialist proverb "time is money". In this context, it is not the reduction of time which increases profits. In slow journalism, "wasting time" can, in fact, produce "added value" by delivering something radically refined compared to the news products that flood the internet.

Conclusion

Studying ethnographic journalists—a tribe within "slow journalism" that takes deceleration to the extreme—this paper has shown how slowness influences journalism practices in three separate temporal registers: regimentation, representation and reorientation. In terms of regimentation, ethnographic journalism abandons the order and discipline imposed by the "urgent fact of deadlines" in favor of time-consuming immersion with local communities and the crafting of elaborate narratives. In terms of representation, these immersive experiences are often designed to help structure the written account and imbue it with narrative arc—"a year of"—exhibiting the ethnographic journalist's dual role as ethnographer and entertainer but also, as Robert Boynton said in a personal interview, that "taking the mundane seriously can be aesthetically rewarding". Reporting on the mundane, ethnographic journalists deal in different "slices of temporality" than news journalists focused on urgency. While journalism studies and the scarce literature on slow journalism have engaged with these first two temporal registers, reorientation has hitherto been neglected as an essential aspect of deceleration in journalism. But as we have seen, a temporality of slowness affords journalists with the ability to *change perspective* not merely in the sense of immersing themselves within a foreign community, but by allowing the passage of time—and with it a host of up-close, personal experiences—to gradually disarm assumptions in favor of a situated point of view. Rather than confirming an angle, ethnographic journalists generate stories about communities through what anthropologists call an "emic" perspective, or what we might describe as the insider's or "native's" point of view. They allow meanings to emerge from the ethnographic encounter rather than imposing meaning from predetermined angles or storylines. Ethnographic journalists describe a critical point during the reporting process beyond which they begin to identify their subjects and abandon certain assumptions about a given phenomenon. We might think of this as a "temporal tipping point". These renewed perspectives propel intentionally subjective reports in which journalists offer autonomous interpretations that, like ethnography, seem valorized by a temporality of slowness. Exchanging traditional journalistic objectivity and the "view from nowhere" with a "native's point of view", these practices stand in stark contrast to the "cognitive cherry-picking" associated with increased tempo within journalism. This "added value" of decelerated reporting may prove important in the press' struggle to compete with amateur reporters in an age of information overload. As such, the neglected temporal aspect of reorientation should be included in addition to the aspects of regimentation and representation in the debate on time in journalism.

DISCLOSURE STATEMENT

No potential conflict of interest was reported by the author.

NOTE

1.   I use the anthropological term "interlocutor" over "informant" or "interviewee" to stress the fact that research took place as semi-structured dialogues rather than structured interviews. It highlights the collaborative construction of knowledge and also that the researcher spent time doing participant-observation with some of the interlocutors. "Interlocutor", unlike "informant", escapes the implication that the interlocutor is somehow "snitching" on his or her community.

REFERENCES

Barnard, Alan. 2000. *History and Theory in Anthropology*. Cambridge, UK: Cambridge University Press.

Bird, S. Elizabeth. 2005. "The Journalist as Ethnographer? How Anthropology Can Enrich Journalistic Practice." In *Media Anthropology*, edited by Eric W. Rothenbuhler and Mihai Coman, 301–308. Thousand Oaks: Sage.

Blommaert, Jan, and Dong Jie. 2010. *Ethnographic Fieldnotes: A Beginner's Guide*. Bristol, UK: Multilingual Matters.

Boyer, Dominic. 2010. "Divergent Temporalities: On the Division of Labor between Journalism and Anthropology." *Anthropology News* 51 (4): 6–9.

Boynton, Robert. 2005. *The New New Journalism: Conversations with America's Best Nonfiction Writers on Their Craft*. New York: Vintage Books.

Campbell, Don. 2012. "Column: Dangers of Speed vs. Accuracy." *USA Today*, April 24. http://usatoday30.usatoday.com/news/opinion/forum/story/2012-04-24/journalism-social-media-giffords-paterno-nikki-haley/54513448/1

Carey, James W. 1997. "The Communications of Revolution and the Professional Communicator." In *James Carey: A Critical Reader*, edited by Eve Stryker Munson and Catherine A. Warren, 128–143. Minneapolis: University of Minnesota Press.

Clifford, James, and George Marcus, eds. 1986. *Writing Culture: The Poetics and Politics of Ethnography*. Berkeley: University of California Press.

Conover, T., ed. 2000 [2001]. *Newjack: Guarding Sing Sing*. New York: Vintage Books.

Conover, T., ed. 2013. "The Way of all Flesh." *Harper's*, April 15.

Cramer, Janet M., and Michael McDevitt. 2003. "Ethnographic Journalism." In *Qualitative Research in Journalism: Taking it to the Streets*, edited by Sharon H. Iorio, 127–143. New York: Routledge.

Dash, Leon. 1997. *Rosa Lee*. New York: Penguin Books.

Dawidoff, Nicholas. 2013. *Collision Low Crossers*. New York: Little, Brown and Company.

Emerson, Robert M., Rachel I. Fretz, and Linda L. Shaw. [2011] 1995. *Writing Ethnographic Fieldnotes*. Chicago: University of Chicago Press.

Fabian, Johannes. 1983. *Time and the Other*. New York: Columbia University Press.

Fadiman, Anne. [2012] 1997. *The Spirit Catches You and You Fall Down*. New York: Farrar, Straus and Giroux.

Finnegan, William. 1993. *A Complicated War*. Berkeley: University of California Pressfr.

Finnegan, William. 2014. "Dignity." *The New Yorker*, September 15. http://www.newyorker.com/magazine/2014/09/15/dignity-4

Fraser, Nancy. 1990. "Rethinking the Public Sphere: A Contribution to the Critique of Actually Existing Democracy." *Social Text* 25/26: 56–80.

Geertz, Clifford. 1973. *The Interpretation of Cultures*. New York: Basic Books.

Geertz, Clifford. 1998. "Deep Hanging Out." *The New York Review of Books*, October 22.

Gitlin, Todd. 1980. *The Whole World is Watching—Mass Media in the Making and Unmaking of the New Left*. London: University of California Press.

Greenberg, Susan. 2007. "Slow Journalism." *Prospect Magazine*. February 25.

Hannerz, Ulf. 2004. *Foreign News: Exploring the World of Foreign Correspondents*. Chicago: University of Chicago Press.

Hartsock, John C. 2000. *A History of American Literary Journalism: The Emergence of a Modern Narrative Form*. Amherst: University of Massachusetts Press.

Harvey, David. 2012. *Education and the Culture of Consumption: Personalisation and the Social Order*. Abingdon: Routledge.

Hermann, Anne Kirstine. 2014. "Ethnographic Journalism." *Journalism*. doi:10.1177/1464884914555964.

Hermida, Alfred. 2012. "Social Journalism: Exploring How Social Media is Shaping Journalism." In *The Handbook of Global Online Journalism*, edited by Eugenia Siapera and Andreas Veglis, 309–328. Sussex, UK: Wiley & Sons.

Hyde, Jon. 2006. "News Coverage of Genetic Cloning: When Science Journalism Becomes Future-Oriented Speculation." *Journal of Communication Inquiry* 30 (3): 229–250.

Jaworski, Adam, Richard Fitzgerald, and Deborah Morris. 2003. "Certainty and Speculation in News Reporting on the Future: The Execution of Timothy McVeigh." *Discourse Studies* 5 (1): 33–48.

Junger, Sebastian. 2010. *War*. New York: Hachette Book Group.

Kotlowitz, Alex. 1992. *There Are No Children Here*. New York: Anchor Books.

Le Masurier, Megan. 2015. "What is Slow Journalism?" *Journalism Practice* 9 (2): 138–152.

Malinowski, Bronislaw. 1922 [1961]. *Argonauts of the Western Pacific*. Hialeah, FL: Dutton.

Marcus, George E. 2003. "On the Unbearable Slowness of Being an Anthropologist Now." *Xcp: Cross Cultural Poetics* 12: 7–20.

Nazario, Sonia. 2007 [2014]. *Enrique's Journey*. New York: Random House.

Neiger, Motti. 2007. "Media Oracles: The Cultural Significance and Political Import of News Referring to Future Events." *Journalism* 8 (3): 309–321.

Neveu, Erik. 2014. "Revisiting Narrative Journalism as One of the Futures of Journalism." *Journalism Studies* 15 (5): 533–542.

Pedelty, Mark. 2010. "Teaching Ethnographic Journalism: Critical Comparison, Productive Conundrums." *Anthropology News* 51 (4): 25–26.

Phillips, Angela. 2009. "Old Sources in New Bottles." In *New Media: Old News: Journalism and Democracy in the Digital Age*, edited by Natalie Fenton, 87–101. London: Sage.

Pratt, Mary Louise. 1986. "Fieldwork in Common Places." In *Writing Culture: The Poetics and Politics of Ethnography*, edited by James Clifford and George Marcus, 27–50. Berkeley: University of California Press.

Reich, Zvi, and Yigal Godler. 2014. "A Time of Uncertainty." *Journalism Studies* 15 (5): 607–618.

Rosen, Jay. 2010. "The View from Nowhere: Questions and Answers." *PressThink Blog*, November 10. http://pressthink.org/2010/11/the-view-from-nowhere-questions-and-answers/

Rosenberg, Howard, and Charles S. Feldman. 2008. *No Time to Think. The Menace of Media Speed and the 24-hour News Cycle*. New York: Continuum.

Sager, Mike. 2008. *Wounded Worriers*. Philadelphia: Da Capo Press.

Schlesinger, Philip. 1978. *Putting "Reality" Together*. London: Methuen & Co.

Schudson, Michael. 1986. "WHEN? Deadlines, Datelines, and History." In *Reading the News: A Pantheon Guide to Popular Culture*, edited by Robert Karl Manoff and Michael Schudson, 79–108. New York: Pantheon Books.

Schudson, Michael. 2001. "The Objectivity Norm in American Journalism." *Journalism* 2 (2): 149–170.

Schwandt, Thomas A. 2007. *The Sage Dictionary of Qualitative Inquiry*. 3rd ed. Thousand Oaks: Sage Publications.

Singer, Jane B. 2009. "Ethnography." *Journalism & Mass Communication Quarterly* 86 (1): 191–198.

Spickard, James V. 2003. "Slow Journalism? Ethnography as a Means of Understanding Religious Social Activism." Paper presented at the Project on Religion, Political Economy, and Society Weatherhead Center for International Affairs Harvard University. September 24th.

Stephens, Mitchell. 2009. "Beyond News: The Case for Wisdom Journalism." Discussion Paper Series, Joan Shorenstein Center on the Press, Politics and Public Policy, Harvard University, John F. Kennedy School of Government.

This American Life. 2013a. "487: Harper High School, Part One." *This American Life*. Accessed April 23, 2015. http://www.thisamericanlife.org/radio-archives/episode/487/harper-high-school-part-one

This American Life. 2013b. "488: Harper High School, Part Two." *This American Life*. Accessed April 23, 2015. http://www.thisamericanlife.org/radio-archives/episode/488/harper-high-school-part-two?act=1

Tuchman, Gaye. 1972. "Objectivity as Strategic Ritual: An Examination of Newsmen's Notions of Objectivity." *American Journal of Sociology* 77 (4): 660–679.

Wolfe, Tom. 1973. *The New Journalism*. New York: Harper and Row.

WHEN SLOW NEWS IS GOOD NEWS
Book-length journalism's role in extending and enlarging daily news

Matthew Ricketson

The imperative on speed in the news media, combined with the inverted pyramid form of news writing, have well-documented strengths, enabling important information to be communicated quickly and clearly. A preoccupation with this part of journalism practice, however, within the news media industry and among scholars, obscures what James Carey has called the "curriculum of journalism." To be properly understood, Carey argued journalism needs to be examined as a corpus that includes a wide range of materials extending to book-length journalism. Longer articles and book-length works add substantially to the store of relevant and newsworthy information. They also significantly enlarge public understanding of people, events and issues of the day by exploring them in depth, usually by taking a narrative approach in the writing. This article brings to the fore the contribution of these slower forms of journalism by examining immediate and longer-term coverage of two historic news events: the dropping of the first atomic bomb, at Hiroshima in 1945, and the invasion of Iraq by United States-led forces in 2003. It argues that the valuable contribution of these forms of journalism has been underappreciated, though recognition is growing.

Introduction

One of the sustaining ideas of journalism is its ability to disclose important information in the public interest, whether from a war zone or in the face of resistance from government. So widespread is this idea, and so well has it been spread by a group who make their living as storytellers, that the phrases to describe it have entered the vernacular—the scoop, the expose, our man on the spot. (At the time these ideas were first nourished, male foreign correspondents far outnumbered females; that has since partly—though regrettably only partly—changed.) This idea is certified in the prizes for journalism, whether the Pulitzers in the United States or the British Press awards in the United Kingdom or the Walkleys in Australia, to name a few. It is enshrined in lists compiled by eminent judging panels of the best journalism of the twentieth century (New York University School of Journalism 1999; RMIT Journalism Program 1999). There is nothing intrinsically wrong with the idea of the big journalistic disclosure, especially when there are so many powerful forces ranged against it, but it significantly underestimates the incremental nature of most journalism and in doing so underestimates the slowness by which information about newsworthy events, issues and people becomes understanding and eventually knowledge.

Take, for example, what is probably the most famous journalistic disclosure of the twentieth century—Watergate by Carl Bernstein and Bob Woodward. There was no single disclosure by the two reporters from *The Washington Post*; rather there were dozens over a period of more than two years between June 1972, when five men were arrested for breaking into the Democratic Party's National Committee headquarters at the Watergate hotel and office complex, and August 1974, when President Richard Nixon, facing impeachment, eventually decided to resign. On their own each news story provides only a fragment of this historic event. From the distance of more than four decades these seem like tiny increments, as can be seen in this lead to one of their news stories:

> Funds for the Watergate espionage operation were controlled by several principal assistants of John N. Mitchell, the former manager of President Nixon's campaign, and were kept in a special account at the Committee for the Re-election of the President, the *Washington Post* has learned. (Bernstein and Woodward 1974, 73)

The provenance of this quotation, which is included in the two journalists' book-length account of their work, *All the President's Men* (Bernstein and Woodward 1974), offers a clue to this process. Much of what is known and remembered today about Woodward and Bernstein's role in uncovering the Watergate scandal comes from their own account. In the book their individual news reports, disconnected from each other and written in the flat, formal style of news, are transformed into a compelling narrative that reads like a detective story. This is actually what the dust jacket on the book's original edition proclaims, describing the book as "the most devastating political detective story of the century." Further, when people think of Woodward and Bernstein today they also think of "Deep Throat," the anonymous source who met Woodward in underground car parks where he provided important leads for Woodward to follow and confirmation for what the two journalists had found. So much mystique grew around the identity of Deep Throat over the next three decades that it is easy to forget the anonymous source had been given a name only for the book. The pair's original news reports never used the name Deep Throat, which may not be surprising given that it was also the title of a contemporaneous pornographic film, but it points to the gap between initial journalistic disclosures and later knowledge. It also draws our attention to the influence of journalism as a storytelling form. Where few would remember the phrase "An anonymous source has told *The Washington Post*," few have forgotten Deep Throat.

The influence of *All the President's Men* in shaping public memory and understanding of the Watergate scandal suggests a need to re-examine how the practice of journalism operates over time, and in the public consciousness. Barbie Zelizer (2004, 6), in *Taking Journalism Seriously*, found that "much existing scholarly work reflects only a portion of that which constitutes journalism and allows it to stand in for the whole." It is primarily hard news, as it is known in the media industry, that has been the portion asked to "stand in for the whole." Hard news has many virtues—to read, it is quick, it cuts to the core of an event or issue, and communicates clearly. The inverted pyramid form in which it is written has proved extraordinarily durable. Even the recently developed communication form—Twitter—is used by journalists to report news as it breaks. But hard news has, if not vices, then shortcomings. It prioritises information over emotion, focuses on the concrete rather than the abstract and values action over reflection. Accordingly, hard news fails to explore events and issues in their complexity and people in their full humanity.

This may well seem a statement of the blindingly obvious. As James Carey (1986, 150) writes: "To expect the dramatic unity of a three-act play in a twelve-paragraph story in a daily newspaper is to doom oneself to perpetual disappointment." News may be presented in fragments but over time journalists actually devote much of their energy, Carey writes, to "keeping significant events afloat long enough so that interpretation, explanation, and thick description can be added" (151).

In his essay "The Dark Continent of American Journalism," Carey (1986) argues that journalism should be examined as a corpus, not a set of isolated stories, and that includes not simply the multiple ways that an individual newspaper covers an issue, with follow-ups, analysis, editorials and so on, but other forms of journalism that "surround, correct and complete" the daily newspaper, such as television, documentaries, newsweeklies, journals of opinion and, finally, book-length journalism (151). Carey was writing before the advent of the internet but the new communication technologies, with their range of new media forms such as blogs and practices such as hyperlinking, have underscored rather than erased his argument for journalism to be seen as a corpus. Journalists not only continue to keep issues afloat over time through news stories that add increments of information, they examine news events and issues at greater length and in greater depth through other forms such as book-length journalism, a genre that since Carey's essay appears to have been expanding alongside the range of new media forms such as blogs (Ricketson 2014, 16). Such examinations are published months or even years after the initial news-worthy event. It might be argued that they are not journalism in the dictionary definition of the word which has its roots in the word diurnal, meaning "of the day." However, they take a journalistic approach and use journalistic methods to inquire more fully into issues "of the day" (Ricketson 2010, 67). In doing this, they may well bring newsworthy reve-lations into the public domain, and generate a fresh round of news coverage of these diurnal preoccupations, as Bob Woodward has done for many years whenever he publishes one of his book-length journalistic accounts (Shepard 2007, 227–228). This would seem to make such works inescapably journalistic but the "slow" gestation of book-length journal-ism offers more than simply fresh fodder for another quick news piece. Yes, it offers fresh information and it offers far more information than can be contained in a news bulletin but equally important it offers information, as I have written elsewhere, that has been set in context and "whose meaning has been mined and shaped into a narrative that fully engages readers' minds and emotions" (Ricketson 2014, 39).

For Carey, the obsessive identification of journalism with a thirst to be first with the news has drastically narrowed public understanding of it as a democratic social practice. The speed imperative, coupled with the professional ethic of presenting news in discrete packages, has foreshortened readers' ability to look across what Carey (1986, 158) calls the "curriculum of journalism" and see the connections between various events, issues and people. The rise of the 24/7 news cycle has intensified the speed imperative and made more urgent the need to explore and advocate for alternative approaches, such as what Thomas Patterson calls "knowledge-based journalism" and media historian Mitchell Stephens terms "wisdom journalism" (Patterson 2013; Stephens 2014). What is yielded when a slower approach and an appetite for context is added to the mix and seen as inte-gral to journalism's overall social purpose? This article examines the question by looking at two major news events. The first is the dropping of the atomic bomb on the city of Hir-oshima in Japan in 1945 and the second is the invasion of Iraq by US military forces in 2003. These events have been chosen for four reasons. First, they are both of historic importance. Second, what is known about these events today and how they are remembered differs markedly from how they were originally reported. Third, journalists played important roles in enlarging public understanding of these events, and, fourth, the two events occurred at different points in the development of journalism. These events affected a number of countries but discussion here will focus primarily on the American media. Implicit in an analysis that stretches as far back as 1945 is the notion that what is termed "slow journalism" is not simply a response to the 24/7 news cycle but is part of a corpus of journalism that has deep historical roots.

Hiroshima

A good way to begin this analysis is to stop for a moment and recall a few top-of-mind facts about the dropping of the bomb on Hiroshima: the image of the mushroom cloud, the heavy number of casualties, the amount of radiation sickness, the appalling suffering of those who survived and the bomb's influence in forcing the Japanese to surrender. It is, of course, difficult to disentangle what we know now about Hiroshima from what was known in the days after the bomb was dropped. To give one example of how easy it is to elide our present knowledge with past knowledge, the unofficial names of the two atomic bombs dropped on Hiroshima and Nagasaki—Little Boy and Fat Man, respectively—are well known today but were kept secret between 1945 and 1960 (Lifton and Mitchell 1995, 265n). Before continuing, it should be noted that the argument here is not that journalism, in all its forms, constitutes the sum total of knowledge about the dropping of the bomb. Far from it. Historians, through careful analysis of declassified documents, have been more diligent and aggressive, according to Lifton and Mitchell, in contesting the received wisdom about the bomb (270–75).

The context of the first news reports about the dropping of the bomb is important. August 1945 was near the end of the sixth year of the Second World War and the Manhattan Project was cloaked in secrecy as scientists raced to build an atomic bomb before the Germans. The dropping of the bomb by the *Enola Gay* high above the Japanese city on the morning of 6 August was done in secret. Even the scientists responsible for its development were not aware initially that the bomb had been dropped (Monk 2012, 447). It was 16 hours later that a lengthy press release was issued in the name of the President, Harry Truman, which read in part:

> Sixteen hours ago an American airplane dropped one bomb on Hiroshima, an important Army base. That bomb had more power than 20,000 tons of TNT. It had more than two thousand times the blast power of the British "Grand Slam," which is the largest bomb ever yet used in the history of warfare. (as quoted in Lifton and Mitchell 1995, 4)

With no other information at hand—the Pentagon also did not release any photographs—the newspapers and radio stations had to rely almost totally on the press release. From the outset, the US government was able to create what Lifton and Mitchell term an "official narrative" which was built on a half-truth. Hiroshima did contain an important military base, with up to 40,000 Japanese soldiers stationed there at the time, but the bomb was aimed at the centre of a city of 350,000. Civilian casualties were inevitable but mention of a military base enabled this to be obscured. Indeed, the number of civilians killed or injured or affected by radiation sickness was continually downplayed or contested by the government, in particular by the director of the Manhattan Project, General Leslie

Groves, who had inserted in the press release at the last minute the reference to Hiroshima as an important military base. It was only in the third paragraph of the press release that Truman said that it was an atomic bomb that had been dropped, and then no mention was made of the possible effects of radiation. Nor was anything said about what would later become a central plank in the government's justification for dropping the first nuclear weapon—that its use would save many American lives by avoiding the need to invade Japan to end the war (Lifton and Mitchell 1995, 3–7).

The following day, the government released a further 14 press releases outlining the background to the Manhattan Project, including the testing of the bomb the month before in New Mexico, which all heralded "the birth of a new age—the age of Atomic Energy." The only photograph it released was of General Groves studying a wall map of Japan. Again, with little else to go on, the newspapers and radio stations ran the government-supplied material, most of which actually had been prepared well in advance, primarily by William Laurence, a journalist seconded to the Manhattan Project from the country's most respected newspaper, *The New York Times*. Laurence's press releases were simply gobbled uncredited by his fellow journalists which he found discomfiting but he ascribed an almost religious significance to the dawning of the atomic age and he had few qualms about its Japanese victims (Lifton and Mitchell 1995, 10–16). On 9 August a second atomic bomb was dropped, on the city of Nagasaki, and within days the Japanese had surrendered. Potential public disquiet about the devastating impact of the two bombs was outweighed by overwhelming relief that the war was over; in any case, the first reports from Tokyo radio about civilian casualties "bloated and scorched" were downplayed by the President in an address to the nation and derided as Japanese propaganda in the press, especially the newspapers owned by William Randolph Hearst (Lifton and Mitchell 1995, 25–28).

Up to this point, journalists had reported little other than what the government fed them, which can be explained partly by the secrecy surrounding the Manhattan Project, partly by relief at the coming peace and partly by the conventions of war reporting at the time (Lifton and Mitchell 1995, 32; Knightley [1975] 2003, 293–364). This pattern looked set to continue when General Douglas MacArthur arrived in Japan in late August 1945 and immediately ordered Hiroshima and Nagasaki off limits. Instead, he invited journalists to report the Japanese signing surrender papers on board the USS *Missouri* on 2 September. Of the hundreds of journalists in Japan all but two did what MacArthur told them. One was George Weller of the *Chicago Daily News*, who visited a kamikaze base near Nagasaki, where he shook off an Army escort and saw for himself the damage wreaked by the second bomb. He sent his lengthy dispatch to MacArthur's headquarters for clearance and that was the last he saw of it (Lifton and Mitchell 1995, 50). It was not published until after he died in 2002 (Weller 2006). The other was an Australian named Wilfred Burchett working for London's *Daily Express* who showed great independence, resourcefulness and courage in making the trip alone from Yokosuka to Hiroshima. He also had good fortune; a *Daily Express* colleague in Japan, Henry Keys, also wanted to go to Hiroshima. They flipped a coin; Keys lost. Burchett's reputation was later tarnished by allegations that in the Korean War (1950–1953) he sided against the allied forces and even interrogated Australian prisoners of war, but that controversy does not tarnish his achievement at Hiroshima. Burchett has recounted in several publications how he became the first western journalist to visit Hiroshima after the bomb; this account draws primarily on the last of his several volumes of autobiography, which was published posthumously, *Memoirs of a Rebel Journalist* (Burchett 2005), and his book *Shadows of Hiroshima* (Burchett 1983).

A representative of Domei, the Japanese news agency, warned Burchett: "Don't go to Hiroshima. Everyone is dying there." Unlike those working on the Manhattan Project he had little idea of the dangers of radiation fallout. He nevertheless engaged in an elaborate ruse to slip away from the other journalists before spending 21 hours getting to Hiroshima. He travelled by train, with much of the trip in the dark as the train swept through long tunnels. At each stop Burchett needed to ask the name of the station. He did not speak the local language and he dared not mention the name Hiroshima as he was sure it would inflame the Japanese soldiers who were crammed into a carriage alongside him. The situation was tense; the Japanese had surrendered but the treaty was just being signed on board the *Missouri*. When Burchett arrived in Hiroshima he was thrown in gaol overnight by two local policemen despite protesting he was a journalist. In the morning, he showed them his letter of introduction to the local Domei representative, which improved his standing in their eyes. Burchett strapped on a pistol lent him by a colleague and simply walked out of captivity. Nobody stopped him. He began walking around the city and was appalled at the level of destruction.

Burchett headed for the city's police headquarters where the Domei representative told Burchett the police wanted to kill him. Astonishingly, it was a member of the Kempeitai, the Thought Control Police, who saved Burchett's life by accepting his pleas to be able to show people around the world what the bomb had done to the city and its citizens. Burchett went to one of the local hospitals, 1.3 kilometres from the epicentre of the blast, and was sickened by the sight of men, women and children dying from what the doctors told him was radiation sickness. He went outside, wrote his report on his battered Baby Hermes typewriter sitting among the ruins and, critically, the local Domei representative tapped it out in Morse code and transmitted it to Tokyo, as arranged with Henry Keys. By now Tokyo had been declared off limits too by General MacArthur and Keys had to get past American Military Police to get into Tokyo by train. He sent another local Domei representative in to pick up Burchett's copy, which finally arrived late on the evening of 3 September. Unfortunately, for reasons that are unclear, only the first 200 words of a 3000-word despatch had come through. It was enough for Keys, though, being the essential eyewitness confirmation of the effects of the bomb. Keys supplemented Burchett's material with his own, but an American censor wanted to stop the story being transmitted. Keys insisted that as the war was over, so was censorship and while the censor went to refer the matter to a higher authority, Keys stood over the telex operator to ensure Burchett's story was sent to London, under Burchett's byline. Burchett was distraught about the missing copy when he learnt this on arriving back at Yokohama and in all his published accounts of the story he has restored it to give readers as much information as possible. The lead paragraph of Burchett's worldwide exclusive report, which was published on the front page of the *Daily Express* on 5 September, is as follows:

> In Hiroshima, 30 days after the first atomic bomb destroyed the city and shook the world, people are still dying, mysteriously and horribly, people who were uninjured in the cataclysm—from an unknown something which I can only describe as the atomic plague.

The story was picked up around the world, aided by the *Daily Express* passing it on free to anyone who wanted it. The American military angrily denied the story. At a press conference held in Tokyo on 7 September, senior US officials, including the deputy head of the Manhattan atomic bomb project, Brigadier-General Thomas Farrell, denied the story and accused Burchett of falling victim to Japanese propaganda. Burchett asked how he explained the fish still dying when they entered a stream running through the city's centre.

> "Obviously they were killed by the blast or overheated water."
> "Still there a month later?"
> "It's a tidal river, so they could be washed back and forth."
> "But I was taken to a spot in the city outskirts and watched live fish turning on their stomachs upwards as they entered a certain patch of the river. After that they were dead within seconds." (Burchett 1983, 22–23)

At this point, the press conference was ended.

Burchett "scooped" his colleagues by getting to Hiroshima first, no doubt, but as John Pilger has written: "In comprehending and identifying an 'atomic plague,' he had rumbled the *experimental* nature of this first use of a nuclear weapon against people." At Burchett's funeral, the eulogy was delivered by an American journalist and author, T. D. Allman, who made the perceptive point: "It was a considerable ordeal to reach Hiroshima but it was an infinitely greater accomplishment, back then, to *understand* the importance of Hiroshima" (Pilger 1986, xii). One of the reasons the US government delayed announcing the dropping of the bomb for 16 hours was to confirm that it had succeeded. As Lifton and Mitchell (1995, 5) write: "Until that moment no one knew for certain that the weapon would work." Those working on the Manhattan Project were well aware of the possibility of radiation fallout from the bomb but the government had already censored a newspaper article that reported radioactivity from the testing of the bomb in July. The press releases written by William Laurence made no mention of it and when he returned to *The New York Times* and wrote a series of articles about the wonders of the atomic age he downplayed early reports of radiation sickness at Hiroshima (Lifton and Mitchell 1995, 19, 42–46; Tanter 1986, 25).

Within days of the disastrous press conference following Burchett's article, President Truman sent a confidential request to American newspaper editors and broadcasters requesting them, for reasons of the "highest national security," not to publish information about atomic bombs without first consulting the War Department. Press coverage virtually ceased for several months (Lifton and Mitchell 1995, 55). Just over a year after the dropping of the bomb, on 31 August 1946, *The New Yorker*, for the first time in its history, put aside all its regular features—the droll cartoons, the arch Talk of the Town pieces—to devote an entire issue to a single piece of reportage. Entitled simply "Hiroshima," the 31,000 word article was the first to report in any sustained way what it had been like to be in the city on the day the bomb was dropped. The article questioned the official estimate of 78,500 killed by the bomb and put it at 100,000 plus. It refuted the claim that poor construction caused most of the destruction at Hiroshima and it cited new information estimating that radiation sickness was responsible for about one in five of the fatalities (Yavenditti [1974] 1998, 293). Valuable though it undoubtedly was to bring this information to public attention, it is not primarily why the article is remembered today, which has more to do with the way the article was written. Earlier in 1946, *Time* had published a firsthand account written by a German priest in Hiroshima, Reverend John A. Siemes, that made some but not much impact (Lifton and Mitchell 1995, 77). "Hiroshima" made an immediate, massive impact. After quickly selling out at newsstands, the entire article was read in a special advertising-free broadcast by ABC over four consecutive evenings. Albert Einstein ordered a thousand copies of the magazine to distribute (Hersey 1946, viii).

By November *Hiroshima* was available as a Penguin book where it became a best-seller and remains in print 70 years later.

It is difficult to discern exactly whether Americans were ready a year after the war to contemplate their former enemy's suffering or whether "Hiroshima" made them do it; more likely it was a combination of the two. The author, a war correspondent and novelist named John Hersey, visited Hiroshima in May 1946 and interviewed between 30 and 40 survivors (Yavenditti [1974] 1998, 291; Sanders 1990, 15) before selecting six whose stories he told in sequential narration. Hersey initially considered an article documenting the bomb's power and its destructiveness but decided he wanted to "write about what happened not to buildings but to human beings" (Lifton and Mitchell 1995, 86–87). Hersey's choice meant that questions about, say, whether the bomb was needed to end the war, would not be considered and he was criticised for this (McCarthy [1946] 1998) but, with the help of the editor of *The New Yorker*, Harold Ross, he saw how important it was to convey the day's events as far as possible through the limited perspective of the survivors (Yagoda 2000, 189).

It would have been entirely understandable if Hersey had felt overwhelmed by the accounts of the *hibakusha* (literally explosion-affected persons). Hersey had felt "a kind of horror" (Yavenditti [1974] 1998, 292) throughout his three weeks in Hiroshima, but this prompted him to reflect: if that was what he experienced eight months afterwards how must those in the city on 6 August 1945 have felt? Instead of expressing directly how *he* felt, though, Hersey channelled his energy into enabling the reader, as far as possible, to sympathise with the bomb survivors' experience. As Jones (1992, 214) writes, the bomb attack demanded Hersey "provide forms for understanding what has been called history's least imaginable event." It could be thought that Hersey's approach is a classic example of Percy Lubbock's "show, don't tell" method of storytelling (as quoted in Herman 2007, 15) but that only partly explains what Hersey did. If the dropping of the atomic bomb was "history's least imaginable event," and if the official narrative had reduced it to more readily imaginable matters—it was a very powerful bomb rather than a qualitatively different kind of bomb, it was necessary to end the war, the Japanese were the enemy—then how does a writer persuade readers to even begin imagining? One, a university student, wrote to *The New Yorker*: "I had never thought of the people in the bombed cities as individuals" (Yavenditti [1974] 1998, 293). If that sounds an odd thing to say, it underscores how we cauterise our imaginations to accept the bombing in the first place, and the chasm we need to cross to empathise with the victims and begin understanding the bomb's impact. Hersey's rare achievement was to be able to do that for millions of people then and since. It is interesting to note, given the difficulties both Burchett and Weller faced with censorship, that Hersey did not submit his article to the government for clearance (Yavenditti [1974] 1998, 292). There were no repercussions, perhaps because restrictions had been eased by August 1946, but when it was published as a book, *Hiroshima* was banned in Japan for two years by the American Occupational authority there, under General MacArthur's command (Sanders 1990, 19–20). The "slowness" of Hersey's journalism, coming as it did a year after the bomb was dropped, is critical to his ability to discover additional information. Equally, if not more important, it gave both him and his readers time to begin seriously contemplating the magnitude of the event.

Iraq

Turning now from a consideration of how understanding developed about Hiroshima to how it has developed about the invasion of Iraq in March 2003, we move from a wartime event the public never knew about to one that it was told well in advance was going to be an awe-inspiring display of American might. Where journalists and editors in 1945 could be partly excused for asking few questions about the government's press releases, no such excuse existed in 2003. The practice of journalism was considerably more advanced and, especially since both the Watergate and Iran–Contra scandals, knowledge of governments hiding information or lying to the American public was well established and widely known. The context is important, to be sure, with the United States traumatised by the terrorist attacks on 11 September 2001 in which just under 3000 innocent people were killed— more than died when the Japanese bombed Pearl Harbor in 1941. Such events impel the news media to mute their questioning and trumpet what Lifton and Mitchell (1995, xiii) term their "patriotic correctness." The 2003 invasion is now widely regarded as a failure, for Iraqis, for American troops and for global opinion of American foreign policy, because of policies and practices that were both misguided and mismanaged. The decision to invade Iraq was grounded in spurious evidence of Saddam's possession of weapons of mass destruction. There was brawling between agencies in the US government that paralysed planning for the post-war period. Lies were told about whether torture was being used on suspected terrorists, at least partly because torture was re-defined to mean any interrogation practice that fell short of killing someone. All these actions by the US government have caused and continue to cause incalculable damage, according to Chris Anderson's (2011) history of the period, *Bush's Wars*. In the months leading to the invasion, however, the overall news media coverage strongly supported the US government's plans, downplayed controversy surrounding the decision to invade and gave little sense of the potential looming pitfalls.

Not surprisingly, commentators and scholars have subsequently sharply criticised the news media for the failures of its coverage (Cunningham 2003; Dadge 2006; Rich 2006; Bennett, Lawrence, and Livingston 2007). At best, too many media outlets reverted to stenography in reporting claims by the Bush administration that Saddam Hussein had close links to those responsible for the 9/11 terrorist attacks and, at worst, newspapers and television stations in Rupert Murdoch's global media empire became cheerleaders for the American President's plans to topple Saddam's regime. In a media conference in early March 2003, where President George Bush laid out the reasons for invading, he mentioned al Qaeda or the September 11 terrorist attacks 14 times in 52 minutes but

> no one challenged him on it, despite the fact that the CIA [Central Intelligence Agency] had questioned the Iraq–al Qaeda connection, and that there has never been solid evidence marshalled to support the idea that Iraq was involved in the attacks of 9/11. (Cunningham 2003, 24)

As David Dadge (2006, 2) writes in *The War in Iraq and Why the Media Failed Us*, even those outlets that did question the official reasons for going to war "often reported them in such a way that they gave credence to the Bush administration's view, while downplaying the view of those who disagreed."

What has so far escaped the attention of most scholars is the breadth and depth of longer articles and book-length journalism books about the war that have added substantially to public understanding of the invasion and its aftermath. Indeed, much of what is known about it comes from the work of journalists, as historian Chris Anderson (2011, x, xiv) specifically acknowledges. The practice of journalism exists along a temporal continuum, of course; the same practitioner may cover news by the hour, write analysis by the day, investigate over weeks and write books over months or years. Even so, it is pertinent to note that in the bibliography of *Bush's Wars* more than one-quarter of the 185 books listed were works of book-length journalism (257–65). Steve Weinberg, a journalist, author and former executive director of Investigative Reporters and Editors in the United States, has reviewed new non-fiction for three decades. In 2007 he wrote: "Far more high-quality, in-depth journalism is being disseminated each year than any individual can absorb, and a great deal of that high-quality, in-depth journalism is arriving in book format" (Weinberg 2007). These works, most of which were primarily aimed at American readers, nevertheless have sold in large numbers abroad. Books about various aspects of the wars in Iraq and Afghanistan sold 1.66 million copies in Australia between 2003 and 2008 (Zwar 2012). Works of book-length journalism comprised a portion of these sales figures (other categories included military studies and political memoirs) but they are important for providing "greater breadth and depth of coverage" and offering an "additional dimension" of the war (330).

One of the books Weinberg admires, Lawrence Wright's (2006) *The Looming Tower: Al-Qaeda and the Road to 9/11*, has won a Pulitzer Prize but it was for general non-fiction, in 2007, which has the effect of obscuring its origins as a work of book-length journalism. Other works of book-length journalism have become bestsellers, such as Ron Suskind's (2006) *The One Percent Doctrine* which reached third spot on *The New York Times* list in 2006 (http://www.hawes.com/2006/2006-08-06.pdf). Some works of book-length journalism may have not sold well but have been critically acclaimed, such as Barton Gellman's (2008) *Angler*, an exhaustively researched portrait of the most influential vice-president in American history, Dick Cheney (https://www.bartongellman.com/angler/news-reviews.php). A number have been praised for the quality of their prose— Sebastian Junger's (2010) *War* is one among several. There is not space in a single article to discuss the range of long-form and book-length journalism about the invasion and its aftermath, at least partly because there has been so much of it. As Weinberg notes, more has been published than all but the closest observers can absorb. So a few examples are chosen to illustrate the argument of how slow journalism adds significantly to the store of knowledge about news events and issues.

Mark Danner, a vocal and early sceptic about the case for war (Danner 2009, 369–71), was commissioned by *The New York Review of Books* to go to Iraq and send back two lengthy despatches headlined "How Not to Win a War" (September 2003) and "Delusions in Baghdad" (December 2003) that combined vivid, on-the-ground reporting with historically informed analysis. What Danner learnt in Baghdad confirmed his scepticism and deepened his fears for the war's disastrous long-term consequences (372–391). Along with Seymour Hersh, Jane Mayer and Dana Priest, Danner has also persistently probed the use of torture in the post-9/11 era, painstakingly documenting it in magazine and book-length accounts despite fierce resistance from the Bush administration (Rich 2006, 221). Some works contained news that had eluded the daily media, such as Ron Suskind's (2006) account in *The One Percent Doctrine* that an Al Qaeda jihadist claimed by the White House to be the organisation's chief of operations on his capture in 2002 turned out to be a mentally ill minor functionary. Abu Zubaydah was subjected to repeated bouts of waterboarding and soon began telling his captors about all kinds of invented terrorist plots. So, writes Suskind, "The United States would torture a mentally disturbed man and then leap, screaming, at every word he uttered" (111).

Thomas Ricks, like Suskind, benefited from lifting his gaze above the daily deadline parapet. Researching the war for his work *Fiasco* (Ricks 2006), he was given thousands of pages of government documents, including the classified plan for the invasion. In 2003, the documents would have been deemed too sensitive, but two years later few in the military were sensitive about it anymore. Ricks was able to write an authoritative—and scathing—account of an invasion that was "launched recklessly, with a flawed plan for war and a worse approach to occupation. Spooked by its own false conclusions about the threat, the Bush administration hurried its diplomacy, short-circuited its war planning, and assembled an agonisingly incompetent occupation" (3–4). Once disclosures such as these are made public and are absorbed in the swift running river of the 24-hour news cycle, it is easy to miss the extent to which they are originally the fruit of longer, slower investigations.

Beyond disclosing news, though, some authors of book-length journalism have substantially enlarged our understanding of the war. The abuse of prisoners at Abu Ghraib by American soldiers rightly provoked a global furore in 2004, but four years later Philip Gourevitch and Errol Morris collaborated on a book and a documentary film, both entitled *Standard Operating Procedure*, because they both believed the core of the Abu Ghraib story had not really been told. In this context, documentary is the visual equivalent of book-length journalism. When the photographs were broadcast on 27 April on CBS's *60 Minutes II* and published by Seymour Hersh in the 10 May issue of *The New Yorker*, Gourevitch was covering the George Bush versus John Kerry presidential campaign for the magazine. Like most people, he thought it an important story that would shape the campaign but it soon disappeared from sight. Gourevitch resists glib excuses such as those broadcast by some right-wing commentators that Abu Ghraib was a case of "a few guys going nuts on the night shift" and the denial of responsibility by the Bush administration, which insisted it was simply a case of "seven bad apples." It disappeared, he says, mainly because the United States was effectively a one-party state. "I'm afraid the real reason Kerry caved in on this issue is that he understood, as the President did, that Americans weren't too exercised about the abuse of prisoners in the war on terror" (Ricketson 2008, 26–27). He argues that all American citizens are implicated because

> we haven't wanted to see ourselves clearly. Everyone across the political perspective found relief in the vilification of a few "rogue" soldiers at Abu Ghraib and looked the other way while far worse was happening as a matter of policy on a continuing basis. (Ricketson 2008, 26–27)

Morris initiated the project and supplied Gourevitch with about 2.5 million words of interview transcripts, more than 25 times the length of the finished book, but Gourevitch was not interested in making "the book of the movie." He did additional research, including drawing on extraordinarily frank interviews given by two soldiers jailed for their role at Abu Ghraib, Charles Graner and Ivan Frederick. They had been unavailable to Morris but had been ordered to co-operate with the Abu Ghraib investigation as part of their sentences and been granted immunity from any further charges as an incentive to be open. Gourevitch also painstakingly re-assembled and parsed the five draft versions of the "standard operating procedure" at Abu Ghraib that subtly but surely shifted the rules of engagement to put the soldiers operating there outside the bounds of the Geneva Convention. This therefore empowered them to use what were euphemistically called enhanced interrogation techniques that were actually torture. Gourevitch in the book and Morris in the film steadfastly step away from passing quick judgement on the low-ranking soldiers and military police involved, such as Lynndie England and Sabrina Harmon. Gourevitch and Morris shared the public outrage but also identified with Harmon's decision to blow the whistle on the atrocities occurring at Abu Ghraib. In one particularly eloquent passage, Gourevitch writes:

> But the complicity, the blind eye and the cover-up, the buck passing and the butt covering, the self-deception and the cowardice, the indiscipline and the incompetence infected every link in the chain of command that ran from the M1 block [at Abu Ghraib] to the Pentagon and the White House—a military bureaucracy that had been politically cowed and corrupted from the top by civilian masters who had no experience of combat. (Gourevitch and Morris 2008, 171)

Standard Operating Procedure, both the book and the documentary, are powerful, disturbing works that ask us to keep looking at things when we would far rather look away—not simply from the shocking images but from the corrosive effect of political corruption. Their commitment to making the time to explore the issues in their complexity and taking the space to reveal the people at Abu Ghraib in their full humanity are shining examples of what can be achieved through longer forms of non-fiction storytelling.

Equally important, Gourevitch and Morris's willingness to return to and delve deeply into an issue, long after its immediate presence in the news cycle has passed, underlines the contribution that slow journalism can make to the overall conception of what Carey calls the corpus of journalism. Their approach is not academic but journalistic. They, along with all the other authors of book-length journalism about Iraq and the dropping of the atomic bomb on Hiroshima, used recognised journalistic methods—gathering documents, interviewing, first-hand observation—and took a recognisably journalistic approach. That is, their approach is imbued with an ethos of holding those in power to account and of making disclosures to a broad audience. And yet they took, or in some cases were given, the time needed to explore further dimensions of the Iraq War and Hiroshima thereby expanding significantly the public understanding of war and its aftermath. At one level, it is entirely unsurprising that these journalists were able to do this—what event yields its full meaning in a matter of hours?—but such is the yen for speed in newsrooms, along with the almost allergic reaction to the virtues of slowness, that the extent to which understanding of events and issues unfolds over time is occluded.

DISCLOSURE STATEMENT

No potential conflict of interest was reported by the author.

REFERENCES

Anderson, Chris. 2011. *Bush's Wars*. New York: Oxford University Press.
Bennett, W. Lance, Regina Lawrence, and Steven Livingston. 2007. *When the Press Fails: Political Power and the News Media from Iraq to Katrina*. Chicago: University of Chicago Press.
Bernstein, Carl, and Bob Woodward. 1974. *All the President's Men*. New York: Simon & Schuster.

Burchett, Wilfred. 1983. *Shadows of Hiroshima*. London: Verso Editions.

Burchett, Wilfred. 2005. "Burchett's Memoir is Hiroshima." In *Memoirs of a Rebel Journalist: The Autobiography of Wilfred Burchett*, edited by George Burchett and Nick Shimmin, 229–244. Sydney: UNSW Press.

Carey, James. 1986. "The Dark Continent of American Journalism." In *Reading the News*, edited by Robert Manoff and Michael Schudson, 146–196. New York: Pantheon Books.

Cunningham, Brent. 2003. "Re-thinking Objectivity." *Columbia Journalism Review*, July/August 24–33.

Dadge, David. 2006. *The War in Iraq and Why the Media Failed Us*. Westport, Connecticut: Praeger.

Danner, Mark. 2009. *Stripping Bare the Body: Politics, Violence, War*. Melbourne: Black.

Gellman, Barton. 2008. *Angler: The Shadow Presidency of Dick Cheney*. New York: Penguin.

Gourevitch, Philip, and Errol Morris. 2008. *Standard Operating Procedure*. New York: Penguin.

Herman, David, ed. 2007. *The Cambridge Companion to Narrative*. Cambridge: Cambridge University Press.

Hersey, John. 1946. *Hiroshima*. Harmondsworth, Middlesex: Penguin.

Jones, Dan. 1992. "John Hersey." In *A Sourcebook of American Literary Journalism: Representative Writers in an Emerging Genre*, edited by Thomas Connery, 213–221. New York: Greenwood.

Junger, Sebastian. 2010. *War*. London: Fourth Estate.

Knightley, Phillip. [1975] 2003. *The First Casualty: The War Correspondent as Hero, Propagandist and Myth-maker from the Crimea to Iraq*. London: Andre Deutsch.

Lifton, Robert Jay, and Greg Mitchell. 1995. *Hiroshima in America: 50 Years of Denial*. New York: Grosset/Putnam.

McCarthy, Mary. [1946] 1998. "The 'Hiroshima' *New Yorker*." In *Hiroshima's Shadow*, edited by Kai Bird and Lawrence Lifschultz, 303–304. Connecticut: The Pamphleteer's Press.

Monk, Ray. 2012. *Inside the Centre: The Life of J. Robert Oppenheimer*. London: Jonathan Cape.

New York University School of Journalism. 1999. "The Top 100 Works of Journalism in the United States in the 20th Century". http://www.nyu.edu/classes/stephens/Top%20100%20page.htm.

Patterson, Thomas. 2013. *Informing the News: The Need for Knowledge-based Journalism*. New York: Vintage.

Pilger, John. 1986. "Preface." In *Burchett: Reporting the Other Side of the World 1939–1983*, edited by Ben Kiernan, ix–xv. London: Quartet Books.

Rich, Frank. 2006. *The Greatest Story Ever Sold: The Decline and Fall of Truth – The Real History of the Bush Administration*. Camberwell: Viking.

Ricketson, Matthew. 2008. "Drawn to trouble." *The Age*, A2, August 16, 26–27.

Ricketson, Matthew. 2010. "The Vibrant State of Book-length Journalism in Australia." *Australian Journalism Review* 32 (1): 67–79.

Ricketson, Matthew. 2014. *Telling True Stories: Navigating the Challenges of Writing Narrative Non-fiction*. Crows Nest: Allen & Unwin.

Ricks, Thomas. 2006. *Fiasco: The American Military Adventure in Iraq*. New York: Penguin Press.

RMIT Journalism Program. 1999. "The Best Australian Journalism of the 20th Century." http://pandora.nla.gov.au/pan/23203/20020122-0000/fifth.estate.rmit.edu.au/November/contentsnov.htm.

Sanders, David. 1990. *John Hersey Revisited, Twayne's United States Authors Series No. 569*. Boston: Twayne.

Shepard, Alicia. 2007. *Woodward and Bernstein: Life in the Shadow of Watergate*. New Jersey: John Wiley.

Stephens, Mitchell. 2014. *Beyond the News: The Future of Journalism*. New York: Columbia University Press.

Suskind, Ron. 2006. *The One Percent Doctrine*. New York: Simon & Schuster.

Tanter, Richard. 1986. "Voice and Silence in the First Nuclear War: Wilfred Burchett and Hiroshima." In *Burchett: Reporting the Other Side of the World 1939–1983*, edited by Ben Kiernan, 13–40. London: Quartet Books.

Weinberg, Steve. 2007. "The Book as an Investigative Vehicle for News." *Nieman Reports*, Spring. http://niemanreports.org/articles/the-book-as-an-investigative-vehicle-for-news/.

Weller, George. 2006. *First Into Nagasaki: The Censored Eyewitness Dispatches on Post-Atomic Japan and Its Prisoners of War*. Edited by Anthony Weller. New York: Three Rivers Press.

Wright, Lawrence. 2006. *The Looming Tower: Al-Qaeda and the Road to 9/11*. New York: Penguin.

Yagoda, Ben. 2000. *About Town: The "New Yorker" and the World it Made*. New York: Scribner.

Yavenditti, Michael. [1974] 1998. "John Hersey and the American Conscience." In *Hiroshima's Shadow*, edited by Kai Bird and Lawrence Lifschultz, 288–302. Connecticut: The Pamphleteer's Press.

Zelizer, Barbie. 2004. *Taking Journalism Seriously: News and the Academy*. Thousand Oaks, CA: Sage.

Zwar, Jan. 2012. "More than Michael Moore: Contemporary Australian Book Reading Patterns and the Wars on Iraq and Afghanistan." *Publishing Research Quarterly* 28 (4): 325–339.

SLOW JOURNALISM IN SPAIN
New magazine startups and the paradigmatic case of *Jot Down*

Alejandro Barranquero Carretero and **Garbiñe Jaurrieta Bariain**

This paper examines the blossoming of slow media practices in Spain within a context of economic and media crisis. After contextualizing the phenomenon and its antecedents, Jot Down Cultural Magazine *is taken as a paradigmatic example of a sustainable journalistic model built on long-form narrative pieces and in-depth reporting. The case study is based on interviews with the magazine's head and staff as well as on an online survey to its collaborators. Its editorial line and collaborative financing system will offer insights into the sustainability of future slow journalism projects.*

Introduction: The Drive for Speed in Contemporary Journalism

The value of information does not survive the moment in which it was new. It lives only at that moment; it has to surrender to it completely and explain itself to it without losing any time. A story is different. It does not expend itself. It preserves and concentrates its strength and is capable of releasing it even after a long time. (Walter Benjamin [1936] 2007, 84)

The temporal dimension of media and communication processes has been traditionally neglected by communication scholars (Sharma 2012, 68), although this concern is present in the works of pioneers such as Harold A. Innis, Charles H. Cooley, Walter Benjamin and Marshall McLuhan. Nevertheless, the field is currently displaying a gradual interest in the issue, as the internet and the Web 2.0 have radically accelerated the processes of journalistic production, distribution and consumption. This preoccupation is thus evident in the new academic debates on the quality of news under time pressure, as well as on the new labor conditions of journalists who are propelled to work in a non-stop digital environment (Cushion and Lewis 2010; Lee 2014; Reich and Godler 2014).

Furthermore, a number of media literacy scholars have turned their attention to the new audience and reception patterns that originate under extreme flexible and accelerated online settings (Carr 2010; Dias 2014; Hassoun 2014), while others propose strategies for media diet and temporal disconnection from new technologies (Brabazon 2013; Serrano-Puche 2013; Sieberg 2011). On the other hand, there is an emergent literature on the material dimensions of computing, telecommunication and ICTs, given that the rates of technological production are reckless and increasing, as well as drive into dramatic consequences for the environment and climate change (Maxwell and Miller 2012; Maxwell, Raundalen, and Lager 2014).

In any case, the drive for speed is nothing new in journalism, as *news* by definition is information that is new. In fact, modern journalism has historically been characterized by the development of technologies that abolish the barriers of time and space. The first substantial leap towards the speeding-up of news came along with the telegraph in the nineteenth century, accurately described as the Victorian internet according to its potential to communicate globally and at real time (Standage 1988). Besides, the wire led to a factory-like reorganization of the newsroom as well as to an abbreviated language that "made prose lean and unadorned … without the luxury of details and analysis" of the former news (Carey 1989, 212).

The invention of radio and television progressively associated journalism with the news value of immediacy and hence to a frequent decontextualized narration of the present. This is particularly noticeable from the development of live television in the 1950s, when broadcasts took the form of non-stop 24-hour and seven-day services (24/7) available at any time and every day (Cushion and Lewis 2010). This tendency has not substantially altered after the adoption of internet and mobile devices by journalists at the end of the twentieth century, since ICTs have rather reinforced the universal and instantaneous access to news production and consumption but just in quantitative terms (Standage 1988). This is to say that the frontiers of space and time have been blurring with the invention of every information technology and there are no radical ruptures in cyberspace despite many claims that the internet brought about the end of history (Mosco 2004, 56).

Within this context, the most relevant accelerating factor can be attributed to the birth of the Web 2.0 and, especially, to social networks, which became an influential media outlet for the delivery of breaking news in real time. In other words, Facebook and Twitter lead to frequent mistakes given that sources are not always verified before publishing and the informative agenda is progressively marked by a non-stoppable flux of reliable and non-reliable sources (Juntunen 2010; Revers 2014; Spence and Quinn 2008). In addition, the endless stream of new data and information makes it harder for journalists to construct a thoughtful and consistent narration of events and this affects the credibility of journalism (Maier 2005; Schmierbach and Oeldorf-Hirsch 2012), as well as discourages investigative reporting (Lee 2014).

In the meantime, there is little evidence for optimism since the demand for high-quality information has not decreased but incremented in recent times (Frijters and Velamuri 2010). This fact is particularly visible in sectors of the audience that specifically demand accurate information and sophisticated designs either through paper, tablets or mobile devices. Moreover, the last few years have witnessed the birth of a large range of journalistic projects that provide depth and reflection beyond the extreme transience and ephemerality of speed-driven audiovisual news.

Objectives and Methodology

The first academic research on slow journalism has essentially focused on English-language magazines and online platforms (e.g., Le Masurier 2015; Meuret 2013). Therefore, the Spanish-speaking context has been neglected to date, with a few recent exceptions (Barranquero and Rosique 2015; Serrano-Puche 2014). Within this context, the aim of this article is to enlarge the scope of the field through an insight into the blossoming of slow journalistic experiences in Spain and Latin America from 2000 onwards.

We will first provide our own definition of slow journalism based on the review of relevant literature. Later, the Spanish-speaking context will be introduced though an approach to a few historical antecedents and paradigmatic cases. The second part of the article analyses the editorial line and financing model of one of the most exemplary slow publications in Spain, *Jot Down Cultural Magazine*, which has been heavily inspired by both the Anglo-Saxon and Latin American slow journalism traditions. Born in 2011 under a context of economic and media crisis, the project has gradually become a highly successful magazine whose online version is currently getting an average of more than one million page views per month, according to OJD Interactiva.[1] We will finally describe another set of Spanish magazines and journals—which are part of *Soidem*, *Jot Down*'s editorial branch—and provide a set of recommendations in order to guarantee the sustainability of future projects as well as to promote further dialogues between journalism and the slow movement.

The case study is based on non-participant observation and in-depth interviews with the magazine's heads and staff between 2014 and 2015. Table 1 shows the names and position of the key informants who were interviewed to construct this article.

Furthermore, a short online questionnaire was sent to 50 journalists who periodically collaborate on *Jot Down*. Through the online platform *e-encuesta*, the survey collected data about the origin of their collaboration, the tasks they are involved in, and whether these journalists are freelance or part of the magazine's permanent staff. We finally got 15 testimonies over two periods running from March to May 2014.

What is Slow Journalism?

Slow journalism is not a new phenomenon since these journalistic practices have lived alongside a more ephemeral journalism throughout the modern history of the profession. Nevertheless, slowness in communication has been little reflected upon. Rather, slow journalistic communication has been usually interpreted either through the lens of its connection with literature (named as narrative, literary, nonfiction or creative journalism), or as journalistic research and in-depth analysis (investigative, immersive, muckracking or watch-dog journalism). In either case, the former adjectives have underlined the idea that there is a sort of journalism that is not guided by a strict and objective coverage of reality. On the contrary, this is marked by high ethical and aesthetic standards as well as by hybrid narration forms, regardless of genre, length or format.

TABLE 1
Conducted interviews

Key informant	Position	Date and place	Interviewer
Olga Sobrido	Assistant editor and content curator	January 25, 2014	Garbiñe Jaurrieta
Carles Foguet	Director of Communication	March 8, 2014	Garbiñe Jaurrieta
Raquel Blanco	Operation Director and Head Director of Soidem, *Jot Down*'s distribution platform	February 27, 2014	Garbiñe Jaurrieta
Ricardo Jonás	Founder and Director	April 13, 2015, Getafe, Madrid	Alejandro Barranquero

What is new, however, is the present revitalization of slow journalistic practices which explore the potentialities of the internet, although this platform has been questioned for its trend to speed and information overload (Freeman 2009; Gitlin 2007). This is notable in the case of literary and immersive journalistic traditions, which have recently incorporated a number of digital tools to animate the field. In fact, many of the new initiatives encompass "more than the fragmented, de-centered, hypertextual blocks of the Web," but also represent "the integration of technology in storytelling that holds literary purposes of its own," as Jacobson, Marino, and Gutsche (2015, 14) have demonstrated in their analysis of 50 long-form multimedia journalism packages, including recent successful platforms such as "Snow Fall," launched by *The New York Times* in December 2012, and *The Guardian*'s 2013 "Firestorm."

The label of slow journalism began to gain popularity at the end of the 2000s in order to describe a variety of blogs and online cultural publications which utilized multimedia and in-depth narrative resources as a challenge to the fetishization of Twitter's 140 characters culture. Scholarly reflection started in 2007 when Susan Greenberg used the term to refer to a growing market of narrative communication practices, such as "essays, reportage and other non-fiction writing of narrative journalism which takes time to find things out and communicates it all to the highest standards" (Greenberg 2007).

In addition, investigative reporter David Leigh (2007, 2009) and journalism scholar Harold Gess (2012) have approached the phenomenon from the perspective of the slow movement and as a reaction to the "McDonaldization" of news, or "McJournalism," a concept coined by Bob Franklin to describe the tabloidization and dumbing down of journalism at the expense of serious analysis (Franklin 2003). As the slow perspectives emphasize values such as quality, deceleration, proximity and creativity (Barranquero 2013), this kind of journalism could be defined by the three main principles encompassed by the slow food movement: good, clean and fair. In other words, this journalism is based on *good* reports for consumers who demand useful information for them and for their community; *clean* and sustainable portrayals of the populations and their natural environments; and *fair* journalism that advocates for social justice and ensures proper conditions of employment and remuneration (Gess 2012, 60).

More recently, Isabelle Meuret (2013) associated slowness with long-form journalism and focused on initiatives that "put the brake" on the "acceleration and overindulgence of the media, taking the time to tell a story." Once again from the principles of the slow movement, Megan Le Masurier (2015) describes this kind of journalism according to how the term is being used on blogs, websites, public forums and producers who self-identify with the notion. The researcher stresses the importance of slow news values and storytelling, and complements the preceding approaches by concentrating on a set of features such as transparency, independence and the relevance of news for a particular community. Both scholars agree that these practices have existed since the early days of journalism and can be traced back to magazines and other publications which historically adopted slower temporalities, such as the muckraking investigative journalism at the end of the nineteenth century (e.g., Ida Tarbell, Lincoln Steffens and Upton Sinclair), and the nonfiction journalistic forms developed by US New Journalism in the 1960s and 1970s (e.g., Tom Wolfe, Norman Mailer and Gay Talese).[2]

In spite of their differences, all these contributions underline the idea that there is a growing emergence of journalistic practices that, opposing the banality and the vertiginous rhythms of contemporary life, take time for reflection and research as well as deciding which is the convenient speed for each context, acting "quickly when it makes sense or be slow when slowness is more convenient," and approaching "what musicians call the *tempo giusto*, or the proper speed" (Honoré 2004, 22).

Therefore, slow journalism is not synonymous with narrative journalism, since there is a lot of "excessively baroque and bad literature dressed as journalism" as well as "neglected and biased reports camouflaged in the form of tales and stories" (27). Neither is long-form journalism equivalent to slowness given that "length is not a virtue in itself" nor "hardly the quality that most meaningfully classify" good stories (Bennet 2013). However, slow journalism usually requires length, as this is needed "for deeper reflection and/or investigation about an original subject" (Le Masurier 2015, 143).

Given the former considerations, we prefer to approximate slow journalism as journalistic products and practices that explicitly emerge as a reaction to the dominant trend to newness, immediacy and a decontextualized narration of the news events. Thus, slow journalism takes the necessary time and length to produce rigorous, diverse and quality information addressed to local or global audiences who express their longing to taste noteworthy information presented with the uppermost ethical and aesthetical standards. Accordingly, this label denotes a kind of journalism that: (1) defies the scoop-driven journalism and the 24/7 cycle and, on the contrary, rescues slower temporalities such as the week or the month; (2) is not concerned with the length *per se* but, in its search for quality, usually takes more than 2000 words in every piece and uses classical genres such as in-depth reports, essays and *crónicas* (chronicles),[3] as opposed to bare news; (3) critique the prevailing news values—immediacy, newness, unusualness, etc.—and, instead, define newsworthiness according to what some audiences demand, what coincides with the traditional criteria promoted by investigative reporting: contextualization, exactitude, balance, diversity, etc.

Slow Journalism Antecedents in Spain and Latin America

From the beginning of the twenty-first century, investigative and narrative journalism have gained an increasing readership in Spain and Latin America, parallel to the birth of a wide range of blogs and print and digital publications whose offer is based on top-quality journalism and refined presentation criteria. Given that chronicles and reports are still a minority genre in the traditional printed press, many reporters and chroniclers have found an important ally in the internet since "there are no limits of space nor borders for creativity" in the online world (Rodríguez and Albalad 2012, 289). Even if many critics thought that the internet would bring about the end of narrative journalism, reporters are stimulating long-form journalism through the progressive integration of multimedia resources (Jacobson, Marino, and Gutsche 2015).

This phenomenon has been identified as a new "boom of narrative journalism" in both Spain and Latin America and a set of recent studies and anthologies diagnose an unprecedented vitality of narrative and investigative journalism on both sides of the Atlantic (Angulo 2013; Carrión 2012; Jaramillo 2012). On the other hand, this phenomenon is deeply rooted in a large variety of journalistic practices that paved the way for the present development of high-quality reports and literary journalism. In Latin America, Claudia Darrigrandi (2013, 124–126) summarizes three key moments in the evolution of the chronicle. The first corresponds to the "modernist Indian chronicle" that emerged at the turn of the nineteenth to the twentieth century and is well represented by pioneers

Jose Marti, Rubén Darío, Amado Nervo or Manuel Gutierrez Najera. These pioneers set the stage for the coming generations through an original combination of journalism and literary techniques in the narration of the major historical events that took place after the decolonization of the subcontinent.

The second moment coincides with the so-called "Latin American literary boom" from the 1960s and 1970s, marked by the internationally known chronicles by Gabriel García Márquez and Mario Vargas Llosa, as well as by other relevant writers whose works fluctuated halfway between literature and nonfiction such as Rodolfo Walsh, Carlos Monsiváis and Tomás Eloy Martínez. This second group has been described by Jorge Carrión as a "silent avant garde or discrete prologue" to US New Journalism, given that Latin American authors have never been included in the English-based canon of New Journalism, despite their stylistic continuities (Carrión 2012, 24).

At the end of the twentieth century, a new cohort of journalists has revitalized the chronicle, fueled by two important landmarks: the educational programs of the Iberoamerican New Journalism Foundation (Fundación Nuevo Periodismo Iberoamericano), founded by Gabriel García Márquez in 1994 in Cartagena (Colombia), and the creation of several flagship publications usually inspired by leading Anglo-Saxon literary journalism magazines such as *The New Yorker*, *Rolling Stone* or *The Atlantic*. Among the founding and most important publications, we can quote: *El Malpensante* (Colombia, 1996), *Letras Libres* (México, 1999), *Gatopardo* (Colombia, 2001), *Etiqueta Negra* (Perú, 2002), *El Marcapasos* (Venezuela, 2007), *La Silla Vacía* (Colombia, 2009), *Pie Izquierdo* (Bolivia, 2010), *The Clinic* (Chile, 2011), *El Puercoespín* (Argentina, 2011), *Orsai* (Argentina, 2011) and *Anfibia* (Argentina, 2012).

The regeneration of Latin American narrative journalism, or the "new Latin American chronicle" (Carrión 2012; Jaramillo 2012), encompasses a large list of authors such as the Argentinian Martín Caparrós and Leila Guerriero and the Mexican Lydia Camacho and Juan Villoro.[4] These chroniclers combine journalism and literary techniques, but, in opposition to US New Journalism, their writings are characterized by new "representations of poverty, exclusion and violence," and an ethical appeal to readers who demand events and stories that are usually silenced and neglected in mainstream media (Callegaro and Lago 2012, 261).

In the case of Spain, the nineteenth century was prolific in the launching of newspapers and miscellaneous illustrated magazines. Propelled by the liberal Printing Act of 1883, these inaugurated the so-called "Golden Age of Spanish Journalism," which extended from the end of the century to the beginning of Spanish Civil War (1936–1939) (Fuentes and Fernández 1997). The Golden Age witnessed the arrival of three prolific generations who experimented with reporting and nonfiction journalism to a greater or lesser extent. Regardless of their differences, the Generation of '98 developed critical analysis on the Spanish political and moral crisis after the loss of Cuba (in 1898). Relevant figures such as Miguel de Unamuno, Pío Baroja and Azorín searched a way out of the '98 Crisis through subjective reporting and a revitalization of traditional Spanish myths and literature.

The Generation of '14—José Ortega y Gasset, Gregorio Marañón, Eugeni D'Ors, for example—shared the '98's concern for the Spanish situation but proposed a more objective, documentary and scientific approach to journalism, guided by European philosophy and journalistic standards in the early twentieth century. Both groups were embedded in the Regenerationist movement, which advocated for the arrival of the Republic and proposed paths to modernize Spanish policies and economy. Regenerationism was not that evident in the more poetic and experimental Generation of '27, although the avant-garde journalistic experiments—for example, Ramón Gómez de la Serna—evolved along with the more political reports by Rafael Alberti or Jorge Guillén, written before and after their exile under the Dictatorship of Franco.[5]

With the arrival of democracy, a reappearance of literary journalism and in-depth reporting can be noticed in a large set of magazines born in the last years of Franco's regime, among which we can quote the satirical publications *Ajoblanco* and *Hermano Lobo* and the political magazines *Cuadernos para el Diálogo*, *Cambio 16* and *Triunfo*. In this context, the chronicle and the report began to experience a sudden revitalization in the work of very well-known writers such as Francisco Umbral, Manuel Vázquez Montalbán, Miguel Delibes, Rosa Montero, Maruja Torres and Manuel Vicent. From the end of the 2000s, although the chronicle is "on the verge of extinction in the Spanish reference newspapers," Rodríguez and Albalad (2012, 293) state that the resurgence of narrative journalism is not just perceivable in Latin America but also in Spain, where they remark upon the blossoming of a large set of new publications based on essays, chronicles and reports.

Jot Down *Culture Magazine: Origin and Evolution*

Within this context, *Jot Down* was launched in May 2011 as an online cultural maga-zine grounded on narrative pieces, interviews and supporting visual resources: photogra-phy, illustrations and graphic humor. As the magazine's founder Ricardo Jonás explained in one of his first interviews, the publication seeks to get away from sensationalism and approach every topic with rigor and independence regardless of newness: "We want the readers to sacrifice their frenetic life style and immerse in the slow motion philosophy" (*Madrilanea*, March 2012).

Jot Down was originally planned to be launched in the form of a printed magazine, but its founders Ángel Fernández and Ricardo Jonás—as well as a group of up to 10 people who joined the project in its early days—preferred to start it as a digital native in order to avoid unnecessary financial risks and reach the first readership. With an initial budget of €30,000, they registered the company within the editorial matrix Wabi Sabi Investments S.C. As one of their first branding strategies, they developed an active online campaign through Twitter and Facebook. The aim was to build up a community of readers that would be willing to pay €15 for a printed quarterly, which was finally released one year after the birth of the online version (May 2012).

During the first year, neither the promoters nor the collaborators received any salary or payment. Nonetheless, the founders received the altruistic collaboration of a large number of widely respected writers and intellectuals such as Enric González, Fernando Savater and Félix de Azúa. They were also accompanied by a large group of less-known bloggers and journalists. Three years after the launching of the online version, *Jot Down* has consolidated a permanent part- or full-time staff of around 20 people on the company's payroll. In fact, the model is still based on a reduced permanent staff as well as on a vast network of freelance collaborators. Depending on the tasks, the collaborators are usually paid between €90 and €150 per piece or picture (Ricardo Jonás, personal communication, April 13, 2015).

The majority of the participants write for both formats: online and print. They joined the project from its foundation, when *Jot Down* offered them a new platform for a kind of narrative journalism that was usually absent in the local or national newspapers, especially in a time of deep professional and economic crisis (Carles Foguet, personal communication,

March 8, 2014). Although the publication started with a fixed group of writers, photographers and graphic designers, two of the interviewees said that they began to collaborate when they offered their service as freelancers. All the same, the online and printed issues usually contain pieces by non-regular writers such as Andrés Trapiello and Maruja Torres, touchstones of Spanish contemporary literature.

Jot Down presented itself as "an ode to slow production" (*ABC*, May 11, 2012), since its subjects are based on long-form pieces that require a paused, careful and leisurely reading. Its varied contents range from in-depth features on arts, literature and music to political analyses. Furthermore, its "Interviews" section plays an important role and the editors request that the interviewers "spend a minimum of one hour with the interviewed" (Carles Foguet, personal communication, March 8, 2014).[6] From the beginning, the publication adopted the form of a characteristic black and white layout inspired by its main referent, *The New Yorker*, although they also admit the influence of the above-described New Latin American Chronicle (Ricardo Jonás, personal communication, 13 April, 2015).

Most of their online pieces usually require more than three scrolls down to be read and there is no concern for length, so articles over 4000 words are accepted for publication. Influenced by the ethics of slowness and thoughtful media production, an average of over 300 pages compose the printed edition and each reader expends an average of around 53 minutes on the online site. The general profile of its readers is marked by urban citizens between 25 and 44 years old that have university degrees and share progressive political views (Carles Foguet, personal communication, March 8, 2014).

So far, *Jot Down* has published 10 printed magazines where a variety of regular, sporadic and new names appear. In the latter they indeed have an open call where people can present new pieces or works. According to the latest audience research, the publication seems to keep on growing and reaching new followers.

An Innovative Financing System

Jot Down's biggest expenditure is aimed at covering the editorial payments for collaborators and staff members, which contrasts with the average 20 percent of the costs expended by the main national newspapers on this budget line (Arrese 2011). In a way, this is possible since the magazine functions as a decentralized online working project that only holds a small newsroom in Barcelona. However, as the online survey demonstrates, 80 percent of the people working for the magazine (writers, journalists, photographers and graphic designers) are freelancers who retain complementary jobs oscillating from traditional journalism to engineering or marketing consultancy, to name a few.

At the moment, *Jot Down*'s main financing system comes from the sale of a €15 printed edition, which is sold both online and in bookstores. The average print run for each issue is around 15,000 copies, which makes more than 70 percent of the magazine's income (Olga Sobrido, personal communication, January 25, 2014). Out of the total, 98 percent of the printed circulation is based in Spain and the biggest demands originate in the largest cities: Madrid and Barcelona. The remaining 2 percent of the sales arises from Latin America, where Argentina and Mexico stand out as the biggest demanders, as well as from Europe, with London and Berlin as the most notable selling points. Nonetheless, the international market remains a minor part of the total (Raquel Blanco, personal communication, February 27, 2014).

The remaining 30 percent of *Jot Down*'s income is obtained through promotions, classical advertisement and profits derived from different editorial projects, as we will further develop. Remarkably, when its first two issues were launched in May and November 2012, there were no advertisements or sponsored content, which were finally introduced from the third issue onwards. One of the most noteworthy strategies was the adding of the Thyssen Museum Foundation's logo on four of their issues' back covers.[7] This was followed by the introduction of banners on the website to promote referential firms, banks and foundations such as Banco Santander Foundation, Barcelona Contemporary Art Center (CCCB), Intermon Oxfam, Bacardi and Viajareuskadi, among others. Depending on their deals, a few companies and organizations just post their banners at the portal while others sponsor articles online (Carles Foguet, personal communication, March 8, 2014).

Since the beginning of the Spanish crisis in 2008, 364 media outlets have been forced to close and 11,875 media workers have lost their jobs. This rate contrasts with the emergence of 331 new media outlets that tend to survive thanks to a combination of hybrid financial models, according to the Madrid Press Association (Asociación de la Prensa de Madrid (APM) 2014). Although classical advertisements still provide the main financial support for many projects, this type of funding is decreasing in favor of alternatives such as sponsored content, *à la carte* subscriptions, crowdfunding and donations. On the other hand, the annual report on Spanish advertising investment published by Infoadex shows how the revenue from advertisements in printed magazines has decreased 17.7 percent, from €313.7 million in 2012 to €253.9 million in 2013. In the case of specialized magazines—labeled as "others" in the report and where *Jot Down* is included—the decrease reached 22.1 percent (Infoadex 2014).

Beside the founder's initial investment, *Jot Down*'s financial viability relies on the revenue provided by the selling of printed copies, sponsorship and other advertising activities. Even though the introduction of a pay-per-view digital version "is not a close future project" (Carles Foguet, personal communication, March 8, 2014), the magazine also relies on the internet to create a community of followers that makes the printed version sustainable. Hence, once they reached 400,000 followers, they decided to develop a network of physical selling points all around Spain through the support of bookstores and specialized newspaper kiosks (Raquel Blanco, personal communication, February 27, 2014). This was the starting point of *Jot Down*'s own editorial and distribution market system with the launching of Jot Down Books first (November 2012) and the distributor Soidem afterwards (June 2013). The latter would encompass a set of partnerships with other Spanish magazines influenced by decelerated ideals.

A New Network of Spanish Slow Publications

In order to face the difficulties of selling a book-like product in the regular newsstands, in June 2013 *Jot Down* built up a network of booksellers under the umbrella of its own distribution system: Soidem (Ricardo Jonás, personal communication, April 13, 2015). After six months of operation and more than 100 selling points around the country, a dozen magazines and journals joined the network (Raquel Blanco, personal communication, February 27, 2014). Along its life, Soidem has distributed or is still distributing a list of publications that share the promotion of slow journalistic practices. Based on the review of the editorial lines of each of the projects, the following publications are briefly described in terms of their origin, slow philosophy and financing model:

- *Alternativas económicas*: Partnered with the French *Alternatives Économiques*, this monthly magazine focuses on the dissemination of economic news from a thoughtful and broad perspective. It is organized as a cooperative and it launched both its online blog and printed version in February 2013. Although its financial model depends on commercial advertising, its editorial principles insist that this revenue must come from socially responsible corporations. This is also why the magazine usually gives preference to the promotion of cultural activities rather than classical advertisements centered on a product or service. The publication is also financed through monthly subscriptions and the selling of printed issues in newsstands and specialized bookstores.
- *Yorokobu*: *Yorokobu* is a monthly magazine born in August 2009 and specializes in new tendencies, technology and startups, as well as in issues regarding the environment and sustainability. Like *Jot Down*, it started online but soon diversified towards different media strategies. This is the case of Brand & Roses S.L., a content edition company that is in charge of *Jot Down*'s graphic design and whose incomes from publicity and branded content are *Yorokobu*'s main revenue, as its cofounder Fermin Arbella states (*Ticbeat.es*, October 2, 2014). *Yorokobu*'s motto, presented not in Spanish but in English, invites the readers to "take a walk on the slow side."
- *La Marea*: The goal of this monthly publication is to cover national affairs in the form of long reports and special issues. *La Marea* is part of the cooperative *Más Público*, which emerged after the 2010 closing of the printed version of the leftist referential newspaper *Público*, which affected 85 percent of the staff. In January 2013 a group of ex-workers decided to create a cooperative to develop a Web publication and a printed newspaper. They both follow the editorial guidelines of *Más Público*, hence: in-depth reports, independence and detachment from political and business interests. As a social economy enterprise, the main capital comes from the investments of their associates, which complements the incomes provided by subscription and direct sale. The minimum budget to become an investor is €500 and this offers the right to take part in *La Marea*'s decision-making processes as well as to access to all online articles and publications.
- *FronteraD*: Founded in November 2009, this online magazine promotes a slow journalistic approach to culture, history and technology, among other subjects. One of its most remarkable characteristics is that there are no word limits for the journalists so its chronicles, reports and features are usually based on non-fiction narrative techniques. The journalists and collaborators thus take the necessary time and space to provide thoughtful reports and chronicles since journalism "is meant for the immense minorities," as the journal's motto states. So far *FronteraD* has only gone online but it has diversified its market through the publishing of e-publications and printed books. The online access to *FronteraD*'s articles is totally free and the financial model is mainly supported by advertisement and the selling of books and printed publications.
- *Mongolia*: Influenced by the historical *Ajoblanco* and *Hermano Lobo*, this humor publication was released in March 2012 and it has evolved as a printed magazine complemented with an online blog. Although it is not strictly a slow journalism publication, its contents promote high-quality graphic humor, political satire and large-scale illustrations. As its director Eduardo Galán declared, *Mongolia* constitutes a "small and humble answer to the current situation that journalism is facing. Actually, no one

earned any money during the first six months" (Abad, Galán, and Jonás 2013). *Mongolia*'s financing system is based on subscription and the selling of printed issues in newsstands and online.

- *Cuadernos*, by *Eldiario.es*: Born in March 2013, this online and printed quarterly pursues the provision of in-depth reports on national and international politics and economy. Its editorial principles are aimed at fostering reflection and empowerment within civil society. As a leftist review, this publication is directed by one of the new leading national newspapers, the digital native *Eldiario.es*, and it shares the three funding resources of its matrix: advertisement, monthly subscriptions and the selling of printed issues.

- *Números Rojos*: This magazine was launched at the beginning of 2012 thanks to a crowdfunding initiative carried out by a group of journalists that came from other media outlets such as the above-mentioned *Público*. Distributed every three months, *Números Rojos* describes itself as a space for political analysis and reviews in which there is no need for financial funding from enterprises or institutional bodies. In fact, the publication has refused to introduce advertisements so far, so it is completely supported by membership fees and subscriptions.

- *Líbero*: Born at the end of 2012, this sports magazine defines itself as an independent publication away from the influence of any media conglomerate. It is specially focused on football but it approaches it from an innovative perspective that promotes cultural and historical frames. Its creators consider themselves as "football fans who don't shout but rather have a taste for beauty and in-depth features" (*libero.com*, 2012). The magazine's main income comes from advertisement and the selling of printed and digital copies. The beautifully edited quarterly has not developed an online version so its issues are still sold in kiosks and through subscriptions.

- *La Ballena Blanca*: This magazine appeared in April 2014 to offer high-quality in-depth reports around economy and environmental issues. It publishes two issues per year. As its blog explains, reading *La Ballena Blanca* implies supporting journalists who are concerned with a critical coverage of ecological news (*laballenablanca.es*, 2014). This magazine mainly finances itself thanks to its subscribers and through the selling of printed issues both online and in bookstores.

- *Fiat Lux*: Since the beginning of October 2012, this printed quarterly aims at providing *crónica roja* (crime chronicles) and information about incidents based on a declared New Journalism-like style. *Fiat Lux* claims to develop a different style of journalism which is not limited to the classical tools of accuracy and narrative resources but also promotes a different temporal conception: "Our features have been written with the necessary slowness that a story needs in order to make them three dimensional" (*fiatlux.es*, 2015). Its income is provided both from subscriptions and the selling of single printed issues online and in bookstores.

All the above-mentioned magazines share a set of parallelisms. First, most of them were created as a printed publication and remain as such. On the contrary, there are also a few that were born as digital natives with the goal of creating a posterior printed version, following the model of *Jot Down*. Second, they were launched as a way to face and challenge a time of severe economic cuts and staff reductions in the journalistic scenario. Although there is not a common financing model, all of them experiment with alternative financing which usually defies corporate advertising as the main financial support.

Third, and what especially connects them, is their philosophy no matter their specialized focus and subjects. As many of them state in their editorial lines, they care for the "process" involved in what they publish as well as for the quality of their articles, regardless of length and immediacy.

Connected to this, most of the publications adapt to the above three-dimensional definition of slow journalism: (1) they promote slow temporalities to disseminate their paper and/or online versions: monthly or more; (2) they are not based on bare news but, unconcerned by length, they usually publish long and in-depth reports, essays and chronicles; (3) they all target specific audience sectors which value investigative reporting and nonfiction pieces presented with high aesthetical criteria. Following this outline, Table 2 provides information about the year of origin and legal form of the magazines, as well as their website and periodicity.

All these magazines are or have been distributed through Soidem, yet this is not the only entrepreneurial project that links them together. In February 2013, *Jot Down* together with *Yorokobu* and three other publications (*Diario Kafka*, *Naukas* and *Politikon*) created the printed book *FIVE* with the aim of merging their audiences. The second issue was published in December 2013 and this time it was formed by other slow magazines, *Alternativas Económicas*, *Periodismo Humano*, *Materia*, *FronteraD* and *Jot Down*. The philosophy behind these partnerships was to unite a readership that has a fondness for alternative ways of journalism and therefore seeks publications that distance themselves from mainstream revenue interests and fast processed information (Carles Foguet, personal communication, March 8, 2014).

Furthermore, in 2014 some of the previously mentioned publications developed a collaborative agreement to launch a re-edition of the historical reference newspaper *Heraldo de Madrid*, closed in 1939 with the advent of Franco's regime. Each magazine

TABLE 2

Magazines and journals integrated in Soidem

Name	Site	Legal form	Format	Origin	Periodicity of print version
Jot Down	www.jotdown.es	Enterprise	Paper and online	2011	Quarterly
Alternativas Económicas	www.alternativaseconomicas.coop	Cooperative	Paper and online	2013	Monthly
Yorokobu	www.yorokobu.es	Enterprise	Paper	2009	Monthly
La Marea	www.lamarea.com	Cooperative	Paper	2013	Monthly
FronteraD	www.fronterad.com	Enterprise	Online	2009	Weekly
Mongolia	www.revistamongolia.com	Enterprise	Paper and online	2012	Monthly
Cuadernos, Eldiario.es	www.eldiario.es/publicaciones	Enterprise	Paper	2013	Quarterly
Números Rojos	www.revistanumerosrojos.com	Enterprise	Paper	2012	Monthly
Libero	http://shop.revistalibero.com	Enterprise	Paper	2012	Monthly
La Ballena Blanca	http://ballenablanca.es	Enterprise	Paper	2014	Biannual
Fiat Lux	http://revistafiatlux.com	Enterprise	Paper	2012	Quarterly

was in charge of covering the theme section they are more specialized in: *FronteraD* wrote the International news section; *Eldiario.es* and *Infolibre* developed the Politics pages; *La Marea* took over Society; *Fiat Lux* wrote the Crime Chronicle section, *Materia* did so with Sciences; *Alternativas Económicas* with Economy; *Líbero* covered Sports; and, finally, *Jot Down* assumed the Cultural section.

As the presentation page in the *Heraldo de Madrid* summarizes, behind all these projects there are journalists that, "far from giving up when the media they were working at closed down, they took the risk to open their own publications, without the impediments that they have had in the previous enterprises: a generation of journalists exempt from editorial obligation" (*Heraldo de Madrid*, March 2014, 13).

Furthermore, they promised to offer readers a sensible information service at a time when the public is overwhelmed by online news fragments that lack contextualization and details. In their content production, they seek to provide antecedents and enlarge the scope of their news, offering the readers a wider and deeper picture of current affairs (*Heraldo de Madrid*, March 2014, 11). Currently, the most remarkable synergy is the partnership between the referential online newspaper *Eldiario.es* and *Jot Down*, which have linked their online spaces providing a supplementary that covers daily events and in-depth features. This cooperation not only enriches Spanish media but also creates a wider working space for the network of professional collaborators who write for these publications. In fact, according to the last 2015 *comScore*'s audience research, *Eldiario.es-Jot Down* is nowadays the online native space with the second highest rate of readership (*comScore MMX Multiplataforma*, May 2015).

Hence, in less than five years, Spanish journalism has managed to put into practice a new way of producing information. By specializing in concrete thematic fields, each publication has been able to provide a more meticulous and engaged coverage of the current issues and this eventually proves the workability of the slow journalism philosophy. Yet, what is at stake is that, thanks to their later alignments through cooperative editorial projects, they have also created a new journalistic network that traces further interesting developments, as the last partnership between *Eldiario.es* and *Jot Down* proves.

Conclusion

According to the case study and the brief profile provided for the rest of the publications, we can affirm that there is no closed model for slow journalism in Spain, since all the above-mentioned projects are characterized by an extreme diversity of content, periodicity or sustainability. Nevertheless, there are a few unifying features such as the inspiration drawn from foreign precedents, developed in the Anglo-Saxon (the case of *Jot Down* and its model, *The New Yorker*), French (*Alternativas Económicas*) and, especially, the Latin American contexts, as acknowledged by almost all the publications.

On the other hand, none of the initiatives are embedded in large media conglomerates. Instead, they are promoted by professionals who "rebel against the mediocrity of the profession" (Rodríguez and Albalad 2012, 306) and try to guarantee independence by avoiding commercial advertisements as their main financial support (Domínguez and Pérez Colomé 2012). This is the case of the described permanent collaboration lines and the launch of joint special issues, such as *FIVE* or *El Heraldo de Madrid*. Nevertheless, most of these publications were born in the context of the economic crisis; and this is why their sustainability is not consolidated and is still subject to the fluctuations of the market. They perceive the importance of creating specialized clubs of readers that, instead of any pay-per-read method, value the presence of free content, as well as special offers, benefits and discounts in cultural consumption, among others (Salaverría 2008). Such readers are situated at the core of the slow journalistic projects, contrary to mainstream reference newspapers whose target comprises an undifferentiated audience. According to Robert S. Boynton (2011), the future of news will probably be determined by two completely opposed economical models: on the one side, publications focused on brief news, easy to produce and consume, particularly with the help of ICTs; on the other, beautifully ornamented long-form and specialized magazines and editorial products, which are more costly but try to amortize their expenses by catching specific communities of readers.

To reach this aim, all the magazines promote active campaigns through social networks (mainly Twitter and Facebook) as well as using the Web from a horizontal perspective that involves a very close interaction with users and followers. Furthermore, most of the magazines combine both online and offline strategies and the online platform usually provides content for the printed edition, although this is deprived of many of the multimedia resources offered by ICTs. Following the example of foreign initiatives—e.g., *Narrative.ly*, *Delayed Gratification*—a decentralized newsroom is highly valued since the expanding strategy is based on counting on a large set of permanent collaborators who are normally paid. Furthermore, their editorial policies explicitly or implicitly reject the journalistic tendency to speed and hyper-fragmentation and combine chronicles, interviews and in-depth reports in a move away from traditional bare news. As the supply of narrative reporting would presumably increase in the following years, these magazines will be able to find new readers when they are "all available on the screens of iPads and tablets" (Neveu 2014, 540). This is so because many of them live in urban environments, hold university degrees and high education levels, and usually consume new technologies (computers, mobile devices, tablets, etc.).

In summary, and as noted in a few preceding works, to communicate slowly means the revalorization of qualitative parameters such as creativity, singularity, sustainability and the world of nuances, networks and high ethical and aesthetical standards (Barranquero 2013, 437). In other words, if the slow food movement has slightly but permanently transformed the way we buy or consume food, it is possible that slow journalism will have an important "impact on our information and entertainment ecosystems, too" (Rauch 2011). Moreover, slow initiatives in Spain are also revitalizing the best journalistic habits, since they incite other professionals and media outlets to go back to the origins and fundamentals of journalism as well as to consider that content and reports should be properly processed by audiences, with time, deliberation, reflection and analysis.

DISCLOSURE STATEMENT

No potential conflict of interest was reported by the authors.

NOTES

1. This rate can be consulted on the OJD site (www.ojdinteractiva.es/medios-digitales/jot-down-cultural-magazine-evolucion-audiencia/totales/anual/3016/trafico-global); besides,

the publication counts of 161,029 followers on Twitter as well as 31,288 likes on Facebook (consulted April 11, 2015).

2.   Although New Journalism can be also traced back to the nineteenth century, from Mark Twain to the Lost Generation—Ernest Hemingway, Francis Scott Fitzgerald, etc., according to Robert S. Boynton (2015).

3.   The presence of the chronicle in the Spanish–Latin American literary and journalistic scene is a cultural phenomenon since the eighteenth century. It can be defined as a hybrid form of writing that, similar to American New Journalism, oscillates between the supposedly objective news and the chronicler's own subjective interpretation of the facts through the use of literary techniques.

4.   A good database to get to know these authors and access to the "New Latin American Chronicle" is the blog "Periodismo narrativo en Latinoamérica" (https://cronicasperiodisticas.wordpress.com), as well as a complete dictionary published in *Frontera D* (González Veiguela 2012).

5.   Clear representatives of these Generations can be traced back to a number of newspapers which claimed for the modernization of Spanish economics and policies, such as the so-called *liberal trust of the press* (*El Liberal, El Imparcial, El Heraldo de Madrid, El Sol*, etc.) (Pizarroso 2010), or the beautifully illustrated literary magazines published by the Generation of '27: *Litoral, Verso y Prosa, La Gaceta Literaria*, etc. (Osuna 1986), preceded by landmarks such as the weekly magazine *Electra* by members of the Generation of '98.

6.   Not only have their founders repeatedly claimed this slogan in several interviews but, when we interviewed them for this research, they also offered at least one hour to answer our questions.

7.   *Jot Down*'s regular graphic designers (the company Brand & Roses) were in charge of this project.

REFERENCES

Abad, Mar, Eduardo Galán, and Ricardo Jonás. 2013. "Medios y remedies." [video] Roundtable at *the Annual Convention on digital culture INTERQUÉ*. Madrid, November 30.

Angulo, María. 2013. *Crónica y mirada. Aproximaciones al periodismo narrativo*. Madrid: Libros del K.O.

APM. 2014. *Informe sobre la protesión periodística*. Madrid: Asociación de la Prensa de Madrid.

Arrese, Ángel. 2011. "Más allá del negocio informativo. Nuevas estructuras de las empresas de información." Presented at *9° Congreso Internacional de Ética y Derecho de la Información*. Valencia, November 11-12.

Barranquero, Alejandro. 2013. "Slow media. Comunicación, cambio social y sostenibilidad en la era del torrente mediático." *Palabra Clave* 16 (2): 419–448. doi:10.5294/pacla.2013.16.2.6.

Barranquero, Alejandro, and Gloria Rosique. 2015. "Periodismo lento (slow journalism) en la era de la inmediatez. Experiencias en Iberoamérica." *El Profesional de la Información (EPI)* 24 (4): 451–462. http://dx.doi.org/10.3145/epi.2015.jul.12.

Benjamin, Walter. 1936/2007. *Illuminations: Essays and Reflections*. Translated by Harry Zohn. New York, NY: Schocken.

Bennet, James. 2013. "Against 'Long-Form' Journalism." *The Atlantic*, December 12. www.theatlantic.com/business/archive/2013/12/against-long-form-journalism/282256

Boynton, Robert S. 2015. *El nuevo Nuevo Periodismo. Conversaciones sobre el oficio con los mejores escritores estadounidenses de no ficción*. Barcelona: Publicacions i Edicions de la UB.

Brabazon, Tara. 2013. *Digital Dieting: From Information Obesity to Intellectual Fitness*. Farnham: Ashley.

Callegaro, Adriana, and María Cristina Lago. 2012. "La crónica latinoamericana: cruce entre literatura, periodismo y análisis social." *Quórum Académico* 9 (2): 246–262. doi:10.5216/cei.v15i1.22496.

Carey, James. 1989. Communication as Culture: Essays on Media and Society. Boston, MA: Unwin-Hyman.

Carr, Nicholas. 2010. *The Shallows: What the Internet is Doing to Our Brains*. New York, NY: W. W. Norton & Company.

Carrión, Jorge. 2012. *Mejor que ficción. Crónicas ejemplares*. Barcelona: Anagrama.

Cushion, Stephen, and Justin Lewis, eds. 2010. *The Rise of 24-hour News Television: Global Perspectives*. New York, NY: Peter Lang.

Darrigrandi, Claudia. 2013. "Crónica latinoamericana: algunos apuntes sobre su estudio." *Cuadernos de Literatura* 17 (34): 122–143. http://revistas.javeriana.edu.co/index.php/cualit/article/view/6242.

Dias, Patricia. 2014. "From 'infoxication' to 'infosaturation'. A theoretical overview of the cognitive and social effects of digital immersion." *Ámbitos. Revista Internacional del Comunicación* 24: 31–40. http://ambitoscomunicacion.com/2014/from-infoxication-to-infosaturation-a-theoretical-overview-of-the-cognitive-and-social-inmersion.

Domínguez, Eva, and Jordi Pérez Colomé. 2012. *Microperiodismos. Aventuras digitales en tiempos de crisis*. Barcelona: UOC.

Franklin, Bob. 2003. ""Mcjournalism": The Mcdonaldization Thesis and Junk Journalism." Presented at Political Studies Association Annual Conference, University of Leicester, Leicester, April 15–17.

Freeman, John. 2009. *The Tyranny of E-mail: The Four-thousand-year Journey to Your Inbox*. New York, NY: Scribner.

Frijters, Paul, and Malathi Velamuri. 2010. "Is the Internet Bad News? The Online News Era and the Market for High-Quality News." *Review of Network Economics* 9 (2): 1–31. doi:10.2202/1446-9022.1187.

Fuentes, Juan Francisco, and Javier Fernández. 1997. *Historia del periodismo español. Prensa, política y opinión pública en la España contemporánea*. Madrid: Síntesis.

Gess, Harold. 2012. "Climate Change and the Possibility of 'Slow Journalism'." *Ecquid Novi: African Journalism Studies* 33 (1): 54–65. doi:10.1080/02560054.2011.636828.

Gitlin, Todd. 2007. *Media Unlimited, Revised Edition: How the Torrent of Images and Sounds Overwhelms Our Lives*. London: Picador.

González Veiguela, Lino. 2012. Diccionario de la crónica hispanoamericana. *FronteraD*, May 1. http://fronterad.com/?q=diccionario-cronica-hispanoamericana.

Greenberg, Susan. 2007. "Slow Journalism." *Prospect Magazine*, 25 February. www.prospectmagazine.co.uk/magazine/slowjournalism/#.U06gsFV_uSo.

Hassoun, Dan. 2014. "Tracing Attentions: Toward an Analysis of Simultaneous Media Use." *Television & New Media* 15 (4): 271–288. doi:10.1177/1527476412468621.

Honoré, Carl. 2004. *In Praise of Slowness: How a Worldwide Movement is Challenging the Cult of Speed*. London: Harper Collins.

Infoadex. 2014. *Estudio Infoadex de la Inversión publicitaria en España 2013*. Madrid: Infoadex.

Jacobson, Susan, Jacqueline Marino, and Robert E. Gutsche. Jr. 2015. "The Digital Animation of Literary Journalism." *Journalism*. doi:10.1177/1464884914568079.

Jaramillo, Darío, ed. 2012. *Antología de crónica latinoamericana actual*. Madrid: Alfaguara.

Juntunen, Laura. 2010. "Explaining the Need for Speed. Speed and Competition as Challenges to Journalism Ethics." In *The Rise of 24-hour News Television: Global Perspectives*, edited by Stephen Cushion and Justin Lewis, 167–182. New York, NY: Peter Lang.

Lee, Angela Min-Chia. 2014. "How Fast is Too Fast? Examining the Impact of Speed-driven Journalism on News Production and Audience Reception." Unpublished PhD thesis. The University of Texas.

Leigh, David. 2007. "Are Reporters Doomed?" *The Guardian*, November 12. www.theguardian. com/media/2007/nov/12/mondaymediasection.pressandpublishing3.

Leigh, David. 2009. "Tracking the Slow Form Journalism." *Campfire Journalism*, July 29. http:// markberkeygerard.com/2009/07/tracking-the-%E2%80%9Cslow-journalism%E2%80%9D-movement.

Le Masurier, Megan. 2015. "What is Slow Journalism." *Journalism Practice* 9 (2): 138–152. doi:10. 1080/17512786.2014.916471.

Maier, Scott R. 2005. "Accuracy Matters: A Cross-Market Assessment of Newspaper Error and Credibility." *Journalism & Mass Communication Quarterly* 82 (3): 533–551. doi:10.1177/ 107769900508200304.

Maxwell, Richard, and Toby Miller. 2012. *Greening the Media*. Oxford: Oxford University Press.

Maxwell, Richard, Jon Raundalen, and Nina Lager. 2014. *Media and the Ecological Crisis*. New York, NY: Routledge.

Meuret, Isabelle. 2013. "A Short History of Long-form Journalism." *INA Global*, December 17. www.inaglobal.fr/en/press/article/short-history-long-form-journalism?tq=6.

Mosco, Vincent. 2004. *The Digital Sublime. Myth, Power, and Cyberspace*. Cambridge/London: MIT.

Neveu, Erick. 2014. "Revisiting Narrative Journalism as One of the Futures of Journalism." *Journalism Practice* 15 (5): 533–542. doi:10.1080/1461670X.

Osuna, Rafael. 1986. *Las revistas españolas entre dos dictaduras, 1931–1939*. Valencia: Pretextos.

Pizarroso, Alejandro. 2010. "El periodismo en el primer tercio del siglo XX." *ARBOR. Ciencia, pensamiento y cultura* 186: 45–54. doi:10.3989/arbor.2010.extrajunion3005.

Rauch, Jennifer. 2011. "The Origin of Slow Media: Early Diffusion of a Cultural Innovation through Popular and Press Discourse, 2002–2010." *Transformation Journal* 20. www. transformationsjournal.org/journal/issue_20/article_01.shtml.

Reich, Zvi, and Yigal Godler. 2014. "A Time of Uncertainty: The Effects of Reporters' Time Schedule on Their Work." *Journalism Studies* 15 (5): 607–618. doi:10.1080/1461670X.2014.882484.

Revers, Matthias. 2014. "The Twitterization of News Making: Transparency and Journalistic Professionalism." *Journal of Communication* 64 (5): 806–826. doi:10.1111/jcom.12111.

Rodríguez, Jorge Miguel, and José María Albalad. 2012. "Nuevas ventanas del periodismo narrativo en español: del big bang del boom a los modelos editoriales emergentes." *Textual & Visual Media* 5: 287–310. doi:10.4185/RLCS-65-2010-885-089-098.

Salaverría. 2008. *Ciberperiodismo: diez años de prensa digital en España*. Madrid: McGraw Hill.

Schmierbach, Mike, and Anne Oeldorf-Hirsch. 2012. "A Little Bird Told Me, So I Didn't Believe It: Twitter, Credibility, and Issue Perceptions." *Communication Quarterly* 60 (3): 317–337. doi:10.1080/01463373.2012.688723.

Serrano-Puche, Javier. 2013. "Una propuesta de dieta digital: repensando el consumo mediático en la era de la hiperconectividad." *Fonseca Journal of Communication* 7: 156–175. http:// revistas.usal.es/index.php/2172-9077/article/view/11710/12121.

Serrano-Puche, Javier. 2014. "Hacia una 'comunicación slow': el hábito de la desconexión digital periódica como elemento de alfabetización mediática." *Trípodos* 1 (34): 201–214.

Sharma, Sarah. 2012. "It Changes Space and Time! Introducing Power-chronography." In *Communication Matters: Materialist Approaches to Media, Mobility and Networks*, edited by Jeremy Packer and Stephen B. Crofts Wiley, 66–77. New York, NY: Routledge.

Sieberg, Daniel. 2011. *Digital Diet: The 4-Step Plan to Break Your Tech Addiction and Regain Balance in Your Life*. New York, NY: Three River Press.

Spence, Edward H., and Aaron Quinn. 2008. "Information Ethics as a Guide for New Media." *Journal of Mass Media Ethics* 23 (4): 264–279. doi:10.1080/08900520802490889.

Standage, Tom. 1998. *The Victorian Internet: The Remarkable Story of the Telegraph and the Nineteenth Century's On-line Pioneers*. New York, NY: Walker & Company.

IS THERE A FUTURE FOR SLOW JOURNALISM?
The perspective of younger users

Nico Drok and **Liesbeth Hermans**

Speed has always been a central part of journalism, and for good reason: people want to be informed about events and threats as soon as possible. Immediacy is seen as one of the key values in journalism's culture. Over the past decade technological and commercial forces have strengthened the speed game. At the same time professional journalism has lost its monopoly on news production; news has become abundant and the value of news diminished along with the attention of the public for news, especially among the younger part of the population. It is hard to tell whether the future of journalism lies in speed strategies like "digital first", in Slow Journalism, or in both. A decisive question is: will the upcoming digital generation be interested in Slow Journalism? Our research among Dutch users in the age range of 15–39 years (N = 2642) showed that—indeed—an overwhelming majority finds that news should be available anytime, anywhere, and for free. However, we also found that a considerable proportion of younger users want journalism to be more investigative, inclusive, co-operative and constructive. These features can serve as substantive building blocks for the emerging concept of Slow Journalism.

Introduction

Professional journalism finds itself in a phase of fundamental transition. It needs to be rethought (Peters and Broersma 2013) or maybe even reinvented (Waisbord 2013). One of the many issues journalism is facing concerns which societal functions journalism should fulfil in the digital era. Some see the digitalization process as a reason for emphasizing the rapid dissemination of information as a central function, for instance through a digital-first strategy. Others, on the contrary, see it as an incentive to give more attention to the function of providing context. These two visions do not necessarily exclude one another, but they do represent different frames of reference for reflecting on the future of journalism.

The question remains: what will the public expect from professional journalism in the longer run? We are especially interested in the younger part of the public, those who use mainstream news media less frequently, supposedly, because they lack interest in society at large. This group is believed to be "tuned out" (Mindich 2005), to be less interested in socio-political issues (Spannring, Ogris, and Gaiser 2008) and to see news primarily as something to check occasionally, just like your e-mail (Associated Press 2008). This article focuses on the question of whether or not—and if so, to what extent—younger users prefer a journalism that takes its time for in-depth content, reflection and investigation, next to their obvious interest in news that is available anytime and anywhere. Consequently, the question is to what extent this preference is connected to their views on the societal function of journalism in the digital age.

Speed and Its Problems

Speed has always been an indispensable component of journalism. People want to be informed about relevant changes in their world as soon as possible and journalism can meet this demand as a social "early warning system". Speed therefore has become an inalienable element of journalistic culture. Deuze (2005, 163) considers "immediacy" as one of the five central values in journalism, next to objectivity, autonomy, public service and ethics. The value that is placed upon immediacy is reflected in the role perceptions of journalists. Across the world, journalists still see the fast dissemination of news as their most important task: "reporting the news quickly had the highest mean score" (Weaver and Willnat 2012, 536). After that, the tasks aimed at deepening of understanding follow, such as providing context and interpretation.

Over the past years the emphasis on speed has further increased in journalism practice as a result of the arrival of interactive and mobile internet, which changed the traditional news cycle with fixed deadlines into a 24/7 news production process with continuous deadlines. The ongoing stress on speed, however, has its downsides. The first is that time pressure can erode journalistic standards of carefulness and precision. In their book *Warp Speed*, Kovach and Rosenstiel (1999, 7) give warning that "In practice, the lowest standards tend to drive out the higher, creating a kind of Gresham's Law of Journalism". Several authors share this concern. In *No Time to Think: The Menace of Speed and the 24-Hour News Cycle*, Rosenberg and Feldman (2008) go one step further, in claiming that every mistake in the newsroom in the end is the result of a too strong ambition to be first. Whether or not that is true, it seems clear that too much emphasis on fastness can harm the most important stock a journalist has in trade: credibility (Laufer 2011, 20). The second drawback of the speed-ambition is that in the race to be the first, journalism is at risk of oversimplification and stereotyping. "The average newsroom is not an environment that nurtures reflection on the complexity of the human race. In the haste to label, categorize and synthesize, the more complex aspects of real life can be overlooked" (Gibbs and Warhover 2002, 85). Furthermore, the emphasis on fastness can strengthen the fixation on clashes, accidents or sensationalism. "A real news story has to be angled on a conflict, a drama, a crook or a victim. And in order for it not to be boring, it has to be written short, square and without too many shades" (Haagerup 2014, 10).

The growing stress on speed in daily practice also has its downsides in the economic field. New technologies have brought an end to the professional monopoly on fast news and the supply of free, "real-time" news has grown considerably. This affects the business model of journalism, as the economic value of fast news is in unremitting decline. A study of the World Association of Newspapers shows that in the area of fast news (who, what, where, when), an overabundance has emerged, "with a value approaching zero" (Erbsen et al. 2012, 7). Scarcity will arise increasingly in the area of reliability, truthfulness, in-depth reporting and analysis. Journalism seems to be getting caught in a paradoxical market logic where high-quality in-depth storytelling could be a unique selling proposition, but at the same time cost savings and speed are used as the main weapons to enhance competitiveness. According to Cooper (2009, 3), this is leading to a kind of schizophrenia among journalists: "On the one hand reporters were sent to journalism conferences to learn how to conduct investigations or write narrative stories. On the other, business managers—and some editors—sought out quick, quicker and quickest stories that were increasingly parochial in scope."

Slow Journalism as a Corrective

Several scholars argue that the time has come for journalism to liberate itself from the pressing world of "McJournalism" (Franklin et al. 2005) or "McNews" (Rosenberg and Feldman 2008). Journalism should leave the "digital fast lane" (Greenberg 2012) and invest its scarce time and money in stories of greater substance that are told in an essayistic, narrative style. This aspiration is referred to by the term "Slow Journalism" (Greenberg 2007; Le Masurier 2015).

In *practice*, Slow Journalism is usually about longer stories on the side-lines of breaking news, often made by using literary principles of narrative structuring and multi-layering. Next to that, publications such as *Ricochet* (Canada), *Long Play* (Finland), *The Atavist* (United States), *XXI* (France), *Delayed Gratification* (United Kingdom) and *De Correspondent* (The Netherlands), almost always mention "deepening" in their mission statements as being distinctive for Slow Journalism. *Delayed Gratification* (2015) states this as follows: "Like the other Slow movements, we take time to do things properly. Instead of desperately trying to beat Twitter to the punch, we return to the values we all want from journalism—context, analysis and expert opinion". There are several other basic principles that are mentioned as characteristic for Slow Journalism, such as transparency and co-operation (cf. the manifesto of *De Correspondent* 2013), but there is less agreement on those. Generally speaking, Slow Journalism is not seen as a model to replace all forms of journalism, but as a corrective.

In the *literature* on Slow Journalism it also is foremost seen as a useful concept to contrast with the dominant trend of acceleration. This is not an isolated phenomenon. In various segments of society resistance to the feverish pace of modern life is growing: "The speed obsession intersects every aspect of contemporary life" (Rosenberg and Feldman 2008, 19). Advocates of Slow Journalism find inspiration in the slow-food movement that wants to create a haven in the frantic world of fast food and ready-made meals by stressing sustainability, transparency about origin and nutritional value, while avoiding the use of unhealthy colourings or flavourings. There is no univocal definition or description of Slow Journalism as yet. In the confined academic literature on Slow Journalism rather divergent features are put forward. Some of these features are mentioned by several authors, who usually do not distinguish between Slow Journalism as a genre and Slow Journalism as an approach. However, to get more conceptual clarity it is useful to make this distinction.

Slow Journalism as a *genre* is about the style and form in which the story is told: essayistic, using long-form formats and principles of narration: "the stylistic focus tends to be narrative storytelling" (Le Masurier 2015, 143). Greenberg (2012, 381), who claims to have coined the term some years ago, describes Slow Journalism as a collection of longer non-fiction genres, like the essay and the reportage. Those genres have to meet the highest standards of the art of storytelling, where "a defining aspect of the genre is that the story works on more than one level" (382; cf. Meuret 2013). Costera Meijer (2007, 112) is primarily focused on audio-visual journalism and finds the narrative dimension distinctive for Slow Journalism in that sector too: "slow news calls for quality images that not just illustrate a story but add their own narrative dimension". The relationship between Slow Journalism and literary journalism is highlighted by various authors (Berkey-Gerard 2009; Donat-Trinidade 2012, 101; Greenberg 2007, 16; Keeble and Wheeler 2007). They do not argue that Slow Journalism should be restricted to the longer, literary forms of journalism, but they acknowledge that these forms often will do it better justice.

Slow Journalism as an *approach* goes beyond style and form and refers to the underlying principles and methods. This aspect is, as yet, less elaborated upon in academic literature. Most of the time it is mainly seen as a type of journalism that takes its time for in-depth reporting, for trying to find nuances and perspectives. "Slow Journalism requires the time for deeper reflection and/or investigation" (Le Masurier 2015, 143; cf. Laufer 2011, 31). It can be of special use when complex and ongoing issues need to be covered, because these kind of issues demand a more analytical and persistent approach than is common in breaking-news journalism (Gess 2012; cf. Sundin 2013).

Out of practice and literature arises an image of Slow Journalism as a counter-movement, a corrective to a kind of journalism that gives priority to the fast spreading of news and pays far less attention to other societal functions of journalism. International research on role perceptions shows that the disseminator-function, which is primarily about getting information to the public quickly, is still seen as the most important one by professional journalists worldwide. However, it also shows that a growing proportion of journalists believe that other societal functions are becoming equally or even more important (Weaver and Willnat 2012). In the first place this relates to the adversarial/watchdog-function and to the interpreter-function of journalism. These are successively focused on scrutinizing the established powers and on analysing and interpreting complex issues. In the second place this relates to the mobilizing-function, which is focused on facilitating citizens to become involved in their community or society (Weaver et al. 2007, 144).

The normative importance that professional journalists attribute to their various roles ("should be") does not always match the actual importance that has to be assigned to them in daily practice ("is"). Research shows that, in practice, less attention can be given to events that can raise the public's awareness of societal issues or the deepening of their understanding. More attention than is desired by the journalists has to be given to events where one's own news organization can be the first, where a press release is available, where celebrities are involved and/or can be covered at low costs. The gap between wish and reality seems to be caused mainly by commercial powers and media logic, which in practice, as a rule, get more weight than the professional ideal of public service (Strömback, Nord, and Shehata 2012, 316).

Slow Journalism and the Digital Generation

Slow Journalism as an *approach* can, in terms of role perceptions, be seen as a plea to resist the increasing stress on the disseminator-function and to strengthen the others; especially the interpreter-function, according to the literature on Slow Journalism. The question remains whether this plea is shared by the audience. Unfortunately neither the academic literature nor the research pays much attention to the public's perspective. However, the answer to the question whether or not Slow Journalism has a future, and if so with which characteristics, largely depends on the extent to which it matches news preferences and public perceptions of journalism's tasks, in particular those of the digital generation.

Younger users have developed a news routine that centres around the frequent and quick checking of the headlines (Associated Press 2008; Costera Meijer 2007; Drok and? Schwarz 2009). It is important to them that news is perpetually and universally available to stay informed about the most important or weird stories, and be able to share them. They have less need for professional news media to fulfil these requirements, because of the availability of mobile and free alternatives. However, this does not seem to be the whole picture. The decline in the use of mainstream news media by the younger part of the population has frequently been the subject of international academic research (Banaji and Buckingham 2013; Drok and Schwarz 2009; Peiser 2000; Pasek et al. 2006). This has led to different kinds of explanations. On the one hand, scholars point at socio-cultural developments, such as a growing orientation of younger people towards popular culture (Van Zoonen 2004; cf. Fiske 1989), an increasing focus on self-realization (Bennett 2008) or a diminishing social engagement by younger people in Western democracies (Skoric and Poor 2013; cf. Buckingham 2000). On the other hand, scholars focus on developments that are more tightly connected to the journalistic process itself. There is a growing feeling of misrepresentation among younger people (Devlin 2006; Wayne et al. 2008), an increasing dislike of the focus by most mainstream media on the institutional side of society (Associated Press 2008; Vogel 2014), as a result of which the bulk of news is seen as boring and irrelevant (Marchi 2012). These findings suggest that the emergence of cheap and mobile devices is not solely responsible for the decline in consumption of mainstream news media.

Research from the times before the iPhone and iPad shows that younger users do not only want fast news, but also profundity: "young people need slow news in order to get the 'deep picture' of something, to hear the complexities" (Costera Meijer 2007, 112). At the Digiday Publishing Summit 2014 on "Myths About Digital Media", the editor-in-chief of Mic—an American media company aimed at the younger share of the public—painted an additional picture: "There is a genuine need for quality content. Young people are curious, engaged and craving for reliable information. The standard image of young people that are only interested in fast news is wrong" (Horowitz 2014). There must at least be some truth in this, as Mic's website attracts 19 million visitors, mostly younger, every month.

Do younger users, the group under 40 that according to Mindich (2005) is "tuned out", indeed want a journalism of two speeds; a journalism that emphasizes the disseminator-function next to a journalism that emphasizes the adversarial-, the interpreter- and the mobilizer-functions?

This article focuses on two interrelated research questions. The answers to these questions should give us more insight into the extent to which Slow Journalism as an approach aligns with younger users' news preferences and with their views on journalism's role in society. The outcomes might help us in working towards a more clear and univocal concept of Slow Journalism. The research questions are:

RQ1: To what extent do the news preferences of younger people indicate an orientation towards Slow Journalism?

RQ2: Is there an association between the degree of preference for Slow Journalism of younger users and their view on the societal functions of journalism?

Method

The data that are used in this article originate from a quantitative investigation into news media use by people in The Netherlands on the basis of a random sample survey ($N =$ 4200). This investigation is part of the Dutch Youth Monitor, a five-yearly inquiry into "Young People, News Media Use and Participation" that started in 2009 and is carried out by the Media and Civil Society Research Centre of Windesheim University of Applied Science.

Sample Characteristics

The sampling and fieldwork were carried out by TNS NIPO. The data concerning the younger users (age 15–39, cf. Mindich 2005; $N = 2642$) were selected from the total sample. Outcomes were weighted for age, sex, family size, educational level and region on the basis of the national data of the Central Bureau of Statistics (The Netherlands) and are therefore representative on these variables. The sample coefficient is 0.97.[1]

Measuring

Slow Journalism Preference is measured by six items that correspond with features of Slow Journalism according to the literature: "News should contain more diversity in sources and perspectives" (cf. Laufer 2011), "There should be more in-depth reporting" (cf. Greenberg 2012), "The content of news should contribute to the solving of societal problems" (cf. Gess 2012), "The news should more often be explained" (cf. Le Masurier 2015), "News should be reported more from the perspective of the people that are involved" (cf. Costera Meijer 2007), "People should be able to contribute to the news more extensively" (cf. Bradshaw 2009). The answering categories are based on a five-point Likert scale, running from (1) "strongly disagree" to (5) "strongly agree". For the purpose of the descriptive analysis these are reduced to a three-point scale: (1) "(strongly) disagree", (2) "neutral", (3) "(strongly) agree". The six items constitute a reliable scale that was named the Slow Journalism Preference Scale (Cronbach's $\alpha = 0.725$; mean $= 3.12$; SD $= 0.53$; $N = 6$). This scale is related to Slow Journalism as an *approach*, not as a genre.

To be able to distinguish the degree to which younger users prefer Slow Journalism, a mean score is calculated for all respondents. Figure 1 shows the frequency distribution of these mean scores (range: (1) "low" to (5) "high"; mean $= 3.12$; SD $= 0.53$; $N = 2642$).

With the use of SPSS the respondents were grouped into four quartiles: 1st quartile ($N = 757$, mean $= 2.50$); 2nd quartile ($N = 544$, mean $= 3.00$); 3rd quartile ($N = 625$, mean $=$ 3.42); 4th quartile ($N = 716$, mean $= 3.75$). In the analysis that was required to answer RQ2, respondents from the 1st quartile ("Low preference") were compared to respondents from the 4th quartile ("High preference").

Views on Journalism's Role in Society is measured by using a selection of items that are commonly used in the research on role perceptions of professional journalists themselves (Weaver and Willnat 2012). The selected items represent the broad spectrum of possible roles. The wording of the items is adapted so that they became suitable for the questioning

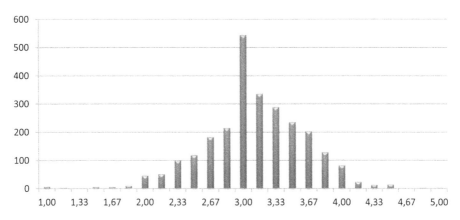

FIGURE 1
Frequency distribution of the scores on the Slow Journalism Preference Scale

of younger users about their views on journalism's societal roles. The selected items were: "Expose social abuses", "Cover deviant events", "Get information to the public quickly", "Provide in-depth background information and analysis", "Give people chance to express views", "Concentrate on news of interest to the widest audience", "Motivate people to get socially involved", "Provide entertainment and relaxation", "Be the first to bring the news", "Point people towards solutions on societal problems", "Cover political debate" and "Provide information that is useful in everyday life". The answering categories are based on a five-point Likert scale, running from (1) "very unimportant" to (5) "very important". For the purpose of the descriptive analysis comparisons were made on the basis of the sum of the percentages of respondents that finds a certain role (4) "important" and (5) "very important". To find out whether or not there would be an underlying pattern in the views of younger people on journalistic roles—in other words, if separate roles would cluster into functions—a factor analysis was carried out. This analysis will be presented in the Results section.

Analysing Process

The analysing process has focused on differences as well as on associations.

Chi-squared (Pearson χ^2 (df = 4), $p < 0.001$) was used to check if there were statistically significant differences with regard to the importance they ascribe to various journalistic roles or functions between respondents with low preference for Slow Journalism and with high preference for Slow Journalism. The outcomes were checked using a t-test. This check gave corresponding outcomes and is therefore not reported in this article.

Pearson correlation, with significance on the $p < 0.01$ level (two-tailed), was used to determine the degree of association between *Slow Journalism Preference* and *Views on Journalism's Role in Society*.

Results

With regard to the first research question, about the extent to which news preferences of younger people reveal an interest in Slow Journalism, the first outcome is that a large majority of respondents find that news should be available anytime and anywhere, preferably on mobile devices (mean = 3.84; SD = 0.998) and for free (mean = 3.59; SD = 0.891). This rather points in the direction of a preference for Fast Journalism than for Slow Journalism. Other potential elements of fast journalism, such as simpler language (mean = 2.74; SD = 0.905) and shorter news items (mean = 2.62; SD = 0.786), on the other hand, get far less support (Figure 2).

Next to these four statements, respondents were presented with six statements that are included in the Slow Journalism Preference Scale. Figure 3 shows that a share of about 30 per cent of younger users have preferences that point in the direction of Slow Journalism. Five out of six items have a slightly positive score, that is a score above the scale average of 3.00. These are: "News should contain more diversity in sources and perspectives" (mean = 3.36; SD = 0.827), "There should be more in-depth reporting" (mean = 3.20; SD = 0.823), "The content of news should contribute to the solving of societal problems" (mean = 3.17; SD = 0.822), "The news should more often be explained" (mean = 3.09; SD = 0.821) and "News should be reported more from the perspective of the people that are involved" (mean = 3.03; SD = 0.781). The sixth item has a slightly negative score: people should be able to contribute to the news more extensively (mean = 2.86; SD = 0.810).

To answer the second research question, about the association between the degree of preference of younger users for Slow Journalism and their view on the societal functions of journalism, 12 different roles were presented and respondents were asked to indicate the importance they attach to each role. The average score on almost all roles lies in between neutral (3) and important (4) on the five-point scale. Figure 4 shows what percentage of younger users find the various roles important or very important, divided into two groups: those that have a low preference for Slow Journalism (1st quartile; $N = 757$) and those that have a high preference for Slow Journalism (4th quartile; $N = 716$). The most substantial differences between the "low" and "high" groups were found for four roles: "Motivate people to get socially involved" ($\chi^2 = 161.7$), "Give people chance to express views" ($\chi^2 = 149.5$), "Point people towards solutions on societal problems" ($\chi^2 = 137.2$) and "Provide information that is useful in everyday life" ($\chi^2 = 107.6$). Next to that, there are significant differences with respect to five other roles, but these are considerably smaller. Finally, there are three roles that show no significant difference (see Figure 4).

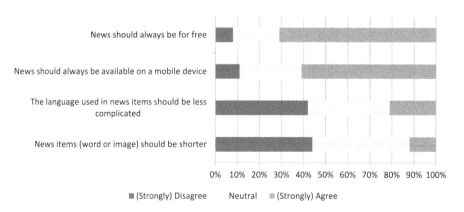

FIGURE 2
News preferences of younger users ($N = 2642$)

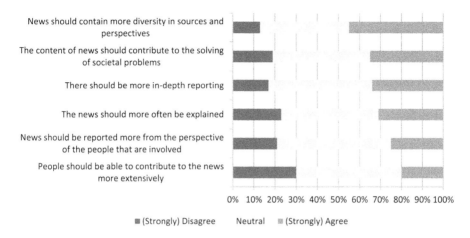

FIGURE 3
News preferences of younger users. The statements are included in the Slow Journalism Preference Scale ($N = 2642$)

Because there appeared to be a pattern in the outcomes, a factor analysis was carried out to enable a more comprehensive interpretation of the differences. After the exclusion of two roles with high loadings on more than one factor, namely "Cover deviant events" and "Provide entertainment and relaxation", three factors emerged. Together they

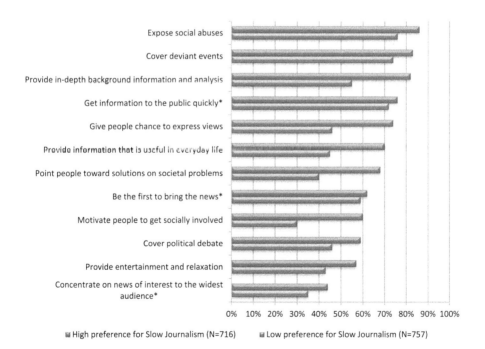

FIGURE 4
Percentage of respondents that finds different journalistic roles (very) important; high versus low preference for Slow Journalism. *Not significant

explain 58.7 per cent of the total variance (Table 1). The first factor contains roles that are related to empowerment: "Point people towards solutions on societal problems", "Give people chance to express views", "Motivate people to get socially involved" and "Provide information that is useful in everyday life". The second factor contains roles that are related to the fast spreading of news to a large audience: "Get information to the public quickly", "Be the first to bring the news" and "Concentrate on news of interest to the widest audience". The third factor contains roles that primarily relate to the classical watch-dog- and interpreter-function of journalism: "Provide in-depth background information and analysis", "Cover political debate" and "Expose social abuses".

With the necessary caution these three factors can be labelled as follows: Factor 1 corresponds with the Mobilizer-function, Factor 2 corresponds with the Disseminator-function, Factor 3 corresponds with the Investigator-function, which combines adversarial and interpretative roles. These factors can be transformed into three scales with sufficient reliability, one for each function:

1. Mobilizer ($\alpha = 0.672$; mean = 3.42; SD = 0.58; $N = 4$).
2. Disseminator ($\alpha = 0.654$; mean = 3.47; SD = 0.66; $N = 3$).
3. Investigator ($\alpha = 0.656$; mean = 3.67; SD = 0.61; $N = 3$).

These three factors show a strong resemblance with the functions that professional journalists around the globe distinguish for themselves (Weaver and Willnat 2012). The main difference is that in the case of the younger users the interpreter- and watchdog/adversarial-functions are combined into one function: the investigator-function. This function has the highest mean score, which means that younger users find the investigator-function of professional journalism the most important one. The disseminator-function comes second and the mobilizer-function comes third.

TABLE 1
Factor analysis for journalistic roles (rotated component matrix)

	Component			Communality
	1	2	3	
Point people towards solutions on societal problems	**0.754**			0.589
Motivate people to get socially involved	**0.750**			0.592
Give people chance to express views	**0.608**			0.437
Provide information that is useful in everyday life	**0.597**	0.327		0.464
Get information to the public quickly		**0.811**		0.726
Be the first to bring the news		**0.802**		0.683
Concentrate on news of interest to the widest audience	0.350	**0.617**	−0.368	0.639
Provide in-depth background information and analysis			**0.780**	0.651
Cover political debate			**0.712**	0.517
Expose social abuses			**0.678**	0.571
Eigenvalue after rotation	2082	1898	1891	
% Variance explained after rotation	20.8	19.0	18.9	

Extraction method: Principal Component Analysis. Rotation method: Varimax with Kaiser Normalization. Rotation converged in six iterations.
Factor loadings < 0.300 are not reported.
Bold scores indicates Factor loadings > 0.400.

TABLE 2
Relationship between Slow Journalism Preference and Functions of Journalism (mobilizer, disseminator, investigator)

	Mobilizer	Disseminator	Investigator
Slow Journalism preference	0.41*	0.08*	0.22*

Pearson correlation ($N = 2642$).
*Correlation is significant at the 0.01 level (two-tailed).

All of these three functions proved to be positively related to a preference for Slow Journalism. However, there appear to be substantive differences in the strength of these relationships (Table 2).

As could be expected, Slow Journalism Preference has the weakest relationship with the disseminator-function (Pearson's $r = 0.08$). The relationship with the investigator-function is considerably stronger (Pearson's $r = 0.22$). The relationship is the strongest with regard to the mobilizer-function (Pearson's $r = 0.41$).[2] This is notable as this function ranks third in the overall importance that the total group of respondents attached to it.

Discussion and Conclusion

In this article, the question is examined to what extent news preferences of younger people reveal a preference for Slow Journalism and, after that, if there is a relationship between this preference and the views younger people hold regarding the functions of journalism in society. From the research, the following conclusions can be drawn.

First of all, it can be concluded that the concept of Slow Journalism is still developing. For the time being it can be seen as a "container construct", maybe not so much with regard to Slow Journalism as a genre (style, form), but as an approach (principles, methods). The lack of conceptual clearness is compensated by the value it can have as a counter-movement, a corrective on a media logic that seems to be pushing journalism further in the direction of speed and haste.

Our research confirms earlier studies that have shown that a large majority of younger users want news to be available mobile and for free. This fits in a news routine where young people habitually pick up bits of news information from various sources, which is referred to by terms such as grazing (Drok and Schwarz 2009), checking (Associated Press 2008) or snacking (Costera Meijer 2007).

Next to that, almost one in three of the younger users show interest in Slow Journalism. This interest is fed by, for one thing, a preference for in-depth stories and context, for another a preference for a greater variety of sources and perspectives, for a stronger orientation towards solutions and for broader use of the perspectives of the people involved.

The degree of Slow Journalism Preference is related to the perception of the functions journalism should fulfil in society: the investigator-function and the mobilizer-function. The investigator-function is commonly recognized as an important element of Slow Journalism (Cooper 2009; Greenberg 2012; Le Masurier 2015), but the mobilizer-function is scarcely mentioned in the literature. This is notable, as it is precisely this function that turned out to be most strongly connected to Slow Journalism (Table 2).

In addition to the investigator-function, the mobilizer-function deserves a more prominent place in the conceptualizing of Slow Journalism. This function is of a relatively recent origin, younger than the disseminator-, adversarial- or interpreter-function. Its rise is strongly connected with the emergence of civic journalism in the United States (Weaver et al. 2007, 174). Civic journalism, according to Schudson (1999, 118) "[the] most impressive critique of journalistic practice inside journalism in a generation", wanted to mobilize people to get involved again and participate in journalism as well as in the public domain (Rosen 1999; Rosenberry and St.John 2010). Therefore, the public has to be engaged in agenda setting and framing, in the process of finding diversity in angles and perspectives, and in the attempt to have a debate on matters of common concern in large sections of the population. Interactive technology can be of great support in the construction and maintaining of a broad range of sustainable contacts and in actualizing different forms of co-creation between professionals and the public. Using interactive technology mainly for the purpose of producing fast news is—from the perspective of civic journalists—by contrast a step backwards in the evolutionary process of journalism (Ryfe and Mensing 2010).

However, the mobilizer-function is not completely absent in the Slow Journalism discourse. Some aspects are mentioned throughout the literature, but rather haphazardly. On the basis of our research, these aspects of the mobilizer-function can be brought together in a systematic way and—next to the investigative element—serve as building blocks for a more comprehensive definition of Slow Journalism.

The first aspect is *inclusiveness*: to facilitate broad deliberation and consider a greater variety of viewpoints than only a bipolar pro and con (Laufer 2011). "Stories that present only two extremes of a complex issue are not only superficial and inaccurate; they also foster polarization among citizens. Stories that present a range of perspectives, however, lead to more constructive public discourse" (Gibbs and Warhover 2002, 168–169). The second aspect is *co-operation*: using the opportunities our twenty-first-century network society has to offer for collaboration with the public and making use of their contributions, from user-generated content to crowdsourcing (Bradshaw 2009). This co-operation is not limited to the production or distribution phase of the journalistic process. The role of the public is of decisive importance in the preliminary phase of agenda setting and framing, where decisions on core issues and angles are made (Berkey-Gerard 2009), and to feed public discourse with a whole range of perspectives (Ananny 2013). What Bradshaw (2009) says about investigative journalism certainly holds for mobilizing journalism too: "it is about enlightening, empowering and making a positive difference. And the web offers enormous potential here—but users must be involved in the process and have ownership of the agenda." The third aspect is *constructiveness*: informing the public about possible solutions to public problems and about possibilities to act. This is a central tenet of the civic journalism movement (Rosenberry and St.John 2010) as well as of the arising constructive journalism movement (Haagerup 2014; Gyldensted 2011). In the literature on Slow Journalism, this third aspect is only mentioned implicitly, in the references to the importance of empowerment (Gess 2012; Le Masurier 2015; Sundin 2013).

Together with the above-mentioned investigator-function, these three building blocks correspond with the description that journalist Susan Moeller gave in the *Huffington Post*:

Slow Journalism is about valuing content over speed. Slow Journalism is about identifying core issues and finding a way to give audiences information of lasting substance—it's not about posting the latest news clip on a 24/7 deadline to "feed the beast." Slow Journalism is about news you can use … to make you a more informed citizen. Slow Journalism is activist journalism; it's journalism that tries to enlighten, and perhaps even empower its audience, often by asking that audience to become collaborators. (Moeller 2010)

Up till now Slow Journalism has been mainly practised in a niche market of literary journalism in a magazine format; online or on paper. In order to develop into a substantial and sustainable alternative for the "digital fast lane" (Greenberg 2012), the wishes and preferences of a far larger audience group should be taken into consideration, especially those of the digital generation. Their preferences seem to point in the direction of a journalism of two speeds, where "fast" probably more often will be associated with free news and "slow" with the kind of journalism one has to pay for (cf. Erbsen et al. 2012). Within this framework of a journalism of two speeds, Slow Journalism should not only be investigative, but inclusive, co-operative and constructive as well. Our research shows that among younger users there is a basis for this.

DISCLOSURE STATEMENT

No potential conflict of interest was reported by the authors.

NOTES

1. A perfect sample has a coefficient of 1.
2. These outcomes are similar in all five underlying age groups: 15–19 years; 20–24 years; 25–29 years; 30–34 years; 35–39 years.

REFERENCES

Ananny, Mike. 2013. "Breaking News Pragmatically: Some Reflections on Silence and Timing in Networked Journalism." *Nieman Journalism Lab*, April 23. http://www.niemanlab.org/2013/04/breaking-news-pragmatically-some-reflections-on-silence-and-timing-in-networked-journalism/.

Associated Press. 2008. *A New Model for News. Studying the Deep Structure of Young-adult News Consumption*. A Research Report from the Associated Press and the Context-Based Research Group. http://rumble.me/wp-content/uploads/2013/02/A-New-model-for-news.pdf.

Banaji, Shakuntala, and David Buckingham. 2013. *The Civic Web. Young People, the Internet and Civic Participation*. Cambridge, MA: The MIT Press.

Bennett, W. Lance. 2008. "Changing Citizenship in the Digital Age." In *Civic Life Online: Learning How Digital Media Can Engage Youth*, edited by W. Lance Bennett, 1–24. The MacArthur Foundation Series on Digital Media and Learning. Cambridge, MA: The MIT Press.

Berkey-Gerard, Mark. 2009. "Tracking Down the 'Slow Journalism' Movement." *Campfire Journalism Blog. Notes on Teaching Digital Storytelling*, July 29. http://markberkeygerard.com/2009/07/tracking-the–journalism-movement/.

Bradshaw, Paul. 2009. "What's been Happening with Help Me Investigate." *Online Journalism Blog*, June 1. http://onlinejournalismblog.com/2009/06/01/whats-been-happening-with-help-me-investigate/.

Buckingham, David. 2000. *The Making of Citizens: Young People, News and Politics*. London: Routledge.

Cooper, Candy. 2009. "The Death of Slow Journalism." *American Journalism Review*, August 6. http://ajrarchive.org/article_printable.asp?id=4789.

Costera Meijer, Irene. 2007. "The Paradox of Popularity; How Young People Experience the News." *Journalism Studies* 8 (1): 96–116.

De Correspondent. 2013. "Our Manifesto." https://decorrespondent.nl/en.

Delayed Gratification. 2015. "Why Slow Journalism Matters." Accessed September 28. http://www.slow-journalism.com/slow-journalism.

Deuze, Mark. 2005. *Mediawork*. Cambridge, MA: Polity Press.

Devlin, Maurice. 2006. *Inequality and the Stereotyping of Young People*. Dublin: The Equality Authority.

Donat Trinidade, Alice. 2012. "What Will the Future Bring?" *Literary Journalism Studies* 2 (4): 101–105.

Drok, Nico, and Fifi Schwarz. 2009. *Jongeren, nieuwsmedia en betrokkenheid* (Youth, News Media and Engagement). Amsterdam: Hogeschool Windesheim/Stichting krant in de klas.

Erbsen, Claude E., Juan Antonio Giner, Juan Señor, and Marta Torres. 2012. *Innovations in Newspapers*. 2012 World Report. London: Innovation Media Consulting Group.

Fiske, John. 1989. *Understanding Popular Culture*. London: Routledge.

Franklin, Bob, Martin Hamer, Mark Hanna, Marie Kinsey, and John E. Richardson. 2005. *Key Concepts in Journalism Studies*. London: Sage Publications.

Gess, Harold. 2012. "Climate Change and the Possibility of 'Slow Journalism'." *Ecquid Novi: African Journalism Studies* 1 (33): 54–65.

Gibbs, Cheryll, and Tom Warhover. 2002. *Getting the Whole Story*. New York: The Guilford Press.

Greenberg, Susan. 2007. "Slow Journalism." *Prospect*, February 26. http://journalism.nyu.edu/assets/BylinePDFs/slowjofeb07.pdf.

Greenberg, Susan. 2012. "Slow Journalism in the Digital Fast Lane." In *Global Literary Journalism: Exploring the Journalistic Imagination*, edited by Richard L. Keeble and John Tulloch, 381–393. New York: Peter Lang Publishing.

Gyldensted, Cathrine. 2011. "Innovating News Journalism through Positive Psychology." Masters diss., University of Pennsylvania. http://repository.upenn.edu/mapp_capstone/20.

Haagerup, Ulrik. 2014. *Constructive Journalism; Why Negativity Destroys the Media and Democracy – And How to Improve Journalism of Tomorrow*. Rapperswil: InnoVatio Publishing.

Horowitz, Jake. 2014. *Untitled*. Key Biscane, Florida: Contribution to the Digiday Publishing Summit, September 2014. http://www.persinnovatie.nl/17590/nl/media-mythes-onthuld http://digiday.com/publishers/mythbusters-digital-medias-biggest-misconceptions/.

Keeble Richard, L., and Sharon Wheeler. 2007. *The Journalistic Imagination: Literary Journalists from Defoe to Capote and Carter*. Oxon: Routledge.

Kovach, Bill, and Tom Rosenstiel. 1999. *Warp Speed: America in the Age of Mixed Media*. New York: Century Foundation Press.

Laufer, Peter. 2011. *Slow News; A Manifesto for the Critical News Consumer*. Corvallis, OR: Oregon State University Press.

Le Masurier, Megan. 2015. "What is Slow Journalism?" *Journalism Practice* 9 (2): 138–152. doi:10.1080/17512786.2014.916471.

Marchi, Regina. 2012. "With Facebook, Blogs and Fake News, Teens Reject Journalistic 'Objectiv- ity'." *Journal of Communication Inquiry* XX (X): 1–17.

Meuret, Isabelle. 2013. "A Short History of Long-form Journalism." *Inaglobal*, December 17. http:// www.inaglobal.fr/en/press/article/short-history-long-form-journalism.

Mindich, David T. Z. 2005. *Tuned Out: Why Americans Under 40 Don"t Follow the News*. Oxford: Oxford University Press.

Moeller, Susan. 2010. "Media Literacy 101: Fast iPad and Slow Journalism (Lessons learned from Gaming)." *Huffington Post*, May 25. http://www.huffingtonpost.com/susan-moeller/media- literacy-101-fast-i_b_525146.html.

Pasek, Josh, Kate Kenski, Daniel Romer, and Kathleen Hall Jamieson. 2006. "America"s Youth and Community Engagement: How use of Mass Media is Related to Civic Activity and Political Awareness in 14 to 22 year olds." *Communication Research* 33 (3): 115–135.

Peiser, Wolfram. 2000. "Cohort Replacement and the Downward Trend in Newspaper Reader- ship." *Newspaper Research Journal* 21 (2): 11–23.

Peters, Chris, and Marcel Broersma, eds. 2013. *Rethinking Journalism. Trust and Participation in a Transformed News Landscape*. London: Routledge.

Rosen, Jay. 1999. *What are Journalists for?* New Haven: Yale University Press.

Rosenberg, Howard, and Charles S. Feldman. 2008. *No Time to Think; The Menace of Media Speed and the 24-hour News Cycle*. New York: The Continuum International Publishing Group.

Rosenberry, Jack, and Burton St.John III, eds. 2010. *Public Journalism 2.0; The Promise of a Citizen- engaged Press*. New York: Routledge.

Ryfe, David M., and Donica Mensing. 2010. "Citizen Journalism in a Historical Frame." In *Public Journalism 2.0; the Promise of a Citizen-engaged Press*, edited by Jack Rosenberry and Burton St.John III, 32–44. NewYork: Routledge.

Schudson, Michael. 1999. "What Public Journalism knows about Journalism but doesn't know about 'Public'." In *The Idea of Public Journalism*, edited by Theodore L. Glasser, 118–133. New York: The Guilford Press.

Skoric, Marko M., and Nathaniel Poor. 2013. "Youth Engagement in Singapore: The Interplay of Social and Traditional Media." *Journal of Broadcasting & Electronic Media* 57 (2): 187–204.

Spannring, Reingard, Günther Ogris, and Wolfgang Gaiser, eds. 2008. *Youth and Political Partici- pation in Europe; Results of the Comparative Study of EUYOUPART*. Farmington Hills, MI: Barbara Budrich Publishers.

Stromback, Jesper, Lars Nord, and Adam Shehata. 2012. "Swedish Journalists: Between Professio- nalization and Commercialization." In *The Global Journalist in the 21st Century*, edited by David H. Weaver and Lars Willnat, 306–319. London: Routledge.

Sundin, Ebba. 2013. "The Concept of 'Slow Journalism'." Paper presented at the Nordic Confer- ence Nordmedia, Oslo, August 2013.

Van Zoonen, Liesbet. 2004. *Entertaining the Citizen: When Politics and Popular Culture Converge*. Lanham: Rowman & Littlefield Publishers.

Vogel, Andreas. 2014. *Talfahrt der tagespresse: eine ursachensuche* (The Daily Press going Down. An Inquiry into the Causes). Bonn: Friedrich-Ebert-Stiftung.

Waisbord, Silvio. 2013. *Reinventing Professionalism; Journalism and News in Global Perspective*. Malden, MA: Polity Press.

Wayne, Michael, Lesley Henderson, Craig Murray, and Julian Petley. 2008. "Television News and the Symbolic Criminalisation of Young People." *Journalism Studies* 9 (1): 75–90.

Weaver, David H., Randal A. Beam, Bonnie J. Brownlee, Paul S. Voakes, and G. Cleveland Wilhoit. 2007. *The American Journalist in the 21st Century: U.S. News People at the Dawn of a New Millennium*. Mahwah: Lawrence Erlbaum Associates.

Weaver, David H., and Lars Willnat, eds. 2012. *The Global Journalist in the 21st Century*. London: Routledge.

EDITING, FAST AND SLOW

Susan L. Greenberg

I first used "slow journalism" in 2007 to describe storytelling that gives equal value to narrative and factual discovery. My contribution was original in one respect: using management theory, it evaluated slow journalism as an example of high-margin journalism at the luxury end of the market, compared to high-volume news at the other, or conventional journalism in the middle. In that sense, slow journalism can be understood as a way of beating the competition through differentiation. An awareness of markets offers an additional frame for understanding slow journalism, alongside others that emphasise its potential as a communal project. However, it is not a binary choice: the best insights arise from understanding the tension between opposites, such as financial and cultural capital (Bourdieu) or ulterior and ultimate motives (Burke). A focus on the editing of slow journalism helps to understand these tensions. It also provides a lens through which to view time. Editing, now commonly seen as an extra stage that slows textual production, first emerged as a way of speeding it up. An historical awareness of the material conditions of production can help distinguish between constraints that are specifically commercial, and those arising from a wider social production of texts.

Introduction

Nearly 10 years ago I started using the term "slow journalism" to describe the kind of storytelling that gives equal value to both factual discovery and narrative technique. On a technical level, the term "narrative nonfiction" is a useful generic term, but in some contexts it lacks precision, as it includes non-journalistic forms. The same problem arises with the umbrella term "creative nonfiction." From the recent past, "the New Journalism" still has resonance, but it acts principally as a historic reference point. In contemporary debate, "literary journalism" vies for purchase with "long form," and argument continues over where to draw the line between literary journalism and "reportage."

Amid such noisy debate, a term like slow journalism—however imperfect—has an evocative and simple appeal. I first gave the name an airing at the founding conference of the International Association of Literary Journalism Studies (IALJS).[1] It reached a wider public in a short article for *Prospect* (Greenberg 2007); then a longer feature (Greenberg 2010) and then finally a book chapter (Greenberg 2012a). More recently, a dictionary entry for the term cited the *Prospect* article as a source (Harcup 2014). My rough and ready definition invoked the "slow food" meme for some forms of journalism on the grounds of transparency about sources and process, and a greater investment of time in discovery and craft. The full definition refers to

> essays, reportage and other nonfiction forms that offer an alternative to conventional reporting … The journalistic equivalent of slow food keeps the reader informed about the provenance of the information and how it was gathered. More time is invested in

both the production and consumption of the work, to discover things we would not otherwise know, or notice things that have been missed, and communicate that to the highest standards of story telling craft. (Greenberg 2012a, 381–382)

Other research since then has documented different media experiments and extended enquiry in many directions, including the ethical potential of the form (Le Masurier 2015) and the role of "slow media" as a counterculture movement that interprets communication as a social good (Rauch 2015).

I cannot claim ownership of the slow journalism idea, which was part of the *zeitgeist* (for a short account, see Greenberg 2011). But I did provide at least one original twist: the use of an old management theory to explain its appeal. The theory is from Michael Porter's 1980 work on competitive strategies (Porter 2004), which identifies the problem of businesses that are "stuck in the middle." They are stuck because they fail to gain an advantage either from offering cheap, high-volume products at the bottom of the market, or from high-margin luxury goods at the top, which beat the competition through differentiation. Outlining his ideas on competitive strategies, Porter says that a firm stuck in the middle

is almost guaranteed low profitability. It either loses the high-volume customers who demand low prices or must bid away its profits to get this business away from low-cost firms. Yet, it also loses high-margin businesses—the cream—to the firms who are focused on high-margin targets or have achieved differentiation overall. (Porter 2004, 41–42)

A firm in this position must either take steps to achieve cost parity or leadership, orientate itself to a particular target, or achieve some uniqueness through differentiation.

If we apply this to journalism, I argue, we get high-volume news bulletins at one end of the market, and high-margin, quality journalism at the top—represented in this case by the concept of slow journalism. The publication offering conventional legacy journalism sits somewhere in the middle. And it is the middle that is suffering.[2]

The "end of the middle" concept does not negate other ways of explaining a multi-faceted phenomenon. Slow journalism takes many different forms and involves a range of players, driven by different motives; sometimes it is published because it makes market sense, but it is also published for its own sake, when enough people in a culture like it and want it to thrive. Occasionally, the two motives overlap. However, an awareness of markets does serve a number of purposes. It reminds us that ambitious nonfiction writing needs first to survive (financially and literally) for other goals to be achievable. Also it can enrich scholarship by reminding us about the material conditions of production.

The focus of this article is on a particular aspect of the material condition of production that is often overlooked—the role of editing in the making and circulation of a text—and what it can tell us about slow journalism. In the process, I will draw selectively on other original work that I have published previously, stitching together arguments and information in a way that helps to introduce editing to the discussion about slow journalism.

Out into the World

A few definitions help to identify the terrain. The words "editing" and "edition" derive from the Latin noun *editor*, someone who "puts forth" or "gives out"—the "e" indicates outwards movement (*Oxford English Dictionary* 1989). My own bespoke definition, developed as a generic benchmark for a wider analysis, describes editing as a decision-making process that aims to *select*, *shape* and *link* content, to help deliver the meaning of the work to its audience. The process involves a relationship between author, editor and text, with the editor embodying the absent reader. The definition points to editing as a state of mind that enables the practitioner to see a text *as if it is not yet finished.*[3]

Editorial selection, in this definition, is understood as a potentially active process of discovery, not just a passive choice. It can take the form of building lists, anthologies and series, assembling contributors, and defining types of content. The editor may develop ideas from scratch or help a writer determine the shape of an idea. The shaping of language includes an engagement with the text's voice; for texts assembled by groups of people—for example, magazines, websites, works of reference or films—a distinctive collective voice is needed, and it is the people doing the editing who create that effect. Linking involves design and paratexts; public perceptions of the publisher or author; and the way a text links to other texts. These are all material conditions of a text's production that can influence its potential meaning.

Since "putting out into the world" entails an understanding of a social dimension, my analysis draws on Pierre Bourdieu's (1993) concept of the "field of cultural production." Bourdieu maps the literary field using the criteria of consecration (cultural capital) on one axis, and market engagement (financial capital) on the other. He proposes that within specific circumstances, different cultural groups create their own social universe in this field, in which they compete for power and influence. My analysis also draws on the work of philosopher and critic Kenneth Burke whose influential *A Rhetoric of Motives*—first published in 1950—describes a spectrum of persuasion, from the "bluntest quest of advantage" to a pure form "that delights in the process of appeal for itself alone, without ulterior purpose" (Burke 1969, xiv). It is the acknowledgement of this range, from "ultimate" to "ulterior" motives, that extends and complicates the discussion of textual mediation in a useful way.

Nowadays, editing is usually seen as an extra layer of activity that *slows* production, for good or ill. But an examination of the practice as it developed through time shows that it developed as a way of *speeding* publication, and releasing resources. What follows is a very brief and telescoped historical account of the period when a recognisably modern editing role first took shape in Europe and North America.

The Uses of Editorial Attention

The emergence of editing as a specific, named professional practice was partly the result of a growing division of labour that could be found in most industries, but it also owes its birth to factors in some ways specific to publishing: in particular, the need for accuracy and speed (initially driven by newspapers); the demand for a consistent voice (magazines); and the technical demands of modern narrative (books). Although each driver is associated with a particular media channel, they influence each other: for example, practices adopted first in magazine publishing are later used for books, and vice versa.

The first English-language magazines in the eighteenth century were "containers" for a jumble of texts, "gathered in a fragmentary way that did not distinguish one field above another or otherwise attempt to group … knowledge" (Butler 1981, 122). This began to change around the turn of the century, as magazines developed a distinctive *persona* of their own. By the mid-nineteenth century, editors "increasingly enforced house forms and styles, often by rewriting contributions to bring them into line with the identity of the periodical" (Liddle 2009, 28).

New genres, such as the editorial, news story, and review, helped to speed up production by simplifying decisions about what was required for a particular form of writing. Like all genres, they developed conventions; usually, the more prescriptive these are, the quicker they are to produce. This made it easier for a wider range of people to act as editorial intermediaries, enabling the recruitment of writers not only from the ranks of literary authors or gentleman-scholars, but also an increasing number of people from the middle and lower classes (Liddle 2009, 31).

Editing helped to achieve consistency of voice; but as periodical circulation grew and publication increased in frequency, it was also needed "to vigorously cut, bulk, reject, censor, and solicit" (Mikaelian 1997, 7). By contributing specialist skills in the selection and shaping of text, to a deadline and for increasingly varied and demanding readers, the editing role helped to confront the material constraints of time and space.

In book publishing, a recognisably modern editor does not appear to emerge until the twentieth century. But the process started long before, driven by greater volume. As the financial stakes grew larger, the potential for disputes between publisher and author increased. The evolution of intermediary roles helped to create a buffer for both parties, and offered an additional selection filter for the burgeoning market. The prototype for the modern book editor is the publishers' "reader," who evolved during the nineteenth century. For inspiration, as the role grew in scope, the protean book editor looked to the thriving world of periodicals,

> borrowing freely from the fraternal role of a magazine or newspaper editor, in that one function is to decide what to print and to supervise the preparation of texts so that they suit the aims and standards of the publisher and the publication. (Sifton 1985, 43)

There was also convergence between book and magazine—not only in the editorial process, but also in the end-product. Throughout the second half of the nineteenth century, magazines published fiction by instalment, providing an entry point for new writers. By the turn of the century, book publishers began to go after mass markets directly, leaving out the periodical as an intermediary, but adopting similar standardised, magazine-like story formats and identities, such as the branded book series with its own specific voice.

By the time the publishing industry resumed business after World War I, a sharp rise in production costs dovetailed with the change in public taste to favour a tighter prose style, replacing the *longueur* of much Victorian and Edwardian literature, which arguably moved it closer to the disciplines of periodical editing. Through the 1920s and 1930s, novelists were urged to reduce their word counts. An article from the time advises that the shorter novel must contain "no loose threads, no bypasses" and warns against writing that produces meaning "only through extreme concentration" (*Publisher's Circular* 1922, 219).

When writers were slow to tackle the problem, publishers felt obliged to step in. In a talk for Oxford University students in 1934, Geoffrey Faber described the questions that arise whenever a publisher considers a new manuscript and finds it wanting: "Can these various faults be put right? Can the author be trusted to put them right himself, or must the manuscript ... be taken home for revision by the publisher's own hand?" (Faber 1934, 121). Faber anticipated resistance to this idea from his audience:

Some of you will be shocked to hear me say so. It is improper, you will think, for a mere man of business to interfere with the artist on his own ground. But what if the artist doesn't know his own ground? The art of authorship must take account of the conditions under which it is practiced. (Faber 1934, 123)

In the United States, the influence of periodicals on literary taste—in this case, a preference for "plain English"—was felt even earlier. As Forde and Foss document, the proportion of the population who read newspapers came close to 100 per cent by 1900, and they became a major vehicle for fiction in serialised form. In both books and periodicals, the connecting thread was a prevailing realism and "mania for facts," understood in the context of a drive for social improvement, which "produced a preference for unadorned language in public expression." As a result, "writing style across print culture … was a popular subject in the early trade journal discourse of the 1880s" (Forde and Foss 2012, 132).

Public debate raged, then as now, about the proper relationship between commerce and culture. But the dividing line is rarely simple. Examples occur throughout the history of publishing, of commercial pressures producing innovations that drive cultural change. The modern editing function may be one such change. Modern professional editing developed for many reasons, but one reason was that it was commercially useful.

From the perspective of today, it is the early part of the twentieth century, and the work of early modernism, that prompts the most resonant stories about a "golden age" of editing. Scholars analysing that moment in literary and publishing history have speculated that there was something about the technical demands of dramatic narrative in modernist fiction, combined with a cultural preference for economical prose and other publishing constraints, that made the uses of a skilled editor more obvious.

Perhaps the most iconic figure from that time is Max Perkins of Schribners' Sons, who worked with writers such as F. Scott Fitzgerald and Thomas Wolfe, among many others. Walter Litz (1969), reviewing the Wolfe–Perkins relationship, speculates that a new tolerance of uncertainty in storytelling at that time created a more urgent need for a perceptive, sensitive textual manager. In Perkins, that is arguably what Wolfe and others found. The documentary evidence supports this view. When Wolfe first sent Perkins a manuscript that had been rejected elsewhere, his "Note for the Publisher's Reader" said: "I need a little honest help. If you are interested enough to finish the book, won't you give it to me?" Perkins agreed, and Wolfe wrote later to a friend in excitement: "For the first time in my life I was getting criticism I could really use" (Bruccoli 2004, xix).

The account above—about the development of editing in book publishing—is worth including in an analysis of journalism to illustrate two points. In part it is an observation about the interconnectedness of art and commerce; the "literary" editing carried out by Max Perkins drew on practices and standards that evolved in the "commercial" editing of periodicals. In the process, it also makes a point about *intermediality*; the "interconnected and shifting relations between media" (Levy and Mole 2015, xv)—in this case, between books and journalism.

How does this discussion about the evolution of editing relate specifically to *narrative* journalism? The question is only recently being broached by scholars, and so any response is likely to be limited. One example that *has* seen some attention is the New Journalism of 1960s and 1970s America. In particular, a recent study by John Pauly (2014)—conceived by Pauly as part of a longer, future work—considers the conditions under which the New Journalism was practised, and the role that magazine editors played in fostering it.

An Enactment of the Social

Pauly argues that analysis of the New Journalism to date has focused, by and large, on the way it arose from the general social and political conditions of the era, including the market and demographic influences that make some styles more commercially viable than others. He is interested in connecting this general level of insight to the "close study of the institutional relationships that gave it life" (Pauly 2014, 591) in order to learn more about how specific, organisational routines shape a story's final form.

The interaction between these two levels is what makes such journalism something that "not only reports on society but enacts the social: in the imagined reader that it addresses, in the authorial voice the writer chooses, in the venue chosen to distribute the story, and in the meaning imputed to its reports" (Pauly 2014, 590). An analysis of non-fiction reporting that came to be described as the New Journalism is particularly suited to providing insights into this interaction, because it "made the interpretive work of [journalism] visible, palpable, and available for comment" (600); and the editor is a key part of the picture, because editors are "the people in a position to negotiate between the different parties and take the lead within editorial institutions" (595). Pauly's study therefore focuses on the material traces of editorial intervention, to see what they contribute to an understanding of this particular enactment of the social, in a particular time and place.

The New Journalism is a literary field that captured the public imagination, partly because of the successful branding provided by Tom Wolfe in his 1973 anthology of that name (Wolfe 1973), and partly because of its secure place in the pedagogy of nonfiction writing. As Pauly records, the term had been in use for some years before it was adopted by Wolfe, arising as part of a wider discussion about how journalism might respond to political conflict and a faster pace of social change. As before, writers considered to be serious literary figures outside journalism found a home in periodicals, only this time with magazines rather than newspapers. The long lead-time needed for this format meant, however, that magazines could not compete on fast news coverage. Instead, editors sought competitive advantage by urging their staff "to watch for trends, and to cultivate writers who … could take an event that had already passed and make it interesting to a reader" (Pauly 2014, 599). Pauly notes:

> By the 1960s, some commentators were arguing that the magazine article, rather than the news story or editorial column, offered the best venue for in-depth reporting … In a 1962 lecture at the University of Minnesota, John Fischer, editor of *Harper's*, said the hectic pace of newspaper reporting had always left him feeling that he had not done his best work [and he found] magazine reporting less formulaic. (Pauly 2014, 598)

This concern chimes with similar comments cited by Le Masurier (2015, 143) about fears that speed can give rise to "sensationalism and herd reporting."

By the early 1960s, says Pauly (2014, 601), American journalists had begun to recognise that they "made interpretations, but not in conditions of their own making." And it is their editors who sought to define the principles that would guide such interpretations, showing not just aesthetic but also ethical concerns. The ethical debate

> was always institutionally situated. It involved not only individual reporters pondering different ways to tell stories, but magazine editors talking to reporters about the social significance of their material and about their choices of story angle, tone, and point of view. (Pauly 2014, 600)

This happens in all professional reporting, but is more obvious in literary journalism, which is more visibly interpretive. A close-up view of the conditions of production in this particular example of the genre therefore "tells us something important about the social construction of moral purpose … the public meanings we attribute to our private ethical choices" (Pauly 2014, 600–601).

A look at the strategies used by *Esquire* under editor Harold Hayes, *Harper's* under Willie Morris, and *New York* under Clay Felker, illustrates how they approached the task of defining their editorial principles and priorities. In a 1960 talk to his sales staff, for example, Hayes described *Esquire* as "a sort of supercharged memorandum routed to the best informed and most curious people in America." At *Harper's*, Morris said he sought an "intelligent and sophisticated reader" who was no longer satisfied with just being informed: the *Harper's* reader "can sense falseness a mile away. He wants to be challenged, enraged, tested, and, most of all, emotionally involved." And Felker's *New York*, read mostly by upscale Manhattanites, hoped to capture the city as a state of mind. In each case, "interpretation" in the sense described by Pauly offered a path to market distinction: "Each magazine promised … a hip, ironic, polished take on social trends; a passionate, literate engagement with current political and social problems; an inside-dopester's account of life in the world's most dynamic city" (Pauly 2014, 599).

Although there were differences in their approach, the editors shared a willingness to depart from genre conventions and mix up old and new practices. Felker ditched the conventions of newspaper neutrality in favour of "sharply angled" stories with a strong personal voice, "in which writers added special insight to their account of an event" (Pauly 2014, 599–600). Hayes experimented with character and tone by making "improbable" matches between writer and subject, as when he invited Jean Genet and William Burroughs to cover the 1968 Democratic National Convention (600). He also experimented with story structure by working closely with writers in the initial stages, to sharpen the story's direction. Hayes coined the term "conceptual editing" for his approach; a more familiar term now might be developmental or structural editing.

I would sum this up by saying that over time, the New Journalism became a recognisable body of work that survived not just financially, because it objectively suited a particular time and place (a conventional, ulterior motive) but also as a marker of cultural value, arising from uncountable decisions by individual editing practitioners. Broad social factors such as political change and the growth of a college-educated readership created necessary conditions for its growth, but on their own, these were not sufficient. A group of magazine editors helped to make it happen, through the selective exercise of their taste, and the shaping and linking expertise of their professional work. They published the work at least in part because they *wanted* to do it (an ultimate motive) and through negotiation and inventiveness found a way to make it pay.

In the very different conditions of post-war Poland, a similar group of like-minded people helped to foster the growth of an entire school of *reportaz;* starting slowly in the 1960s, and picking up speed in the post-revolutionary 1990s. As with other examples of literary journalism, Polish *reportaz* came to the fore in periods of intense uncertainty and conflict and it performed an ethical role; in this case, as I put it in an earlier work, by connecting facts and feelings through documentation, on one hand, and a recognition of personal experience, on the other (Greenberg 2012b, 134). And as with the New Journalism, the institutional support of periodicals such as *Gazeta Wyborcza* was crucial. Philip Gwyn Jones, who has published English translations of contemporary Polish writers, comments:

Like others, I would point to the role of a great, cosmopolitan, cultured newspaper, which has championed and—crucially—funded so much of the best contemporary Polish reportage. Its existence is not a given; if it hadn't had such a temperament, might many of these writers have floundered longer in obscurity? (as quoted in Greenberg 2012b, 129)

Slow Editing in the Digital Present

For the print magazines that fostered the New Journalism, a strategy of differentiation appeared to make sense on both financial and cultural levels. Is that still true for narrative nonfiction in the digital publishing environment of today?

The answer seems to be "yes"—all other things being equal. One contemporary example is *The Atavist*, an app-based publication that provides original multimedia reporting, made with very high production values. Economic survival for both contributor and publisher depends on subscriptions, the sale of rights to other formats, and cross-subsidy from distribution of the app software. The model is working for now, says co-founder and editor-in-chief Evan Ratliff, but it is still too early to know if that will continue. "People always ask, is this model working?," he says. "But the model never worked … Everyone's cobbling together different ways of making it work. There's no golden age when people made amazing wages by being freelance writers" (as quoted in Greenberg 2015, 178).

The Atavist aims to be profitable, but would never have been launched without its founders' love for the form, and a desire to produce more of it. Its focus on reporting rather than, say, the popular (and less expensive) genre of memoir still involves a high level of risk—for example, of being scooped—because the kind of story that it publishes takes a long time to produce. And if a shorter version gets out first, says Ratliff, the worry remains: will people still bother with the longer one, even if it is better in every way?

Now, as in the 1960s, differentiation involves the investment of extra time, and editing is a key element of that investment. When *Buzzfeed* launched a new strand of longer, researched features, Ben Smith explained that the aim was

> to take the best of the former tradition, and bring it to the new medium. That meant a kind of patience … it meant magazine-style fact-checking, which is really another round of reporting; it meant a copy desk; it meant loving attention to design. (Smith 2014)

Patience in production was matched by the encouragement of "dwell time" in reading, with some success: longer articles in the "BuzzReads" section were given "twice the site's average" amount of attention, he reported, and new tools allowed them to learn "how much time readers spend on a story, and where they exit it. It offers a deep satisfaction when a high percentage of people make it to the end." However, technology was a side issue: "We want people to linger, and there's no technical trick to that" (Smith 2014).

Smith raised another issue, which prompted wide debate at the time. He noted that "long form" was being used as a synonym for good, but questioned whether "long" was a good in itself: "Some of them were long only because they hadn't been edited" (Smith 2014). Ratliff agrees:

> The problem is that people are writing longer and longer on the web, but in a lot of cases it's not edited … There's a danger that readers will say, "It's great that you're running these long pieces," when they're dumbing down people's understanding of an in-depth piece. (as quoted in Greenberg 2015, 182)

The account so far has provided some examples of the way in which journalism has looked for a way out of the dangerous "middle." In theory, a commitment to high standards of editing is not attached to a specific business model. If publishers and authors are convinced that it should happen, they can find a way to make it possible, as previous examples indicate. But under current prevailing business models, the funding of professional editing presents a challenge.

The connection between editing and slow journalism may not be obvious at first glance, but there is a logical overlap of concerns. Intensive, ground-level reporting should be an ingredient of all quality journalism, but one can argue that it is a foundational condition of the "slow" variety, which puts so much stress on original factual discovery. To make such discoveries, and communicate them in a way that is transparent to readers, requires skills that take time to learn and time to practise.[4] This explains why both editing and slow journalism are understood as labour-intensive luxuries.

For both reporting and editing, the way to survive and even prosper is to make the case for value. But while good reporting comes with a ready-made set of arguments about an informed citizenry and the public good, the case for good editing has been, to date, more fragmentary. If anything, editing has seen a fall in its cultural capital; positioned as it is by some new media ideologies as an oppressive handmaid of the mainstream media.[5] As a result, the motivation to make room for high-quality editing, in the face of financial pressures, cannot be taken for granted. A fuller analysis of editing's cultural capital and the challenges it faces, is something I will consider in a future work.

Conclusion

The title of this paper is "Editing, Fast and Slow." By now, the reader may wonder: where has this idea taken us? Is editing fast, or slow; or is it both?

In *A New Republic of Letters* we learn from Jerome McGann,[6] a leading scholarly editor and theorist of editing, that Nietzsche proposed the study of philology as an antidote to the pressures of what he called "an age of work; that is to say, of haste, of … 'getting things done' at once." Nietzsche sees in philology a discipline that "teaches how to read well; i. e. slowly, profoundly, attentively" (as quoted in McGann 2014, 54).

It is not a stretch to say that many forms of editing also offer connoisseurship of the word, albeit working to different purposes and timescales. In my research on the subject, a consistent imagery emerges of editing as an intense form of reading. One interviewee says: "To explain what I do, I say that I read and I decide. I read in order to figure out what we might publish" (as quoted in Greenberg 2015, 51). And deliberate reading involves slowness. Another interviewee recounts, for example, that someone

> saw all my books, and said, "Oh you must read very fast" and I said, "No, it's just the opposite." When you're reading to edit, and you're going to speak to the person who wrote it the next morning, you have to read very carefully, and reading becomes slower. (Greenberg 2015, 118)

On one level, therefore, the answer to the question above is simple: editing is slow. Although the professionalisation of ever-more specialised functions during the nineteenth century meant that the publishing process became quicker overall, the cumulative time spent by all the people hired to practise different forms of editing amounted to a significant investment of extra time and labour. Further research is needed to confirm the anecdotal evidence that overall levels of investment in professional editing have fallen since that time, and what implications a drop may have; bearing in mind that not all acts of editing are called by that name, now or in the past. If the "end of the middle" hypothesis holds up, the intriguing possibility arises that the "differentiated" world of slow journalism may be one of editing's rare, future fields of practice.

As a contribution to future research, however, it seems fitting to end with a speculative note about the complications of the subject, beyond any simple response; in particular, the meanings given to "slow" and "fast."

The association of "slow" with value is an understandable one, but one cannot say that slow is *always* a good. Just as "long form" can be long for no reason other than that it is not edited, "slow" can be another word for "unfocused" or "not finished." And what is slow for one person or genre can be quick for another.

In the working definition offered at the start, editing is described as a state of mind that enables the person doing it to see a text as if it is not yet finished. In this sense, the creative potential of the practice lies in its ability to open up possibilities, and therefore choice, which is widely considered a condition for originality. That is why genres perceived as formulaic tend to have less cultural status than those perceived as artistically free. But the argument can be made that all editing involves the entry into another dimension of text, ripe with potential for infinite tinkering. When the mind is in that zone, it can and must —at least for a period—resist the arbitrariness of a "final version." When asked, "When are you finished?," the answer given by practitioners, across the board, can be summed up in one word: "Never."

However, even slow work needs a deadline—a constraint—to become something that exists in the world, shared with others. Also, as I have noted elsewhere, "[t]he idea of completion, however imperfect, is still useful because it allows for failures to be absorbed and something new to be born" (Greenberg 2015, 188). The truly rare skill that a good editor offers is this: the ability to hold two different possible worlds in mind at the same time. The text is opened up, and then—sometimes sooner, sometimes later, depending on circumstances—it is closed down again, so that the text can move across the dotted line, from private to public. It is the tension between speed (constraint) and slowness (freedom)—not just slowness alone—that helps to foster creativity.

For similar reasons, complications arise in the other direction, over negative assumptions about speed. One obvious influence here is the association of speed with mass production. The manner in which slow media defines itself against mass media has been explored in the topic's literature. Perhaps most relevant to note here is Rauch's extension of Walter Benjamin's aura—a term used to distinguish the cult value of original "art" from objects with commodity value—to anything that represents an escape from narrow "usefulness." In prioritising cult value over commodity value, slow media therefore serves as pushback against the built-in obsolescence generated by media businesses designed to enhance profitability (Rauch 2015, 574).

If the "end of the middle" argument is accepted, however, the link between profit and obsolescence applies only to the bottom end of the market; cult value and profit are still potentially compatible at the top. That is assuming, of course, that media forms do not continually influence each other, and that business always acts in an entirely rational manner. From the perspective of Bourdieu's fields, the extent of sheer jostling for cultural capital (rather than the literal kind) is not to be underestimated. In the space created by the contest, individual editors—acting with ultimate motives as well as ulterior ones—have some influence. This applies to slow media as well. If they have any cult value, it derives as much from their *process* (including the work of editors) as it does from the existence of a slow media *object*.

Bourdieu's work reminds us of another reason for humility in assigning values to media forms, including the positive value assigned to slow journalism. This is the self-reflexive thought that it is a rare social group which does not—like those 1960s magazine readers (ironic, engaged and in-the-know)—pride itself on its good taste and *avant garde* daring. In Bourdieu's (1993, 66) explanation, groups seeking "consecration" make a virtue out of necessity by bidding for *avant-garde* status, "defined mainly negatively, by their opposition to the dominant positions." This description seems relevant to our subject and, in my view, an analysis of slow journalism as one specific battle for cultural capital among others only adds to the richness of the analysis.

In the case of literary or slow journalism, the "dominant positions" to be challenged are typically located in the "industrial" mass media. But it is always sobering to put such struggles into an historical perspective. John Hartsock, for example, charts the emergence of the institutional and cultural divide between literature and journalism, noting the changing language used to put journalism into its place once it ceased to be produced for an elite readership only. Underlying the different forms of critique, he says, is a shared reluctance to consider as art any "text that acknowledges its origins of production;" and reporting, as a form of bearing witness, must by nature acknowledge its "phenomenological origins" (Hartsock 2000, 225). Here the "origins of production" echoes my own earlier reference to "material conditions of production," albeit with a new emphasis (via phenomenology) on the author's subjectivity. I introduce the analysis not only for its historical perspective, but also for the reminder it provides of the emotional dimension in social, Bourdieusian struggles over taste. We can aim to connect fact and feeling, not only in our narrative journalism, but also in our analysis of the form.

To continue the complication process, we can examine the relation between speed and motive in editing practices. Speed often relies on tacit patterns of thought. Because such thought patterns are often used at an instinctive, "gut" level, they are open to interpretation as secret or opaque.[7] And indeed, there are many reasons why tacit knowledge can be problematic, or why it can benefit from reflection and challenge. It is helpful, however, to maintain a careful distinction between "tacit" and "secret." The latter implies a dyslogistic motive (deliberate concealment) whereas the former is more value-neutral. It potentially refers to a speeded-up version of accumulated knowledge, common to many forms of specialist practice. In other words, speed can reflect experience; a professional pride in the ability to act fast without loss of skill or attention. A further complicating distinction is that between "secret" and "hidden." Many forms of mediation are hidden not out of choice, but as an inherent consequence of occupying a backroom role that attracts no intrinsic interest from the non-specialist.

This paper has set out to focus on the role of editing as a specific material condition of production, to see what insights it might offer on the subject of slow journalism. An awareness of material conditions implies above all an awareness of constraints, including the constraint of economic survival. It is argued that constraints can be painful, but can also be a spur to creativity. The promise of this approach may lie in embracing the complication, and working to distinguish what is specifically commercial about constraints and what is a more general consequence of publishing as a material practice—and an inherently social one.

DISCLOSURE STATEMENT

No potential conflict of interest was reported by the author.

NOTES

1. For more information about the IALJS founding conference, see http://ialjs.journalism. ryerson.ca/wp-content/uploads/2011/07/IALJS-1_Conference_Program_2006_v02.pdf.
2. A version of the argument, applied to digital business models, was made by Jeff Bezos in a much-quoted interview: "On the Internet, companies are scale businesses, characterised by high fixed costs and relatively low variable costs. You can be two sizes: You can be big, or you can be small. It's very hard to be medium. A lot of medium-sized companies had the financing rug pulled out from under them before they could get big" (Hof 2001).
3. For longer examinations of editing by the author, see Greenberg (2018, 2015).
4. I have argued elsewhere (Greenberg 2014) that the ethical goal of discovery and the aesthetic goal of storytelling are intertwined: among other things, the pleasure we derive from language is connected to its precision, which is a form of reporting about the world.
5. In an indicative early polemic, for example, *Wired* journalist Jon Katz (1997, 7) praises the unfiltered nature of new technology which he describes as a return to the conditions of the US founding fathers, when "there was almost no distinction between citizens and journalists".
6. McGann is one of the interviewees in *Editors Talk About Editing* (Greenberg 2015).
7. Le Masurier (2015, 147) refers, for example, to "secrecy in the decision-making process to feed this illusion of total coverage."

REFERENCES

Bourdieu, Pierre. 1993. *The Field of Cultural Production*. Cambridge: Polity Press.

Bruccoli, Matthew. 2004. *The Sons of Maxwell Perkins: Letters of F. Scott Fitzgerald, Ernest Hemingway, Thomas Wolfe, and Their Editor*. Columbia, SC: University of South Carolina Press.

Burke, Kenneth. 1969. *A Rhetoric of Motives*. Berkeley: University of California Press.

Butler, Marilyn. 1981. *Romantics, Rebels and Reactionaries: English Literature and its Background 1760–1830*. Oxford: Oxford Paperbacks.

Faber, Geoffrey. 1934. *A Publisher Speaking*. London: Faber & Faber.

Forde, Kathy Roberts, and Katie Foss. 2012. "'The Facts—the Color!—the Facts': The Idea of the News Report in America, 1885–1910." *Book History* 15: 123–151.

Greenberg, Susan. 2007. "Slow Journalism." *Prospect*, Accessed February. http://www. prospectmagazine.co.uk/magazine/slowjournalism/#.UzAX0F7j744.

Greenberg, Susan. 2010. "Poetics of Fact." *Times Higher Education*, Accessed August 12. https:// www.timeshighereducation.com/features/poetics-of-fact/412982.article.

Greenberg, Susan. 2011. "The 'Slow Journalism' Meme." *Oddfish*, Accessed February 11. http:// oddfish.co.uk/2011/02/11/slowjournalism/.

Greenberg, Susan. 2012a. "Slow Journalism in the Digital Fast Lane." In *Global Literary Journalism: Exploring the Journalistic Imagination*, edited by Richard L. Keeble and John Tulloch, 381– 393. New York: Peter Lang.

Greenberg, Susan. 2012b. "The Polish School of Reportage." In *Global Literary Journalism: Exploring the Journalistic Imagination*, edited by Richard L. Keeble and John Tulloch, 123–140. New York: Peter Lang.

Greenberg, Susan L. 2018. *A Poetics of Editing*. London: Palgrave.

Greenberg, Susan. 2014. "The Ethics of Narrative: A Return to the Source." *Journalism: Theory, Practice, Criticism* 15 (5): 518–532. doi 10.1177/1464884914523091.

Greenberg, Susan L. 2015. *Editors Talk about Editing: Insights for Readers, Writers and Publishers*. New York: Peter Lang.

Harcup, Tony. 2014. *The Oxford Dictionary of Journalism*. Oxford: OUP.

Hartsock, John C. 2000. *A History of American Literary Journalism: The Emergence of a Modern Narrative Form*. Amherst: University of Massachusetts Press.

Hof, Robert D. 2001. "Online Extra: Q&A with Amazon's Jeff Bezos." Accessed March 25. http://www.businessweek.com/stories/2001-03-25/online-extra-q-and-a-with-amazons-jeff-bezos.

Katz, Jon. 1997. *Virtuous Reality: How America Surrendered Discussion of Moral Values to Opportunists, Nitwits, and Blockheads Like William Bennett*. New York: Random House.

Le Masurier, Megan. 2015. "What is Slow Journalism?" *Journalism Practice* 9 (2): 138–152. doi:10.1080/17512786.2014.916471.

Levy, Michelle, and Tom Mole, eds. 2015. *The Broadview Reader in Book History*. Ontario: Broadview Press.

Liddle, Dallas. 2009. *The Dynamics of Genre: Journalism and the Practice of Literature in Mid-Victorian Britain*. Charlottesville, VA: University of Virginia Press.

Litz, Walter. 1969. "Maxwell Perkins: The Editor as Critic." In *Editor, Author, and Publisher*, edited by William James Howard, 96–112. Toronto: University of Toronto Press.

McGann, Jerome. 2014. *A New Republic of Letters: Memory and Scholarship in the Age of Digital Reproduction*. Cambridge, Mass: Harvard University Press.

Mikaelian, Allen. 1997. "Middlemen by profession: popular fiction and the rise of the in-house book editor." MA diss., University of London.

Oxford English Dictionary. 1989. "Editor." Second Print Edition. http://www.oed.com/viewdictionaryentry/Entry/59553.

Pauly, John J. 2014. "The New Journalism and the Struggle for Interpretation." *Journalism: Theory, Practice, Criticism* 15 (5): 589–604.

Porter, Michael. 2004. *Competitive Strategy: Techniques for Analysing Industries and Competitors*. New York: Free Press.

Publishers' Circular. 1922. March 4.

Rauch, Jennifer. 2015. "Slow Media as Alternative Media: Cultural Resistance Through Print and Analogue Revivals." In *The Routledge Companion to Alternative & Community Media*, edited by Chris Atton, 571–581. London: Routledge.

Sifton, Elizabeth. 1985. "The Editor's Job in Trade Publishing." In *The Business of Book Publishing: Papers by Practitioners*, edited by Elizabeth A. Geiser Arnold Dolin, and Gladys S. Topkis, 43–61. Boulder, CO: Westview.

Smith, Ben. 2014. "What the Longform Backlash Is All About." *Medium*, Accessed January 26. https://medium.com/journalism-deliberated/958f4e7691f5.

Wolfe, Tom. 1973. "The New Journalism." In *The New Journalism*, edited by Tom Wolfe and E. W. Johnson, 3–52. New York: Harper & Row.

NETWORKED NEWS TIME
How slow—or fast—do publics need news to be?

Mike Ananny

What kind of news time does a public need? The production, circulation, and interpretation of news have always followed timelines and rhythms, but these have largely been seen as artifacts of press sociology, not central aspects of journalism's public mission linked to the design and deployment of journalism infrastructure. Since different types of news time make possible different kinds of publics, any critique of the press's material cultures of time-keeping is a critique of the press's power to convene particular people and issues, at particular times. Motivated by the temporal needs of one type of public (a pragmatic public that ensures a public right to hear), this paper proposes a unit for studying news time (the temporal assemblage), and traces it across four intertwined sites in the contemporary, networked press: labor routines, platform rhythms, computational algorithms, and legal regulations. Beyond this article's investigation of this public in relation to these dynamics, my aim is to contribute to the emerging "slow journalism" movement by asking: how slow—or fast—do different publics need news to be? And how are networked press paces set?

Introduction

What kind of time does the public need from networked news? If publics emerge, in part, because people come to see individual concerns as common causes and inextricable consequences of social life, how does the networked press's time-keeping make some kinds of commonalities and consequences more likely to emerge than others?

This article proposes an answer to this question by examining how one mission of the networked press—its role guaranteeing a public right to hear—appears in its temporal infrastructure. Specifically, following critical legal scholarship and pragmatic philosophy, I argue that collective self-governance requires the press not only to call a public to action at key moments, but also to provide publics time for uncertainty, self-doubt, and listening. I ground this rhythm in a branch of US legal theory and emerging political philosophies; argue that the press's time-keeping functions are best understood as a sociotechnical assemblage; and trace the making of networked press time through the press's labor routines, platform rhythms, computational algorithms, and legal regulations.

Beyond this article—exploring the networked press's guarantee of a public right to hear through its assemblage of temporal elements—my aim is to suggest a general, theory-driven approach to studying news time: for any normative theory of the press, identify the time-keeping dynamics that instantiate that theory empirically, and suggest a framework for evaluating—and making interventions into—both how well those dynamics enact the theory and how they suggest new normative models of press time. My aim is to contribute to emerging conversations on the study and practice of "slow journalism" (Craig 2015; Le Masurier 2015), "slow news" (Shapiro 2010), and online breaking news (Hartley 2011; Saltzis 2012; Thurman and Newman 2014) by asking: how slow—or fast—do publics need the networked press to be, why, and what regulates its speed?

What is a Public Right to Hear and What Kind of News Time Does it Need?

Communication scholars have long studied how to connect normative goals to institutional conditions. As Baker (2002, 125) asks: "What type of free press does democracy need and why does democracy need it?" Different versions of democracy assume seemingly self-evident and unassailable definitions of press freedom: *pluralist liberals* want "partisan and segmented" journalism to mobilize people and advocate for interests; *administrative liberals* see the press as a "check on power" that covers "crises and campaigns" and exposes government abuse; and *republicans* want journalists to amplify citizens' voices, facilitate discussion, and manage debate forums (Christians et al. 2009, 97). Any interference with—or failure to support—one of these models is seen as infringing upon press freedom.

Throughout US history, scholars, journalists, and audiences alike have either attacked or celebrated different ideals of the press. It was only in the 1940s that critiques of the media's "excessive commercialism" spurred policy interventions to "ensure that profit was not the sole imperative of the American news media" (Pickard 2014, 3) —that the rights of media owners to be free of state intervention did not trump the *public*'s freedom to self-govern *through* the press. The challenge of this "central image" of press freedom is to ensure that the public "receive[s] all the information it needs— about government actions or public issues—to exercise its sovereign powers" (Bollinger 1991, 1). If democratic self-governance requires not only the *absence* of unreasonable restrictions on individual speakers, but also the "right to hear the views of others and to listen to their version of the facts" (Emerson 1970, 3) then, as legal philosopher Alexander Meiklejohn (1948, 25) famously wrote, the "point of ultimate interest is not the words of the speakers, but the minds of the hearers." Contemporary philosophers continue this line of inquiry, arguing that *listening* is a legitimate and necessary form of political participation in its own right (Lacey 2013). Without listeners, speakers lack power and are effectively mute (Macnamara 2013); and political ends achieved through listening are more legitimate, efficacious, and sustainable (Dobson 2012) than those reached through speech marketplaces that leave no time for listening.

Compelling as these theories and critiques may be, we are left with the problem of how to create the institutional conditions for listening. Especially in an era of seemingly endless opportunities to speak, how can the press make *time* for the "type of press freedom" that values the "minds of the hearers?" Answering this question requires two steps. First, operationalizing the concept of listening into practices and values that show why a right to hear matters to democratic self-governance; and, second, connecting this operationalization to the material cultures—tools, systems, artifacts—that the contemporary, networked press uses to convene publics in time.

Giving Publics Time to Hear

A public right to hear requires not only the right to receive information from state officials, or access libraries, archives, and courtrooms (Lee 1987). Rather, it is a broader entitlement to meaningfully consider perspectives on the social conditions that people create and share with others. Distinct from individual and private interests, what "have to be taken care of, looked out for, and call a public into being" (Dewey 1954, 27) are the indirect and unplanned consequences of associational life. Consequentialist publics emerge from—and are *contingent* upon—the description and experience of inextricable social relationships that lead some consequences to be believed and acted upon over others. For Dewey (1910), the only *legitimate* way to believe or reject a consequence as relevant and "reasonably probable or improbable" (4) is through "active, persistent, and careful consideration of … the grounds that support it, and the further conclusions to which it tends" (6).

People need time to reflect before believing a consequence, appreciating its relevance, and seeing its social dynamics. The experiences of "perplexity, hesitation, doubt, [and] suspended belief" (Dewey 1910, 9) are politically powerful because they help people to "digest impressions, and translate them into substantial ideas" (37). Only when "general summaries are made from time to time does the mind reach a conclusion or a resting place" (212).

To be sure, not all types of publics require this kind of time. A "representative liberal theory endorses a norm of closure—a time at which all concerned can agree that the matter has been decided and the system moves on" (Ferree et al. 2002, 294), while Habermas's (1996) ideal speech situation permits infinite rational deliberation. Pragmatist publics similarly need ongoing communication and material action, but they see them as less linear and isolated; pragmatists see communication and action as inseparable because they both "help us get into satisfactory relation with other parts of our experience" (James 1997, 100). To a pragmatist, communication only ends too quickly —or goes on too long—if it creates *unsatisfactory* relationships among people and social consequences. The *temporal* challenge facing institutions acting in a pragmatic tradition is to enlist memory, empathy, and foresight (Belman 1977) quickly enough so that shared consequences can be seen and acted upon—but not *so* quickly that people divert their attention or act before having had time to reflect upon the significance of those consequences. Incessant talk delays necessary action, but peripatetic communication creates unsatisfactory ends and incoherent justifications.

Time is not only a requirement *for* publics—it is also a product *of* publics. As Sharma (2014) shows, an individual's freedom to imagine consequences emerges from a "politics of time" that sees "time, not as being singularly yours or mine for the taking but as uncompromisingly tethered and collective" (149–150). No single person can control time because time is only meaningful when it is collaboratively made and interpreted. For example, although some people have the power to pause or delay action to enjoy "a sort of distance from the world that makes it possible to assess one's place in it" (111), slowness is a "privileged tempo" that shows the inequalities of "democracy and the public sphere" (110). Dewey may want his publics to have time to hesitate, doubt, digest, translate, and rest, but Sharma reminds us that the power to slow time is unevenly distributed and asks:

> what new forms of vulnerability are necessitated by the production of temporal novelties or resistances to speed. Whose time and labor is reorchestrated by changes in pace, whether sped up or slowed down? (Sharma 2014, 150)

Materials for Making Temporal Publics

Answering Sharma's question does not require abandoning Dewey's ideal, but it does mean critiquing the material conditions of the politics of time. Specifically, it means examining how time is governed by sociotechnical relationships that communicate consequences—how people and materials intermix to keep time in ways that make some shared conditions more believable, visible, actionable, acceptable, or relevant than others.

The sociotechnical power to make time is long-standing and well-studied. Farmers in the Middle Ages had to coordinate their church bells with the townspeople's mechanical clocks; fourteenth-century French vintners destroyed the centralized clocks that tracked their hourly wages (de Vaujany et al. 2014); wrist watches began as symbols of wealth but, later, *not* wearing one signified the privilege of living without schedules (Thompson 1967); clock towers became "logistical media" that both told time and assembled groups (Peters 2009); and even in seemingly rational contemporary organizations, managers regularly re-set workers' clocks and calendars in response to events they judge significant (Orlikowski and Yates 2002). Time is never just time: it always "functions as a context for anchoring the meaning of social acts and situations" (Zerubavel 1981, xiv), meanings that take *material* form as "artificial signs to remind ... in advance of consequences, and of ways of securing and avoiding them" (Dewey 1910, 15).

Drawing upon Latour's (2005) actor-network theory and DeLanda's (2006) assemblage theory, the study of networked news time is the study of "temporal assemblages": networks of humans and non-humans continuously creating and adapting to forces that control the speed of actions, and the significance of that speed. The unit of analysis is the *network* of relations; the network can never be stopped or bracketed without changing it; both people and artifacts have agency; and the primary objects of study are not only *control* of speed (how quickly or slowly a network produces action) but *interpretations* of speed (the significance a network of actors gives to speed). Rhythms, interruptions, beginnings, and ends of temporal assemblages are not intrinsic to networks, but *second-order* constructs created by the humans and non-humans (including researchers studying assemblages) describing a network's control and interpretation of speed. The political economy of this assemblage is the distribution and application of power that sets speeds or defines their significance.

Two issues are at stake for the public significance of temporal assemblages. First, if a public right to hear requires that people who inextricably share social conditions have time to encounter, doubt, revise, and act upon beliefs, then we need to ask whether any given temporal assemblage's political economy makes time for this kind of self-governance. Second, the temporal assemblage *itself* may be an inextricable condition of associational life. It is impossible for publics to simply *use* a temporal assemblage to govern themselves without eventually wondering about the political economy of the assemblage itself. For example, part of understanding the pace and significance of climate change means appreciating how a powerful network of journalists, press ideals, lobbyists, policy-makers, advertising, and consumer preferences let climate change go underreported for so long. Temporal assemblages matter not only because they have the power to set rhythms for listening out for and self-governing consequences—they also involve powerful forces that require oversight if new forms of listening are to be invented and new types of consequences are to be recognized.

A *consequentialist* theory of publics, then, is concerned not only with giving individuals time to reflect on the origins and probability of outcomes, but also with the network (Latour 2005) of time-keeping people, practices, norms, and objects that control the timeframe over which a controversy becomes a "matter of concern" (Latour 2004). If a network is defined too broadly, or a timeframe stretched too far, an issue can be seen as *irrelevant*: a product of niche interests, unimaginable futures, or incessantly intractable debates (Edwards 2003). If it is defined too narrowly or too immediately, matters are private and without public relevance. Connecting Dewey's focus on consequences with Latour's network, Marres (2012) defines the contemporary problem of the public as *relevance*: "the more inclusively we define the set of actors that may take an interest in the matter at hand, *the less relevant* the issues are likely to be to them" (51, emphasis in original).

The problem of relevance assumes a temporal dimension when assemblages have power to determine *which* and *when* consequences get attention by convening people and timescales. Some argue that separations between space and time collapse as information technologies "annihilate time" by "squeezing more activity into a given time" and "blurring" the "past, present, and future in a random order" that resists coherent sequencing (Castells 2009, 35). But space and time may normatively *need* separating in order to sustain a diversity of timescales. A *range* of temporal publics—constituents considering consequences in the short, middle and long term—require temporal assemblages with "resistances to speed" (Sharma 2014, 150) and the ability to counter "timeless" and "undifferentiated time, which is tantamount to eternity" and perpetual immediacy (Castells 1996, 494). Diverse publics require diverse timescales.

Such assemblages—and the potential for annihilation, resistance, and diversity—now exist not only in traditional institutions (work, religion, schools) and biological rhythms (sleeping, eating), but also consumer devices omnipresent on our bodies (Wajcman 2014), social media platforms pushing immediacy and newness (Kaun and Stiernstedt 2014), infrastructures for synchronizing distributed labor (Irani 2015), and real-time machine learning algorithms driving online surveillance, search, and advertising (Weltevrede, Helmond, and Gerlitz 2014). Normative interventions into these networks require descriptions and justifications of *ideal* temporal assemblage configurations—a typology of the power and associations needed to make normative times possible.

An ideal temporal network for realizing pragmatic publics gives people enough time to surface, reflect, and act upon the social conditions that create inextricable, shared consequences. Akin to Silverstone's (2003, 473) argument that media can create "proper distance"—configurations of space and meaning that are "distinctive, correct, and ethically or socially appropriate"—the press might help to create "proper time" for pragmatic publics if it creates assemblages that both control speed and articulate that speed's significance. "Proper" is a charged word. My aim is not to argue that journalists should paternalistically govern time but, rather, to point out that the power to make time is the power to make publics. The networked press might do so purposefully, for example, configuring its temporal elements to ensure a pragmatic, public right to hear.

Historical Forces Governing News Time

A complete history of news time is beyond the scope of this article, but it has always emerged from material cultures that make, circulate, and signify news. In the 1820s, New York City newspapers banded together to buy a "fast boat" (Schudson 1978, 26) that could meet ships with news arriving from England faster than their competitors' slower fleets. US news organizations were initially slow to use telegraphs because the companies that owned them insisted on "giving each station a turn at transmitting a bundle of accumulated dispatches without interruption"; instead of using telegraphs to create "two-way … real time" (Blondheim 1994, 36) as they originally wanted, papers instead synchronized their printing schedules with their telegraph turns or only printed telegraph news that was ready at press time. Even the *breaking* of news rhythms to signify novelty took material form as early radio broadcasters standardized the "bulletin": short introductory sirens, breathy announcers, and dead air with background noises all built anticipation. The new genre signified the unrehearsed importance of everything from the Lindbergh baby's kidnapping to the *Hindenberg* explosion and *The War of the Worlds*. The making, distribution, and interpretation of news have always depended on how journalists used materials to compress, organize, and puncture time.

Studies of news work (Boczkowski 2010; Gans 1979; Molotch and Lester 1974; Schudson 1986, 2000; Tuchman 1972) identify inside-out and outside-in forces governing news time. *Inside-out* time emerges from within news organizations. The need to start a press run and coordinate with circulation logistics might pause or stop reporting; a desire to conserve resources might halt expensive, long-term investigative work; competition can mean speeding up to scoop a rival, minimally updating a story to make it seem novel, or delaying publication until an exclusive news hole opens up; and an editorial judgment of a time-sensitive public need may mean issuing a bulletin, interrupting an audience, or hurrying publication before an election. *Outside-in* time, though, is set by forces beyond the news organization. For example, a morning government press briefing may drive a day's news cycle; a natural disaster can unexpectedly dominate coverage for days or weeks; election cycles reorient journalism toward political issues; and quarterly earnings reports, monthly economic metrics, State of the Union addresses are all anticipated and highly ritualized events that organize press schedules. Many of the tensions of news time are about synchronizing inside-out and outside-in forces—making sure that sources, beats, journalists, advertisers, and audiences all share rhythms.

But these temporal relationships are simply traditions that have become fixed in materials and practices, not recipes for how news time *should* work. As Birth (2012, 2) puts it, the "artifactual determination of time does not represent a coherent, consistent cultural system," but "the sedimentation of generations of solutions to different temporal problems." As journalism changes so too do the boundaries (Carlson 2015, 2) separating inside-out and outside-in time, making this a moment to normatively critique the material forces governing assemblages of networked news time and, thus, making temporal publics.

Contemporary Forces Governing Networked News Time

Following the operationalization of the contemporary press as the networked production, circulation, and interpretation of news, networked news time is a function of at least four dynamics: labor routines, platform rhythms, computational algorithms, and legal regulations. I do not suggest that these four capture all aspects of networked news, but propose them as a starting point for tracing the networked rhythms of the contemporary press. Together, they represent major forces driving journalistic work, publishing mechanisms, audience modeling, and regulatory oversight.

Labor Routines

Research suggests that many online journalists, worldwide, work under a "tyranny of immediacy" (Le Cam and Domingo 2015). Studies of French, Spanish, Danish, German, UK, and US newsrooms (Domingo 2008; Hartley 2011; Le Cam and Domingo 2015; Saltzis 2012; Usher 2014) describe journalists working under a complex mix of inside-out and outside-in time pressures inextricable from digital materials: an ever-present wire service driving continuous site updates; fear of a seemingly stale homepage and a need to continually reorder stories according to ever-changing importance; all-hours feedback from editors sending texts and mobile emails; an expectation to start shifts already aware of social media trends; awareness of competitors' posts and audience traffic metrics; multitasking across media and publishing platforms; pressure to trust wire services without verification; confidence that website errors can be deleted without having to issue formal corrections; distinguishing among a story update, a new story, and a completed story; and coordinating with coworkers and audiences in other time zones. Indeed, *The New York Times* recently foregrounded immediacy in its organizational structure when it created an "Express Team": specialists in fast reporting who act as an "early-warning system" to "cover news that readers are searching for and talking about online," designed to "supplement—not supplant—the work of desks and departments" (Wemple 2015).

Such patterns suggest that online news rhythms emerge more from brokering *among* networked forces than using internal power to tame outside forces into predictable, coherent schedules (cf. Molotch and Lester 1974). Individual journalists and news organizations cannot slow news *themselves* because they often lack the "allocative" power to set rhythms independent of the networks in which they are embedded —and usually always lack the "operational" power (Murdock 1982) to unilaterally reshape networks and independently marshal platforms, audiences, algorithms, and laws to control when news circulates.

Platform Rhythms

Many networked news rhythms are now set by social media sites that solicit, curate, and govern engagement with online news (Clark et al. 2014). Such platforms are not just publishing channels, but places where journalists source, disseminate, and compete with people and information that have not historically been part of the press. Social media rhythms influence press rhythms when platforms change the making and meaning of news time. This influence comes not only in the form of technological power to deliver content faster, but also cultural power to suggest that social media represent public concerns—that social media rhythms *should* be press rhythms.

For example, as part of its "Instant Articles" initiative, Facebook hosts the stories of some news organizations directly on its servers; the company says this is to ensure that articles "load up to 10 times faster than they normally would" (Goel and Somaiya 2015) if served from news organizations' own servers. The new Google-led "Accelerated Mobile Pages Project" (2015) similarly lets publishers speed up their mobile site load times in exchange for letting data brokers cache news content. News organizations trade their content for access to speedier platform infrastructures they hope will drive traffic and advertising revenue to *their* sites—but early evidence suggests that "Instant Articles" sequestered within *Facebook*'s infrastructure are shared more frequently than links to news organizations' own sites (Hazard Owen 2015a). Infrastructures with the fastest load times garner the most traffic, making speed a commodity for partnerships between news organizations and social media platforms.

In addition to the distribution speed, platforms also regulate memory. A past story can suddenly resurface and seem novel because platform forces make it newly visible: e.g., a well-connected user reposts it, a recommendation algorithm resurrects it as relevant to current coverage, or Facebook deems it an "anniversary" event. News organizations also regulate and encounter archives through application programming interfaces (APIs)—software controlling and regulating database access. For example, *The Guardian* (2015) requires that users of its "Open Platform" API refresh content every 24 hours, discouraging content from being cached beyond its servers and ensuring that *its* database contains the most current version of any story. News organizations also depend upon *other* platforms' archiving policies. This was the case when journalists suddenly lacked a full history of politicians' public statements after Twitter rescinded API access to the Sunlight Foundation's Politiwoops project, an initiative to archive politicians' deleted tweets (Bondioli 2015).

Platform dynamics can also impact reporting rhythms on and beyond news sites. Immediately after the 2013 Boston Marathon bombings, hastily assembled Reddit and Twitter groups identified innocent people as suspects and circulated false information based on rumors. News organizations were triply ill-equipped to deal with this speedy crowdsourcing: they reported unconfirmed social media information far earlier than their editorial standards officially allowed; once discovered, news organizations struggled to correct errors faster than platforms propagated them; and news media who purposefully paused before reporting were seen as slow-moving, overly cautious official information sources out of step with what audiences wanted during the crisis (Starbird et al. 2014; Tapia, LaLone, and Kim 2014). Reporters not only compete with and publish on platforms during crises, they consult them for background information (Machill and Beiler 2009), potentially adopting their temporal properties: Wikipedia pages on unfolding crises are moderated by a small group of densely connected power users (Keegan, Gergle, and Contractor 2013) who are most often men with high levels of internet skill (Hargittai and Shaw 2014). Wikipedia may be invaluable for reporting breaking news but the demographics of those willing and able to edit newsworthy pages during crises may skew journalists' contextualizations of quickly unfolding events.

Platforms can also influence when news circulates. Approximately 33 percent of Americans access online news sites throughout the day (American Press Institute 2014), but they also encounter news when platforms reveal it. Platform designs structure time: tweets appear in reverse chronological order; recency influences Facebook's newsfeed; SnapChat and Periscope stories are framed as more ephemeral than those on other platforms; some mobile news apps only show breaking news to people in the relevant locations (Ellis 2014a); and, after two US television journalists were shot, video of the killings not only circulated on Facebook and Twitter but *automatically* played when users encountered it in their tweet streams and news feeds (Valinsky 2015). It was impossible to avoid the video by not clicking on it, or choosing a different time to watch it. *The New Yorker* even anticipates if a reader is about to leave an article before finishing and asks if she or he wants an email reminder to return (Lichterman 2015). Many sites also optimize their publishing times—Vox updates at 8 pm daily and Toronto's "lunchtime tabloid" at precisely 12:36 pm (Hazard Owen 2015b)—in part due to global platform rhythms: the most popular times to tweet are 9 am Pacific, 8 am in Hong Kong, and 9 pm in China, but to get clicks on tweeted links 2 am Pacific, 11 pm Eastern, and 8 pm Eastern European are best (Lee 2015).

Press time is inextricable from platform time. Circulation, archiving, crisis reporting, global distribution, and viewing times are all beyond the control of any single news organization, or even the field of organizations that have historically defined the press. For the press to create the time a public right to hear requires, it must adopt, coopt, and challenge how forces existing beyond newsrooms and in platforms both control and signify speed.

Computational Algorithms

Networked news rhythms also appear in the "technological dramas" (Carlson 2014) driving the largely invisible networked information algorithms that semi-autonomously make, organize, and disseminate online news. An emerging set of predictable, event-driven news stories are written by algorithms that parse databases in near real-time to data-driven natural language narratives. The news beats of these "robot journalists" are defined by the rhythms and changes of databases that algorithms have been programmed to query regularly.

Such temporal encodings exist within news organizations' own algorithms and para-journalistic social media platforms. The Associated Press partners with Automated Insights to algorithmically generate stories on companies' quarterly reports (Miller 2015); *The Los Angeles Times* (Meyer 2014) and KPCC (Take Two 2014) regularly query the United States Geological Services's (USGS) data to algorithmically generate stories on seismic activity; and *The New York Times*' "Watching" and "Trending" projects (Ellis 2014b) continuously monitor social media platforms for changes, alerting audiences to patterns in near real-time. The Google News crawler uses, among other factors, "freshness" to rank search results (Google 2015); Facebook's news feed algorithm considers not only how recently a story has been shared but how much time people spend on it and whether older stories are popular enough to be resurfaced (Yu and Tas 2015; Backstrom 2013).

No single algorithm governs news time. Algorithms both inside and outside of newsrooms are sustained by a largely invisible set of real-time computational relationships: code talking to code nearly instantaneously and often without close human oversight. Such assemblages are often only visible as temporal infrastructure when they fail (Star 1999, 382)—when they err so egregiously that audiences, editors, and programmers alike agree that networked news time broke.

For example, in 2008, United Airlines' stock price dropped 75 percent after Google's crawler mistakenly interpreted a *Florida Sun-Sentinel* story about the airline's 2002 bankruptcy as a *new* story, not of a six-year-old report (Cohen 2008). Search results for "United Airlines" on Google News listed the archived story as the most relevant, leading some investors to trust the *algorithm's* sense of time and sell their stocks before confirming the story's veracity (Baer 2008).

News organizations' own algorithms are not immune to such temporal errors. Prior to publication, *The Los Angeles Times* reviews all stories its "Quake Bot" algorithm writes in response to the USGS automatically generated earthquake data. But, in July 2015, the USGS database failed to issue a data "deletion notice" after mistakenly locating two earthquakes in California and thus trigging "Quake Bot" to write a story. After no reports of damages, no tweets from the area tagged #quake, and an Associated Press story questioning *The Los Angeles Times* report, it took several hours for the paper to issue a correction—but not before *The Los Angeles Times'* own tweets of its erroneous stories were retweeted 148 times. In the aftermath of this error, *The Los Angeles Times* and USGS announced they would collaborate to design a less error-prone data flow (CBS San Francisco 2015). The stories and their corrections revealed: poorly synchronized data structures without consistent human oversight; reliance on audience reports, platform patterns, and competitors to identify errors; and the impossibility of issuing timely corrections that could propagate quickly across multiple distribution channels. Algorithms write quickly, but corrections require human judgment and platform control that move more slowly than errors spread.

When computational infrastructures automatically publish stories, news time becomes algorithmic time. News organizations may be able to design editorial pauses into their own algorithms, but their review, publication, and correction rhythms are effectively at the mercy of other organizations' algorithms, databases, and fact-checking standards. Networked news time entails negotiating with non-journalists *and* their code.

Legal Regulations

Finally, networked news time intersects with legal doctrines regulating the frequency, timing, and archiving of news stories. For several years, US shield laws have prevented journalists from being compelled to testify in state courts but, in attempts to update or pass statutes for *online* journalists not officially employed by traditional news organizations, a temporal element to the protection has emerged. For example the proposed US federal shield law defines a "journalist" as someone who, before an incident in question, practiced for one continuous year within a 20-year period, three consecutive months within five years, or produced a significant amount of work in the last five years (Schumer 2013). State statutes similarly contain temporal references that need interpretation in online contexts: Alaska, Illinois, Florida, Louisiana, and Oklahoma protect someone who "regularly" collects or writes news; Indiana and Rhode Island protect journalists at organizations where news is "issued at regular intervals," whereas in New York protected newspapers must publish "not less frequently than once a week" for "at least one year"; and Delaware only protects someone who during "the preceding 8 weeks had spent at least 20 hours" doing journalism (Digital Media Law Project 2013). Journalism is protected only if journalists have worked recently, often, and long enough; journalists who are too slow, infrequently publishing, or novice may not be shielded.

Online news can also effectively disappear if journalists depend upon circulation infrastructures that become illegal. Although news organizations are exempt, the European Union's "right to be forgotten" legislation requires that "data controllers" like Google remove from their search indices "inadequate, irrelevant or no longer relevant" information (Arthur 2014). Since news organizations receive anywhere from 5 to 40 percent (Benton 2014) of their traffic from Google, in practice this means that de-indexed news stories have limited circulation. The BBC, *The Guardian*, and *The New York Times* have all had stories de-indexed (Cohen and Scott 2014), with the BBC keeping a public record of removed stories (McIntosh 2015). Past news stories are only *effectively* visible if archival infrastructures stay legal.

Lastly, some publishers are attempting to resurrect time-sensitive news laws. The "hot news" doctrine emerged when, in 1918, the Associated Press (AP) "challenged International News Service's (INS) use of its newswire stories, attacking INS's ability to take advantage of the time difference between the East and West Coasts by immediately rewriting AP's stories and distributing them at the same time AP was able to distribute them on the West Coast" (Sherrod 2012, 1209). The US Supreme Court agreed that because the AP had invested in infrastructure to quickly gather and disseminate breaking—"hot"—news, it not only had copyright to its wire stories but, for a short period of time, it also *owned* the *facts* within those stories. The ruling recognized that material investments in news time can create a time window within which news organizations have a right to use temporal infrastructures for competitive advantage.

Though it might seem antiquated today, the doctrine lives on. In 2009, in *AP v. All Headline News*, a United States District Court recognized that the AP's claim of "misappropriation of [their] hot news remains viable" (Castel 2009, 9) as grounds for claiming time-limited ownership over news facts. Also, in 2010, the same court required that online financial news site FlyOnTheWall.com wait to release facts about the firms it analyzed "until at least thirty minutes after the market opened" or "two hours after the firms first released" the information (Harrison and Shelton 2013, 1659). Though controversial and rarely invoked in an age of global and nearly instantaneous news circulation, the "hot news" doctrine's continued relevance shows courts' willingness to slow news to the pace set by the media companies creating and controlling time-keeping infrastructures.

Conclusion

In their landmark study "It's About Time: Temporal Structuring in Organizations," Orlikowski and Yates (2002) find that successfully sharing time depends upon how many people belong to a group, how geographically widespread it is, how common time-keeping artifacts are, how taken-for-granted and embedded time-keeping is in everyday lives, and how many *other* groups depend upon that group's version of time. Time only "works" when all these factors are accounted for.

This definition of success, though, leaves largely undeveloped the question of whether one type of time might be normatively better than another. We could complement descriptions of *how* networks create time with ethics of how they *should* create time. In the context of contemporary news time, the challenge is to connect accounts of how press assemblages create journalistic rhythms with theories of what publics need from networked news time. If networked news rhythms are set by labor, platforms, algorithms, and laws, then forces with the power to do so need to configure them in ways that realize the time required for a public right to hear—pauses to reflect, hesitate, and doubt *and* make timely interventions into the inextricable consequences of shared social life.

Different temporal assemblages create different types of news time and, thus, different types of consequences. Some shared social conditions may never be realized or debated because the temporal assemblages governing public discourse never surface them—because the power to speed up or slow down collective time is unevenly distributed or systematically oppresses the realization of diverse timescales. The responsibility for ensuring that temporal assemblages enable listening cannot simply mean asking individual readers to "speed up" or "slow down." Personally offloading accountability is too common in neoliberal models that expect individual consumers to (impossibly) define their own social conditions, or create their own time. The responsibility to create temporal assemblages that ensure a public right to hear lies with those who wield assemblage power. In the case of networked news, those with power are increasingly technologists and advertisers—not journalists—whose platforms and commodifications control how and when news circulates.

Since different types of publics require different types of time—the consequentialist public foregrounded here is only one—each theory of the public requires different temporal assemblages; and since assemblages intertwine technologies, practices, and values that constantly change, each new seemingly independent innovation of a particular actor—e.g., a change to Facebook's newsfeed algorithm, or Twitter's introduction of the "Moments" feature—will influence how news time is collectively made and thus which publics are possible. Temporal assemblages become analytics for tracing the power of the networked press to convene publics by managing timescales.

Integrating the forces discussed here, a public need to pause and reflect during breaking news may only be realized if news organizations reward journalists for slower publishing, if platforms suspend auto-playing videos, if story-writing algorithms pass a higher standard of error-checking or extra round of editorial review, and if news organizations see delayed publishing as a public duty, not property right. Similarly, a temporal assemblage might help publics relate historical patterns to contemporary events if it uses archived traffic data to reassemble past audiences, reorients social media platforms' recommendation algorithms, and gains exceptions to the "right to be forgotten."

No single assemblage element can change news time, but a public right to hear may provide an impetus for new types of coordination among the parts.

Such experiments in news time require both power to configure networks and normative arguments for doing so. Scholars and practitioners defining the *field* of journalism might examine what types of networked news time are possible, what types are needed, and how the power to make news time is distributed among diverse actors. The emerging "slow journalism" movement might ask: "how slow—or fast—do different publics *need* news to be?" and how can networked news paces be set?

DISCLOSURE STATEMENT

No potential conflict of interest was reported by the author.

REFERENCES

Accelerated Mobile Pages Project. 2015. "Frequently Asked Questions." Accessed October 20.

American Press Institute. 2014. "Americans Are Accessing the News throughout the Day and across Devices." Accessed August 5. http://www.americanpressinstitute.org/publi cations/reports/survey-research/how-americans-get-news/

Arthur, Charles. 2014. "Explaining the 'Right to Be Forgotten'." Accessed May 20. http://www. theguardian.com/technology/2014/may/14/explainer-right-to-be-forgotten-the-newest-cultural-shibboleth

Backstrom, Lars. 2013. "News Feed Fyi: A Window into News Feed." Accessed July 3. https:// www.facebook.com/business/news/News-Feed-FYI-A-Window-Into-News-Feed

Baer, Justin. 2008. "United Airlines Shares Plunge 75% after Six-Year-Old Bankruptcy Story." Accessed July 5. http://www.ft.com/cms/s/0/a2653cb6-7e07-11dd-bdbd-000077b07658. html#axzz3pu46CXY1

Baker, C. Edwin. 2002. *Media, Markets, and Democracy*. Cambridge, UK: Cambridge University Press.

Belman, Larry S. 1977. "John Dewey's Concept of Communication." *Journal of Communication* 27 (1): 29–37.

Benton, Joshua. 2014. "How Much of Your News Site's Search Traffic Comes from Google News?" Accessed March 3. http://www.niemanlab.org/2014/12/how-much-of-your-news-sites-search-traffic-comes-from-google-news-probably-5-to-25-percent/

Birth, Kevin K. 2012. *Objects of Time: How Things Shape Temporality*. London, UK: Palgrave Macmillan.

Blondheim, Menahem. 1994. *News over the Wires: The Telegraph and the Flow of Public Information in America, 1844–1897*. Cambridge, MA: Harvard University Press.

Boczkowski, Pablo. 2010. *News at Work: Imitation in an Age of Information Abundance*. Chicago, IL: University of Chicago Press.

Bollinger, Lee C. 1991. *Images of a Free Press*. Chicago, IL: The University of Chicago Press.

Bondioli, Sara. 2015. "Tweet and Delete: Politwoops' Demise Means Less Transparency in Politics." Accessed September 30. http://www.huffingtonpost.com/2015/06/04/twitter-re vokes-politwoops_n_7512892.html

Carlson, Matt. 2014. "The Robotic Reporter: Automated Journalism and the Redefinition of Labor, Compositional Forms, and Journalistic Authority." *Digital Journalism* 3 (3): 416–431. doi:10.1080/21670811.2014.976412.

Carlson, Matt. 2015. "The Many Boundaries of Journalism." In *Boundaries of Journalism: Professionalism, Practices and Participation*, edited by Matt Carlson and Seth C. Lewis, 1–18. New York: Routledge.

Castel, P. Kevin. 2009. "Memorandum and Order." In *08 Civ. 323*, edited by Southern District of New York United States District Court.

Castells, Manuel. 1996. *The Rise of the Network Society*. London: Blackwell.

Castells, Manuel. 2009. *Communication Power*. Oxford, UK: Oxford University Press.

CBS San Francisco. 2015. "Two Powerful Earthquakes Did Not Hit Northern California." Accessed June 4. http://sanfrancisco.cbslocal.com/2015/05/30/4-8-and-5-5-magnitude-earthquakes-did-not-hit-northern-california-automated-quake-alerts-fail-usgs-la-times-a-2nd-and-3rd-time/

Christians, Clifford G., Theodore L. Glasser, Denis McQuail, Kaarle Nordenstreng, and Robert A. White. 2009. *Normative Theories of the Media*. Urbana, IL: University of Illinois Press.

Clark, Jessica, Nick Couldry, Abigail T. De Kosnik, Tarleton Gillespie, Henry Jenkins, Christopher Kelty, Zizi Papacharissi, Alison Powell, and José van Dijck. 2014. "Participations, Part 5: Platforms." *International Journal of Communication* 8: 1446–1473.

Cohen, Josh. 2008. "Update on United Airlines Story." Accessed October 3. http://googlenewsblog.blogspot.com/2008/09/update-on-united-airlines-story.html

Cohen, Noam, and Mark Scott. 2014. "Times Articles Removed from Google Results in Europe." Accessed January 5. http://www.nytimes.com/2014/10/04/business/media/times-articles-removed-from-google-results-in-europe.html

Craig, Geoffrey. 2015. "Reclaiming Slowness in Journalism." *Journalism Practice*: 1–15. doi:10.1080/17512786.2015.1100521.

DeLanda, Manuel. 2006. *A New Philosophy of Society: Assemblage Theory and Social Complexity*. New York: Bloomsbury Academic.

Dewey, John. 1910. *How We Think*. Boston, MA: DC Heath &.

Dewey, John. 1954. *The Public and Its Problems*. New York: Swallow Press.

Digital Media Law Project. 2013. "State Shield Laws." Accessed July 5. http://www.dmlp.org/state-shield-laws

Dobson, Andrew. 2012. "Listening: The New Democratic Deficit." *Political Studies* 60 (4): 843–859.

Domingo, David. 2008. "When Immediacy Rules: Online Journalism Models in Four Catalan Online Newsrooms." In *Making Online News: The Ethnography of New Media Production*, edited by Chris Paterson and David Domingo, 113–126. New York: Peter Lang Publishing.

Edwards, Paul. 2003. "Infrastructure and Modernity: Force, Time, and Social Organization in the History of Sociotechnical Systems." In *Modernity and Technology*, edited by T. J. Misa, P. Brey and A. Feenberg, 185–225. Cambridge, MA: The MIT Press.

Ellis, Justin. 2014a. "The Notification Knows Where You Are: Breaking News Debuts News Alerts Tied to Your Location." Accessed July 2. http://www.niemanlab.org/2014/06/the-notification-knows-where-you-are-breaking-news-debuts-news-alerts-tied-to-your-location/

Ellis, Justin. 2014b. "Watching What Happens: The New York times is Making a Front-Page Bet on Real-Time Aggregation." Accessed September 30. http://www.niemanlab.org/2014/09/watching-what-happens-the-new-york-times-is-making-a-front-page-bet-on-real-time-aggregation/

Emerson, Thomas I. 1970. *The System of Freedom of Expression*. New York: Random House.

Ferree, Myra Marx, William A. Gamson, Jürgen Gerhards, and Dieter Rucht. 2002. "Four Models of the Public Sphere in Modern Democracies." *Theory and Society* 31: 289–324.

Gans, Herbert. 1979. *Deciding What's News*. New York: Vintage.

Goel, Vindu, and Ravi Somaiya. 2015. "Facebook Begins Testing Instant Articles from News Publishers." Accessed May 14. http://www.nytimes.com/2015/05/13/technology/facebook-media-venture-to-include-nbc-buzzfeed-and-new-york-times.html

Google. 2015. "About Google News." Accessed October 3. https://support.google.com/news/answer/106259?hl=en&ref_topic=2428790

Habermas, Jurgen. 1996. *Between Facts and Norms: Contributions to a Discourse Theory of Law and Democracy*. Cambridge, MA: MIT Press.

Hargittai, Eszter, and Aaron Shaw. 2014. "Mind the Skills Gap: The Role of Internet Know-How and Gender in Differentiated Contributions to Wikipedia." *Information, Communication & Society*. doi:10.1080/1369118X.2014.957711.

Harrison, Jeffrey L., and Robyn Shelton. 2013. "Deconstructing and Reconstructing Hot News: Toward a Functional Approach." *Cardoza Law Review* 34 (5): 1649–1692.

Hartley, Jannie Møller. 2011. "Routinizing Breaking News: Categories and Hierarchies in Danish Online Newsrooms." In *Making Online News: Newsroom Ethnography in the Second Decade of Internet Journalism*, edited by David Domingo and Chris Paterson, 73–86. New York: Peter Lang.

Hazard Owen, Laura. 2015a. "Instant Articles Get Shared More than Old-Fashioned Links, plus More Details from Facebook's News Push." Accessed October 27. http://www.niemanlab.org/2015/10/instant-articles-get-shared-more-than-old-fashioned-links-plus-more-details-from-facebooks-news-push/

Hazard Owen, Laura. 2015b. "Is There an Ideal Time of Day to Read News?" Accessed October 30. http://www.niemanlab.org/2015/10/is-there-an-ideal-time-of-day-to-read-news-a-site-called-twelve-thirty-six-has-one-idea-youll-never-guess/

Irani, Lilly. 2015. "The Cultural Work of Microwork." *New Media & Society* 17 (5): 720–739. doi:10.1177/1461444813511926.

James, William. 1997. "What Pragmatism Means." In *Pragmatism: A Reader*, edited by L. Menand, 93–111. New York: Random House.

Kaun, Anne, and Fredrik Stiernstedt. 2014. "Facebook Time: Technological and Institutional Affordances for Media Memories." *New Media & Society* 16 (7): 1154–1168. doi:10.1177/1461444814544001.

Keegan, Brian, Darren Gergle, and Noshir Contractor. 2013. "Hot off the Wiki: Structures and Dynamics of Wikipedia's Coverage of Breaking News Events." *American Behavioral Scientist* 57 (5): 595–622. doi:10.1177/0002764212469367.

Lacey, Kate. 2013. *Listening Publics: The Politics and Experience of Listening in the Media Age*. Cambridge, UK: Polity.

Latour, Bruno. 2004. "Why Has Critique Run out of Steam? From Matters of Fact to Matters of Concern." *Critical Inquiry* 30 (2): 225–248.

Latour, Bruno. 2005. *Reassembling the Social: An Introduction to Actor-Network-Theory*. Oxford, UK: Oxford University Press.

Le Cam, Florence, and David ,Domingo. 2015. "The Tyranny of Immediacy: Gatekeeping Practices in French and Spanish Online Newsrooms." In *Gatekeeping in Transition*, edited by Timothy Vos and François Heinderyckx, 123–140. London, UK: Routledge.

Le Masurier, Megan. 2014. "What is Slow Journalism?" *Journalism Practice*. doi:10.1080/17512786.2014.916471.

Lee, William E. 1987. "The Supreme Court and the Right to Receive Expression." *The Supreme Court Review* 1987: 303–344.

Lee, Kevan. 2015. "The Best Time to Tweet." Accessed August 4. https://blog.bufferapp.com/best-time-to-tweet-research

Lichterman, Joseph. 2015. "Can't Finish a New Yorker Story Online?" Accessed October 30. http://www.niemanlab.org/2015/10/cant-finish-a-new-yorker-story-online-the-magazine-will-now-send-you-an-email-reminder-to-come-back/

Machill, Marcel, and Markus Beiler. 2009. "The Importance of the Internet for Journalistic Research." *Journalism Studies* 10 (2): 178–203. doi:10.1080/14616700802337768.

Macnamara, Jim. 2013. "Beyond Voice: Audience-Making and the Work and Architecture of Listening as New Media Literacies." *Continuum: Journal of Media & Cultural Studies* 27 (1): 160–175.

Marres, Noortje. 2012. *Material Participation: Technology, the Environment and Everyday Publics*. London, UK: Palgrave Macmillan.

McIntosh, Neil. 2015. "List of Bbc Web Pages Which Have Been Removed from Google's Search Results." Accessed June 27. http://www.bbc.co.uk/blogs/internet/entries/1d765aa8-600b-4f32-b110-d02fbf7fd379

Meiklejohn, Alexander. 1948. *Free Speech and Its Relation to Self-Government*. New York: Harper.

Meyer, Robinson. 2014. "How a California Earthquake Becomes the News: An Extremely Precise Timeline." Accessed March 22. http://www.theatlantic.com/technology/archive/2014/03/how-a-california-earthquake-becomes-the-news-an-extremely-precise-timeline/284506/

Miller, Rosa. 2015. "Ap's 'Robot Journalists' Are Writing Their Own Stories Now." Accessed March 23. http://www.theverge.com/2015/1/29/7939067/ap-journalism-automation-robots-financial-reporting

Molotch, Harvey, and Marilyn Lester. 1974. "News as Purposive Behavior: On the Strategic Use of Routine Events, Accidents, and Scandals." *American Sociological Review* 39 (1): 101–112.

Murdock, Graham. 1982. "Large Corporations and the Control of the Communications Industries." In *Culture, Society and the Media*, edited by Michael Gurevitch, Tony Bennett, James Curran and Janet Woollacott, 118–150. New York: Methuen.

Orlikowski, W., and J. Yates. 2002. "It's about Time: Temporal Structuring in Organizations." *Organization Science* 13 (6): 684–700.

Peters, John Durham. 2009. "Calendar, Clock, Tower." In *MiT 6: Media in Transition, Stone and Papyrus Storage and Transmission*. Cambridge, MA: Massachusetts Institute of Technology. Accessed January 21, http://web.mit.edu/comm-forum/mit6/papers/peters.pdf

Pickard, Victor. 2014. *America's Battle for Media Democracy: The Triumph of Corporate Libertarianism and the Future of Media Reform*. Cambridge, UK: Cambridge University Press.

Saltzis, Kostas. 2012. "Breaking News Online: How News Stories Are Updated and Maintained around-the-Clock." *Journalism Practice* 6 (5-6): 702–710.

Schudson, Michael. 1978. *Discovering the News: A Social History of American Newspapers*. New York: Basic Books.

Schudson, Michael. 1986. "Deadlines, Datelines, and History." In *Reading News*, edited by Robin K. Manoff and Michael Schudson, 79–108. New York: Pantheon Books.

Schudson, Michael. 2000. "The Sociology of News Production Revisited (Again)." In *Mass Media and Society*, edited by James Curran and Michael Gurevitch, 175–200. London: Arnold.

Schumer, Charles. 2013. "Free Flow of Information Act of 2013." https://www.congress.gov/bill/113th-congress/senate-bill/987

Shapiro, Walter. 2010. "After Breitbart and Shirley Sherrod, We Need a Slow-News Movement." Accessed October 1. http://www.politicsdaily.com/2010/07/27/after-breitbart-and-shirley-sherrod-we-need-a-slow-news-movemen/

Sharma, Sarah. 2014. *In the Meantime: Temporality and Cultural Politics*. Durham, NC: Duke University Press.

Sherrod, Heather. 2012. "The "Hot News" Doctrine: It's Not 1918 Anymore-Why the "Hot News" Doctrine Shouldn't Be Used to save the Newspapers." *Houston Law Review* 48 (5): 1205–1240.

Silverstone, Roger. 2003. "Proper Distance: Towards an Ethics for Cyberspace." In *Digital Media Revisited: Theoretical and Conceptual Innovations in Digital Domains*, edited by Gunnar Liestol, Andrew Morrison and Terje Rasmussen, 469–490. Cambridge, MA: MIT Press.

Star, Susan Lee. 1999. "Ethnography of Infrastructure." *American Behavioral Scientist* 43 (3): 377–391.

Starbird, Kate, Jim Maddock, Mania Orand, Peg Achterman, and Robert M. Mason. 2014. "Rumors, False Flags, and Digital Vigilantes: Misinformation on Twitter after the 2013 Boston Marathon Bombing." Paper presented at the iConference 2014.

Take Two. 2014. "Introducing Kpcc's New Earthquake Tracker." Accessed October 3. http://www.scpr.org/programs/take-two/2014/01/14/35528/introducing-kpcc-s-new-earthquake-tracker/

Tapia, Andrea H., Nicolas LaLone, and Hyun-Woo Kim. 2014. "Run Amok: Group Crowd Participation in Identifying the Bomb and Bomber from the Boston Marathon Bombing." Paper presented at the 11th International ISCRAM Conference, University Park, PN, USA.

The Guardian. 2015. "Terms and Conditions of Use - Open Platform." Accessed September 2. http://www.theguardian.com/open-platform/terms-and-conditions

Thompson, Edward P. 1967. "Time, Work-Discipline, and Industrial Capitalism." *Past and Present* 38: 56–97.

Thurman, Neil, and Nic Newman. 2014. "The Future of Breaking News Online? A Study of Live Blogs through Surveys of Their Consumption, and of Readers' Attitudes and Participation." *Journalism Studies* 15 (5): 655–667. doi:10.1080/1461670X.2014.882080.

Tuchman, Gaye. 1972. "Objectivity as Strategic Ritual: An Examination of Newsmen's Notions of Objectivity." *American Journal of Sociology* 77: 660–679.

Usher, Nikki. 2014. *Making News at the New York times*. Ann Arbor, MI: University of Michigan Press.

Valinsky, Jordan. 2015. "News Crew Shooting Shows Perils of Auto-Play Videos on Twitter, Facebook." Accessed September 5. http://digiday.com/platforms/news-crew-shooting-shows-perils-auto-play-videos-twitter-facebook/

de Vaujany, Francois-Xavier, Nathalie Mitev, Pierre Laniray, and Emmanuelle Vaast. 2014. "Introduction: Time and Materiality." In *Materiality and Time: Historical Perspectives on Organizations, Artefacts and Practices*, edited by Francois-Xavier de Vaujany, Nathalie Mitev, Pierre Laniray and Emmanuelle Vaast, 1–13. New York: Palgrave Macmillan.

Wajcman, Judy. 2014. *Pressed for Time: The Acceleration of Life in Digital Capitalism*. Chicago, IL: University of Chicago Press.

Weltevrede, Esther, Anne Helmond, and Carolin Gerlitz. 2014. "The Politics of Real-Time: A Device Perspective on Social Media Platforms and Search Engines." *Theory, Culture & Society* 31 (6): 125–150. doi:10.1177/0263276414537318.

Wemple, Eric. 2015. "What is the New York times Doing with Its New Breaking-News Unit?" Accessed October 14. https://www.washingtonpost.com/blogs/erik-wemple/wp/2015/10/14/what-is-the-new-york-times-doing-with-breaking-news-unit/

Yu, Ansha, and Sami Tas. 2015. "News Feed Fyi: Taking into Account Time Spent on Stories." Accessed August 5. http://newsroom.fb.com/news/2015/06/news-feed-fyi-taking-into-account-time-spent-on-stories/

Zerubavel, Eviatar. 1981. *Hidden Rhythms: Schedules and Calendars in Social Life*. Berkeley, CA: University of California Press.

MULTIMEDIA, SLOW JOURNALISM AS PROCESS, AND THE POSSIBILITY OF PROPER TIME

Benjamin Ball

Digital communication is fast and easy; but as a cultural process communication is difficult, especially when it engages with strangers and strangeness. Roger Silverstone describes the space necessary for respectful communication as a "proper distance" vis-à-vis mediated Others —neither too far away, nor too close to see the Other, and to recognise in her our own inherent Otherness. What Silverstone describes in terms of distance can also be considered in relation to time. This article builds on Silverstone's ideas to outline a working definition of slow journalism as process, and it is argued that multimedia journalism provides a platform for communication that approximates "proper time"—journalism that is fast enough to engage, surprise and retain our attention, yet slow enough to respect a story's nuance and complexity. It is argued that the poetics of photography provides a subversive logic of efficiency, capable of both revelation and evocation, and of helping us hear the Other; and that audio can expand our vision beyond the photographic frame, providing us with the necessary context and narrative to properly see. This is a narrative warp and weft. The trajectory of one form crosses and expands the narrative arc of the other, providing colour, depth, and nuance. Multimedia journalism can be quick and profound, fast and slow, short-form and long-form, thus occupying a critical middle ground between the impenetrable overloads and binary simplifications of digital communication, and opening a space and a time for mediated Others.

Introduction

Between a morning train and an office in central Sydney, I walk, mulling over the words and ideas that might begin this article. In front of me, two men approach an escalator ascending from a crowded pedestrian tunnel. The first man walks awkwardly on to the steps and presses the handrails with the palms of his hands, his fingers splayed upwards. The man is motionless except for his head, which jolts to one side as though emptying water from his ear. Four other people follow behind him before the second man, power walking in a power suit, boards the escalator and clambers past the other pedestrians. He reaches the first man and taps him on the shoulder. "Excuse me, please."

Nothing.

The suited man shakes his head and swears under his breath as though to himself, but audible to those of us around him. Within seconds both men are at the top of the escalator. The first man steps on to the peak-hour pavement, his rigid legs moving from the hips, his shoulders alternately facing the direction in which he walks, with skill and resilience, with a body not entirely at his command.

The second man surges past and continues on his way. No looking back.

Digital media make communication fast, cheap, easy, and ubiquitous. So constant and pervasive is our communication that Mark Deuze (2011) proposes a new ontology in which we no longer live with media, but *in* media. Smartphones shape our landscapes like the weather, each device a symbolic universe from which we retrieve information and conversations like Mary Poppins pulls hat stands from her carpetbag.[1] Except that her bag was fabulous—an enchantment—and our smartphones, by contrast, are entirely normal. So normal that we readily forget that communication is *not* easy at all, that as a process that lies at the heart of human culture, and at the core of journalism as a craft, communication is difficult, because understanding is difficult (Carey 1992). It is hard enough to understand one another in material spaces like trains, pedestrian tunnels, and streets, as my morning commute daily demonstrates; and the difficulty is amplified as the communication extends across distance and time, as it travels across the media that connects us to the world beyond our geographical neighbourhoods.

In what follows I argue that the difficulty of understanding one another in media is an essential part of what slow journalism is, and—perhaps more importantly—an essential element of *why* it is. That is, why slow journalism has emerged as a topic of professional and academic interest, and why as a practice it is socially valuable and morally important. My premise is simple. Our communication is fast and technically easy, but understanding one another in media is a task that requires time. In addition to providing information, journalists face the unfamiliar task of providing sufficient time for what Roger Silverstone (2007) describes as "proper distance" *vis-à-vis* mediated Others. Here I argue that Silverstone's spatial metaphor ought also be expressed temporally, as "proper time." My concern is theoretical and practical. Engagement with slow journalism requires thought, imagination, and emotion—it requires a degree of commitment from the readership or audience—but the amount of time that is committed need not reflect the depth of emotion that a person will experience, or the degree of understanding that will be achieved (Cramerotti 2009, 22). "Proper time" is therefore not a question of perfect duration, pace, tempo, or length, but—instead—it is about reflexive consideration, on the part of journalists, for how understanding can be achieved in, and through, journalism. I am interested in slow journalism as a necessary process, rather than as a thing. Also, as a critical practitioner of slow journalism, my intention is to outline how and why photography provides an important platform for slow journalism, as well as for the possibility of proper time. This article argues that multimedia photo essays provide a subversive logic of efficiency that achieves a sort of Goldilocks length: neither too short to exclude nuance, complexity, or profound responses, nor too long to preclude the engagement with entire narratives that storytelling and proper distance require.[2] But to reach that argument, I must first provide some context.

Proper Distance

A poignant starting place for a discussion of proper distance and its relationship to slow journalism lies flat amongst subsistence crops in northwest Pakistan, where in the past decade military drones have killed an estimated 3600 people, including as many as 951 civilians and 200 children (Meyer 2014). According to drone operators, taking a human life, when seen through the pixelated greyscale of a drone's camera, looks like squashing a bug, a description that provides the name for a collaborative art project designed to speak directly to the operators of military drones. *Not A Bug Splat*, led by French photographer JR, expands the vision of drone operators beyond what is normally seen—pixelated homes, buildings, and crops—to include a massive black and white photograph of a child whose parents were killed in a drone strike. *Not A Bug Splat* is an open letter that interrogates the moral character of contemporary warfare and questions issues of accountability, mediation, international justice, silence, and memory; but connecting and underscoring each of these issues is the project's fundamental subject: distance.

In a media life, the meaning of distance is altered, and because everything we know of the world beyond our geographical neighbourhoods is known through the media (as well as an increasing amount of what we know of life within our geographical neighbourhoods), our communication, experiences, and decisions in media take on a moral dimension. Depth, shallowness, meaning, superficiality, understanding, and incomprehension are all relative and relational measures of our mediated world, and are therefore abstract and ultimately *moral*, understood here as existing within a social code that is impervious to empirical measurement, but nevertheless comprehensible through judgements based on first principles (Silverstone 2007, 7). For Roger Silverstone (2003, 473–474), "distance" ought not to be deemed a material, geographical or social category, but—precisely because the word infers and interrelates each of these—it should be considered a moral category of life in media. Distance allows or denies speech and determines the quality of our listening—the ability to hear, the expectations for being heard, and the willingness to listen. "Proper," then, is a description and moral evaluation of distance. It can be understood as a synonym for "correct," as in, "now is the *proper* time to act," and by extension it can describe and judge something as proper, or improper, in relation to social norms and expectations (Silverstone 2003, 473). Silverstone writes:

> Proper distance is the critical notion that implies and involves a search for enough knowledge and understanding of the other person or the other culture to enable responsibility and care, as well as to enable the kind of action that, informed by that understanding, is in turn enabling. We need to be close but not too close, distant, but not too distant. (Silverstone 2007, 172)

The cameras of military drones mediate the world through a cultural lens of *improper* distance, and not simply because the vision they provide is inherently macabre, remote, or incapable of listening and thus also incapable of understanding; but also, and especially, because there is insufficient insight into these mediating effects, and thus of the moral character of the communication involved (Butler 2010, 14). Through the lens of the drone the Other is shunned: knowable, but refused hospitality, and excluded from the expectations of *normal* life. For Mexican poet Octavio Paz, this shunned Other is not simply a stranger, but a "Nobody," of whom he writes:

> It would be a mistake to believe that others prevent him from existing. They simply dissimulate his existence and behave as if he did not exist. They nullify him, cancel him out, turn him to nothingness. It is futile for Nobody to talk, to publish books, to paint

pictures, to stand on his head. Nobody is the blankness in our looks, the pauses in our conversations, the reserve in our silences. He is the name we always and inevitably forget, the eternal absentee, the guest we never invite, the emptiness we can never fill. He is an omission, and yet he is forever present. He is our secret, our crime, and our remorse. Thus the person who creates Nobody, by denying Somebody's existence, is also changed into Nobody. (Paz 1985, 45–46)

It is in this sense, too, that the drone embodies improper distance. The drone operator nullifies the subjects that appear to her or him through the camera and in so doing she or he, too, is diminished; as I am diminished at this very moment, writing about drone operators and Pakistani orphans of whom I know so little! And so I arrive at the central point, because proper distance is vital precisely because it is unattainable. Proper distance is not a thing to be had or achieved, but a process based on an ideal that allows us to think critically about our own place, and work, in media (Silverstone 2007).

We cannot attend to the presence of every person we encounter, in digital media or in the street. And yet, just as inhabitants of dense urban dwellings can choose to know something of their neighbours—or not—and imagine life beyond their suburb— or not—so too can we move towards a moral relationship with Others in the digital spaces of a media life. For Max Weber, moral communication requires empathic understanding, or *verstehen* in the original German, and this in turn requires putting aside one's own vision of the world and adopting the framework of the Other (as quoted in Chang 2008, 27). Perfect *verstehen* is impossible, but, as is the case with proper distance, any attempt to apply the idea opens the possibility and likelihood of rich intercultural dialogue. Silverstone writes:

> There can, of course, be no reasonable and sustainable expectation that audiences and users as participants in the mediapolis can or should take responsibility for everything they see and hear on television or which they access on the internet. This would be both absurd and crippling. Yet to expect that they should never take any responsibility for what they see and hear in the mediapolis would be equally crippling. News really would then become merely spectacle, and the world would disappear into the realms of fantasy. (Silverstone 2007, 134)

Proper Time and Slow Journalism as Process

Slow journalism is exciting and necessary because it provides a framework for media production that approximates (by which I mean, "moves towards") proper distance. Critically, this practice-based framework concentrates on reflexive consideration for how media is received—for how mediated Others are seen, heard, and understood, in media—which has historically been a blind spot in the fields of media studies and journalism studies, precisely because moral understanding is so hard to measure (Silverstone 2007). As theorists we can gain an empirical sense of social understanding through longitudinal studies of empathy (Turkle 2011, 293; Immordino-Yang et al. 2009, 3–5), or through neurological assessments of how multitasking affects our capacity to follow and comprehend a story (Greenfield 2009, 71; Zanto and Gazzaley 2009, 3065); but the study of listening as a moral category, the analysis of its social quality and character, is like measuring tension by pushing on a string. As David Harvey (2006, 141–142) laments, "try measuring any social relation directly and you always fail." If, as Silverstone (2007, 4) claims, mediated images of strangers increasingly define what constitutes the world, a reflexive approach to journalism that allows, respects, and celebrates difficulty may provide a practical response to this theoretical gap, prompting us to see mediated images as more than fleeting, two-dimensional *things*, and recognise them instead as processes that begin with a person who, like us, is vulnerable to the traumas of misunderstanding (Butler 2010). What I am beginning to outline, then, is a possible definition for slow journalism that focuses on its social processes rather than its formal characteristics. In this understanding, slow journalism is not about reaching a particular word-count, duration, or production time, but about reaching an audience, and not only reaching an audience *technically*, but also, and more importantly, engaging the audience intellectually and emotionally. "Slow" describes the extent and moral tenor of the communicative process, rather than its duration or tempo.

Not a Bug Splat says nothing directly. It carries no caption or story, and for that reason the project is hard to recognise as journalism in the traditional sense. Additionally, because the photo was first exhibited in a field and not in a newspaper or website, and because it was published in the absence of audio or graphics, it is difficult to recognise as multimedia; but from the field, the photograph quickly migrated to make newspaper headlines around the world.[3] From within a media life perspective, in which the material world and the symbolic world overlap, our understanding of "multimedia journalism" needs to be reconsidered, and arguably expanded, as theorists such as Mark Deuze (2012) and Alfredo Cramerotti (2009) are beginning to hint at, and as some research on cross-platform and transmedia journalism suggests.[4] Nevertheless, as a case study for slow journalism, *Not a Bug Splat* is useful, for several reasons. The first is that its temporality is difficult to define. Photography is ephemeral *and* lasting—an idea I will return to shortly; the second is that the project presents the portrait of a boy who is otherwise invisible and unknown. We see him, and seeing him is easy; yet his presence in media challenges us with the *possibility* of further understanding. The photographic medium precludes the possibility of speech, and so the medium becomes part of the message, part of the recognition that understanding is both possible and difficult. We see, *and* we are made aware of the limits of our vision. Difficulty itself becomes productive.

This is an old idea, but in the context of the ever-increasing technological ease of digital communication, it takes on additional gravity. Slow journalism as process requires of journalists that we provide a view of the world, as we have always done, and additionally that we provide insight into the mediating process, or what Alfredo Cramerotti (2009, 28) in his outline of aesthetic journalism calls the "view of the view." This is an idea that Cramerotti draws from modern art, but its application extends into other fields. For example, Michael Taussig writes:

> Indeed, what is anthropology but a species of translation made all the more honest, all the more truthful, and all the more interesting by showing showing—i.e., showing the means of its production? (Taussig 2004, 313–314)

Replace "anthropology" with "journalism," or with "documentary," or with "art," and the question holds true, because the sentence is not about anthropology at all; it is about understanding and its processes. The methodological challenge for slow journalism is to provide a view of the view in digital media, to show showing in a way that is honest, yet that proves sufficiently engaging on the screen to ward off distraction. A reflexive and transparent account of the world that approximates proper distance is arguably a reasonable expectation within the contemplative spaces of an art gallery or the pages of an anthropological text, but journalists typically work with and against time, and even the most honest story is of little value if it is left unfinished and unresolved. Hence the importance of proper time, which in essence is proper distance recast with rhetorical emphasis on the temporal qualities of life in media.

The idea's importance, however, exceeds rhetoric. Dialogue with difficulty is a necessary precondition for a productive civic culture (Calhoun 1998). As places where contesting ideas collide, cities have always been hubs for creativity and social change, and—increasingly—we experience cities through digital media (Deuze 2012). Smartphones reshape our notions of being "together," or "alone," and alter our understandings of public and private spaces. The distinction between what is "real" and what is "virtual" is rendered redundant. Digital and material spaces fold across one another, and—at least in part—this is what Mark Deuze (2012) means when he describes a life *in* media.

In media, the world becomes smaller, easier, and more manageable. City maps are in our pockets, and we can place ourselves upon them; but increased control brings with it the temptation to shelter from strangers and strangeness, and it is from within this media life perspective that time as a moral variable must be reappropriated, re-emphasised, and rethought (Cramerotti 2009, 104–105). Cramerotti writes:

> At the moment there is simply not enough [time] to stroll around like a flaneur. All information, any object or experience has to be instantaneously at hand. Our techno-cultural default is one of temporal intolerance … Usability experts measure the fractions of a second in which we decide whether the information on the screen is what we are looking for. If we're dissatisfied, we click further. Serendipity requires a lot of time … With Lev Manovich and other colleagues I argue that we need to invent new ways to interact with information, new ways to represent it, and new ways to make sense of it. (Cramerotti 2009, 104–105)

Photography and Multimedia

Photography does not hold a monopoly on how slow journalism is, or ought be practised; but as I have begun to suggest, photography provides a subversive logic of efficiency that facilitates the reappropriation of time that slow journalism requires in digital media—an "achievement of stillness in the midst of chaos" (Saul Bellow, as quoted in Honoré 2004, 199). This subversive logic begins with one of photography's inherent limitations: its inability to provide context. "Only that which narrates can make us understand," writes Susan Sontag ([1977] 2008, 23), and photography, she says, is too static and too idiosyncratic a medium to coherently communicate the fluidity and complexity of peoples, places, and events. This remains true of still photographs when seen individually and in isolation, but the marriage of documentary photography with audio storytelling provides a platform for slow journalism that begins to address Sontag's concern.

In the multimedia context photography speaks, and provides through the human voice, what Walter J. Ong describes as "interiority" (as quoted in Soukup 2005, 4). Soukup writes: "For Ong, interiority represents what persons reveal to each other, an individual's self-consciousness, that which makes a claim on another" (4). The voice implies and creates a listener; it claims our attention and creates a relationship based not on abstract knowledge *of* somebody, but on an empathic belief *in* that person (Butler 2010; Soukup 2005, 4). Just as a photograph can never fully capture the reality of a given moment, Ong describes the voice as an abstract that cannot fully be contained within a media form. A voice may be recorded and broadcast, but its tone and timbre extend beyond the words that are expressed to the realm of supposition and possibility.

Importantly, however, the spoken word can also be written, typically as prose, opening with an uppercase letter and ending with a full stop. That is, a voice provides narrative. It tells a story, creates suspense, presents an opinion, or canvasses an idea. In contrast, still photography has neither uppercase letters nor full stops. It is mute, abstract, and flawed. Neil Postman writes:

> By itself, a photograph cannot deal with the unseen, the remote, the internal, the abstract. It does not speak of "man," only of a man; not of "tree," only of a tree. You cannot produce a photograph of "nature," any more than a photograph of "the sea." You can only photograph a particular fragment of the here-and-now—a cliff of a certain terrain, in a certain condition of light; a wave at a moment in time, from a particular point of view. And just as "nature" and "the sea" cannot be photographed, such larger abstractions as truth, honor, love, falsehood cannot be talked about in the lexicon of pictures. (Postman 1987, 73)

Postman (1987, 73) concludes that where the photograph presents the world as object, language gives us the world as idea. But it is precisely photography's inability to provide a complete picture that makes the multimedia photo essay such a potent platform for slow journalism. The form is necessarily incomplete, but it need not be superficial; indeed, as W. J. T. Mitchell argues, no amount of description adds up to a depiction:

> A verbal representation cannot represent—that is, make present—its object in the same way a visual representation can. It may refer to an object, describe it, invoke it, but it can never bring its visual presence before us in the way pictures do. Words can "cite", but never "sight" their objects. (as quoted in Campbell 2003, 74)

As an art of evocation, photography is akin to poetry, its message both literal and metaphorical. A good photograph relies on what lies outside the frame, drawing on the viewer's imagination to create an image larger than what is visually stated. Photographs give evidence of the world and enable questions to be answered, but, like the timbre of the human voice, photography's innate open-endedness influences its ability to speak to our emotions, prompting outrage or laughter (Bock 2011, 603). As Van Assche remarks, "that which lies outside of the image can be conceived as a more mental terrain and remains to be explored" (as quoted in Curran 2008, 146–147). Photography not only gives evidence but also, and more importantly, asks questions, opening up meanings and challenging assumptions, and photography is much more than "object," and can be abstract in ways that Postman does not allow for. At its best, photography is difficult, and—importantly—the human voice helps photography perform at its best, juxtaposing narrative expression against the frame of a mute moment in time.

In digital media, it is this poetic quality that imbues photography with a subversive logic of efficiency. A still photograph is worth a thousand words, and when combined with audio narratives its ability to evoke as well as show lends itself to communication that defies the logic of truncation. Multimedia photo essays provide context and coherence yet retain the poetry of photography's non-literality. Tom Kennedy asserts that photojournalism is reinventing itself by blending "the best practices from still photojournalism, broadcasting, and independent films" (as quoted in Newton 2009, 240). Kennedy continues:

> The Internet permits us to blend still photographs with audio, text, video, and databases to make compelling content that is far richer than print or broadcasting typically deliver. This new world of visual story telling gives us a chance to reinvent the form and to adapt integration of various media types to tell the most compelling possible story. (in Newton 2009 240)

An important aspect of the photojournalism that Kennedy describes is that it has evolved with the internet. It is still rare to find multimedia photo essays on any other medium, even though there is nothing to impede such stories from being broadcast on television, or exhibited in gallery spaces. Photographers who produce images for digital photo essays enjoy greater freedom to communicate the nuances of a story, because photo editors are less likely to discard the photos that do not cause an immediate reaction, and there is therefore more freedom to produce what John Pilger describes as "slow" stories that for lack of immediate newsworthiness would not otherwise be published (Bock 2011, 610–611; Pilger 1998, 1).

One in Eight Million, a 52-part multimedia series produced for *The New York Times* online throughout 2009, is an early illustration of both these points. Collaborating with *New York Times* reporters, staff photographer Todd Heisler produced one story every week for a year. Each story is an intimate, three-minute portrait of a New York resident combining first-person narrative, ambient sound, and 20–30 monochrome photographs. If one wants to know what life in New York City was like in 2009, it is hard to imagine a more engaging or informative resource, and it is also difficult to imagine how the series could have been produced without the internet. The public comments that follow each of the *One in Eight Million* stories are also worthy of reflection. Some of the comments compliment Todd Heisler for his outstanding photography, or are directed to *The New York Times* to thank it for producing the series, but a significant number of comments are addressed directly to the individuals portrayed. Responding to the story of community gardener Mr English, for example, Gail Madden of Lacey, WA, writes:

> Great work, Mr. English. I listened to your story after harvesting tomatoes from my own garden. It made me think that it is truly a small world where we are all much more alike than we are different … Keep up the good work Mr. English—you are a treasure. (http://community.nytimes.com/comments/www.nytimes.com/packages/html/nyregion/1-in-8-million/1in8_buster_english.html)

Such personal messages illustrate engagement, imagination, and empathy, and, like all of *One in Eight Million*, they are also evidence of photography's growing ability to communicate literary stories on the internet, slowly. It is a sign of evocative storytelling when the storytellers—in this case, the photographer and journalists—disappear.

Multimedia photo essays have also been employed to give voice and context to issues that historically have proved problematic. In June 2010, Médecins Sans Frontières (MSF) began publishing a multimedia report on global malnutrition, produced in collaboration with the VII photo agency (http://www.starvedforattention.org/). *Starved for Attention: The Story of Global Malnutrition* attempts to address the media's inability to explain the root causes of famine and malnutrition, of which David Campbell writes:

> The African food crises of the 1980s fundamentally transformed the academic consensus on the nature of famine. In place of timeworn assumptions about the naturalized occurrence of shortages, famines were recognised as human productions, engendered as much by asymmetrical power relations in the economic, political and social environment as by the continent's ecology. What did not change in this period, however, were the images of African famine. (Campbell 2003, 69)

Starved for Attention was produced because little has changed since 1980 in terms of media representation of starvation, but also, and more importantly, because two things have changed: organisations like MSF are not only producers of media content, but also publishers of content; and still photographs can be combined with voices, video, music, and text to represent and explain the realities of starvation more incisively, ethically, and evocatively than was previously possible. Just as viewers empathise with the subjects of *One in Eight Million*, organisations like MSF employ multimedia photo essays to challenge traditional media representations of vulnerability and suffering in a form that is engaging for an audience that is geographically distant and socially removed.

Photography's ascendance in such contexts is spurred by empirical evidence that people watch multimedia photo essays from beginning to end. *Kingsley's Crossing* is a 21-minute long photo essay about a young man's journey to Europe from his small coastal village in Cameroon (http://mediastorm.com/publication/kingsleys-crossing). In a 2009 interview with *The Nieman Report*, Brian Storm, executive producer of *Kingsley's Crossing*, says that 65 per cent of viewers watch the essay in its entirety, despite its length (Storm 2009).

Photo essays provide a moment of calm in the maelstrom of digital immediacy, and an important differentiation should be made here between still photography and video. Digital photo essays ostensibly share more with television than with the printed book, however, still photography's rhythm is slower than that of the moving image, asking of the viewers that they explore each photograph, scan it, enter into it, and imagine its outer edges. Photography's literal meaning is "writing with light," which—as a definition—is inclusive of the video that photographers increasingly include in their work; but, just as poetry renders language strange, beautiful, and problematic, providing insight into the *process* of expression, so too can photography be considered an aesthetic insight into the process of seeing, as, in fact, the two words, "video"—which is literally, "to see"—and "photography" imply. In the documentary tradition, *photography* is not simply that which is seen; it is the aesthetic expression of what is seen, written through the lens of a critical observer.

In the multimedia context, this visual expression becomes multidimensional. Narrative always requires a forward motion along an axis; but crossing this narrative axis are multiple other axes that provide context and perspective and without which a story cannot approximate proper distance. This relationship between flow and counter-flow is the narrative dance between complexity and simplicity, nuance and speed, proper distance and improper distance; it is (and looks like) rhythm—a wavelength with peaks and troughs. How much detail and how many divergent arguments can I provide in this article, for example, before it is dismissed or abandoned for lack of coherent narrative, or—conversely—before it is criticised for opening questions that are not properly resolved? Proper distance requires lateral movement along a narrative axis—it requires waveforms with large amplitudes—and proper time requires that the amplitude is not so great that the story itself is abandoned. There is a necessary tension here, much like the tension that exists between dancers as they maintain a space between them that is neither too close nor too distant. Movement requires space *and* time, and it also requires tension, because without tension the dance collapses, and the same is true of stories. It is within the sphere of tension that a story unfolds. In fact, to an important degree the tension *is* proper distance, and the tension *is* proper time, or—more exactly —it is within the sphere of tension that proper time is possible. In a multimedia photo essay, for example, a story is heard. It moves along an axis from beginning to end, and the same is true of that story that is *seen*. Turn the audio off, and a story still unfolds; close your eyes, and a story is still heard. Combine the two stories, and you have a narrative that travels in multiple directions, interrogating and expanding upon its own assumptions and processes.

Hearing photography helps us see what is shown, helps us analyse how it is shown, and helps us to reflect on what is not shown; and photography does the same for the spoken word—each provides lateral motion across the narrative axis of the other. Through photography we can appreciate the silence of another, and recognise that communication, and even speech, cannot be reduced to the mouth. To understand the Other properly we must hear and appreciate her silence as well as her words —what goes unsaid as well as what is expressed—and to properly see the Other we must be able to travel towards her beyond the superficiality of image, towards the joy or grief that an image may express.

The ability to comprehend the silence of a mediated Other is arguably a yardstick for proper distance and proper time, but only when the silence exceeds the two-dimensionality of an image, and challenges its clichés (Rajchman 2000, 10). Silence in isolation is only a reason or an excuse to ignore the Other, to create another Nobody. And, of course, what most people "are" in media *is* silent. Without the giant image in the field, the orphan in northwest Pakistan has no presence, and no narrative; he is a Nobody, and his presence—or lack thereof—provides no challenge. The indignity of comfort in a troubled world continues undisturbed.

Roland Barthes famously laments photography's inability to traumatise the viewer, regardless of how gruesome an image might be (Barthes [1980] 2000). Press photography is contemplated for the duration of a second, and is rarely retained; but multimedia photo essays do not aim for, or rely on the retention of any single image, because their subject matter is always, to an important degree, *distance*; they interrogate how we see and hear each other in a contested world. An image can bring the world closer to us, to a distance *apparently* within reach, like looking at the world through binoculars; and audio can remind us that what we see is in fact a distorted vision—that what we see is *not* within physical reach, but *is* within symbolic reach. This is a productive difficulty, because the potential for, and inherent difficulty of understanding is presented in a package that is enjoyable, and evocative. At their best, photo essays approach what James Joyce calls "aesthetic arrest"—a state in which the mind is elevated above desire or loathing, to where it is possible to see the essence, or "being" of another person (as quoted in Wesch 2009, 27). For Judith Butler (2010), this essence is our common vulnerability, the recognition that we are all susceptible to the traumas of misunderstanding.

Conclusion

Multimedia photo essays present a platform for the production of slow journalism that builds on a foundation of productive difficulty, and—as process—slow journalism provides a framework for approximating proper distance and proper time *vis-à-vis* strangers and strangeness in digital media. A final example of this is *Living in the Shadows*, a photo essay by photographer David Maurice Smith that explores life in the remote Australian indigenous town of Wilcannia (https://vimeo.com/74436566). In the essay's four-minute duration we see and hear a complex web of thought and possibility, and we also realise that what is seen is a profound glimpse of life that otherwise—and for most Australians—is heard only as a sound bite, and seen only from behind the window of a car travelling along a highway, if it is seen at all. *Living in the Shadows* expands photography beyond the frame, and grounds spoken stories in the abstract possibilities of stillness and silence. *Living in the Shadows* is a digital poetry book: a multi-dimensional story that is quick and profound; short-form and long-form; simple and complex; ephemeral and lasting; difficult, but not too difficult; and slow, but not too slow. It allows us to *hear* photography, and to *see* audio, and in doing so it problematises both, without diminishing the story's overall impact. *Living in the Shadows* is a demonstration of slow journalism as method, and an approximation of proper time in a media life.

DISCLOSURE STATEMENT

No potential conflict of interest was reported by the author.

NOTES

1. Notwithstanding the rapid increase in smartphone ownership and subsequent digital connectivity in many parts of the world that have hitherto been on the information-scarcity side of the digital divide, my concern here is for how those of us in media-rich societies live with, and relate to, mediated Others. The first-person plural is not intended to be an exclusive mode of expression, nor is it intended to disregard distinct relationships to media—the opposite is the case—but it does necessarily represent a particular experience of "normal" that is specific to those of *us* who typically consume the journalism that foreign correspondents produce (for example), rather than those who appear, mediated, within the correspondence.

2. By "multimedia photo essay" I mean a story in which still photographs are combined with audio, and sometimes with video, to produce a linear non-fiction story. Other common names for the form include audio slideshows and digital photo essays.

3. See, for example, http://www.independent.co.uk/news/world/asia/giant-not-a-bug-splat-art-installation-takes-aim-at-pakistans-predator-drone-operators-9246768.html, and http://www.theatlantic.com/technology/archive/2014/04/for-shame-the-giant-poster-that-shows-drone-pilots-the-people-theyre-bombing/360257/.

4. The argument for an environmental understanding of "multimedia" lies beyond the scope of this article, but in the context of what Scott Lash (2007) and Mark Deuze (2012) describe, in their different ways, as our *new new media ontologies*, it is an important idea to consider. For relevant research on transmedia storytelling, good starting places include Jenkins (2010) and Scolari (2009).

REFERENCES

Barthes, Roland. 2000. *Camera Lucida*. London: Vintage.

Bock, Mary A. 2011. "Newspaper Journalism and Video: Motion, Sound, and New Narratives." *New Media & Society* 14 (4): 600–616.

Butler, Judith. 2010. "Precarious Life." In *Radicalizing Levinas*, edited by Peter Atterton and Matthew Calarco, 3–20. Albany: State University of New York Press.

Calhoun, Craig. 1998. "Community without Propinquity Revisited: Communications Technology and the Transformation of the Urban Public Sphere." *Sociological Inquiry* 68 (3): 373–397.

Campbell, David. 2003. "Salgado and the Sahel: Documentary Photography and the Imaging of Famine." In *International Politics and Social Meaning*, edited by Francois Debris and Cynthia Weber, 69–96. Minneapolis, MN: University of Minnesota Press.

Carey, James W. 1992. *Communication as Culture: Essays on Media and Society*. New York: Routledge.

Chang, Heewon. 2008. *Autoethnography as Method*. Walnut Creek: Left Coast Press.

Cramerotti, Alfredo. 2009. *Aesthetic Journalism: How to Inform without Informing*. Bristol and Chicago: Intellect.

Curran, Mark. 2008. "The Breathing Factory : Locating the Global Labouring Body." *Journal of Media Practice* 9 (2): 139–152.

Deuze, Mark. 2011. "Media Life." *Media, Culture & Society* 33 (1): 137–148.

Deuze, Mark. 2012. *Media Life*. Cambridge and Malden: Polity Press.

Greenfield, Patricia M. 2009. "Technology and Informal Education: What is Taught, What is Learned." *Science* 323 (5910): 69–71.

Harvey, David. 2006. *Spaces of Global Capitalism: Towards a Theory of Uneven Geographical Development*. London and New York: Verso.

Honoré, Carl. 2004. *In Praise of Slow: How a Worldwide Movement is Challenging the Cult of Speed*. London: Orion.

Immordino-Yang, Mary Helen, Andrea McColl, Hanna Damasio and Antonio Damasio. 2009. "Neural Correlates of Admiration and Compassion." Proceedings of the National Academy of Sciences of the United States of America, First published online 20 April 2009, viewed 2 March 2011. http://www.pnas.org/content/early/2009/04/17/0810363106.abstract.

Jenkins, Henry. 2010. "Transmedia Storytelling and Entertainment: An Annotated Syllabus." *Continuum: Journal of Media and Cultural Studies* 24 (6): 943–958.

Lash, Scott. 2007. "Power after Hegemony: Cultural Studies in Mutation." *Theory, Culture & Society* 24 (3): 55–78.

Meyer, Robinson. 2014. "For Shame: The Giant Poster That Shows Drone Pilots the People They're Bombing." *The Atlantic* April 7.

Newton, Julianne H. 2009. "Photojournalism." *Journalism Practice* 3 (2): 233–243.

Paz, Octavio. 1985. *The Labyrinth of Solitude*. New York: Grove Press.

Pilger, John. 1998. *Hidden Agendas*. London: Vintage.

Postman, Neil. 1987. *Amusing Ourselves to Death: Public Discourse in the Age of Show Business*. London: Metheun.

Rajchman, John. 2000. *The Deleuze Connections*. Cambridge and London: The MIT Press.

Scolari, Carlos Alberto. 2009. "Transmedia Storytelling: Implicit Consumers, Narrative Worlds, and Branding in Contemporary Media Production." *International Journal of Communication* 3 (2009): 21.

Silverstone, Roger. 2003. "Proper Distance: Toward an Ethics for Cyberspace." In *New Media Revisited: Theoretical and Conceptual Innovation in Digital Domains*, edited by Gunnar Liestøl, Andrew Morrison and Terje Rasmussen, 469–490. Cambridge and London: The MIT Press.

Silverstone, Roger. 2007. *Media Morality: On the Rise of the Mediapolis*. Cambridge: Polity Press.

Sontag, Susan. 2008. *On Photography*. London: Penguin Modern Classics.

Soukup, Paul A. 2005. "Looking is Not Enough: Reflection on Walter J. Ong and Media Ecology." *Proceedings of the Media Ecology Association* 6: 1–9.

Storm, Brian. 2009. "Long-Form Multimedia Journalism: Quality is the Key Ingredient." *The Nieman Report* Spring 2009. http://www.nieman.harvard.edu/reportsitem.aspx?id=100937.

Taussig, Michael. 2004. *My Cocaine Museum*. Chicago, IL: The University of Chicago Press.

Turkle, Sherry. 2011. *Alone Together: Why We Expect More from Technology and Less from Each Other*. New York: Basic Books.

Wesch, Michael. 2009. "YouTube and You: Experiences of Self-Awareness in the Context Collapse of the Recording Webcam." *Explorations in Media Ecology* 8 (2): 19–34.

Zanto, Theodore P., and Adam Gazzaley. 2009. "Neural Suppression of Irrelevant Information Underlies Optimal Working Memory Performance." *The Journal of Neuroscience* 29 (10): 3059–3066.

THE SOCHI PROJECT
Slow journalism within the transmedia space

Renira Rampazzo Gambarato ⓘ

The Sochi Project is a distinguished example of slow journalism. The project, a transmedia experience built by Dutch photographer Rob Hornstra and journalist Arnold van Bruggen, depicts the hidden story behind the 2014 Winter Olympic Games in Sochi, Russia. The project involves an interactive documentary, numerous print media extensions, digital publications, and an exhibition. Transmedia storytelling involves the unfolding of a storyworld in which instalments of the narrative are distributed across different media platforms to engage the audience and offer a meaningful experience. The case study paper aims to discuss the premises of slow journalism within the transmedia space as the theoretical background on which the analysis of the project is founded. The transmedia analysis delineates how The Sochi Project is developed and, consequently, how slow journalism can benefit from multiplatform media production. In conclusion, slow journalism is not necessarily attached to traditional media, but the opposite: it is aligned with the new possibilities offered by novel technologies. The relevance of the paper relies on the exemplification of slow journalism within transmedia dynamics.

Introduction

The Sochi Project is a transmedia experience built by Dutch documentary photographer Rob Hornstra and journalist/filmmaker Arnold van Bruggen to depict the hidden story behind the 2014 Winter Olympic Games in Sochi, Russia. Since Sochi was announced as the Olympics host in 2007, the two worked together to tell the complicated story of the region.

> Never before have the Olympic Games been held in a region that contrasts more strongly with the glamour of the Games than Sochi. Just twenty kilometers away is the conflict zone Abkhazia. To the east, the Caucasus Mountains stretch into obscure and impoverished breakaway republics such as North Ossetia and Chechnya. On the coast, old Soviet-era sanatoria stand shoulder to shoulder with the most expensive hotels and clubs of the Russian Riviera. By 2014 the area around Sochi will have been changed beyond recognition. (van Bruggen 2013)

The project's tent pole, an interactive documentary (iDoc), is accompanied by numerous print media extensions, digital publications, and an exhibition. Hornstra and van

Bruggen are practitioners of so-called slow journalism, which involves an in-depth, investigative approach to storytelling. This approach provides a solid research foundation for the project. The Sochi Project, the result of their investigation, is described as "a remarkable exercise in photojournalism, a transmedial stream of photobooks, catalogues, exhibitions and online documentaries that has set new standards in modern journalism" (Ferri 2014).

In this context, the paper aims to discuss the premises of slow journalism within the transmedia space as the theoretical background on which the transmedia analysis of the project is founded. Although the transmedia phenomenon is not new, as a concept, a discipline, transmedia storytelling (TS) is still elusive. Consequently, it remains open and does not yet have its own consolidated analytical methods. Therefore, the methodological approach chosen to explore the case of The Sochi Project is the original transmedia project design analytical model by Gambarato (2013), aimed at outlining the essential features of the process of developing transmedia projects.

Slow Journalism Within the Transmedia Space

TS involves the unfolding of a storyworld (Jenkins 2006) in which instalments of the narrative are distributed across different media platforms in order to engage the audience and offer a more meaningful experience. "Transmedia enriches story by activating the human affinity toward shared experience" (Bernardo 2014, 150). Bernardo also emphasizes: "In the past decade, transmedia has proved invaluable as a communication strategy. Its real value lies in its prioritization of a dynamic storytelling experience as opposed to a more or less static broadcast" (125). The classic examples of TS are often related to entertainment, as the case of *The Matrix* (1999) by the Wachowski brothers. "In between each feature film, additional content (including graphic novels, animations, video games and memorabilia, for instance) were released to give the audience a richer understanding of the storyworld and to help keep fans engaged" (Gambarato 2013, 85). An example beyond fiction is the British project Fish Fight (http://www.fishfight.net/). It was produced by Channel 4 and hosted by chef Hugh Fearnley-Whittingstall as a transmedia experience designed to draw the audience's attention to the reckless discarding of caught fish because of the quota system intended to conserve fish stocks in the domain of the European Union and, consequently, to pressure the authorities to change the European Common Fisheries Policy. The story unfolded on various media platforms and involved multiple extensions, such as a television series, a mobile application, websites, newspaper advertisements, and social media profiles. The result was massive public participation demonstrating support for the project with an online petition to end fish discarding. In 2013, the parliament voted to ban this wasteful practice, and amend the fishing policies. Nevertheless, it still must be passed into law (Gambarato and Medvedev 2015b).

Therefore, TS is connected to fictional and nonfictional forms, embracing interactivity and participation. Interactivity is a notion in vogue in contemporary communication strategies, and to a certain extent, every computer user seems to be interacting with the computer interface. However, this general assumption is not exactly the focus of interactive storytelling. Jensen's (1998, 201) definition, which considers the user's perspective and the technological dimension, portrays interactivity as "a measure of a media's potential ability to let the user exert an influence on the content and/or form of the mediated communication." The close relationship between the story and the audience is a TS principle.

In interactive stories, such as The Sochi Project, the audience can act/react/interact without interfering with the creation of the narrative, which would characterize participation (Gambarato 2012). It is a matter of choice: the audience decides the path by which the story is experienced. Crawford (2012) considers three main factors involved in the aesthetics of interactivity: (1) speed, (2) depth, and (3) choice. The first is related to the degree of responsiveness of users' actions, the second is about the subject material being significant to the user, and the third is what really matters because the choices should work together to satisfy the audience's needs. The transmedial environment seems the ideal place for interactivity to flourish because "transmedia space appears as a notion that integrates meta- and intercommunicative levels, presuming the interpretation of the same message as the sequence of proto- and metatexts described in different discourses and fixed in different signs systems and media" (Saldre and Torop 2012, 41).

The Sochi Project is referred to as an eximious example of slow journalism (Colberg 2013). Inspired by the slow food movement (Petrini 2007) from the 1980s, in contrast to fast food, slow journalism is, according to Paul Salopek, "the process of reporting at a human pace of three miles an hour" (Osnos 2013). Among multiple facets of journalism, slow journalism is defined by Greenberg as:

> essays, reportage and other nonfiction forms that offer an alternative to conventional reporting, perceived as leaving an important gap in our understanding of the world at a time when the need to make sense of it is greater than ever. The journalistic equivalent of slow food keeps the reader informed about the provenance of the information and how it was gathered. More time is invested in both the production and consumption of the work, to discover things we would not otherwise know, or notice things that have been missed, and communicate that to the highest standards of storytelling craft. (Greenberg 2012, 381–382)

Cooper (2009) describes the 1980s, on the one hand, as "days of 'takeouts,' stories that might take days, weeks, or months to report and that were carefully written and edited for maximum effect magazine style writing for newspapers." On the other hand, she emphasizes that although the slow food movement was ascendant at that very moment, journalism was suffering what "would become the age of 'charticles,' or presentations of news that combined words with data and graphics into a journalistic form" (Cooper 2009). She strongly criticizes "a declining industry moving toward … what? Tidiness? Word Counting? Charticles?" and decrees "the death of slow journalism" (Cooper 2009).

However, Greenberg (2012, 382) stresses the aspect that could perfectly place slow journalism within the contemporary transmedia space: "Often, a defining aspect of the genre is that the story works on more than one level so that the specific subject matter leaves openings to other, more universal themes." That is the case of The Sochi Project. The 2014 Winter Olympic Games open doors to other stories, characters, conflicts, and feelings connected to the Olympics, such as the reality of the neighbouring (largely unrecognized) small state of Abkhazia, where disputes have originated since time immemorial. The unfolding of other extensions of the project takes advantage of the characteristics of different media platforms.

Gerard (2009) summarizes the distinctiveness of slow journalism as follows: it (1) is not focused on beating the competition; (2) values accuracy, quality, and context, not just being fast and first; (3) avoids celebrity and sensationalism; (4) takes time to discover the context; (5) seeks out untold stories; (6) relies on the power of narrative; and (7) sees the audience as collaborators. Dallman (2012) adds that slow journalism is about: (8) longer articles that rely on excellent narratives; (9) taking the time and effort to construct reliable and credible stories; (10) more likely to source information that fast media does not; and (11) embraces the new digital technologies, such as smartphones and tablets. In addition, Le Masurier highlights (12) transparency:

> Slow journalism would lay bare the way stories are reported, by, for example, crediting all sources, being clear about what is original journalism and what is reproduced PR copy, being clear about how information is obtained, and in digital journalism by linking readers to source documents, background research and other relevant stories. (Le Masurier 2015, 142)

Pertinent initiatives of the genre are expressed, for instance, by the Finnish online publication longplay.fi, the American news site salon.com, the global magazine monocle.com, the American and European editions of politico.com, the British magazine *Delayed Gratification*, the Spanish yorokobu.es, the American narrative.ly, and the Dutch decorrespondent.nl.

In the midst of fast-paced media, *churnalism* (Davies 2009, 59), i.e. press release material turned into news, and robot journalism (Fresneda 2015), slow journalism seems to provide information with added value without flirting with Luddism. In addition, this genre is not necessarily attached to traditional media but the opposite: it is aligned with the new possibilities offered by novel technologies.

> The word slow is often associated with print media but a print story is not automatically slow journalism and slow journalism is certainly not limited to just print stories. Slow journalism could equally take the form of an extended online overview on a particular topic covering a longer time period, comment pieces or analyses or even a carefully edited video. The emphasis here is on quality, that particular knack of journalism to tell a good story, to identify the core issues and to present them to the reader in an accessible form. (Kauhala 2013)

Matti Posio, newspaper editor in Finland, states that slow stories are often shared throughout social media networks because these stories help people forge their own identities by doing so. It characterizes the search for more extensive and in-depth content. He concludes that slow journalism could transform media in two ways: "by causing existing products to evolve and by establishing brand new channels" (Kauhala 2013).

The connections between TS and slow journalism start from the focus on the story and the power of narrative. The story is number one and works on multiple levels, or dimensions, creating a dynamic storytelling experience and leaving space for the content to expand across different media platforms. A storyworld is developed to support the expansion of content and multiplicity of media channels. Both TS and slow journalism embrace new technologies (mobile, locative media, for instance) and devices (smartphones, tablets, etc.) to tell compelling stories able to reach a diversified public. The audience engagement is a central point for both to involve the audience as collaborators and create a more valuable experience. In order to do so, more time is invested from the side of authors/producers as well as from the public.

Transmedia Project Design Analytical Model

Although the analytical procedures of TS remain undefined, the analytical model developed by Gambarato (2013) is the method chosen to develop the case study of The Sochi Project because this model contributes to a qualitative understanding of the design process of projects that unfold across multiple media platforms. The model was elaborated in 2013 as a tool to facilitate the analysis of transmedia projects in the fictional and nonfictional realms. For other analyses applying this analytical model see Gambarato (2014) and Gambarato and Medvedev (2015a, 2015b). The structure of the model involves 10 specific topics that are guided by a series of practicable questions. A brief description is presented in Table 1.

The Sochi Project

Premise and Purpose

The Sochi Project, a nonfictional narrative, documents the location at which the 2014 Sochi Winter Olympics take place beginning more than five years before the Games. The project reflects on the transformations of the area and presents a different perspective from the official image portrayed by the Olympic Committee and President Vladimir Putin's propaganda machine. The Sochi Project takes advantage of the inherent characteristics of slow journalism, such as deep research and credible compelling narratives, to engage the audience across multiple media platforms and offers a more purposeful and significant experience. The designer Arthur Herrman, part of the project's team, states that the "long-term approach [of The Sochi Project] contributes to deepen the story. It's a form of *slow journalism* that doesn't show solely *what* is happening but also *why* it's happening. It doesn't avoid complex matters" (Ferri 2014, original emphasis).

The project aims to inform the audience not only about Sochi, the site of the most expensive Olympic Games ever, but also about neighbouring regions, such as Abkhazia, which normally does not attract media attention. Abkhazia declared independence from Georgia in 1999. However, this small and impoverished country is recognized by only five nations, including Russia. In addition, the project also documents the North Caucasus and Chechnya, poor Russian regions stigmatized by Islamist rebels, terrorism, and female suicide bombers. Hornstra states: "If you look a little bit farther than the stadium, you'll see different things. I think it's important for people to know what's going on over there, that it is part of this facade, the Putin show" (Teicher 2014).

Narrative

The geopolitics of the Sochi Winter Olympics is the focus of the narrative. The iDoc is organized into eight chapters: (1) the summer capital, (2) a paradise lost, (3) on

TABLE 1
Concise description of the transmedia project design analytical model

Topic	Practicable questions
1. Premise and purpose State clearly what the project is about and why it exists.	What is the project about? Is it a fiction, nonfiction, or mixed project? What is its fundamental purpose? Is it to entertain, to teach, or to inform? Is it to market a product?
2. Narrative It is the structure that storyworlds evoke in the transmedia milieu.	What are the narrative elements of the project? What is the summary of its storyline? What is the time frame of the story? What are the strategies for expanding the narrative? Are negative capability and migratory cues included? Is it possible to identify intermedial texts in the story?
3. Worldbuilding A storyworld or story universe should be robust enough to support expansions, going beyond a single story.	When does the story occur? Which is the central world where the project is set? Is it a fictional world, the real world, or a mixture of both? How is it presented geographically? Is the storyworld large enough to support expansions?
4. Characters The features of the characters and how they appear across all the platforms should be consistent.	Who are the primary and secondary characters of the story? Does the project have any spinoffs? Can the storyworld be considered a primary character on its own? Can the audience be considered a character as well?
5. Extensions Transmedia storytelling involves multiple media in which the storyworld will unfold and be experienced.	How many extensions does the project have? Are the extensions adaptations or expansions of the narrative through various media? Is each extension canonical? Does it enrich the story? Are the extensions able to spread the content and provide the possibility to explore the narrative in-depth?
6. Media platforms and genres A transmedia project necessarily involves more than one medium and can also embrace more than one genre (science fiction, action, comedy, etc.).	What kind of media platforms (film, book, comics, games, etc.) are involved in the project? What devices (computer, games console, tablet, mobile phone, etc.) are required by the project? How does each platform participate and contribute to the whole project? What are their functions in the project? Is each medium really relevant to the project? What is the rollout strategy to release the platforms? Which genres (action, adventure, detective, science fiction, fantasy, etc.) are present in the project?

(Continued)

TABLE 1. (*Continued*)

Topic	Practicable questions
7. Audience and market Scoping the audience is fundamental for a more appropriate delivery of the transmedia experience. The TS involves some level of audience engagement.	Who is the target audience for the project? What kind of "viewers" (real-time, reflective, and navigational) does the project attract? Do similar projects exist? Do they succeed in achieving their purpose? What is the project's business model? Was the project successful revenue-wise? Why?
8. Engagement All the dimensions of a transmedia project, at a lower or higher level, are drawn into the experience of people when engaging with the story.	Through what point of view does the audience experience this world: first person, second person, third person, or a mixture of them? What role does the audience play in this project? What are the mechanisms of interaction in this project? Is there any participation involved in the project? Does the project work as a cultural attractor/activator? Is there user-generated content related to the story (parodies, recaps, mash-ups, fan communities, etc.)? Does the project offer the audience the possibility of immersion into the storyworld? Does the project offer the audience the possibility to take elements of the story and incorporate them into everyday life? Is there a system of rewards and penalties?
9. Structure The organization of a transmedia project, the arrangement of its constituent elements, and how they interrelate can offer concrete elements for analysis.	When did the transmediation begin? Is it a proactive or retroactive project? Is this project closer to a transmedia franchise, a portmanteau transmedia story, or a complex transmedia experience? Can each extension work as an independent entry point to the story? What are/were possible endpoints of the project? How is the project structured?
10. Aesthetics The visual and audio elements of a transmedia project should also contribute to the overall atmosphere and enhance the experience spread throughout multiple media platforms.	What kinds of visuals are used (animation, video, graphics, a mix) in the project? Is the overall appearance realistic or a fantasy environment? Is it possible to identify specific design styles in the project? How does audio work in this project? Are there ambient sounds (rain, wind, traffic noises, etc.), sound effects, music, and so forth?

the other side of the mountains, (4) always troubled, (5) building the winter capital, (6) the Abkhazian Olympic dream, (7) injustice breeds unrest, and (8) Putin's private project. The chapters describe Russia's summer capital since Soviet times, "its history as the site of a genocide, its development into a tourist destination, and recent changes made in anticipation of the Olympic Games" (Teicher 2014). Homophobic issues, a topic that permeated the 2014 Winter Olympics, are also discussed in the project. The Sochi Project documents the very existence of homosexuals in Sochi, which was completely denied by the authorities, especially the mayor of Sochi, Anatoly Pakhomov, who declared that "there are no gay people in the city [of Sochi]" ("Sochi 2014: No Gay People in City" 2014).

The iDoc is available in Dutch, English, and Russian, and includes text, videos, photos, and hyperlinks to other extensions of the project, such as online publications of books and catalogues. The hyperlinks work as migratory cues to redirect the audience to other expanded parts of the story. Conflicts in the region are alive even now, after the Winter Olympics. Georgia continues to claim that Russia, ahead of the Olympic Games, moved the "border line 11 kilometers deeper into Georgia's breakaway region of Abkhazia" ("Georgia Claims Russia Grabbed Abkhazia Land" 2014). Internally, shortly after the Games, demonstrators stormed the presidential building and demanded the resignation of Abkhaz President Alexander Ankvab due to corruption allegations (Rutland 2014). The story goes on.

Worldbuilding

The storyworld of the project develops around the city of Sochi, in the Krasnodar Krai region of Russia, and neighbouring regions, especially Abkhazia, North Caucasus, and Chechnya. Sochi, a subtropical resort on the Black Sea, was the favourite location for summer holidays for Soviet citizens in the past and remains the favourite among Russians today, although it is no longer affordable for all of them. Sochi was a socialist paradise for the proletariat, the dream of Soviet citizens, and a symbol of all that was good in the Soviet Union: sun, warm temperatures, beach, good food, music, strip clubs, and rest provided by the state. Then Sochi was an inexpensive option for workers, and now is a luxurious place for wealthy Russians.

Sochi is "the Florida of Russia, but cheaper" (Byrnes 2013). Therefore, the site is a peculiar choice to host the Winter Olympic Games. This decision was made by President Vladimir Putin, who spends time at his opulent house in Sochi and stated: "I chose this place personally" (Murray 2014). Hornstra states that "it's Putin's project. The people there, they don't care about these Games. They were complaining about too much traffic, dust, and construction work" (Teicher 2014). Putin, himself a winter sports lover, seems to have used the Olympics to polish his image and distract the world from more serious issues in the country, such as human rights violations (Caryl 2014). As The Sochi Project documents, the Olympic Games was pure propaganda (Gray 2014). The open-air winter sports venue was located in the Caucasus Mountains, 50 kilometres from Sochi, but the indoor stadiums for the Games were built in the city at sea level.

Why Sochi then? This site was not chosen by chance. Several reasons for this controversial choice include the following. (1) The Olympic bid was launched in 2006, when Putin was being heralded as a hero who had conquered the rebels in Chechnya; thus, it would be his triumph over the enemies to have the Olympics in the Caucasus Mountains. (2) After the collapse of the Soviet Union and the historical battles in the Caucasus, the Sochi Olympic Games is an effort to elevate the country's morale. (3) The Olympics ended on 23 February, a symbolic date. On the same day 70 years ago, Joseph Stalin deported Chechens to Siberia, Kirghizstan, and Kazakhstan; genocide ensued (Caryl 2014). Due to all the battles for independence in the region, Hornstra refers to the area as "a black hole on Earth" ("Dutch Journalists Bring Sochi to America" 2014). In this scenario, the storyworld of The Sochi Project is rich and robust enough to support numerous expansions.

To build a world around the story that can provide different entry points to the story universe is a key characteristic of transmedia projects. Slow journalism can benefit from this project-based approach from TS to extend the content and amplify the reach and impact of the story through diversified media platforms and audience engagement.

Characters

The primary character of the project is the storyworld itself: Sochi and the region portrayed across multiple media platforms. The storyworld is inhabited by simple but definitely emblematic personae, such as the singer, the prostitute, the retired worker, the widow, and the wrestling pupils, for instance. Their colours are mixed to compose a portrait of what life is really like in this naturally beautiful and historically troubled part of the world. "It bears little resemblance to the place presented during the Games" ("The Art of Slow Journalism" 2014).

The authors play an essential role in this long-term project because of the subjectivity in telling the stories of the Sochi universe visually. The Sochi Project is the result of the creative and journalistic work of Rob Hornstra (born in Borne, the Netherlands, 1975) and Arnold van Bruggen (born in Texel, the Netherlands, 1979) in association with the design team Kummer & Herrman. Hornstra is a slow-form documentary photographer, and van Bruggen is a writer/filmmaker and founder of the journalistic production agency Prospektor. Various extensions of the project won relevant prizes, such as the New York Photo Book Award 2010; the Magnum Expression Award 2011; the Sony World Photography Award 2012; the World Press Photo Award for Arts & Entertainment Stories 2012; the European Design Awards 2014; and the Canon Prize for Innovative Journalism 2014, among several others.

Extensions

The project involves the online iDoc, printed books, e-books, sketchbooks, catalogues, billboard, newspapers, cards, an exhibition, and social media profiles. The exhibition has travelled to the Netherlands, Canada, the United States, Ireland, Italy, Belgium, Austria, and Spain thus far. An exhibition stop planned for Moscow in 2013 was cancelled because the authors' visa applications to re-enter Russia were rejected. The catalogues *Empty Land* (2011) and *No Fixed Format* (2013) accompany the exhibition. Newspapers are connected to the exhibition as well: *On the Other Side of the Mountains* (2010) and *Paris Photo Newsprint Exhibition* (2012). The *Billboard Sochi Singers (Lilya/Olymp)* (2013), composed of 42 A3 pieces, was also produced. The designer Arnold Herrman explains that a series of sketchbooks was developed because "the 'sketchbooks' were too small for being a *year publication*, but too beautiful not to share, so we decided to start a new smaller series" (Ferri 2014). The series encompasses *Safety First* (2011), *Life Here is Serious* (2012), and *Kiev* (2012).

The final publication of The Sochi Project is the book *An Atlas of War and Tourism in the Caucasus* (2013). Other books are *Sanatorium* (2009), *Empty Land, Promised Land, Forbidden Land* (2010, 2013), and *The Secret History of Khava Gaisanova* (2013). In 2010, The Sochi Project printed a small documentary story displayed as a series of six Christmas cards. The main publications are also available as special editions, most of them finely displayed in boxes.

The Facebook page (https://www.facebook.com/thesochiproject?fref=ts) for The Sochi Project, as the main social media extension, is updated with the latest news about exhibition venues, lectures performed by the authors, links to reports and interviews related to the project, and nominations and prize ceremonies, and had more than 8700 "likes" in February 2015. Therefore, the Facebook page collaborates to keep the project alive, add value to the community interested in the project, and function as a migratory cue to point the audience in the direction of other extensions connected to the project.

Overall, the extensions contribute to expanding the narrative through online and offline platforms, providing the possibility of exploring in-depth dimensions of the story, a key feature of slow journalism and TS. Although all the extensions are canonical (maintain the coherence and respect the logic of the story) and enrich the project, not all necessarily offer new content. For instance, the printed and electronic versions of the books have the same content, and the images incorporated in the iDoc are available in the books and exhibition. In this context, The Sochi Project has also characteristics of crossmedia (Davidson 2010), a broader concept than TS that presupposes the repetition of content in different media platforms. Crossmedia is a more generic term that "includes the whole process of communication and interactivity not restrict to audio-visual industry, and the main difference would be the emphasis of TS on the narrative" (Gambarato 2013, 83). Herrman states that "the storylines of the final publication (*An Atlas of War and Tourism in the Caucasus*), the traveling overview exhibition and the web documentary are largely the same. The experience for each platform, however, is entirely different" (Ferri 2014). The different types of media have their own affordances and limitations, therefore, the transmedia producers/slow journalists should be aware and take advantage of it. To read a book is a different kind of experience than visiting a photo gallery exhibition. Reading is a lively experience for the imagination; visiting an exhibition is a physically immersive experience; and accessing an online documentary offers an audio-visual interactive experience of moving through the story linearly or non-linearly. "In the ideal form of transmedia storytelling, each medium does what it does best" (Jenkins 2006, 96), contributing to a more rewarding experience.

Media Platforms and Genres

As a long-term project that unfolded over more than five years, The Sochi Project incorporated the logic of releasing the story via instalments in print media (books, catalogues, newspapers, cards) and on the internet (e-books and iDoc), with each extension focusing on a particular facet of the people, the geography, and the history of the region. Social media networks are modestly involved in the project. The main role of Facebook, Twitter, and Pinterest is sharing and spreading the word about the project. To facilitate this action, social media buttons are embedded in the documentary website.

The documentation nature of the project is anchored in the specific aspects of the slow journalism genre. "Although not in any way channel-dependent, slow journalism represents a lifeline for one medium in particular: It is an opportunity for print journalism to redefine its role in the world" (Kauhala 2013). The Sochi Project places great emphasis on print media and incorporates digital media well.

The website https://www.thesochiproject.org presents the iDoc, which includes an online shop/donation section. Herrman describes the development of the website as follows:

> Because of its narrative form, it feels like reading a book. It's shaped as a long read divided in eight chapters, ranging from *The Summer Capital* to *Putin's Private Project*. Lots of imagery, audio and video content and detailed maps accompany the stories. Obviously, audio and video make a substantial difference in comparison with printed matter; but the interactivity ensures you that a connection can be made. [The purpose is] [t]o add urgency and importance [and] to make it an experience rather than "just" a story, or a narrative. (Ferri 2014)

Audience and Market

The authors are independent professionals without any links to media corporations and financed the project entirely with small grants and online crowdfunding. The funds came from Dutch institutions, such as Stichting Democratie en Media, Mondriaan Fund, Stichting Sem Presser Archief, Fonds Bijzondere Journalistieke Projecten, and Dutch Culture and Postcode Loterijfonds voor Journalisten. However, the project "has been largely crowdfunded by more than 650 private donators over the years 2009–2013. With individual yearly donations between 10 and 1500 they have made this project possible" (van Bruggen 2013).

Greenberg (2012, 382) suggests that "there appears to be a public appetite for 'slow journalism' when it becomes available," which could justify the successful crowdfunding model used in this case. In the website online shop, in the donation section, the audience can easily donate by adding the amount to the shopping cart. If It Is the first donation, the user is invited to subscribe to The Sochi Project and will be included among the other donors in the list displayed on the website.

The potential audience interested in the project is broad since the Olympic Games are a fascinating topic and Sochi is mostly unknown in Western countries, which could raise curiosity. Nevertheless, the project scale is small, and The Sochi Project is a niche production focused on a community interested in the geopolitical dimension of the Winter Olympics to the exclusion of sports *per se*. From young to mature adults, the target audience is international, especially European countries and the United States. The massive media attention directed at the controversies, allegations of corruption, misleading administration, and homophobic issues, for instance, that surrounded the 2014 Winter Olympics benefited The Sochi Project.

The multiplatform production attracts various kinds of users/viewers, and this is a special bonus for slow journalism, which has the potential for exploration by different audiences. In Murray's (1997) terms, the project comprises real-time (who accessed the content), reflective long term (who followed the entire development of the project), and navigational viewers (who explored the connections between different instalments of the project).

The Sochi Project is not the only initiative to portray the challenges of the region. The project Grozny Nine Cities (http://www.mediapart.fr/documentaire/interna tional/grozny-derriere-la-facade-russe) by Olga Kravets, Maria Morina, and Oksana Yushko, is also a long-term slow journalism production in the transmedia space that explores particular aspects of Grozny, the capital of turbulent Chechnya, including the issues around the Sochi Olympic Games.

Engagement

The mechanisms of interactivity in the iDoc involve the selection of the chapters to be explored; the option to read the text; watch the videos; enlarge and see pho-tographs; access the maps; clink on the hyperlinks and be redirected to other exten-sions of the project, such as e-books; and share information through embedded social media buttons. The maps that contribute to the understanding of the conflicts in the region, for instance, can be shared via Facebook, Twitter, and Pinterest. Photos, includ-ing historical ones, can be easily shared via Facebook and Twitter buttons as well. The project, however, does not presuppose participation, in the sense that the audience cannot co-create and modify the story. Thus, the project functions more as a cultural attractor (being able to congregate a community around the topic depicted in the pro-ject) than a cultural activator (giving this community the opportunity to participate) (Jenkins 2006). Ryan believes interactivity affects narrative discourse and the presenta-tion of the story when:

> the materials that constitute the story are still fully predetermined, but thanks to the text's interactive mechanisms, their presentation to the user is highly variable. Narratologists would say that interactivity operates here on the level of narrative dis-course, as opposed to the level of story. This type of interactivity requires a collection of documents interconnected by digital links, so that, when the user selects a link, a new document comes to the screen. This type of structure is widely known as hypertext. (Ryan 2005)

In addition, among the four modes of interaction (conservational, hitchhiking, par-ticipatory, and experiential) proposed by Gaudenzi (2013, 37–71), The Sochi Project iDoc is predominantly characterized by the hitchhiking mode. The hitchhiking (or hypertext) mode presupposes the rearrangement of a fixed storyline within a closed system:

> What is arguably more essential is an interesting narrative or a well-defined topic for the user to explore. Because the user's personal interest in the topic is often what motivates her to explore, the sense of freedom of action is less significant, and a low level of agency will still make for a satisfying experience. Indeed it may allow the user to concentrate on the content without being overly distracted by navigation. (Gaudenzi 2013, 51–52)

One of the main extensions of The Sochi Project is an offline exhibition, which offers the audience the condition to be immersed into the story by being surrounded by large-scale photographs. However, the audience can extract elements of the story-world, such as printed books, catalogues, and cards, and incorporate them in their everyday life. As a slow journalism project, the story can be experienced in the first-person point of view with the direct narrative of the characters and in third person through the eyes of the narrator.

Structure

The Sochi Project is a proactive transmedia production that from the beginning was planned to spread the story in various instalments. Although the framework was clear, not all the planning was done in advance mainly because of funding limitations, uncertainties, and the story itself, which depended on the reality found *in loco*. Herrman explains the process:

> Not willing to be dependent on grants only and having the idea that there was a crowd out there interested in the stories Rob and Arnold wanted to bring across, we introduced a crowdfunding platform from the very first start. Inspired by the Obama campaign (largely funded with small donations) *we came up with a yearly donation system in three levels*. Referencing the Olympic medals, donors were subdivided in gold, silver and bronze supporters for respectively 10, 100 and 1,000 [actually 1,000, 100, and 10] Euro. (Ferri 2014, original emphasis)

The main extensions of the project are the iDoc, the books, and the exhibition, but the structure started very small with the authors building the visual identity, publishing an introductory newspaper, and launching the website to start the crowdfunding and distribute the first journalistic stories (Ferri 2014). The Sochi Project is a transmedia franchise with each extension functioning as an independent entry point to the storyworld. The endpoint of the project remains open, as the authors intend to return to the region soon. Hornstra comments: "We have seen many more subjects that we want to cover. What we have done is just one chapter in our final project. When the authorities give me the possibility," he says without hesitation, "I'll go back immediately" ("The Art of Slow Journalism" 2014).

Aesthetics

Arthur Herrman and Jeroen Kummer are the designers of the entire project and stress the relevance of The Sochi Project, which "has become a leading model on how to disseminate and present documentaries in a transmedial manner" (Ferri 2014). In addition, Hornstra's photographic approach combines slow journalism with documentary storytelling and portraits. The text, in the iDoc and in most of the books, highlights the use of quotes (in red), which calls attention and emphasizes the first-person point of view of a documentary, bringing intimacy to the experience. Herrman states:

> *"People are trying to organize Winter Games in a subtropical conflict zone"* was one of the very first quotes we've been using. *In terms of communication about the project, this was a very powerful move.* In just one sentence, it summarizes the core of the project: a small yet incredibly complicated region suddenly finds itself in the glare of international media attention. (Ferri 2014, original emphasis)

Text and image coexist as inseparable parts and there are no fixed formats to restrain the organic development of designing the stories (Ferri 2014). The design of each extension emerged from the stories themselves, and the strongest element of unification is the overall subject of the project: "there are some elements contributing to this effort: the use of *bold and penetrating quotes*, the frequent use of *newspaper print* which often very well suited the nature of the stories, and of course the use of *typography*" (Ferri 2014, original emphasis). The materials used in the print media extensions, especially the roughness of newspaper print in contrast to the glossy photo paper, also reinforce the authenticity and (slow) journalistic aura of the project.

Conclusion

The Sochi Project brings to the surface the deeply rooted struggles of a turbulent region historically immersed in disputes for independence, divided by different ethnic groups and religious expression, and relegated to mixed feelings of pride and hopelessness. This multiplatform slow journalism production functions as an appropriate canvas to paint, with a variety of colours, the neglected stories behind Sochi and the odyssey of the Winter Olympic Games in this lost land. The project explores online as well as offline outcomes in order to embrace the diverse facets of the project and the audience, elevating the slow journalism experience. The Sochi Project incorporates the main principles of TS and slow journalism combined: emphasis on the quality of the story, multiple media platforms, expansion of content throughout a storyworld, investment of time for production/consumption, usage of new technologies and devices, the project is neither focused on beating the competition nor on being fast and first, the characters are not celebrities, and the project portrays untold stories. However, the principle of having the audience as collaborators, which is key for TS and slow journalism, is not fully developed in The Sochi Project. The interactive mechanisms used in the project are limited without the full exploration of either interaction or participation. For instance, the maps displayed in the iDoc are crucial for understanding the region, the distances, the neighbours, and the conflicts, but are extremely generic and grey without enough detail. The user can zoom in and out and can share them via social media networks, but that is all. In this case, the maps do not capture the whole potential of interactivity as it could be experienced in other iDocs, such as Bear 71 (http://bear71.nfb.ca) and Farewell Comrades (http://www.farewellcomrades.com). The interactive result is probably closer to what Ingrid Kopp, the director of digital initiatives at New York's Tribeca Film Institute, refers to as "scrollytelling projects" (Cheshire 2014) in the realm of journalism, such as the acclaimed *New York Times* Snow Fall (Branch 2012).

The ability to engage the audience and allow them to participate is underestimated in The Sochi Project and could be improved in future developments. This would help intensify the slow journalism feature of considering "the audience as collaborators" (Gerard 2009) or "a practice of responsible citizenship" (Le Masurier 2015, 149).

Although the authors were arrested multiple times in the North Caucasus, they plan to return: "We want to follow up on specific main characters in the project. We want to see how the region around Sochi is dealing after the games, how it's developing after the games" (Teicher 2014). The potential to continue to unfold the story is a relevant aspect of transmedia spaces that can contribute to the development of slow journalism.

Greenberg (2012, 389) argues about the possible conflict in the realm of journalism regarding the attempt "to offer original and documented writing that aims for a high level of craft" in opposition to "the move into a digital environment … that makes a virtue of its raw and instantaneous nature." This assertion does not apply to the case of The Sochi Project. As the analysis demonstrates, the usage of digital tools does not decrease the high-quality craft of journalism achieved by the project. On the contrary, the online outcomes reinforce the level of in-depth information made available for a diverse audience.

In this context, transmedia strategies combined with slow journalism practices can actually take full advantage of the possibility to offer high-quality content via a digital environment with "a good dose of pleasurable narrative style" (Le Masurier 2015, 149). The Sochi Project exemplifies this trend.

DISCLOSURE STATEMENT

No potential conflict of interest was reported by the author.

REFERENCES

Bernardo, Nuno. 2014. *Transmedia 2.0—How to Create an Entertainment Brand Using a Transmedial Approach to Storytelling* [Kindle version]. Lisbon: BeActive Books.

Branch, John. 2012. "Snow Fall: The Avalanche at Tunnel Creek." *The New York times*, December 21. http://www.nytimes.com/projects/2012/snow-fall/#/?part=tunnel-creek.

van Bruggen, Arnold. 2013. "The Sochi Project." Accessed January 20. https://www.thesochiproject.org/en/about/.

Byrnes, Mark. 2013. "Like the Florida of Russia, but Cheaper." *The Atlantic CityLab*, December 12. http://www.citylab.com/design/2013/12/florida-russia-cheaper/7789/.

Caryl, Christian. 2014. "Why Sochi?" *The New York Review of Books Blog*, February 5. http://www.nybooks.com/blogs/nyrblog/2014/feb/05/why-sochi-russia-olympics/.

Cheshire, Tom. 2014. "Documentary Storytelling with You Directing the Action." *Wired*, July 5. http://www.wired.co.uk/magazine/archive/2014/07/features/docu-storytelling.

Colberg, Jörg. 2013. "The Sochi Project and the Future of Storytelling." *Conscientious Photo Magazine*, October 21. http://cphmag.com/sochi-project-storytelling/.

Cooper, Candy. 2009. "The Death of Slow Journalism." *American Journalism Review*, June 8. http://ajrarchive.org/Article.asp?id=4789.

Crawford, Chris. 2012. *Chris Crawford on Interactive Storytelling*. Indianapolis, IN: New Riders.

Dallman, Deano. 2012. "Slow Journalism—It is Still Relevant?" *Deano Dallman Blog*, November 1. http://deanodallman.wordpress.com/2012/11/01/slow-journalism-is-it-still-relevant/.

Davidson, Drew, ed. 2010. *Cross-media Communications: An Introduction to the Art of Creating Integrated Media Experiences*. Pittsburgh, PA: ETC Press.

Davies, Nick. 2009. *Flat Earth News: An Award-winning Reporter Exposes Falsehood, Distortion and Propaganda in the Global Media*. London: Vintage.

Dutch Journalists Bring Sochi to America. 2014. *Here & Now*, January 16. http://hereandnow.wbur.org/2014/01/16/the-sochi-project.

Ferri, Graziano. 2014. "The Sochi Project—An Interview with Designer Arthur Herrman." *Fotografia Magazine*, February 7. http://fotografiamagazine.com/the-sochi-project-de signers/.

Fresneda, Carlos. 2015. "En Defesa Del Periodismo Sin Prisa." *El Mundo*, February 1. http://www.elmundo.es/television/2015/02/01/54cbad25ca47419e058b4579.html.

Gambarato, Renira R. 2012. "Signs, Systems and Complexity of Transmedia Storytelling." *Estudos Em Comunicação* 12: 69–83.

Gambarato, Renira R. 2013. "Transmedia Project Design: Theoretical and Analytical Considera-tions." *Baltic Screen Media Review* 1: 80–100.

Gambarato, Renira R. 2014. "Transmedia Storytelling in Analysis: The Case of Final Punish-ment." *Journal of Print and Media Technology Research* 3 (2): 95–106.

Gambarato, Renira R., and Sergei Medvedev. 2015a. "Grassroots Political Campaign in Russia: Alexei Navalny and Transmedia Strategies for Democratic Development." In *Promoting Social Change and Democracy through Information Technology*, edited by Jakob Svens-son and Vikas Kumar, 165–192. Hershey: IGI Global.

Gambarato, Renira R., and Sergei Medvedev. 2015b. "Fish Fight: Transmedia Storytelling Strategies for Food Policy Change." *International Journal of E-Politics* 6 (3): 43–59.

Gaudenzi, Sandra. 2013. "The Living Documentary: From Representing Reality to Co-creating Reality in Digital Interactive Documentary." PhD diss., University of London.

Georgia Claims Russia Grabbed Abkhazia Land. 2014. *Aljazeera*, January 21. http://www.al jazeera.com/news/europe/2014/01/georgia-claims-russia-grabbed-abkhazia-land-201412 1173742751456.html.

Gerard, Mark B. 2009. "Tracking the 'Slow Journalism' Movement." *Campfire Journalism Blog*, July 29. http://markberkeygerard.com/2009/07/tracking-the-%E2%80%9Cslow-journal ism%E2%80%9D-movement/.

Gray, Jules. 2014. "Western Scepticism Vs Putin Propaganda: Reporters React to Sochi." *Euro-pean CEO*, April 04. http://www.europeanceo.com/business-and-management/western-scepticism-vs-putin-propaganda-reporters-react-to-sochi/.

Greenberg, Susan. 2012. "Slow Journalism in the Digital Fast Lane." In *Global Literary Journal-ism: Exploring the Journalistic Imagination*, edited by Richard L. Keeble and John Tulloch, 381–393. New York: Peter Lang.

Jenkins, Henry. 2006. *Convergence Culture: Where Old and New Media Collide*. New York: New York University Press.

Jensen, Jens F. 1998. "Interactivity: Tracing a New Concept in Media and Communication Studies." *Nordicom Review* 1 (19): 185–204.

Kauhala, Anna. 2013. "Slow Journalism Spreads Fast." Accessed January 20. http://www.alma media.com/investors/quarterly/Slow-journalism-spreading-fast/.

Le Masurier, Megan. 2015. "What is Slow Journalism?" *Journalism Practice*, 9 (2): 138–152. doi: 10.1080/17512786.2014.916471.

Murray, Janet. 1997. *Hamlet on the Holodeck: The Future of Narrative in Cyberspace*. Cambridge, MA: MIT Press.

Murray, Don. 2014. "The Costly Distraction That is Vladimir Putin's Sochi Olympics." *CBC News*, February 04. http://www.cbc.ca/news/world/the-costly-distraction-that-is-vladi mir-putin-s-sochi-olympics-1.2521816.

Osnos, Evan. 2013. "On Slow Journalism." *The New Yorker*, January 31. http://www.newyorker. com/online/blogs/comment/2013/01/on-slow-journalism.html.

Petrini, Carlo. 2007. *Slow Food Nation*. New York: Rizzoli.

Rutland, Peter. 2014. "Abkhazia's Crisis Not over Yet." *The Moscow times*, June 9. http://www.themoscowtimes.com/opinion/article/abkhazias-crisis-not-over-yet/%20501782.html http://www.themoscowtimes.com/opinion/article/abkhazias-crisis-not-over-yet%20/501782.html.

Ryan, Marie-Laure. 2005. "Peeling the Onion: Layers of Interactivity in Digital Narrative Texts." http://users.frii.com/mlryan/onion.htm.

Saldre, Maarja, and Peeter Torop. 2012. "Transmedia Spaces." In *Crossmedia Innovations: Texts, Markets, Institutions*, edited by Indrek Ibrus and Carlos Scolari, 25–44. Frankfurt: Peter Lang.

"Sochi 2014: No Gay People in City, Says Mayor." 2014. *BBC*, January 27. http://www.bbc.com/news/uk-25675957#TWEET1024869.

Teicher, Jordan G. 2014. "An Uncensored Look at the Real Sochi." *Slate*, February 5. http://www.slate.com/blogs/behold/2014/02/05/rob_hornstra_photographs_changes_to_sochi_russia_in_the_years_leading_up.html.

The Art of Slow Journalism: Rob Hornstra. 2014. *Border Crossings* 130. http://bordercrossingsmag.com/article/the-art-of-slow-journalism.

ORCID

Renira Rampazzo Gambarato ⓘ http://orcid.org/0000-0001-7631-6608

SLOWING DOWN MEDIA COVERAGE ON THE US–MEXICO BORDER
News as sociological critique in *Borderland*

Stuart Davis

This article argues that though loosely configured and encapsulating a variety of approaches, the "slow journalism" movement offers a useful set of techniques and tools for critiquing the way print and television news currently represents the US–Mexico border. Working against the sensationalism and lack of introspection in contemporary news media, slow journalism advocates champion projects that focus on developing innovative techniques for providing deeper coverage of social issues. Drawing on Borderland: Dispatches from the US–Mexico Border, *a multimedia collaboration launched by National Public Radio's (NPR) Morning Edition staff and the Center for Investigative Reporting (CIR) in 2014, I will address the interaction between two complementary "slow" strategies: an ethnographic strategy that draws heavily on extensive interviews with individuals whose everyday lives are affected by border issues and an analytical strategy featuring visualizations created by processing large datasets related to annual seizure figures, ownership information, and demographics of border crossers Drawing on content analyses of newspapers and television programs on the US–Mexico border, in-depth interviews with staff members from NPR and the CIR, and a visual/textual analysis of the* Borderland *website, I hope to advance a strategy that incorporates multiple genres of journalistic coverage together in order to deepen and sharpen news' investigative potential.*

Introduction

Anxieties around the US–Mexico border weigh prominently in contemporary news media within the United States. Between 2010 and 2014, the number of print news stories by local, regional, and national newspapers referencing issues related to the US–Mexico border (including topics ranging from illegal immigration, corruption, and political violence by trafficking cartels in border areas to military and Drug Enforcement Agency initiatives) numbered over 200,0000 (The Opportunity Agenda 2014). Furthermore, in the last five years there have been three reality television series focusing exclusively on the border (ABC's *Homeland Security USA*, 2009; National Geographic's *Border Wars*, 2010; and A&E's *Bordertown: Laredo*, 2011), as well as special episodes of news and reality programs ranging from *20/20* to the "extreme documentary" series *Vice* on HBO. Characterized by sensationalist storytelling, a heavy focus on controversial themes like illegal immigration and organized crime, and a disproportionate reliance on official or police sources, a significant amount of media coverage of the border follows a similar formula albeit with certain medium-specific differences (Andreas 2000; Branton and Dunaway 2009a, 2009b).

Sifting through these layers of media coverage, this article discusses a recent project that utilizes storytelling practices resonant with the growing "slow journalism" movement (Greenberg 2007; Le Masurier 2015) to complicate and deepen how audiences conceptualize border issues. Analyzing audiovisual storytelling strategies in *Borderland: Dispatches from the US–Mexico Border*, a 2014 multi-platform collaboration between National Public Radio's (NPR) *Morning Edition* program and the Center for Investigative Reporting (CIR), I argue that this type of project mobilizes some of the key elements of the recent "slow journalism" movement in order to promote a deeper and more sustained form of engagement between media source and audience. Through this project I hope to create a conversation around how the aesthetic strategies of the slow movement might be adapted to create a more complex model for advocacy or social change-oriented news production—a pressing issue given the ever-growing number of sensationalistic or melodramatic stories published or aired about the border region.

Launched between March 18 and April 10, 2014 and based around a two-week driving tour, from Brownsville, Texas, to San Diego, California, undertaken by *Morning Edition* host Steve Inskeep and crew, *Borderland* addresses a range of social, political, and economic issues experienced by individuals living in this region. Typically centering on a single individual, the stories address both social issues like the perils of illegal immigration and human-interest topics such as street food in cities or popular festivals that bring together communities on each side of the border. The main stories are presented in the typical NPR format of five- to seven-minute segments read by a narrator supplemented by direct quotes. The website, however, offers multiple other layers of information and experience to users. Created in collaboration with the San Francisco-based CIR, the website offers a series of innovative features including personal photos and artifacts provided by individuals interviewed, a highly detailed series of maps showing the historical evolution of the US–Mexico border fence created using a combination of satellite imaging, digitized maps dating back to the early twentieth century, and census and other demographic information generated onto maps using geographical imaging systems (GIS), and a timer that tracks the number of legal versus illegal entries and quantities of cocaine and marijuana seized during the time the user has been on the site. As a collaborative creation between *Morning Edition* staff and the CIR, the site combines material intended to both deepen personal stories and provide quantitative data to back up assertions made in the stories regarding drug seizures, nationality of border crossers, and other issues.

Slow Journalism as Sociological Critique: Triangulating Ethnographic and Analytical Elements

Before analyzing how *Borderland* distances itself from other forms of media coverage of border issues through adopting strategies resonant with the "slow journalism" movement, this emergent and yet-to-be heavily theorized concept must be unpacked

Coined by British journalist and academic Susan Greenberg in 2007, slow journalism has generally been conceptualized as an extension of the Slow Food movement (Le Masurier 2015). Established in the 1980s as part of a larger critique of the potential impact of American mass culture, the Slow Food movement argues that the increasing global popularity of pre-packaged and fast food risks destroying local food traditions (Petrini 2007). Extending that movement's critique to news, advocates of slow journalism are highly critical of the sensationalism, lack of investigative reporting, and reduction of complex stories into tiny sound bites that characterizes the contemporary global news environment. In response, these supporters call for the expansion of a subsection of the journalism market reserved for material of high literary or aesthetic value: "At the luxury end, there should be a growing market for essays, reportage and other non-fiction writing that takes its time to find things out, notices stories that others miss, and communicates it all to the highest standards" (Greenberg 2007, 15). In essence, she is arguing for an aesthetic alternative to the kind of "junk food" journalism dominating print, television, and online news).

Moving beyond theorizations of the aesthetic function of slow journalism, we can see within this new practice the potential to utilize the extra time and space to produce a form of "news as sociological knowledge" resonant with the theories of the Chicago School of Sociology. Drawing on the city's urban spaces as "laboratories for investigating macro-level social issues embedded in the minutia of everyday life" (Robert E. Park, as quoted in Marx 2002, 109), researchers launched a series of in-depth studies from the 1920s to the 1940s examining immigrant life in urban slums, juvenile street gangs in downtown areas, and other problematic urban issues of the day (Rogers 1997). Often combining intensive ethnographic fieldwork aimed at producing life stories and a detailed mapping process aimed at integrating the qualitative material with census and other survey data on the ethnic and socio-economic breakdown of the city, the Chicago School bridged *ethnographic* and *analytical* approaches. In "News as a Form of Knowledge," Robert E. Park (1940), considered one of the intellectual architects of the school, posits these two types of investigation in terms of "knowledge of" and "knowledge about." The first ("knowledge of") refers to the production of deeper understanding about a population through life histories, extensive oral interviews, and participant observation. The second ("knowledge about") relates to the processing of triangulating ethnographic information into theoretical positions or postulates by incorporating a quantitative approach (Park 1940). Later studies in this tradition, like Gary Marx's *Muckraking Sociology: Research as Social Criticism*, formulate this dual aim in terms of "detailed documentation and the use of the analytical tools of social science to investigate in everyday life the consequences of social action inequality, poverty, racism, exploitation, opportunism, neglect, and denial of dignity" (Marx 1972, 3). Importantly for our discussion, Park and colleagues advocated this dual approach for news media as well as academic inquiry. For Park (himself a former journalist), the application of a social scientific approach to news productions was crucial in re-modeling how citizens understand information. In *The City*, he explicitly connects research with strengthening journalistic coverage:

> The real reason that the ordinary newspaper accounts of the incidents of ordinary life are so sensational is because we know so little of human life that we are not able to interpret the events of life when we read them. (Park and Burgess [1925] 1984, 97–98)

Adapting a social scientific methodology for journalism strengthens the quality and analytical precision of news stories.

Borderland utilizes a combination of the ethnographic/"knowledge of" and analytical/"knowledge about" approaches in a manner resonant with the Chicago School. Without compartmentalizing the contributions of both organizations into strict categories, each strongly exhibits resonant characteristics. The Morning Edition element offers interviews and personalized vignettes designed to deepen the listener/viewer's conceptualization of the US–Mexico border through exposure to individual's life stories (Inskeep 2014; National Public Radio 2014). CIR's contribution to Borderland consisted of a series of interactive visuals created through processing expansive datasets. Ranging from the real-time border crossing/drug seizure counter to a multi-layered map illustrating the physical composition of every section of the border wall, these visuals served to reinforce the stories' claims to the complexity of the border region as a human, economic, political, and cultural ecosystem (A. Becker, personal communication, September 2, 2015).

Read through the optic of slow journalism as sociological critique, the experience presented by projects like Borderland can be seen as a pedagogical tool where the anecdotal, personalized elements of Morning Edition are reinforced by the data-driven contributions of the CIR. Working in unison, they offer a complicated picture of the border region that could potentially begin to dismantle stereotypes that often color how audiences understand sociological questions including poverty, crime, immigration, and violence in this region.

Research Approach

In order to discuss how these "ethnographic" and "analytical" elements are deployed within the Borderland project, I draw on a qualitative case study approach combining focused interviews with NPR and CIR staff members responsible for creating the project and a textual analysis of the interactive website. The interview guide is divided into two sets of questions related to the "technical" and "conceptual" background of the project. Technical questions spoke to issues related to the division of labor and responsibility in the production process, choices of certain technologies over others, and the popularity of this type of multi-media production within each of the organizations. The conceptual questions were more specifically directed towards elaborating participants' views regarding the position of the US–Mexico border in the American cultural and political imaginary, media representations of the area, and the potential role of Borderland in re-orienting general conceptions of the border. The textual analysis component analyzes the Morning Edition and CIR portions of the site through the critical literature on the genre each of these approaches represents. I will argue that the Morning Edition elements are resonant with a genre of personalized, anecdotal journalism in line with shifts in post-World War II American journalism away from objectivity and reportage towards interpretation (Barnhurst 2003; Schudson 1982). The CIR contributions resonate with computational, quantitative elements of the burgeoning data journalism sub-field (Mair and Keeble 2014).

My discussion also relies on data generated by other sources. The discussion in the next section draws on content analyses of border newspapers conducted by the

Observatory of Culture and Lawfulness at the Monterrey Technological Institute and by the Texas A&M International MA Program in Latin American and Border Media Studies. Furthermore, my discussion of *Morning Edition*'s role in the project cites at length interviews with Steve Inskeep conducted with other media outlets in 2014 and available through their sites. Finally, the conclusion cites analytics from the *Borderland* site generated by NPR staff and shared with me for the purposes of writing this piece.

An Overview of Representations of the Border in Print and Television Media

The innovative approach adopted by *Borderland* diverges drastically from the kind of coverage offered by mainstream American news outlets. Though multi-generational research projects conducted within trans-border metropolitan regions including El Paso–Ciudad Juarez (Collin 2011; Ortiz-Gonzalez 2003), San Diego–Tijuana (Florida 2014), and Laredo–Nuevo Laredo (Kilburn, Miguel, and Kwak 2013) have illustrated a long history of economic, cultural, and political linkages, contemporary media coverage largely focuses on the sensationally violent struggle between American law enforcement and Mexican organized crime. Content analyses of print and broadcast news media over the last 15 years present findings that corroborate this idea of the border. For example, a study by Branton and Dunaway of over 1500 news stories from California newspapers in 2004 and 2005 found that newspapers spatially proximate to the California–Baja California border feature a very high volume (25–30 occurrences per month) of articles on "negative aspects of immigration" including illegal immigration, violence related to drug trafficking, and political corruption of border officials (Branton and Dunaway 2009b, 289–290). Using a similar set of composite measures for "negative aspects," Lozano Rendon et al. (2015) find resonant patterns in border newspapers in McAllen, Brownsville, and other Texas border cities. A study by the Observatory of Culture and Lawfulness at the Monterrey Institute of Technology published similar findings regarding coverage by US and Mexican newspapers in border cities (Lozano Rendon et al. 2012). Beyond the generally high levels of coverage of "negative aspects," another significant aspect pointing to the rise of the military border apparatus is the *heavy reliance on official sources* in print and television coverage. In their content analysis, Lozano Rendon et al. (2015) found that less 5 percent of the stories they found covering "negative aspects" actually included citations from anyone other than a police, immigration, or border patrol official. In a 2014 content analysis of media coverage specifically related to the immigration of unaccompanied children that sampled *The New York Times*, *USA Today*, and other heavily distributed papers, the advocacy organization Opportunity Agenda found that residents comprised less than 1 percent of sources cited in national papers and 29 percent in regional papers. While it is impossible to give a definitive prognosis given the huge potential sample, these reports suggest that border coverage in print news is largely focused on negative aspects of immigration and that most newspapers draw their source information from some form of public official or security agent.

Recent reality television programs like A&E's *Bordertown: Laredo* and HBO's *Witness* depict the border and its cities in an even more sensationalistic and melodramatic fashion. Both programs pitch themselves as insider looks at what it is "really like" in border cities (Laredo, Texas, for *Bordertown* and Ciudad Juarez, Chihuahua for *Witness*). However, this claim to capture what it is "really like" is already heavily shaded by the occupations of the shows' respective protagonists: one focuses on a detective working in an anti-narcotics task force and the other on a photojournalist embedded with the Mexican Army's anti-gang unit. *Bordertown*, which debuted in 2011 and was canceled after one season due in part to local protests, creates a vision of Laredo, Texas, that resonates closely with how international relations theorists like Achille Mbembe (2001) describe failed states: public security has broken down in this "city under siege" (as promotional materials for the show labeled it), citizens live in a constant state of fear due to the spillover of drug-related violence, and the only way to preserve lawfulness is through a series of increasingly over the top and constitutionally ambiguous police raids on drug stash houses conducted by the Laredo Police Department's narcotics enforcement unit. As the show bounces from raid to raid, the only reference point to let viewers know that the show is set in Laredo is a long shot of the US–Mexico Bridge in the opening credits; the rest of the show exists wholly in the world of the police raids (Gonzalez 2014). Though *Witness* purports to offer a ground-level view of everyday citizens suffering because of the decades-long cycle of violence in Ciudad Juarez, its fascination with the breakdown of public security mirrors that of *Borderland*. The show is centered on Eros Hoagland, a photojournalist famous for his work embedded with military battalions and police contingents in Iraq, Afghanistan, and other areas with extreme security issues (Kamber 2013). Though the point of the show is to present the impressions of the everyday people Hoagland meets through his work, it constantly frames their narratives in terms of Hoagland's own experience of traveling with a military battalion to investigate gang activity. Unsurprisingly, the contributions of everyday citizens reinforce Hoagland's own description of the warzone qualities of the city. Though they focus on different cities, both programs fall neatly within what Mexican activist Sergio Gonzalez Rodriguez (2009, 21) calls "the 'Gringo Formula' for Mexico: a coupling of yellow journalism and extreme tourism."

Borderland: Interweaving Ethnographic and Analytical Approaches

If mainstream print and television coverage of border issues is governed by sensational aesthetics, what form might a potential counter-strategy take? Attempting to speak back to dominant media sources of the print and audiovisual kind discussed earlier in this article, *Borderland* directly addresses popular conceptualizations of the border itself. In the introduction to the first segment from March 19, 2014, host Inskeep offers a very different picture of the border than the type propagated by mainstream media:

> Many people think of the *Borderland* as a single region—north and south—linked by history, trade and often by blood ties. Of course the two sides of the border are different in many ways, but they were bound by a single shared experience, the border itself. We will hear their stories in days to come. (Inskeep 2014)

Without directly attacking or critiquing dominant trends in border coverage of the media, he sets up *Borderland* to address a different objective: offering a complex and historically informed view of the economics, culture, and politics of regions on both sides. In order to expand the listener's experience of the border as "a constantly shifting, living organism," the project augments radio segments with an interactive website. As key participants from both NPR and CIR point out in interviews, the central target of *Borderland* was the *body of preconceptions* about the US–Mexico border (Inskeep 2014; K. Amaria, personal correspondence, August 30, 2015). In this pursuit, each of the organizations adopts a different approach. For *Morning Edition* staff, the goal is to curate personal stories about life on the border in a way that helps familiarize and personalize macro-level issues (Inskeep 2014). For the CIR, the goal is to provide quantitative data to back claims made through the anecdotal vignettes (A. Becker, personal communication, August 22, 2015). From the beginning, the project was conceptualized as a collaborative endeavor between these two different sets of journalists with different skills. Before conducting any of the interviews for the radio program, *Morning Edition* staff reached out to the CIR to start planning the site (K. Amaria, personal correspondence, August 30, 2015). As the project developed to fruition, a team of 11 journalists from NPR and four from the CIR (with data visualization expert Michael Corey acting as a bridge between both groups) worked together to coordinate the contributions of each team (National Public Radio 2014). The next two sections will describe in detail some of the cardinal contributions of the *Morning Edition* and CIR journalists to *Borderland*.

Morning Edition *and the Documentation of the "Living Border".* The radio segments and audiovisual materials presented by *Morning Edition* follow the model established over the program's 35-year tenure. As Barnhurst (1994, 2003), Schudson (1982), and others have argued, the growing prominence of NPR within the American journalism industry points to a shift towards a more reporter/presenter-centered, interpretative approach to reporting where standards of objectivity and detachment are replaced by personal investment. The overarching architecture of *Borderland* works closely within this model as the project is introduced as reflections and insights presented by Inskeep and colleagues, reflecting their trip along the border. The segments themselves are consistently framed through personal interactions between NPR staff and participants. Topics under discussion range from lighter stories about the history of the Alamo as a tourist site or the popularity of the heavy metal band Fix to more serious fare addressing the militarization of border towns and cities, diffuse fears over drug-related violence, and the physical and psychological difficulties facing illegal immigrants. Regardless of topic, each story is presented in a highly personalized manner that focalizes the issue under discussion on a single individual or group through extensive use of quotes and personal reflections—a practice that embodies *Morning Edition*'s mantra of "people not policy" (K. Amaria, personal correspondence, August 30, 2015).

The website reinforces the stories presented in the audio segments (though it is possible to read and understand the site without recourse to the radio stories). Each of the 11 sections (listed completely in Appendix A) corresponds to a discrete element of the border experience. The most direct translation of the interpretative approach to reporting comes in sections of the site that retell the first-person narratives from the radio broadcasts in visual language. The first section sharpens personal narratives as part of a larger critical project. The first story, titled "Just Getting There," offers a potent example of this technique. It focuses on Inskeep's discovery of and first meeting with Saraa Zewedi Yilma, an Ethiopian asylum seeker caught while trying to cross illegally into the United States in Brownsville, Texas. Told through a series of slides featuring photographs and figures, the story lays out her entire journey from Ethiopia to Brownsville. The lynchpin slide for the whole story is a flow chart visualization of Saraa's journey (Figure 1).

As the foundation for the entire story, this image captures the cost and geographical expansiveness of immigration. First, it shows that for this immigrant the "easy route" cost a significant amount of money. The flow chart then tracks the progress from nation to nation through northern Africa, South America, Central America, and Mexico. The website diagrammatically reinforces the narrative presented in the radio story in a subtle yet crystalline critique of media portrayals.

While less anchored to a first-person storytelling approach, the use of photographic portraiture in numerous sections re-iterates tropes of familiarity and intimacy. The fourth section, entitled "What is it Like?," most heavily utilizes this approach. This section contains 12 images of individuals representing different socio-economic, cultural, and professional demographics ranging from teenagers preparing for their *quinceanera* to border patrol and customs agents to ranchers. Each picture is accompanied by a quote from the individual pictured. Most of the portraits focus on *the familiarization of the precarious*.

Figure 2 features Ralph Cowen, the US Port Commissioner for Brownsville, Texas, standing in front of his home with a quotation reading "People have this idea that this part of the country is full of drugs and violence, but every day, moms take their kids to soccer, people go to work, go to church..." (National Public Radio 2014). The contrapuntal relationship between the precarious "official role" of this individual as a law enforcement official and the visual and narratively disarming nature of the portrait hints at the complex and often mundane character of life on the border. Other portraits in this section also serve a familiarizing function as they provide snapshots of everyday life below the level of public policy or mainstream media coverage.

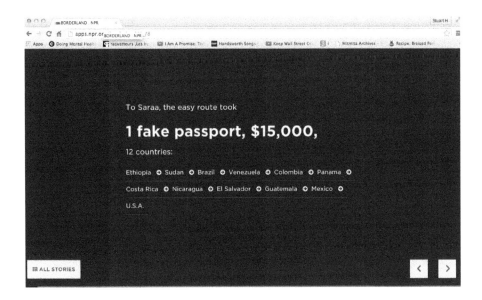

FIGURE 1
This slide from "Just Getting There" visualizes Saraa's trip from Ethiopia to Brownsville

FIGURE 2
This slide from "What is it Like?" illustrates the portraiture style of the section

Perhaps the most ambitious example of *Borderland*'s strategy for drawing on detailed accounts of individual experience to raise larger social queries comes through the use of embedded home videos produced in coordination with participants from the stories. Shot in a style reminiscent of amateur media (cf. Zimmerman 1995), these films feature characters from the radio stories talking about their lives within intimate settings. These segments, which often supplement the stories, present a more personalized version of the radio stories. For example, the section "Junior's Story" is composed entirely of a video created by Junior, a teenager born in Mexico but living illegally in Anthony, Texas, whose father was caught engaging in criminal activities and was permanently deported. Drawing on Junior's personal history, the video attempts to capture some of the feelings experienced by teenagers growing up in border areas with families and identities split between the United States and Mexico.

Giving Junior the space to tell his story captures the ambivalent situation facing some living in the US–Mexico border areas. He is caught in a series of double binds. Though seeking asylum, he cannot leave the United States because he would not be able to return. At the same time, his father and a large number of his extended family members are on the other side of the border. This feeling of being in-between also translates into Junior's aspirations: he feels caught between a desire to stay in the United States and continue his education and the emotional difficulty of dealing with the stereotypes and prejudice that come with being an illegal alien in a border community (Figure 3).

The Center for Investigative Reporting: The Analytical Approach. If *Morning Edition* offers the ethnographic component of *Borderland*, the visual materials provided by the CIR provide the analytical or synthetic element that incorporates the narratives into a more directed and pointed political critique (A. Becker, personal communication, August 26, 2015). For the CIR, the *Borderland* collaboration resonates with the group's larger professional and aesthetic strategies. On an operational level, the group's

FIGURE 3
In this video capture from "Junior," Junior shows the camera a family portrait. A central element of this story is the emotional difficulty of having family members living on both sides of the border

approach to investigative journalism reflects central concerns of slow journalism by privileging the production of a smaller number of laboriously researched pieces instead of a steady flow of short pieces published or posted at a more rapid rate. According to staff members, this approach leverages the group's unique structure where each of the reporters or analysts are first encouraged to become specialists in a few topical areas and then allowed the opportunity to write a few heavily researched stories in that area. Recognizing that it will never be able to compete with larger news outlets, wire services, or news sites in the market of breaking coverage, the group instead focuses on producing fewer stories generally crafted through a combination of extensive background research, the processing of large amounts of data, collaboration with journalists and concerned citizens in areas covered by stories, and distribution of materials used in producing the story (public records, policy reports, etc.) for readers to peruse (M. Corey, personal communication, September 20, 2015). As its stories are often constructed through the processing of data, the organization might be more suitably characterized as a type of media observatory that analyzes large swathes of data in order to track trends or expose new correlations than a traditional news outlet (e.g. Schudson 2008).

Reflecting on the CIR's role in *Borderland*, project lead Andrew Becker connects it to recent CIR projects aimed at "demystifying popular myths" about law enforcement on the US–Mexico border (A. Becker, personal communication, August 26, 2015). Before participating in the Borderland collaboration, the CIR launched an exposé on drug busts in Texas. Created by Becker (the CIR's border and homeland security specialist), G. W. Schulz, and staff from *The Daily Beast*, the project began when Becker and a team of data analysts processed six years' worth of arrest records obtained from US Customs and Border Protection using the Freedom of

Information Act. While processing raw data, they noticed that a disproportionate number of individuals arrested and booked for illegal narcotics were American citizens (Becker, Schulz, and Ghose 2013). The reporters then analyzed press releases from Customs and Border Protection to address a potential correlation between the number of Americans arrested and the frequency of these arrests being mentioned in press releases. They found that despite the high number of American citizens being arrested, press releases referenced the arrest of Mexican nationals at a disproportionately higher rate. Based on this data, the piece argued that public officials and security forces working in border regions needed to substantiate their press releases and media relations with a closer analysis of the data at hand.

In *Borderland*, the CIR's central contribution came through helping the NPR team *connect* personal narratives about individuals living in the border region to larger arguments about the complexity of life on the border and the general lack of public understanding about the region. In this pursuit, they created three visualizations that were interwoven into the stories presented on the site. The first, a multi-layered map of the history of the border, is connected to the site's second section, "Why the Border is Where it is." Produced through combining a series of maps going back to when Mexico achieved independence from Spain in 1821 and ending with the Gasden Purchase in 1852, the map illustrates the evolution of the border in order to refute the notion that the present border between the United States and Mexico is eternal and unchangeable (M. Corey, personal communication, September 20, 2015). "Fence Facts," the next section of the website, further complicates the "naturalness" of the border by illustrating how different the actual border fence is in different areas. Created by combining images from OpenStreetMap and Google Maps with images taken by staff photographers, this section offers a visual catalogue of the different types of "fence" along the border as well as a map of the entire border area with the areas covered by an actual physical fence shaded in Figure 4.

These images and maps are used together to reiterate the impossibility of referring to or creating a single "fence" along the border.

The third visualization is a "border counter" used to introduce the site (Figure 5). Drawing on algorithms created by dividing the 2013 annual statistics on human and commercial border traffic taken from Customs and Border Patrol and the Department of Transportation by the number of seconds in a year, the counter presents a real-time depiction of border crossing and enforcement. Once opening the site, the counter begins to track how many vehicles and individuals have crossed the border, how many arrests for illegal entry have been made, and how much cocaine and marijuana have been seized during the time the user has been on the site.

Figure 5 gives an example of the counter after approximately two minutes on the site. While local newspapers might dedicate a front-page story and reality shows like *Bordertown: Laredo* an entire segment to a cocaine or marijuana seizure, the border counter here reflects 14 pounds of marijuana and two ounces of cocaine being seized in two minutes. The counter is designed to emphasize the *repetitive nature* of border security and governance (A. Becker, personal communication, August 22, 2015). By observing the frequency at which these events occur on the border, the user gets an idea about how routine these activities actually are.

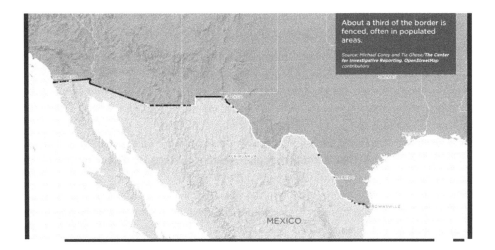

FIGURE 4
This slide from "Fence Facts" contains a map showing the relatively small amount of the border "fence" that is actually covered by a physical fence. This illustration was created through aggregating a large number of images of different sections of the border fence taken from OpenStreetMap onto a single map

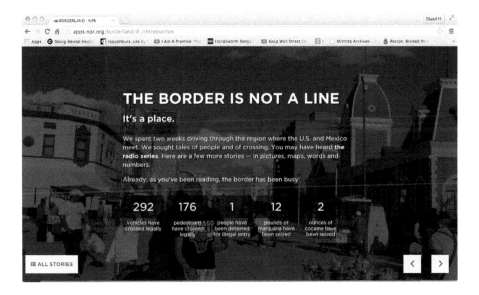

FIGURE 5
The border counter from the introductory slide of *Borderland* tracks the number of pedestrians and vehicles crossing, number of people detained, and amount of marijuana and cocaine seized while the viewer was on the site. The screen capture was taken after approximately two minutes on the site

These three visualizations (especially the border counter) help demonstrate the CIR's role in the project. By presenting data in an innovative way, it reinforces the anecdotal or personalized information provided by *Morning Edition*'s stories.

Borderland *and Slow Journalism: Innovation and the Problem of Cultural Change Within News Production and Consumption*

Moving out from a discussion of *Borderland* to think about its position within the forms of border media coverage described in the earlier sections of this article, we can see innovations related to content and professional practice. In terms of content, *Borderland* shows how two very different approaches to slow journalism might work together to enhance the impact of each. Both have a distinctive strategy: *Morning Edition* attempts to familiarize audiences through personalized stories while the CIR breaks down data into ways that critique popular misconceptions. However, together they serve a similar purpose in problematizing popular myths about crime, violence, drugs, and security on the border. Returning to the idea of slow journalism as a form of sociological investigation, we can see each component drawing on a different methodological approach. The *Morning Edition* team draws on qualitative tools including open-ended questions and maximal room for respondents to guide the conversation during interviews. These represent an inductive approach to the border issues under examination: narratives or arguments about border issues are constructed from the bottom up around the complicated experience of the participants. The CIR utilizes a deductive approach that processes large datasets into clear and concise visualizations like the border fence composition map and the border ticker. The symbiotic interaction between the two resembles the process of *triangulation* in academic research (Lazega 1997; Lindlof and Taylor 2011) where the "depth" of qualitative methodology (the richness of lived experience it can capture) is combined with the "breadth" of quantitative methodology (its ability to apply formulas to enormous amounts of data in order to create legible patterns) to strengthen the arguments of each. Triangulating between both of these reinforces *Borderland*'s central argument regarding the complexity of political, economic, and cultural life in the US–Mexico border region.

While this project offers innovative strategies for cultivating a sociological focus in news reporting, questions of reception or audience response raise potential issues. More specifically, problems with legibility could arise when audiences are faced with a multimedia interface and storytelling approach radically different from current conventions or norms. During interviews, NPR staff members registered concern about the potential that the complexity of the website as compared to the radio broadcasts might potentially confuse or disorient casual readers. Christopher Grosskeep, the lead visual design specialist from NPR working on the project, raises this concern through the problem of "context switching":

> If the transitions aren't especially clear we can lose readers at those moments we force them to "context switch." We've collected extensive analytics on our slide-based projects and what we've found is that for many stories there are "drop off" points where we abruptly lose a large number of folks. Sometimes these occur in sync with the audio, but in *Borderland* it was the video where this was a problem. We lost a much larger number of users on the video slide than at any other single point in the story— probably because we did a poor job setting up the expectation that there would be video in the story and communicating to the user why the experience had suddenly changed so drastically. (Personal correspondence, September 11, 2015)

Though in this case he was speaking specifically about the drop in viewership during the video portion of the "Junior" segment, this issue reflects a larger problem for slow journalism practitioners. If audiences are used to consuming news in a certain fashion, a radical departure from this formula risks creating disorientation. The problem becomes one of cultural change within the news industries. As Schudson (1982) and other scholars who interrogate the institutional and industrial history of American journalism argue, certain professional standards and practices calcify as an industry matures. Breaking away from these calcified habits provides both the aesthetic and political challenge of slow journalism of the kind outlined here. However, anchoring it between the more normalized form of anecdotal storytelling popularized by NPR and the experimental tendencies of Web-based journalism and data visualization presented by the *Borderland* site might offer one way to bridge both the old and the new.

DISCLOSURE STATEMENT

No potential conflict of interest was reported by the author.

REFERENCES

Andreas, Peter. 2000. *Border Games: Policing the US-Mexico Divide*. Ithaca, NY: Cornell University Press.

Barnhurst, Kevin. 1994. *Seeing the Newspaper*. New York: St. Martin's Press.

Barnhurst, Kevin. 2003. "The Makers of Meaning: National Public Radio and the New Long Journalism, 1980-2000." *Political Communication* 20: 1–22. doi:10.1080/10584600390172374.

Becker, Andrew, G. W. Schulz, and Tia Ghose. 2013. "Four out of Five Border Patrol Busts Involve US Citizens, Records Show." The Center for Investigative Reporting. http://cironline.org/reports/four-five-border-patrol-drug-busts-involve-us-citizens-records-show-4312

Branton, Regina, and Johanna Dunaway. 2009b. "Spatial Proximity to the US- Mexico Border and Newspaper Coverage of Immigration Issues." *Political Research Quarterly* 62: 289–302. doi:10.1177/1065912908319252.

Branton, Regina, and Johanna Dunaway. 2009a. "Slanted Newspaper Coverage of Immigration: The Importance of Economics and Geography." *Policy Studies Journal* 37 (2): 62–79. doi:10.1111/j.1541-0072.2009.00313.x.

Collin, Martina. 2011. *Entre el sueno y la Pesadilla: La Frontera Ciudad Juárez-El Paso*. [Between the dream and the nightmare: The Ciudad Juárez-El Paso border]. Querátero, Mexico: Editorial Endira.

Florida, Richard. 2014. *From Border Barriers to Bi-National Futures*. Toronto, CA: Creative Class Reports.

Gonzalez, Ariadne. 2014. "*Bordertown Laredo*: Manufacturing Mexicanness in Reality Television." In *How Television Shapes Our Worldview: Media Representations of Social Trends and Changes*, edited by Deborah Macey and Kathleen Ryan, 228–240. Lanham, MD: Rowman and Littlefield.

Gonzalez Rodriguez, Sergio. 2009. *The Femicide Machine*. New York: Semiotext(e) Foreign Agents Series.

Greenberg, Susan. 2007. "Slow Journalism," *Prospect*, February 25, 2007. http://www.prospectmagazine.co.uk/opinions/slowjournalism

Inskeep, Steve. 2014. "Introduction to *Borderland*: Dispatches from the US-Mexico Border." http://www.npr.org/series/291397809/Borderland-dispatches-from-the-u-s-mexico-boundary

Kamber, Michael. 2013. *Photojournalists on War: The Untold Stories from Iraq*. Austin, TX: University of Texas Press.

Kilburn, John, Claudia San Miguel, and Dae Hoon Kwak. 2013. "Is Fear of Crime Splitting the Sister Cities? The Case of Los Dos Laredos." *Cities: The International Journal of Urban Policy and Planning* 34: 30–36. doi:10.1016/j.cities.2012.11.00

Lazega, Emmanuel. 1997. "Network Analysis and Qualitative Research: A Method of Contextualization." In *Context and Method in Qualitative Research*, edited by Gale Miller and Robert Dingwall, 119–134. Thousand Oaks, CA: Sage Publications.

Le Masurier, Megan. 2015. "What is Slow Journalism?" *Journalism Practice* 9 (2): 138–152. doi:10.1080/17512786.2014.916471.

Lindlof, Thomas, and Bryan Taylor. 2011. *Qualitative Communication Research Methods*, 3rd Edition. Thousand Oaks, CA: Sage Publications.

Lozano Rendon, José Carlos, Jesus Gonzalez, Pablo Reyes, and Monica Castellanos. 2015. "A Content Analysis of the Coverage of 'Border Issues' in Border Newspapers: Provisional Findings." Paper presented at Lamar Bruni Vergera Annual Conference, Texas A&M-International University.

Mair, John, and Richard Keeble. 2014. *Data Journalism: Mapping the Future*. Suffolk, UK: Abramis Academic Publishing.

Marx, Gary. 1972. *Muckraking Sociology: Research as Social Criticism*. New York: Transaction/Society Books.

Marx, Gary. 2002. "Looking for Meaning in All the Wrong Places: The Search for Academic Satisfaction." In *Lessons of Criminology*, edited by Gilbert Geis and Mary Dodge, 109–137. London: Routledge.

Mbembe, Achille. 2001. *On the Postcolony*. Berkeley, CA: University of California Press.

National Public Radio. 2014. *Borderland: Dispatches from the US-Mexico Border*. http://apps.npr.org/borderland/.

Ortiz-Gonzalez, Victor. 2003. *El Paso: Local Frontiers at a Global Crossroads*. Minneapolis, MN: University of Minnesota Press.

Park, Robert E. 1940. "News as a Form of Knowledge: A Chapter in the Sociology of Knowledge." *American Journal of Sociology* 45 (5): 669–686.

Park, Robert E., and Ernest Burgess. 1984 [1925]. *The City: Suggestions for Investigation of Human Behavior in the Urban Environment*. Chicago, IL: University of Chicago Press.

Petrini, Carlo. 2007. *Slow Food Nation: Why Our Food Should Be Good, Clean, and Fair*. New York: Rizzoli Publications USA.

Rendon, Lozano, José Carlos, Francisco Martínez Garza, and Fernando Abiel Rodriguez Elizonda. 2012. *Border News Media Coverage of Violence, Organized Crime, the War on Drugs, and a Culture of Lawfulness: A Content Analysis and Discussion of Possible Policy-Oriented Measures*. Houston, TX: The Puentes Consortium.

Rogers, Everett. 1997. *A History of Communication Study: A Biographical Approach*. New York: The Free Press.

Schudson, Michael. 1982. "The Politics of Narrative Form: The Emergence of News Conventions in Print and Television." *Daedalus* 3: 97–112.

Schudson, Michael. 2008. *Why Democracies Need an Unlovable Press*. London, UK: Polity Press.

The Opportunity Agenda. 2014. *Media Analysis: Coverage of the US-Mexico Border and Unaccompanied Child Migrants*. New York: Opportunity AgendaReports.

Zimmerman, Patricia. 1995. *Reel Families: A Social History of Amateur Films*. Bloomington, IN: University of Indiana Press.

Appendix A

Section Titles for the *Borderland* Site (http://apps.npr.org/borderland)

1. Just Getting There
2. Why the Border is Where it is
3. Fence Facts
4. What is it Like?
5. Empty Houses
6. Junior
7. Snack Time
8. Toothbrushes
9. Apprehension
10. Wanna Buy a Hammock?
11. Palabras/Words

RESILIENCY IN RECOVERY
Slow journalism as public accountability in post-Katrina New Orleans

Jan Lauren Boyles

Hurricane Katrina thoroughly restructured New Orleans as a news environment. In the recovery period, New Orleans also lost its daily, printed newspaper when the venerated, Pulitzer Prize-winning Times-Picayune *transitioned to a reduced print delivery, digital-driven format. At the same time, the uptick in public interest surrounding institutional corruption post-Katrina left a heightened civic need for newswork that fulfills the social responsibility ethic of journalistic practice. This research—founded upon 92 days of on-the-ground fieldwork and 60 in-depth interviews with newsworkers—explores the nature of accountability reporting post-Katrina. More specifically, this work traces three phases of ecological restructuring that reordered practitioner routines, fostering the growth of slow journalism in the Crescent City.*

Introduction

After Hurricane Katrina's landfall, entire neighborhoods in New Orleans were flooded. As the waters slowly receded, residents of the Crescent City began a long and painful process of sense making. The city's journalists, acting as "first informers," helped citizens navigate through the physical and emotional process of recovery (May 2006). Immediately after the storm, news actors throughout New Orleans—particularly the city's newspaper, *The Times-Picayune*—provided dependable coverage upon which residents could rely. Collectively, the city's news producers fulfilled the social responsibility ethos of newswork by serving the informational needs of news consumers at a time of crisis.

In the years that followed, however, significant industry and cultural shifts would restructure the New Orleans news ecosystem (the collective array of news producers within the city), bolstering its ability to produce in-depth journalism that became so vital to communities after Katrina (Robinson 2009a, 2009b; Usher 2009). In this period, *The Times-Picayune*'s leadership scaled back its print publication loads (Chittum 2013). Seven years after the storm, New Orleans became the largest American city without a daily printed paper (Carr 2012). At the same time, the importance that the city's residents placed upon the circulation of local news had greatly accelerated, as residents had to navigate complex bureaucracies to rebuild their homes and their lives. Also as political malfeasance abounded after the storm, New Orleanians say they needed investigative newswork to animate the city's path back to health (Boyles 2014). Analyses of the paper's content, however, illustrate that *Times-Picayune* journalists scaled back coverage (Bockino 2015). As a result, the city's residents vocally questioned if the shrinking breadth and depth of the newspaper's accountability reporting was fostering a dearth of knowledge about the local community (Theim 2013).

As New Orleans rebuilt itself structurally and emotionally, new entrants to the city's news ecosystem concurrently challenged *The Times-Picayune*'s position as primary provider of accountability reporting. After the crisis of Katrina, the restructuring of the city's news ecology led to creative approaches to content production. Fueled by philanthropic funding, these emergent, digital-only outlets placed significant support behind investigative stories that uncovered corruption post-Katrina. New Orleans became a testing ground for the expansion of slow journalism. Beyond informing audiences about occurrences in their local communities, slow journalism places a high priority upon the circulation of narratives that are both transparent and collaborative. In the case of New Orleans, journalists are increasingly working with their former competitors to co-produce in-depth reporting across media platforms.

Using the ravages of Katrina as a critical juncture in the city's recent history, this case study tracks how the city's journalists stumbled upon slow journalism and integrated its practice into everyday newswork. More specifically, this study identifies three phases of transition (competitive chaos, territorial exclusivity and collaborative newswork) that fostered the growth of slow journalism in the city. This research—founded upon 92 days of on-the-ground fieldwork and 60 in-depth interviews with newsworkers —also identifies how the restructuring of the city's news ecology has altered day-to-day practitioner routines in the production of slow journalism. Interrogating New Orleans as a case study sheds light, more broadly, on how the entry of slow journalism shifts newswork at both organizational and practitioner levels, yielding accountability reporting that fulfills citizen needs.

Tracing the Lineage of Slow Journalism

In Western media outlets, the social responsibility construct of the press has historically suggested that journalists bear a moral duty to the audience, arising from their position as societal knowledge producers (Christians and Nordenstreng 2004; Hanitzsch 2007; Schramm, Siebert, and Peterson 1956). This ethic of news production did not originate with the foundations of journalistic practice in Western newsrooms. In the United States, for instance, publishers of the penny press once used their publications to wield political influence by setting the news agenda (Christians 2009; Nerone 2013). The notion that journalists bore a societal obligation to inform audiences began to crystallize as the twentieth century progressed (Schramm, Siebert, and Peterson 1956). Scholars have traced this spirit to muckraking—a movement in which reformers sought to illustrate counterpoints to Gilded Age decadence by exposing daily hardships of the lower classes (Schudson and Tifft 2005). This movement left its imprint upon journalistic practice, for reporters developed a shared mission that expansive institutional power must be checked by the press (Aucoin 1995; Christians and Nordenstreng 2004). This social responsibility orientation further sharpened in the mid-twentieth century. Some scholars link the resurgence of social responsibility newswork to the media's engagement in the McCarthy hearings (Aucoin 1995), while others point to the press's entanglement in the Watergate saga (Schudson and Tifft 2005). Since the 1970s, American newsgathering organizations have been increasingly institutionally oriented to "speak truth to power" as the newsroom maxim relates (Bennett 1990; Bennett and Serrin 2005).

At a practitioner level, journalists engaging in *accountability reporting*—the types of in-depth news stories that act as a check on institutional power—are often viewed not only as caretakers of democracy, but also as guardians of the public's trust (Nerone 2013). Journalists, in this best case, should provide audiences with a forum for debating and engaging in civic life, and for learning about their local community (Christians and Nordenstreng 2004). Historically, reporters toiling for newspapers (which still today produce the vast amount of original reporting) have been most explicitly charged with meeting this editorial mission of social responsibility (Anderson 2013; Downie and Schudson 2009; Robinson 2007).

Today, the roots of social responsibility newswork can be further advanced in elements of the emerging slow journalism movement. Practitioners are coalescing around a set of principles (adapted from the slow living and slow food movements) that suggest newswork should be "good, clean and fair." In its ideal form, slow journalism centers upon the construction of quality narratives that are highly explanatory in nature (Parkins 2004; Gess 2012; Le Masurier 2015). On its surface, slow journalism is most broadly characterized by its temporal dimension, which presents a counterbalance to the accelerated nature of the modern news cycle (Gess 2012). In both its production and consumption, slow journalism requires a significant investment of time (Greenberg 2012). On the consumption side, slow journalism requires sustained engagement, contemplation and reflexivity, in which audiences gain pleasure in the ability to leisurely interact with the narrative (Le Masurier 2015). Also on the production side, such deep journalistic dives stand as directly oppositional to the ephemeral, speedy "scoop" of breaking news (Gess 2012; Le Masurier 2015). The construction of these stories is often rich, layered and lengthy. But the facet that appears to set slow journalism apart from prior movements of practice surrounds the manner in which the narrative is manufactured. To some practitioners, slow journalism is nearly ethnographic in its approach. Journalists ascribing to this view are challenged to provide nuanced portraits of complex phenomena, while also acknowledging any practitioner subjectivity or bias that contributes to the narrative.

In its execution, slow journalism (in many, but not all forms) builds upon the social responsibility tradition in newswork in two respects. First, proponents of slow journalism advocate that narratives be constructed with enhanced notions of transparency (Greenberg 2012; Le Masurier 2015); and second, an anti-competitive orientation is inherent in producing slow newswork (Gess 2012; Le Masurier 2015). Drawing from the slow food approach, narratives should ideally serve as a "shared table," in which content is communally co-produced. The labors of the audience are not a prerequisite for production, however. This is a clear point of distinction from citizen journalism, in which audiences are actively expected to contribute content (Le Masurier 2015). In the context of slow journalism, co-production often equates to collaboration between newsgatherers across media platforms. Circling back to the social responsibility notion of newswork, slow journalism values the circulation of news as shared sustenance for a community, not as a rival commodity for individuals.

To understand better how slow journalism operates in the context of a local news community, this research adopts a case study approach. Such research affords a strong sense of naturalism where scholars can evaluate phenomena within their "real-life context" (Yin 1981, 59). While researchers generally aim to select representative cases (Flyvbjerg 2006), in practice, these typical cases may not possess clear or illustrative qualities. In this study, the city of New Orleans as a case carries greater explanatory power because Katrina's aftermath restructured the city's "storytelling neighborhoods" in such an extreme way (Ball-Rokeach 2001, 5). This critical juncture in the city's history clearly and powerfully illustrates how slow journalism works in practice.

The Supply and Demand of Slow Journalism in New Orleans

After Katrina, media producers of New Orleans emerged not only as an informer of civic knowledge, but also as a rescuer and as a consoler for the community. In Katrina's wake, thousands of New Orleanians drowned in their own homes, while others remained trapped for days. In this hour of need, the city's news providers acted as a literal lifeline for residents. With emergency 911 phone lines unresponsive, residents turned to the media for help—including relaying information directly to public officials (Macias, Hilyard, and Freimuth 2009; Moody 2009).

> We know that a number of people died listening to us on the air shortly after they got off the phone, said WWL's Garland Robinette. We'd just put on anyone [on-air] who called and hear: "Help! I'm trapped in an attic." "Help! I'm in a boat." "Help! I'm trapped in my home." (Sylvester 2008, 95, 97)

In producing journalism directly after the storm's approach, local newsworkers could provide value where public officials could not (Miller and Goidel 2009). Writing immediately after the storm, *Times-Picayune* managing editor Jim Amoss stated that, "This is the newspaper's great strength: reporting knowledge of your own backyard, and the need to tell your readers what is going on in the intimate corners of their neighborhoods" (Sylvester 2008, 3). Journalists, in short, not only provided societal knowledge; they enabled collective survival by adhering to the mission of social responsibility.

The Times-Picayune's newswork during and immediately following Katrina aligned with its public-facing editorial orientation, which had long been tethered to a social responsibility ethic (Dabney 1944; Usher 2009). In its post-Katrina editions, the paper became a vocal and urgent advocate for the rebuilding of New Orleans (Theim 2013; Usher 2009). Editor Jim Amoss, in fact, described the paper's writers as "crusaders" in the post-Katrina aftermath (Sylvester 2008, 7). The character of the journalists' narratives also changed post-Katrina, with reporters writing first-person posts from their own perspectives in the weeks following the storm, eschewing detached objectivity for passionate accountability reporting (Birch and Wachter 2006). Journalists also encouraged New Orleanians to tell their own stories of survival, leveraging the ability of newsmakers to cultivate "storytelling neighborhoods" within urban space (Ball-Rokeach 2001, 5; Robinson 2009b).

In the subsequent years after Katrina, the paper's ability to conduct its social responsibility mission would be challenged, however. In 2012, *The Times-Picayune* entered the national spotlight as one of the first newspapers in the country to retract from a daily, printed product. Preemptively, leaders at *The Times-Picayune* assured city residents that the paper's journalistic output would remain steady, as editors planned to increase the size of the paper's three editions to span a week's worth of news (Amoss 2012). But between 2007 and 2013, the number of journalists working for the New Orleans publication steadily declined—ranks thinned by rounds of downsizings and departures (Chittum 2013; Theim 2013). Writing on the paper's Web portal nola.com, T-P publisher Ricky Mathews noted the interplay between reduced staffing and content: "Your *Times-Picayunes* have been getting smaller and smaller," Mathews penned. "They are being produced by a staff that has also been getting smaller and smaller" (Mathews 2012). The paper's editorial content concurrently decreased (Bockino 2015).

The timing of the paper's restructured coverage coincided with an increased demand for accountability reporting within the city of New Orleans. Vulnerable in the years after the storm, thousands of New Orleanians requested funding from the Road Home program (Federal block grants administered through the local Louisiana Recovery Authority), which disbursed $11.1 million to residents wishing to rebuild their businesses and homes (Norcross and Skriba 2010; Olshansky et al. 2008). In practice, the complexity of the Road Home's guidelines for aid left New Orleanians mired in red tape (Norcross and Skriba 2010; Usher 2009). Numerous city residents also fell prey to complex scams by private contractors, intended to further defraud residents (Leeson and Sobel 2008). At the same time, dozens of local politicians took advantage of the federal largess—nearly $33 billion from the Federal Emergency Management Agency alone—that flowed into the region (Leeson and Sobel 2008). The myriad of schemes perpetrated upon the city's residents contributed to a lack of institutional trust—broadening the social responsibility role of practitioners and the need for accountability reporting in the city.

In New Orleans today, residents are still actively navigating the recovery—a term that implies not only the physical act of reconstructing the city, but also the emotional repair of lives after the flood. Citizens are also still demanding answers for the post-Katrina greed, turning to the media for support in rooting out institutional corruption. Given the instability at *The Times-Picayune*, new entrants into the New Orleans news ecosystem began placing significant energy behind in-depth investigations that form one of the core approaches of slow journalism. Philanthropic interest in the region's rebuilding has led to the sprouting of numerous news nonprofits designed around missions of slow newswork. To better understand the shifting news ecology at hand, this research outlines recent transitions in the city's organizational landscape and practitioner routines surrounding the production of slow journalism in post-Katrina New Orleans.

Methods

Case studies generally encompass a "comprehensive research strategy," fusing multiple methods together (Flyvbjerg 2006; Yin 2003, 14). Conceptually, this case views the city of New Orleans as a news ecosystem, looking at the city's "communicative infrastructure—the invisible system of communication set within a community's residential environment" (Ball-Rokeach 2001, 5). This perspective examines the journalism outlets creating original news content within New Orleans, and assesses how these journalistic outputs align with the maintenance of an informed citizenry (Anderson 2013; Scolari 2012). Such ecological approaches have been applied in prior studies of Los Angeles (Ball-Rokeach 2001), Baltimore (Pew Research Center 2010), Chicago (Chicago Trust 2011), Philadelphia (Anderson 2013) Denver/Macon/Sioux City (Pew Research Center 2015) and three communities in New Jersey (Napoli et al. 2015). The current case study of the New Orleans news ecosystem draws upon 92 days of fieldwork conducted between August and November 2013. In addition to on-the-ground observation, 60 in-depth interviews were conducted. Initial interview subjects were identified through a process of *networked ethnography*—a strategy that applies elements of social network analysis to identify and map news producers operating in the city's ecosystem (Anderson 2013; Howard 2002).

In-depth interviewing formed the primary data collection technique of the research. In digital spaces, those producing original journalistic content are connected by links (Howard 2002). By applying graph theory (the study of network architecture), a small-scale network analysis of the New Orleans news ecosystem was conducted. In a process of networked ethnography, seed sites (the original list of links to news knowledge producers' sites) were only included if the news knowledge producer updated content at least weekly (Howard 2002). For each major, active node identified in the social networking mapping, an interview subject was contacted. From this initial list of major interlocutors, snowball sampling was also employed, in attempts to locate all active news producers operating in New Orleans, including: newspapers, alternative weeklies, niche print publications, local television, public access television, news radio, radio talk shows, college newspapers and digital native publications. Of the 60 interview subjects, 19 journalists worked primarily for print publications, 13 journalists worked primarily for digital native publications, nine worked for radio broadcasts, eight worked for television broadcasts, seven were community activists and four were local academics.

Conversations with interview subjects were informal, following a semi-structured interview schedule (Berger 2000; Soss 2006) about information needs in the community, the fluctuations of *The Times-Picayune*'s daily coverage, and how the roles, expectations and coverage have changed in the period since Katrina's landfall. To assure both frankness and confidentiality, all interview subjects were granted complete anonymity, if requested. All direct quotes and identities used in the narrative were verified with interview subjects prior to publication.

This study also features a 92-day period of direct field observation in the community-gathering spaces in which residents share news (coffeehouses, churches and libraries, for instance). In many instances, the in-depth interview subjects cued the researcher to sites of observational inquiry. Because the practice of slow journalism often mirrors fieldwork, this quasi-ethnographic method aligns with the need to understand the "storytelling neighborhoods" of New Orleans (Ball-Rokeach 2001). The fieldwork began with a period of "enculturation"—or "the natural process of learning a particular culture" (Spradley 1979, 47). To build a corpus of ethnographic observations, the environmental conditions for news within the city's gathering spaces were recorded as field notes.

The analysis of the qualitative findings began inductively by examining interview notes and field notes. From this inspection, the data was categorized into patterns of responses (Creswell 2012; Emerson, Fretz, and Shaw 1995; Yin 2003). The researcher relied upon triangulation, in which each important finding must be observed in three (or more) separate instances to be incorporated into the resultant narrative (Stake 2006). Taken together, the overarching goal of the study stands to place readers in the "storytelling neighborhoods" of New Orleans, delving deeper into the production of slow journalism, post-Katrina (Ball-Rokeach 2001, 5).

Advancing Slow Journalism Organizations in the News Ecology

Ten years after Katrina, the public's demand for accountability reporting—coverage that forms the core of a publication's social responsibility mission—remains particularly strong. As Lee Zurik, chief investigative reporter and anchor for the city's Fox affiliate, WVUE, said in an interview on October 1, 2013:

> Katrina changed everything here. I think one thing that it did … it pulled the Band-Aid off the city and the region, really. I think people reacted differently to everything that they saw—they used to accept things before. But then, they evacuated to different parts of the country, and they came back and had more of a distaste for corruption.

The public's "distaste for corruption," compounded by the shortfall of content from *The Times-Picayune* (Bockino 2015), led to significant shifts in news production within New Orleans after the storm.

Organizationally, the city's news ecology migrated through three phases of restructuring. The *Times-Picayune*'s publication fluctuations acted as the initial catalyst for the first phase of ecological change. In this period of *competitive chaos*, organizations vigorously pursued news scoops. At the same time, news outlets in the Crescent City began placing a stronger emphasis upon the process and products of slow newswork. The entry of a competing print newspaper from neighboring Baton Rouge led to the second phase of ecological restructuring. *The Advocate* began producing a New Orleans-based edition, further reordering the production of the city's news. The focus on longform narratives accelerated in this second phase, in which news organizations developed *territorial exclusivity* surrounding specific beats. News outlets identified that slow journalism could be used to competitive advantage, enabling organizations to carve out distinguishing areas of editorial focus. Given this entrepreneurial energy, philanthropic support heavily increased, leading to the third and most recent phase of ecological restructuring. Today, news actors now actively engage in co-production routines of *collaborative newswork* in which content is shared between newsworkers and across platforms. Taken together, the trio of phases has advanced the slow journalism movement in the Crescent City.

Phase 1: Competitive Chaos

The *Times-Picayune*'s publication fluctuations created an opening for new approaches to newswork and new journalistic ventures to thrive in the Crescent City, as readers were angered and frustrated by *The Times-Picayune*'s transition into a thrice-weekly newspaper (Theim 2013). News outlets were competing to attract readers who were looking for new sources of journalism in the wake of *The Times-Picayune*'s transitions. Tapping into this perceived void in the marketplace, a handful of print legacy outlets—mainly city magazines and business journals—began building their slow journalism presence in New Orleans. At *New Orleans CityBusiness*, for instance, writers were directed to cover the financial angles of the city's rebuilding, unpacking complex trends and analysis through more comprehensive news analysis pieces. Similarly, entrepreneur Smith Hartley, who previously worked as a hospital administrator, identified a gap in the paper's in-depth coverage of healthcare. Consequently, he founded the *Healthcare Journal of New Orleans*, a print magazine with a niche audience. In an interview on September 4, 2013, Hartley said, "I wanted to provide coverage of healthcare that would be specific to the city. The paper's coverage of healthcare was not that effective or deep."

As legacy outlets reformulated their approaches, the competitive environment was enhanced by the entry of several digital-only journalism startups, which emerged as serious challengers to institutional news outlets. At the time, these startups were regarded as challengers to legacy producers, who believed that the new entrants would siphon off readers, and in turn, lure away lucrative advertisers. The newest additions to the city's news environment, in fact, built their entire brands around socially responsible works of slow journalism. *The Lens*, the city's first nonprofit news outlet, entered the market by focusing on five, primary public affairs beats: criminal justice, schools, government and politics, land use and the environment. Funded through a mix of foundation support and crowdfunded donations, the storytelling model of *The Lens* prioritized longform, in-depth investigative coverage that would expose and track the city's post-Katrina corruption. *The Lens* was joined online by news provider, *Uptown Messenger*. Its blend of hyperlocal and longform journalism concentrated upon the city's Uptown district, in efforts to expand accountability reporting to a neighborhood level. The site draws financial support from local advertising and private donations. Monthly "subscribers" are recognized on the hyperlocal site.

The growth in such digital-only platforms led to more choice for consumers seeking slow journalism content. "Each of us represents a different entrepreneurial approach to the news," says *Uptown Messenger*'s publisher, Robert Morris, "but we are all working to ensure that New Orleanians are better informed than ever before" (New Orleans Digital News Alliance 2012). The influx of content has also expanded the range of local news coverage within the domain of slow newswork. In an interview on September 12, 2013, WSGO radio talk show and "Politics with a Punch" host, Jeff Crouere said:

> People in the media are not all following the same story, So you're getting different kinds of information because not everyone [news actor] follows every issue. Overall, I think it's a big positive, because it lets the consumer have more choice.

This influx of content, however, meant that newsworkers began to compete more vigorously for stories in a crowded and competitive media environment. As the 2010s progressed, the city's burgeoning reporting corps—both legacy and digital—actively fought to stake out pieces of the longform news ecosystem, applying a territorial approach to newswork in New Orleans.

Phase 2: Territorial Exclusivity

Given the increase in both news outlets and news reporters in New Orleans, strains were placed upon the city's journalists to land stories first. To directly compete with *The Times-Picayune*, *The Advocate*—a newspaper from neighboring Baton Rouge—began producing a New Orleans-based print edition. In this climate of heightened competition, nearly all reporters in the city referred to the palpable "fear of getting scooped." Journalists across news organizations were explicitly instructed to avoid the production of formulaic stories deemed "routine" (event-based stories drawn from traditional, newsprint beats). Such stories were ceded to the city's paper. Instead, news organizations encouraged their staff to focus upon "exclusive" stories that yielded a competitive advantage, in that these detailed pieces would be difficult for competitors to replicate. In short, practitioners heavily capitalized upon the temporal quality of slow newswork for competitive advantage.

In this period, news organizations also began building their brands around more specialized content that leveraged slow journalism—acting to distinguish competitors in the crowded marketplace. Digital-only outlet *NolaVie* embraced this ethos. The site, which focuses upon arts and lifestyle accounts, entered the news ecology "to fill the gap in diminished cultural coverage" (*NolaVie* 2015). Like other Web-based outfits in the city, *NolaVie* depends on private donations as well as corporate/nonprofit partnerships to fuel the site. Unlike its competitors, however, *NolaVie* contributors often write from first-person perspectives, acknowledging the interplay between their own points of view and the narrative. In this light, *NolaVie*'s coverage comports with some practices of slow newswork, in which journalists openly disclose their own biases in the production process. *NolaVie* fought to claim a space for slow journalism in the city's increasingly crowded news market.

As media outlets developed distinguishing brands of content, news organizations in the city (particularly in broadcasting) concurrently made "deliberate" and "aggressive" efforts to expand accountability coverage. Unlike "routine" stories, pieces constructed with investigative tools are more difficult for competitors to scoop because the time horizon is longer. The process of arranging and conducting interviews, logging field tape and editing video is incredibly lengthy. Building rapport with sources is also time-intensive, and requires labor in the field cultivating contacts. "I've always liked to do bigger projects—digging deep into data and documents that people couldn't do in a day," broadcaster Lee Zurik said. But as the concentration in longform investigations increased, news organizations uncovered that the significant time investment also equaled a significant financial investment as well. The solution to promoting slow journalism in the city's news ecology rested in a counterintuitive approach to journalistic routines: collaboration among the city's newsworkers.

Phase 3: Collaborative Newswork

The slow journalism movement, which took hold in New Orleans in 2013, can be traced to an uptick in collaborative newswork. Conducting team-based reporting projects can help news organizations shoulder the weighty financial burden linked to investigative stories, in particular. The costs of accountability reporting, such as obtaining public records or keeping legal counsel on retainer, can be cut in half by joining forces with former media rivals.

Beginning in 2013, two types of collaborative newswork emerged: alliances between legacy outlets and alliances that converged legacy and digital operations. The city's primary print organizations both aligned with local television networks to bolster accountability reporting in the city. *The Times-Picayune* entered a content-sharing agreement with Fox 8. The television station also inked an agreement with *New Orleans CityBusiness*, in which the two news organizations collaborate on longform financial stories. Also *The New Orleans Advocate*—the new, daily newspaper that entered from neighboring Baton Rouge—announced a formal, longform content-sharing partnership with television broadcaster WWL. On air, the partnership's first story—an investigation into a scholarship program at Tulane University—yielded a seven-minute and 40-second nightly news package—an expansive length for a 22-minute newscast that must also accommodate sports and weather. (Generally speaking, broadcast segments last two minutes or less). The collaborative nature of the package was emphasized throughout the segment. On screen, the chyron featured the logos of both *The New Orleans Advocate* and WWL. To emphasize the partnership, the anchor's copy began, "Tonight, in a special investigation with *The New Orleans Advocate*…" At the piece's end, viewers were reminded that, "Tomorrow morning, *The New Orleans Advocate* is breaking new details on our joint investigation." In the print edition of the story, a slideshow of stills from the television broadcast accompanied the lengthy 3420-word narrative—a story for which WWL broadcaster Mike Perlstein also received a 1A byline.

Mainline news knowledge producers have also formed partnerships to integrate digital-only content into the raw materials of slow newswork. *NolaVie*, for instance, has a "handshake agreement" to share content with *The Times-Picayune*. The newspaper created a special landing page on its Web portal, nola.com, for *NolaVie* stories. Also CBS affiliate WWL formed a content-sharing agreement with hyperlocal site, *Uptown Messenger*, to facilitate more extensive, neighborhood-level coverage.

Digital-only news nonprofits are forging alliances as well. Fueled by a $100,000 Knight Foundation Community Information Challenge grant, the city's largest content-sharing partnership tethers WWNO (the city's National Public Radio affiliate) to a patchwork of independent, digital-only news organizations, including *NolaVie*, *The Lens* and the Greater New Orleans Data Center. For each collaborative story brainstormed between *NolaVie* and WWNO, two journalistic products are typically constructed: a longform piece for circulation on nolavie.com and a longform radio segment intended for broadcast on WWNO and its website, wwno.org. A prime example of this collaborative effort would be *The Lens* reporter Bob Marshall's series "Last Call," which studied the geological and environmental causes behind the erosion of the Southeast Louisiana coastline. Marshall's work at *The Lens* was complemented by the talents of Fred Kasten, a veteran radio producer for WWNO who reshaped Marshall's detailed print narrative for a slow journalism piece on public radio.

In the hypercompetitive media environment of New Orleans, such partnerships are particularly vital to emerging digital-only outlets, as the collaborative efforts increase visibility for journalism startups. Furthermore, collaborative newswork can amplify the reach and audience of the news story itself. In this sense, the collaborative aspects of the slow journalism movement have fused with the culture of open source reporting. *The Lens*, for instance, publishes all of its news stories under a Creative

Commons license. To reprint a *Lens* story, a news organization must use the nonprofit's byline as credit. As evidence to the anti-competitive nature of slow newswork that has developed in the city, stories from *The Lens* have run in both *The Times-Picayune* and *The New Orleans Advocate*. Of the nearly 1000 stories filed online by the news nonprofit in 2013, more than 50 were picked up and redistributed by local media. Beyond regional ties, *The Lens* signed a content-sharing deal with *ProPublica*, and has redistributed its stories nationwide.

From Katrina onward, the evolution of the city's approach to slow journalism—born from enhanced competition and fully-formed from expanded collaboration—has yielded a vibrant ecosystem of content producers. Within these nimble news organizations, journalists have responded to the evolving landscape by altering their day-to-day routines in producing slow newswork.

Co-producing Socially Responsible News

At the level of individual practitioners, the process of manufacturing slow journalism often runs counter to deeply ingrained notions of practice, which value competition. Interactions at the heart of collaborative newswork stand as diametrically opposed to the ethos of territorial exclusivity. Unlike traditional structures of newswork, journalists engaging in content partnerships generally share the raw content of reporting (audio files from interviews or breaking news video from the scene, for instance) in the process of co-production. In New Orleans, numerous journalists referred to this process as the "report once, produce twice" model of reporting. In many cases, collaborative news products make more news knowledge available to the end consumer, because the collective raw materials of newswork can be stretched across multiple platforms for divergent audiences.

The foundation of collaborative, co-produced slow journalism in practice rests upon fostering strong interpersonal relationships among the reporting team's members. Collaboration, in the context of slow journalism, mandates relinquishing sole control over the ultimate editorial product(s), which can prove difficult. As digital works of slow journalism meld text, images and video into new, longform packages, team-based reporting requires working with journalists across media platforms, each with varying routines and norms of practice. Journalists in New Orleans described their initial encounters with their former competitors as "adversarial" and "challenging." But as closer partnerships developed, journalists began sharing and exchanging complementary skills. "For a long time, the print journalists kind of looked down on TV journalists," broadcaster Lee Zurik said. "In some cases now, there's a newfound respect. They're [print journalists] trying to do in-front-of-the-camera things and video. And they bring different perspectives, too."

For journalists engaging in collaborative newswork, open lines of communication are critical. Several journalists in the city referred to this as the "trust factor"—the promise that works will foster collaboration, not competition. Within the news ecosystem of New Orleans, all journalists engaged in team-based slow journalism had weekly editorial meetings to shape the product(s). But in between these sessions, reporters may independently receive tips from sources that may advance the story. For collaborative works of slow journalism to succeed, however, the leads must be incorporated back into the workflow of the collective reporting team. To heighten trust among collaborative reporting teams, the city's public radio affiliate WWNO has embedded its producers across platforms, placing journalists in the newsrooms of its partners. Such engagement reflects the "shared table" of slow journalism, which favors co-production approaches and shared models of newswork.

Toward Resilience and Sustainability

Immediately after the flood, the communicative architecture of New Orleans rested in ruins. Once residents returned to the city, however, New Orleanians also longed to return to "normal life" in all its forms. Ten years after the flood—after periods of competitive chaos, territorial exclusivity and collaborative newswork—the city's news ecosystem has demonstrated an ability to bounce back from crisis. Journalists effectively stumbled into the practice of slow journalism, which reordered practitioner routines in the digital age. While this case study approach is limited by its focus upon the Crescent City, this resurgence of news production post-Katrina more broadly suggests an underlying resilience of a city's news ecology. In the context of New Orleans, this resilience can also be witnessed in the adaptation and adoption of slow journalism that has reshaped organizational structures and practitioner routines post-Katrina.

The continued ability to produce longform works of slow journalism rests upon larger issues of the ecosystem's long-term sustainability, however. Digital producers of slow journalism in the city rely heavily, if not entirely, upon funding from private-sector philanthropists. Most of the outreach has been in the form of short-term grants. Without dependable, annual funding, news organizations engaging in slow newswork remain in states of perpetual fundraising. If these resources are threatened, accountability reporting that, in the case of New Orleans, forms the core of slow journalism may substantially diminish. Beyond the city of New Orleans, the underlying tension between resilience and sustainability merits further academic inquiry. Future research is also needed to better understand how audiences, like news consumers in New Orleans, engage with slow journalism in urban spaces.

In the mid-2010s, the expansion of news startups, digital-only outlets and other entrepreneurial publications centered upon slow journalism has led to more journalistic oversight of the city's institutions, sharpening the long-standing journalistic commitment to social responsibility. Reporters, like WAFB's lead investigative reporter Kiran Chawla, have integrated notions of the social responsibility ethos into their execution of slow journalism products. In an interview on September 25, 2013, Chawla said, "I see myself as a public servant. I don't wear a badge, but I see myself as serving the public." In the city of New Orleans, slow journalism has acted as another tool to check institutional power. This orientation toward enhanced public service, born of the ecosystem's upheaval post-Katrina, has enhanced the ability to which New Orleanians are informed about the community in which they live. It has also shifted the work routines of reporters, who now engage in acts of co-production with colleagues. In the city's restructured news ecology, slow newswork has emerged as another tool of accountability reporting, which advances the social responsibility mission of newswork in the digital age.

ACKNOWLEDGEMENTS

Thank you to Declan Fahy, Matthew C. Nisbet, Kathryn Montgomery and Sue Robinson for reading and providing feedback on early drafts of this work.

FUNDING

This work was supported by American University under a Doctoral Student Research Award.

DISCLOSURE STATEMENT

No potential conflict of interest was reported by the author.

REFERENCES

Amoss, Jim. 2012. "The Message for Our Organization is Clear: Adapt, or Fade Away." *The Times-Picayune*, June 13. http://www.nola.com/opinions/index.ssf/2012/06/post_153.html.

Anderson, C. W. 2013. *Rebuilding the News: Metropolitan Journalism in the Digital Age*. Philadelphia, PA: Temple University Press.

Aucoin, James L. 1995. "The Re-emergence of American Investigative Journalism 1960-1975." *Journalism History* 21 (1): 3–15.

Ball-Rokeach, Sandra J. 2001. "Metamorphosis: Transforming the Ties That Bind." University of Southern California White Paper Series, June 12. http://www.metamorph.org/images/uploads/The_challenge_of_belonging_in_the_21st_century.pdf.

Bennett, W. L. 1990. "Toward a Theory of Press-state Relations in the United States." *Journal of Communication* 40 (2): 103–127.

Bennett, W. L., and William Serrin. 2005. "The Watchdog Role." In *The Institutions of American Democracy: The Press*, edited by Geneva Overholser and Kathleen H. Jamieson. 141–155.

Berger, Arthur A. 2000. *Media and Communication Research Methods: An Introduction to Qualitative and Quantitative Approaches*. Thousand Oaks: Sage Publications.

Birch, Eugenie, and Susan Wachter. 2006. *Rebuilding Urban Places after Disaster: Lessons from Hurricane Katrina*. Philadelphia, PA: University of Pennsylvania Press.

Bockino, David. 2015. "Times-Picayune Coverage Differs Print to Online." *Newspaper Research Journal* 36 (1): 58–74.

Boyles, Jan Lauren. 2014. When the Newsprint Fades: How the Media Ecology of New Orleans Produces News Knowledge. PhD diss. American University.

Carr, David. 2012. "New Orleans Paper Said to Face Deep Cuts and May Cut Back Publication." *The New York Times*, May 23. http://mediadecoder.blogs.nytimes.com/2012/05/23/new-orleans-paper-said-to-face-deep-cuts-and-may-cut-back-on-publication/?_r=0.

Chicago Trust. 2011. "Linking Audiences to News: A Network Analysis of Chicago Websites." http://www.cct.org/sites/cct.org/files/CNM_LinkingAudiences_0611.pdf.

Chittum, Ryan. 2013. "The Battle of New Orleans: Is Advance Publications Securing the Future of Local News—Or Sacrificing It?" *Columbia Journalism Review*, March/April. http://www.cjr.org/feature/the_battle_of_new_orleans.php?page=all.

Christians, Clifford G. 2009. *Normative Theories of the Media: Journalism in Democratic Societies*. Urbana: University of Illinois Press.

Christians, Clifford, and Kaarle Nordenstreng. 2004. "Social Responsibility Worldwide." *Journal of Mass Media Ethics* 19 (1): 3–28.

Creswell, John W. 2012. *Qualitative Inquiry and Research Design: Choosing among Five Approaches*. Thousand Oaks: Sage.

Dabney, Thomas E. 1944. *One Hundred Great Years-The Story of the Times Picayune from Its Founding to 1940*. Baton Rouge, LA: Louisiana State University.

Downie, Leonard, and Michael Schudson. 2009. "The Reconstruction of American Journalism." *Columbia Journalism Review*, November/December. http://www.cjr.org/reconstruction/the_reconstruction_of_american.php.

Emerson, Robert M., Rachel I. Fretz, and Linda L. Shaw. 1995. *Writing Ethnographic Fieldnotes*. Chicago, IL: University of Chicago Press.

Flyvbjerg, Bent. 2006. "Five Misunderstandings about Case-study Research." *Qualitative Inquiry* 12 (2): 219–245.

Gess, Harold. 2012. "Climate Change and the Possibility of 'Slow Journalism'." *Ecquid Novi: African Journalism Studies* 33 (1): 54–65.

Greenberg, Susan. 2012. "Slow Journalism in the Digital Fast Lane." *Global Literary Journalism: Exploring the Journalistic Imagination*. Edited by Richard Lance Keeble and John, Tulloch, 381–393

Hanitzsch, Thomas. 2007. "Deconstructing Journalism Culture: Toward a Universal Theory." *Communication Theory* 17 (4): 367–385.

Howard, Philip N. 2002. "Network Ethnography and the Hypermedia Organization: New Media, New Organizations, New Methods." *New Media & Society* 4 (4): 550–574.

Le Masurier, Megan. 2015. "What is Slow Journalism?" *Journalism Practice* 9 (2): 138–152.

Leeson, Peter T., and Russell S. Sobel. 2008. "Weathering Corruption." *Journal of Law and Economics* 51 (4): 667–681.

Macias, Wendy, Karen Hilyard, and Vicki Freimuth. 2009. "Blog Functions as Risk and Crisis Communication during Hurricane Katrina." *Journal of Computer-Mediated Communication* 15 (1): 1–31.

Mathews, Ricky. 2012. "The Times-Picayune and nola.Com Are Here to Stay." *The Times-Picayune*, June 27. http://www.nola.com/opinions/index.ssf/2012/06/the_times-picayune_and_nolacom.html.

May, Albert L. 2006. *First Informers in the Disaster Zone: The Lessons of Katrina*. Queenstown, MD: Aspen Institute.

Miller, Andrea, and Robert Goidel. 2009. "News Organizations and Information Gathering during a Natural Disaster: Lessons from Hurricane Katrina." *Journal of Contingencies and Crisis Management* 17 (4): 266–273.

Moody, Reginald F. 2009. "Radio's Role during Hurricane Katrina: A Case Study of WWL Radio and the United Radio Broadcasters of New Orleans." *Journal of Radio & Audio Media* 16 (2): 160–180.

Napoli, Philip M., Sarah Stonbely, Kathleen McCollough, and Bryce Renninger 2015. "Assessing the Health of Local News Ecosystems: A Comparative Analysis of Three New Jersey

Communities." http://wp.comminfo.rutgers.edu/mpii-new/wp-content/uploads/sites/129/2015/06/Assessing-Local-Journalism_Final-Draft-6.23.15.pdf.

Nerone, John. 2013. "The Historical Roots of the Normative Model of Journalism." *Journalism* 14 (4): 446–458.

New Orleans Digital News Alliance. 2012. "Online Publishers to Promote Each Other's Work, Strengthen Digital News." http://www.poynter.org/wp-content/uploads/2012/07/New-Orleans-DNA-release.pdf.

NolaVie. 2015. "About *NolaVie*." *NolaVie*, April 27. http://nolavie.com/about/.

Norcross, Eileen, and Anthony Skriba. 2010. "The Road Home: Helping Homeowners in the Gulf after Katrina." In *The Political Economy of Hurricane Katrina and Community Rebound*, edited by Emily Chamlee-Wright, 185–214. Cheltenham: Edward Elgar Publishing Ltd.

Olshansky, Robert B., Laurie A. Johnson, Jedidah Horne, and Brendan Nee. 2008. "Longer View: Planning for the Rebuilding of New Orleans." *Journal of the American Planning Association* 74 (3): 273–287.

Parkins, Wendy. 2004. "Out of Time: Fast Subjects and Slow Living." *Time & Society* 12 (2–3): 363–382.

Pew Research Center. 2010. *How News Happens*. Washington: Pew Research Center.

Pew Research Center. 2015. *Local News in a Digital Age*. Washington: Pew Research Center.

Robinson, Sue. 2007. "'Someone's Gotta Be in Control Here': The Institutionalization of Online News and the Creation of a Shared Journalistic Authority." *Journalism Practice* 1 (3): 305–321.

Robinson, Sue. 2009a. "A Chronicle of Chaos: Tracking the News Story of Hurricane Katrina from The Times-Picayune to Its Website." *Journalism* 10 (4): 431–450.

Robinson, Sue. 2009b. "'If You Had Been with Us': Mainstream Press and Citizen Journalists Jockey for Authority over the Collective Memory of Hurricane Katrina." *New Media & Society* 11 (5): 795–814.

Schramm, Wilbur, Fred S. Siebert, and Theodore Peterson. 1956. *Four Theories of the Press*. Urbana: University of Illinois Press.

Schudson, Michael, and Susan E. Tifft. 2005. "American Journalism in Historical Perspective." In *The Institutions of American Democracy: The Press*, edited by Geneva Overholser and Kathleen H. Jamieson, 17–47. Oxford: Oxford University Press.

Scolari, Carlos A. 2012. "Media Ecology: Exploring the Metaphor to Expand the Theory." *Communication Theory* 22 (2): 204–225.

Soss, Joe. 2006. "Talking Our Way to Meaningful Explanations." In *Interpretation and Method: Empirical Research Methods and the Interpretive Turn*, edited by Dvora Yanow and Peregrine Schwartz-Shea, 127–149. London: M.E.Sharpe.

Spradley, James P. 1979. *The Ethnographic Interview*. New York: Holt, Rinehart and Winston.

Stake, Robert E. 2006. *Multiple Case Study Analysis*. New York: Guilford Press.

Sylvester, Judith. 2008. *The Media and Hurricanes Katrina and Rita: Lost and Found*. New York: Palgrave Macmillan.

Theim, Rebecca. 2013. *Hell and High Water: The Battle to Save the Daily New Orleans Times-Picayune*. New Orleans: Pelican.

Usher, Nikki. 2009. "Recovery from Disaster: How Journalists at the New Orleans Times-Picayune Understand the Role of a Post-Katrina Newspaper." *Journalism Practice* 3 (2): 216–232.

Yin, Robert K. 1981. "The Case Study Crisis: Some Answers." *Administrative Science Quarterly* 26 (1): 58–65.

Yin, Robert K. 2003. *Case Study Research: Design and Methods*. Thousand Oaks: Sage.

TIME TO ENGAGE
De Correspondent's redefinition of journalistic quality

Frank Harbers

This article explores De Correspondent as a specific example of slow journalism that aims to establish an alternative for quality journalism governed by the objectivity regime. It offers an analysis of the way the platform redefines journalism's quality standards against the background of the tension between traditional modernistic claims to truth and competing postmodern ideas on the social construction of knowledge. Moreover, the article examines how these ideals are translated into journalistic texts. The article argues that both in its rhetoric and in its actual practice, the articles in De Correspondent deviate from the principles of quality journalism under the objectivity regime. They are structured around the mediating subjectivity of the journalists and are thus openly subjective. Yet, they also draw on empirical research and scientific knowledge. Moreover, they are transparent about the reporting process, which through their reflection becomes an integral part of the story itself. Thus, being transparent about their combination of different forms of knowledge, rooted in more traditional rational-positivistic inquiry as well as in personal experience and emotion, they try to reconcile the tension between the modernist and postmodernist claims to truth.

Introduction

Within eight days former editor-in-chief of *NRC.Next* Rob Wijnberg crowdfunded the necessary 1,000,000 to realize his idea of an innovative, online-only platform for quality journalism: *De Correspondent* (Van der Valk 2015a). Wijnberg's plan was based on the idea that nowadays quality journalism is held hostage by increasing commercial pressures, temporal demands of around-the-clock coverage, and outdated journalistic values and practices. In his view this has led to hasty, superficial, formulaic and uncritical journalism that only focused on a limited selection of events that were out of the ordinary. According to Wijnberg, this has resulted in quality journalistic outlets squandering their fundamental role of showing and explaining what is happening in the world. Moreover, they are scaring away a younger generation of news consumers (Wijnberg 2013a).

With this criticism Wijnberg joins the ranks of several journalists and scholars who have reproached journalistic developments since roughly the 1990s for its growing commercial or tabloid logic. With obvious disappointment, they argue how even quality news media are increasingly being determined by scandal-oriented click bait, forms of "churnalism," journalism of assertion, infotainment, and soundbite culture (Davies 2009; Franklin 2008; Sparks 2000; Williams 2010). Their disqualification of the current developments in journalism is rooted in their—implicit or explicit—adherence to the core values of the objectivity regime (Hackett and Zhao 1998), such as independence, factuality, impartiality, neutrality, and detachment. This set of norms has been the dominant professional framework and quality standard for a large part of the twentieth century and shaped the routines and textual forms of journalism accordingly (Broersma 2010a; Harbers 2014; Schudson 2001; Ward 2004).

Although he agrees with the diagnosis, Wijnberg's critique is not so much a nostalgic lament for the crumbling professional standards revolving around objectivity (cf. Harbers 2014; Le Masurier 2015). On the contrary, he sees objectivity as part of the problems journalism is currently facing and as an important part of the explanation why the younger generation is "tuning out."

> Objectifying news makes it much harder to feel engaged with what the news is about. Removing the narrator from the story, and thus the one that can establish engagement with the world, means creating a distance between the public and the world. That is exactly why *De Correspondent* says goodbye to the traditional objectivity ideal. Not only because objectivity is to a certain extent always *feigned* (that the subjective choices and considerations that precede every story remain implicit, doesn't mean they are not there), but first and foremost because *De Correspondent* wants to close that gap between public and world (and public and journalist). (Wijnberg 2013b)[1]

Wijnberg envisions an alternative form of journalism that is more in touch with the cultural customs and technological possibilities of our current network society, shaped by postmodern culture (see Castells 1996; Bogaerts and Carpentier 2013).[2]

With his journalistic platform *De Correspondent*, Wijnberg proposes an alternative and antidote to the news coverage of established quality news media. The way Wijnberg has conceived his new medium as going against the emphasis on speed and immediacy that has become such an integral part of contemporary journalism clearly relates to a broader discourse and practice of "slow journalism" (Greenberg 2011; Le Masurier 2015)—a predicate that is often used by others to typify the start-up as well as by *De Correspondent* itself (Njotea 2013; *De Correspondent* 2013). Slow journalism has emerged in response to the increasing importance of "fast and instantaneous journalism and the concerns about the deleterious effects of speed" (Le Masurier 2015, 138). Le Masurier defines it as a form of journalism that devotes time to in-depth research and verification; draws on the tradition of storytelling; is transparent about its journalistic methods and procedures; does not strive to score off their competition; is focused on a specific community; and draws on the input of an active public. The journalistic conception of *De Correspondent* seems to fit quite well into this broad concept with its emphasis on quality over quantity and speed, societal relevance over current events, on context over bare facts, on participation over consumption, and on professional independence over commercial gain (Wijnberg 2013a, 2013b).

The principles of slow journalism can be seen as a particular response to journalism's struggle with its transition from an industrial towards a post-industrial logic. This development entails the shift from a top-down, one-size-fits-all way of producing and distributing news towards an approach centering on a more bottom-up, collaborative, and personalized form of news coverage and dissemination. Yet, what is too often disregarded is that these changes also challenge the corresponding core values of journalism, revolving around objectivity (Broersma and Peters 2013; Singer 2010). Although the emphasis on storytelling and transparency might be seen as signs that indicate that slow journalism distances itself from the objectivity regime's attempt to hide the fact that the representation of reality is rooted in the mediating subjectivity of the reporter (Wahl-Jorgensen 2013; Karlsson 2010), it has not been researched yet to what extent slow journalism can be seen as a challenge to the objectivity regime. It is therefore interesting to analyze an example of slow journalism like *De Correspondent*, which explicitly rejects objectivity as a professional ideal and instead embraces a more personal and engaged approach to the news.

Next to an exploration of *De Correspondent* as a particular type of slow journalism, which aims to establish an alternative for quality journalism governed by the objectivity regime, the article also hopes to act as a further invitation to examine to what extent slow journalism is redefining journalism's traditional core values. By offering analysis of the journalistic accounts published in *De Correspondent*, it elucidates the way Wijnberg *cum suis* redefine journalism's quality standards against the background of the tension between traditional modernistic claims to truth and competing postmodern ideas on the social construction of representation and knowledge.

For this purpose a textual analysis was performed on the 63 major "stories of the day" produced in 2014 by six regular correspondents (16 stories by Rutger Bregman, 15 stories by Maurits Martijn, 9 stories by Lennart Hofmann, 9 stories by Maite Vermeulen, 7 stories by Joris van Casteren, and 7 stories by Vera Mulder). In addition, I have mapped the genre labels of the articles, the use of hyperlinks, the number of readers' comments, and the number of times journalists interact with their readers of all the articles that these six correspondents have written throughout 2014 (406 articles). These particular correspondents were chosen because they offer a representative cross-section of the range of content in *De Correspondent*: the more analytic and investigative form of journalism by Bregman and Martijn, the on-site reportage of Hofmann and Vermeulen, and a form of narrative journalism by Van Casteren and Mulder. In addition, to gain more insight into the way their newsroom and content flow is organized and structured, *De Correspondent*'s senior editor, Andreas Jonkers, was interviewed.

Based on this analysis, I argue that both in its rhetoric as in its actual journalism practice, *De Correspondent* indeed deviates from the principles of quality journalism under the objectivity regime. As I will outline below, *De Correspondent* tries to reconcile the tension between the modernist trust in the positivist nature of journalism's basic reporting routines and the competing postmodern perspective on the socially constructed nature of representation and knowledge by combining different types of information that are the result of rational-positivistic inquiry as well as experiential and emotion-based forms of information.

Post-industrial Logic and Postmodern Culture

According to several critics and scholars, the growing commercialization of the media and the rise of online media outlets turned quality journalism into a crowd-pleaser and eroded the professional quality standards (Davies 2009; Franklin 2008; McNair 2013). This critique generally points to three intricately related causes for this deterioration. (1) In order to keep attracting a large audience, quality news media adopted the logic of the lowest common denominator (Biressi and Nunn 2008). As a result news coverage became more focused on topics such as lifestyle, human interest, and celebrity culture, which was packaged in a more sensational way. This pressure to keep appealing to the public was exacerbated by (2) the rise of online news and the growing "culture of connectivity" (Van Dijck 2013), which also contributed to this growing pressure on quality journalism. Not impeded by set publishing deadlines, online media could immediately publish the news and update it 24/7. Being the first with a certain news story put a strain on the factual accuracy and exhaustiveness of the coverage (Kovach and Rosenstiel 1999). Finally, (3) the possibilities to actively contribute to the news that social media offered also made the—already not that sharply delineated—difference between amateurs and profession-als fuzzier (Singer 2003). Subsequently, the blurring of this distinction put a strain on dominant professional quality standards, which started to lose prominence.

The critics subscribing to this "narrative of decline" (McNair 2010) try to find a cure by looking for economic and technological solutions to this problem. Yet, as Broersma and Peters (2013) point out, this perspective on the developments of the quality news media fails to question whether the state of turmoil (quality) journalism is in, is rooted in the core values of the journalistic profession itself. It assumes a static and self-evident set of professional quality standards firmly rooted in the objectivity regime. From this perspective, the "traditional" is basically equated with the "natural" and thwarts a fruitful debate on evolving professional journalistic standards (Schudson 2013).

The changes in journalism's media ecology, however, are so fundamental that its modernistic professional framework is being uprooted (Bogaerts and Carpentier 2013; Broersma and Peters 2013). Journalism is in the course of a transformation from an industrial production logic to a post-industrial logic, in which well-known news con-sumption rituals, such as reading the newspaper at breakfast, are quickly dissolving. Based on standardization and economies of scale, the industrial logic in journalism refers to a top-down dissemination of "a limited amount of identical information in a fixed order to a mass audience in an effective, attractive, relatively cheap and conve-nient way" (Broersma and Peters 2013, 4). This production logic was conducive to the rise of the objectivity regime and was simultaneously reinforced by it. The norms of providing the bare facts in a detached, unbiased, and neutral fashion basically meant filtering out the "mediating subjectivity" (Chalaby 1996) of the reporter and provided a successful framework to hierarchically enforce editorial uniformity (Broersma and Peters 2013; Harbers 2014; Schudson 2001).

The post-industrial logic revolves around a personalized and on-demand supply of news, which draws heavily on a more bottom-up participatory culture of liking and sharing of news content and commenting on or contributing to it (Broersma and Peters 2013; Deuze and Bardoel 2001; Jenkins 2006). Part of the reason why particularly estab-lished media are having a hard time adapting to this new logic is that they fail to acknowledge that not only the consumption patterns have changed, but also the way news is conceived of by the public (Broersma and Peters 2013; Deuze 2008).

An important factor in the transformation to a post-industrial logic that is seldom discussed is the rise of postmodern ideas about epistemology, knowledge production and truth (Bogaerts and Carpentier 2013).The professional framework of journalism under the objectivity regime is rooted in a modernist faith in people's ability to provide a truthful and coherent representation of reality (Bogaerts and Carpentier 2013; Zelizer 2004). Subsequently, this ability enabled people to overcome the problems society is facing (Welsch 2002). Yet, literary and philosophical postmodernism cast doubt on the influential epistemological assumption that a combination of rational inquiry and posi-tivistic methods makes it possible to represent reality in a coherent and universally truthful manner. Any representation is inherently partial and ideologically infused (Welsch 2002). Such ideas were conducive to the rise of a postmodern society and cul-ture, doubting progressivist ideas about the ability of "grand narratives" to explain the world in a coherent and encompassing way (Welsch 2002; Van Zoonen 2012). This emerging culture is typified by a decline in people's trust in core institutions, such as parliament, universities, and banks, and their ability to safeguard or improve fundamen-tal aspects of life, like individual freedom, labor, welfare, safety, and prosperity (Beck 1994).

For journalism this meant that the objectivity regime and its underlying assump-tions lost their self-evidence and increasingly met with critique. Scholars have pointed to the untenable oppositions between fact and value, detachment and engagement, neutrality and commitment, public and private, reality and story, and between informa-tion and entertainment that are foundational to the regime's truth claim. They question the validity of the distinction between hard and soft news, often used as synonyms for quality and popular (i.e. low-quality) journalism, which is also based on these opposi-tions (Conboy 2008; Van Zoonen 2012; McNair 2013).

Van Zoonen (2012) argues that new forms of personalized and experience-based journalism are gaining prominence and should not immediately be disqualified as lack-ing quality in the traditional sense. She coined the telling term "*I-Pistemology*" to refer to a journalism practice and culture in which personality and individuality play a pivotal role: "the self [has become] the source and arbiter of all truth" (56–57). Her analysis is indebted to research by well-known cultural sociologists Ulrich Beck and Anthony Gid-dens. They both argue that professionals, like politicians, scholars, and also journalists, are losing authority, because for every analysis, argument, or assessment they offer it is possible to find somebody else who states the opposite. As a result, the routines and methods of knowledge production are hollowed out (Beck 1994; Giddens 1994). This has not resulted in the rejection of such "modern" institutions altogether, but to what Beck (1994, 25, 29) calls the "self-opening of the monopoly on truth" or the "demonop-olization of expertise." With this he means that the traditional domains of knowledge production have become more pervasive and that the accepted forms in which knowl-edge is disseminated are complemented with new ones.

Beck emphasizes the opportunities of these developments rather than pointing to possible detriments. Whereas in modern society such fundamental doubts about the possibility of a unifying and monolithic understanding of the reality was always felt as a loss, he embraces the rejection of this idea as an opportunity—or liberation even—within the context of postmodern society and culture (Beck 1994; Welsch 2002). He envisions a shift in knowledge production in general towards a more diverse, modest, cautious, and open-ended process. His idea of demonopolization can explain the declining authority of the objectivity regime and the (re)emergence of a range of alternative forms of reporting that fundamentally challenge the modernist rhetoric of journalism (Bogaerts and Carpentier 2013; Broersma 2013).

Slow Journalism Between Tradition and Innovation

Although postmodern culture has eroded the self-evidence of journalism's traditional professional standards, several scholars have pointed to the remaining centrality of a universalistic truth claim in the way journalism has acquired and maintains its position and authority within society at large (Broersma 2010b, 2010a; Zelizer 2004). Marcel Broersma (2010a) argues that journalism's authority centers on its ability to convince its audience that they are able to represent reality in a truthful way. According to him, the rejection of the objectivity norm would mean confessing its inability to depict reality accurately, thereby refuting its own truth claim. He thus points to the inherent tension between journalism's goal to provide information that is accepted as truthful by as many people as possible and the realization that it cannot escape the inherent subjectivity of the reporting process. This leaves contemporary journalism with a structural tension between competing conceptions of what quality journalism should look like (Bogaerts and Carpentier 2013).

In her nuanced attempt to delineate what slow journalism is about, Megan Le Masurier (2015, 148) asks herself whether slow journalism actually offers a solution to the felt need to reassess journalism practice or if it is "just elitist, 'nostalgic modernism' pining after a simpler slower existence?"—indeed reflecting this broader tension within contemporary journalism. In her answer she shows the complex relation forms of slow journalism have with their faster counterparts. Le Masurier points out how slow journalism adopts traditional and broad criteria, such as independence, in-depth research, proportional coverage, thorough analysis, and contextualization, which are also fundamental to the norms of objectivity (McNair 2013; Ward 2004). Yet, the fact that these criteria are operationalized as transparent, reflective, interactive, and compelling forms of reporting (Le Masurier 2015) suggests that slow journalism is geared towards forms of reporting that do not conceal the underlying aspects of the reporting process in order to maintain the illusion of objective truth. Taking *De Correspondent* as a case study, I will further explore this way of conceptualizing slow journalism and illustrate how slow journalism might be regarded as an attempt to move beyond the idea that the objectivity regime is journalism's self-evident professional framework.

The Guiding Principles and Institutional Structure of *De Correspondent*

Wijnberg clearly presents his new journalistic platform as an alternative form of journalism in comparison to traditional quality journalistic outlets. *De Correspondent* is a journalistic platform without any advertisements (not including self-advertisements for the books some of their correspondents have written and which *De Correspondent* has published) to ensure journalistic independence. It is a commercial enterprise, but making a profit is not its primary aim. To make sure that profit maximization will never overhaul journalistic considerations as the driving force behind the platform, the profit distribution is capped at 5 percent of the gross revenue (Van der Valk 2015a). As their senior editor Andreas Jonkers mentioned, this freedom from such commercial pressures allows *De Correspondent*, for example, to largely ignore metrics about the popularity of articles as a criterion for what they publish and how they package a story.

What Wijnberg envisions is a journalism practice in which a reporter no longer only delivers a final product, which in its presentation is disconnected from the process of reporting. Instead, journalists should take their readers along on their attempt to make sense of the issue. This way Wijnberg aims to re-engage his readership by offering stories that capitalize on the reporter's mediating subjectivity. Reporters are encouraged to write from their own personal fascination and motivation, in which they do not have to maintain a neutral perspective. Based on thorough reporting and in-depth background research, they ultimately choose sides in a certain matter or determine what the best point of view is. The authority of the accounts is thus inextricably bound to the individual behind it.

The journalists are expected to give their readers access to their train of thought leading up to the definitive story, including their potential puzzlement, frustration, fascination, or commitment. This way, reporters can be open about any problems they have with truth verification and about the troubles they have to interpret what they learn, observe, or experience. Moreover, the readership is envisioned as actively contributing and discussing the reporter's depiction and analysis of the issue at hand. In short, Wijnberg aims to move away from presenting a finalized and monolithic representation of reality towards a way of reporting that is transparent about its constructional character and invites the reader to actively engage with the reporter's inquiry into an issue (cf. Karlsson 2010; Singer 2010).

Wijnberg is quick to emphasize that this conception of journalism should not be equated with partisan reporting or with the "journalism of assertion" for that matter. Although subjectivity and personality is embraced, independent truth verification remains at the heart of *De Correspondent*'s journalism practice (Wijnberg 2013b). Wijnberg's emphasis on the reverence for the truth shows once more how fundamental this claim is in legitimizing journalism (Zelizer 2004; Broersma 2010a, 2010b; Bogaerts and Carpentier 2013). Yet, by acknowledging the participatory culture and collective intelligence (Jenkins 2006), Wijnberg (2013b) tones down the universalistic connotation of "the truth" a notch and characterizes the current culture as "an era in which truth is no longer set in stone, but can be constantly updated. And subsequently contested in thousands of responses below the article."

This is why Wijnberg deliberately chose an online-only platform—besides avoiding the large costs that accompany any form of print journalism. He saw the opportunities of an online platform as a much better way to highlight the individuality and personal approach of the correspondents and to facilitate the actively participating readership he envisioned. In addition, it also allowed for more and more advanced ways to create digital files of interlinked and multi-media stories (Van der Valk 2015a, 2015b; Wijnberg 2013a). As a result, *De Correspondent* has an interface that shows the daily newsfeed, displaying the selection of stories for that day, but the platform is also structured through the personalized interest of their readers, who follow their handpicked selection of correspondents. These correspondents each have a so-called "garden," in which they write about a specific, but broad theme that relates to their expertise or fascination, such as "technology & surveillance," "conflict & development," "progress," or more unconventional "extraordinary and extra-terrestrial life." These gardens function as a sort of dossier, in which the correspondents can shed light on these themes from different angles, delve into a specific phenomenon or ongoing development or event to build up expertise and gain in-depth insight. In other words: the gardens create the conditions for in-depth issue-based journalism (Haas and Steiner 2006). In addition, it offers a space for other voices in the form of guest correspondents.

According to Jonkers, the platform publishes approximately four articles on every working day, two or three on Saturdays, and one or two every Sunday. This obviously relates to the much smaller size of the editorial staff, which makes it impossible to even come close to the amount of articles that newspapers publish. Jonkers stated that *De Correspondent* employs about 10 full-time journalists and has a larger and fluctuating network of part-time journalists and freelancers. But this publishing rhythm is also a deliberate choice. Jonkers disclosed that full-time correspondents are roughly expected to produce two larger "stories of the day" every month and preferably also two follow-ups on earlier pieces. This is clearly a big change of pace compared to daily newspaper journalism. It allows journalists to take their time to really delve into a story, to research it thoroughly, and to think about a fitting narrative form. This results in articles that are often substantially longer than average newspaper articles. The "stories of the day"—basically their most substantial and eye-catching stories that draw on and synthesize smaller stories about specific aspects or elements of an issue—that I have analyzed, for instance, have an average length of almost 2500 words.

How the Ideals Translate into Stories

To see how the correspondents shape the journalistic ideals of *De Correspondent* in their everyday practice the focus needs to be on their journalistic output. The analysis shows that what is common in the pieces of all the authors is their struggle to find a solid foundation for the truth claim of their accounts. They search for a way to present their stories without relapsing into a modernistic framework of providing finalized and monolithic representations of reality. Yet, they also stay clear from relativistic or solipsistic positions, in which any representation is only one possibility among many equally valid alternatives. I will analyze and illustrate this by discussing three aspects of the stories of the selected six correspondents: (1) the mediating subjectivity of the journalist, (2) factuality, and (3) transparency and reflection.

The Mediating Subjectivity of the Journalist

Contrary to the objectivity regime, factual information is not separated from the values and opinions of the reporter or from the level of experience and emotion (Chalaby 1998). In the accounts of *De Correspondent* these traditional oppositions are rejected and truthful information is not restricted to the "bare facts." This is not to say that all articles are an even mix of reportage, opinion or commentary, and personal experience. Some articles are predominantly analytic, written in a discursive mode, whereas others are clearly descriptive, written in a narrative mode (cf. Broersma 2010a). Nevertheless, in all accounts it is clear that the consciousness of the correspondent is the organizing principle of the story. He or she operates overtly as "mediating subjectivity" between reality and the reader. *De Correspondent* thus clearly moves away from the way stories governed by the objectivity regime are presented—as a "unified text which conceals the editor's intervention" (Bell, as quoted in Bogaerts and Carpentier 2013, 65). In no way do they hide that the representation of reality that is put forward is theirs, inherently influenced by their values, beliefs, impressions, and experiences. On the contrary, the correspondents employ several narrative techniques to signal to the readership that they are actively shaping the story.

The most basic way the correspondents do this is by using a first-person perspective in their stories instead of filtering out their presence in the text. It is a clear sign that the journalist has a role in the story. They exploit this technique to intervene in the story to explain the approach to the story, to share their impressions and experiences concerning a certain event or person, or to convey their thoughts on the matter at hand. It is a way for them to share their personal fascination or interest for a certain topic and explain to their readers why they think it is an important issue to focus on. Take the article by Vera Mulder (issue focus: society, behavior, and groups) on sexual intimidation of men. She starts out by describing how she was baffled by the machismo in the responses to an incident at her old high school where a female teacher sexually harassed a 16-year-old boy; the boy was generally characterized as a sissy. Her puzzlement about such responses and personal engagement sets off a broader inquiry into the sexual harassment of males and how it is viewed in society (Mulder 2014a).

At times the correspondents also relate their stories to their own personal experiences, which they share with their readers. This strategy enables them to elucidate abstract ideas or to convey their response to certain information or experiences. In his piece on the performative power of ideas in shaping society, Rutger Bregman (issue focus: progress) discusses Leon Festinger's famous research that shows how hard it is to change peoples' minds when it comes to their fundamental beliefs. To elucidate this mechanism he takes himself as an example:

> Half a year ago I wrote a piece about why we should shorten the working week. I had found all sorts of supporting arguments … I had to think about that piece while I read about Festinger's work. And particularly about the article I had come across at that time. The title read "Shorter Workweek May Not Increase Well-Being". It was an article in *The New York Times* about a study from the Republic of Korea where they had shortened the working week by 10 percent, without increasing the happiness of people. When I googled some more I read in *The Telegraph* that working less could even be bad for people's health … I immediately set off a few defense mechanisms … How certain were these research results exactly? Furthermore, I thought: ah well, those Koreans are total workaholics, they probably kept on working when they were off. And happiness, are we really able to measure it? Not really, right?
>
> I did not study the research any further. I had already convinced myself it wasn't relevant. (Bregman 2014a)

Next to their illustrative use, such personal elements make the journalist in question come across as more authentic; not just as a distant figure, but as an actual person. It therefore helps to build up a relation between the journalist in question and his or her readers.

This is reinforced by the writing style of the articles, in which the reader is regularly—explicitly or implicitly—addressed by the correspondent. Particularly the more analytic pieces by Rutger Bregman or Maurits Martijn make use of this strategy to make their readers part of their train of thoughts. They call out their readers by integrating short interjections in their stories, such as "Sounds plausible right?" (Bregman 2014a), "short question" (Bregman 2014b), or "Do you still remember?" (Martijn 2014a). In addition, in the way they set up their story and formulate their argument, it sometimes seems as if certain ideas are based on the input of their readers. When Martijn (issue focus: technology & surveillance) discusses the wiretapping policy of Obama he conveys that Obama has promised not to listen in on his allies unless there was "a compelling national security purpose." When he returns to this particular statement to point out the broad way this can be interpreted he formulates it as follows: "And yes, a 'compelling national security purpose' obviously offers a lot of space for a broad interpretation of this 'prohibition' [to tap the phones of his political allies]" (Martijn 2014b). The authors deliberately employ such a conversational register to make the readers part of the way they set up their argument and draw their conclusions. This is also why both correspondents occasionally move from the first-person singular ("I") to the first-person plural ("we"). The "we" refers to the correspondent and the readers together and suggests a shared perspective. By doing so, the correspondents implicate their readers in their implicit or explicit moral stand they take in the accounts.

The correspondents of the reportage pieces do not address the reader as often, but also try to involve their readers by providing them with a vicarious experience. Their on-site presence lies at the heart of their accounts. By detailed observations and in-depth interviews about the experiences of the people involved they try to depict concrete situations that shed light on an encompassing issue. On top of describing and explaining what is going on, they write in a way that aims to lend their senses to their readers and thus convey their impressions. When Maite Vermeulen (issue focus: conflict & development) examines how and why a large part of the humanitarian aid supplies that different humanitarian institutions distribute at different places all over the world comes from Dubai, she starts her account by sketching the environment:

> A brand new patch of asphalt draws a straight line through the desert of the United Arab Emirates as far as the eye can see. The skyline of Dubai disappears in the rearview mirror; the long antennas of an infinite number of skyscrapers fade away in the dusty air. The sand has paled all colors. It isn't summer yet, but the temperature outside moves close to 40 degrees [centigrade]. Nothing but low and gray vegetation, electricity cables and an occasional camel. (Vermeulen 2014)

Such accounts not only share information with the readership, but also aim to convey events and situations that are largely alien to the readership, such as the Papua New Guinean battle for independence and the Yezidi massacre by Islamic State, but also more mundane things like being part of a subculture of funfair attraction owners, on an emotional and experiential level (cf. Harbers 2014; Wahl-Jorgensen 2013; Zelizer 2007).

In both cases the correspondent acts as some sort of "witness-ambassador" who observes—and researches and analyzes in this case—on behalf of the readership. Muhlmann (2008, 21–22), who coined this term to characterize a type of reporting in which the journalist keeps on "reminding us, more or less implicitly, that they see *in all our names*, hence reminding us of the pact which binds them to 'us'."

Between Detached Fact and Lived Experience

The merging of factual information and commentary or personal experience is usually criticized as the deterioration of journalism, contributing to a "fact-free" democracy in which "truthiness," i.e. truth based on a gut feeling rather than on well-researched factual information, dominates (Ettema 2009; Van Zoonen 2012). Although the journalists of *De Correspondent* challenge the God-like status of detached fact, they do not reject the concept of factuality altogether (cf. Zelizer 2004). They are well aware of the potential critique of only offering unfounded statements based solely on punditry or personal experience or shortsighted and purely emotionally driven commentary; Wijnberg's discursive strategy to carve out a position within the field of quality journalism is partly built on the same reproach concerning the established media. It thus shows the split these journalists are in: they need to honor their constructivist reflexivity without abandoning the basic positivist principles of referentiality and vice versa. Their attempt to tackle this problem centers on the juxtaposition and merger of lived human experience—their own or that of their sources—and more abstract and encompassing quantified data and background information.

The critique of the superficiality and predictability of the choice of news topics as well as the coverage by the established media is both implicitly and explicitly voiced in the articles in *De Correspondent*. The following remark by Lennart Hofmann (issue focus: forgotten wars) in his reportage on the emancipatory effects of the participation of Kurdish women in the war against Islamic State exemplifies what all the correspondents aim for:

> In western media women such as Selgan are often portrayed as glamorous Amazon horsewomen who fight fearlessly for the survival of their people. Hidden behind this stereotype is an entirely different reality. A reality in which women use their new prominent role in society to free them of the patriarchal yoke. (Hofmann 2014a)

Rutger Bregman especially makes no secret of his attempt to go beyond the common interpretations and explanations concerning broad social-political issues. He extends the critique on the press to the domain of politicians and policy-makers, constantly pointing out where they go wrong. What is striking is the way he cements his analyses and arguments, for he strongly relies on and emphasizes the necessity of sound empirical research to base policy on—implicitly criticizing "fact-free politics." In his pieces he therefore strongly relies on scientific research and interviews mostly researchers for their expert perspective. In one of his articles about income inequality he introduces the research of Thomas Piketty as more or less the first one who sought to base his analysis of income inequality on sound empirical data.

> Forty years later Piketty realized that no decent historical research into inequality had been conducted since 1953. The debate was based on an abundance of prejudices and a *chronic absence of facts*. Kuznets [a Nobel prize-winning economist] himself had even written that his theories consisted of "5 percent empirical information and 95 percent speculation." (Bregman 2014c, italics added)

This emphasis on facts—in the sense of detached facts obtained following the standard scientific method adhering to the strict demands of reliability and validity—is exemplary for his stories. They are often set up as a way to debunk conventional wisdom, which, as Bregman then comes to show, lack a valid empirical basis. Moreover, he rhetorically presents his diverging take on the matter as quite obvious or even almost self-evident as long as the facts are taken into account. He also actively attempts to show that his alternative explanations are not only compelling from a left-oriented political position, but that they exceed conventional oppositions such as right versus left or conservative versus liberal. Bregman is the strongest representative of this reverence for a solid factual foundation, but the importance of first getting the facts straight underlies the stories of all the correspondents. All six journalists regularly draw on research and interview scholars and experts to cement their analyses, arguments or to contextualize their on-site observations and experiences.

Still, even the most analytical accounts in *De Correspondent* are never solely logical-abstract treatises or aloof contemplations. Such an abstract approach to reality on a macro-level is not considered to convey the entire picture. This comes to show that detached facts are considered important, but certainly not the only source of trustworthy knowledge. The correspondents also rely on lived experience. Firstly, they go to great lengths to carefully portray their sources. By giving them space to tell what happened and how it affected them and by describing their facial expressions while they do their story, they aim to convey the emotional impact of events, such as war, or the way they perceive reality. In that sense they bring cultures and events that are alien to a western public closer. As Karin Wahl-Jorgensen (2013) has shown, this "strategic ritual of emotionality" is not uncommon in quality journalism. By outsourcing the emotions to the people they talk to, this way of integrating the subjective level of the personal experience remains within bounds of the objectivity regime.

Many of the articles in *De Correspondent* go a step further though. The journalists also convey their own experience—which is directly related to their mediating subjectivity as organizing principle of their accounts. In an attempt to grasp the state of mind of George Orwell while he wrote 1984, Joris Van Casteren (2014a) traces Orwell's steps to the Scottish island Jura, where he wrote most of this seminal novel. Such accounts clearly value a more experience-based inquiry, which can convey knowledge in a much more concrete and applied way. Illustrative for this approach is Maurits Martijn's (2014c) story on the risks of public Wi-Fi networks. Instead of just analyzing the various risks, he asked a hacker to join him on a tour of several of Amsterdam's cafés and terraces to learn how easy it is to hack the computers, smartphones, or whatever kinds of device using public Wi-Fi. Martijn himself is the first guinea pig and experiences firsthand how easy it is to be hacked. Consequently, he makes the unknown or abstract risk of being hacked almost tangible. Such an approach adds to his authority in these matters and enables him to put more weight behind his moral appeal to the readers to take better care of their online privacy in an age of increasing surveillance.

Towards a Transparent Reporting Practice

Arguably the most innovative aspect of *De Correspondent* is its attempt to be transparent in the way journalists do their research, reach their conclusions, and construct their stories. The correspondents do so in several ways. Firstly, they make clear on which information they base their accounts and when possible enable the readership to consult it by integrating a link to the source. On average every article contains about three links and the "stories of the day" contain even more than double that number. This way the readers can actually verify the information the correspondents use to construct their story or just out of curiosity delve further into the topic.

Furthermore, the "garden structure" of the platform enables journalists to keep their readers updated about their progress on a story or to follow up on the story after publishing it. The journalists clearly exploit this opportunity as approximately 45 percent of the stories of the six correspondents is devoted to what I will call "process pieces." Such articles are labeled as "updates," "notes," "calls" (for input), and "suggestions." In anticipation of a larger story, Lennart Hofmann, for instance, writes a daily "note," which he uses as a sort of journalistic diary. This way he makes his readers part of his reporting process. Yet, this strategy is not restricted to such process pieces. One of the stories of the day by Maurits Martijn can be read as an encompassing follow-up on his older article on the risk of public Wi-Fi networks. The account starts off with a quick recap of the preceding story, but then Martijn pauses to seriously reflect on his own role:

> I formulate it as "we", but my role was rather limited. To prepare myself I had delved into technology and software the hacker would use, and during the story I kept on researching as well. That way I could grasp enough of the matter at hand to confidently write the story. But the hacker performed the actual fieldwork. I couldn't do what he could. I could only sit and watch. (Martijn 2014d)

The rest of the story is basically a summary of his experiences at a course to enhance his knowledge and skills of digital network technology. The article therefore conveys interesting information about how digital networks operate and simultaneously also gives the readers insight in the way Martijn goes about his journalistic work.

Making the reflection on the reporting process part of the story is something all correspondents do—though some correspondents more frequently or elaborately than others. The first-person perspective the correspondents employ already highlights their active presence and implicitly draws the attention to the reporting process. In addition, they also draw attention to their journalism practice in a more explicit way. Their accounts are interlaced with short moments of reflection on their own conduct. This ranges from a subtle comparison between the conventional coverage of the mainstream quality media and their own way of approaching a story (Bregman 2014d), conveying how they approached or experienced an interview (Martijn 2014e; Mulder 2014b) or by emphasizing the on-site presence of the reporter (Vermeulen 2014; Van Casteren 2014b; 2014a; Hofmann 2014b). The reporters exploit this reflection generally as a way to reinforce their authority by making clear how thoroughly and independently they examine an issue. Subsequently, it adds weight to the status of the value judgments they make in their accounts and the conclusions they draw.

Conclusion

Clearly, slow journalism offers a fruitful perspective through which to examine *De Correspondent*. Not only does Wijnberg's basic conception of journalism match the premises of slow journalism, but the actual journalism practice also lives up to these ideals. It would stand firm against the credo of "good," "clean" and "fair," which can be translated in terms of journalism as referring to careful research, nuanced and ethical coverage, and independent but morally engaged reporting (Le Masurier 2015). Yet, as Le Masurier acknowledges, this combination is not necessarily very innovative and has a long tradition in forms of quality journalism such as investigative reporting and long-form or narrative journalism.

What makes *De Correspondent* innovative is its explicit rejection of the objectivity regime as a suitable professional standard for our current digital and postmodern era. According to Wijnberg, this professional framework has become outmoded as it cannot adapt to a post-industrial production logic and as such fails to engage a new generation of news consumers (Wijnberg 2013a, 2013b; Broersma and Peters 2013). The alternative Wijnberg proposes is more in touch with the epistemological affordances of postmodern culture, yet does not accept a relativistic perspective on truth and knowledge. *De Correspondent* has traded in a top-down "Truth" for a work-in-progress aggregative truth with an overt moral grounding. The articles revolve around the mediating subjectivity of the journalist, who guides the readers through the relevant information and research, observes and experiences reality *in lieu* of the public, and implicates the reader in their moral judgments. On the one hand, the reporters show an unwavering faith in scientific empirical research, which they use to cement or contextualize their analyses, arguments, and experiences. Yet, they acknowledge the partiality of the information on this level and try to juxtapose it to or even fuse it to the more concrete level of human experience and emotion—either their own or that of their sources.

In their stories they are clearly aware of their subjective position, which manifests in the implicit and explicit reflection on their own position. The journalists of *De Correspondent* mainly use this reflection to be transparent about their reporting practice, thereby building their authority as well-informed and thorough professionals.

DISCLOSURE STATEMENT

No potential conflict of interest was reported by the author.

NOTES

1. All translations into English are the author's.
2. In this article, I use the term "postmodern" to refer to changes with regard to ideas on epistemology and knowledge production. I am well aware that it is only one option and is closely related to notions such as "liquid modernity" and "reflexive modernization" (see Bauman 2000; Beck, Giddens, and Lash 1994).

REFERENCES

Bauman, Zygmunt. 2000. *Liquid Modernity*. Cambridge: Polity Press.

Beck, Ulrich, Anthony Giddens, and Scott Lash, eds. 1994. *Reflexive Modernization. Politics, Tradition and Aesthetics in the Modern Social Order*. Cambridge: Polity Press.

Beck, Ulrich. 1994. "The Reinvention of Politics: Towards a Theory of Reflexive Modernization." In *Reflexive Modernization. Politics, Tradition and Aesthetics in the Modern Social Order*, edited by Ulrich Beck, Anthony Giddens and Scott Lash, 1–55. Cambridge: Polity Press.

Biressi, Anita, and Heather Nunn. 2008. "Introduction." In *The Tabloid Culture Reader*, edited by Anita Biressi and Heather Nunn, 1–4. New York: Open University Press.

Bogaerts, Jo, and Nico Carpentier. 2013. "The Postmodern Challenge to Journalism. Strategies for Constructing a Trustworthy Identity." In *Rethinking Journalism. Trust and Participation in a Transformed News Landscape*, edited by Chris Peters and Marcel Broersma, 60–72. New York: Routledge.

Bregman, Rutger. 2014a. "Hoe Ideeën De Wereld Veranderen." *De Correspondent*. April 24.

Bregman, Rutger. 2014b. "Waarom Een Uitdijende Overheid Geen Ziekte Maar Een Zegen is." *De Correspondent*. June 9.

Bregman, Rutger. 2014c. "Al Onze Theorieën over Het Kapitalisme Weerlegd in één Grafiek." *De Correspondent*. March 24.

Bregman, Rutger. 2014d. "Waarom Politieke Partijen Steeds Meer Op Elkaar Lijken." *De Correspondent*. July 16.

Broersma, Marcel. 2010a. "Journalism as a Performative Discourse. the Importance of Form and Style in Journalism." In *Journalism and Meaning-Making: Reading the Newspaper*, edited by Verica Rupar, 15-35. Cresskill: Hampton Press.

Broersma, Marcel. 2010b. "The Unbearable Limitations of Journalism: On Press Critique and Journalism's Claim to Truth." *International Communication Gazette* 72 (1): 21–33.

Broersma, Marcel. 2013. "A Refractured Paradigm: Journalism, Hoaxes and the Challenge of Trust." In *Rethinking Journalism. Trust and Participation in a Transformed News Landscape*, edited by Chris Peters & Marcel Broersma, 28–44. New York: Routledge.

Broersma, Marcel & Chris Peters. 2013. "Introduction: Rethinking Journalism: The Structural Transformation of a Public Good." In *Rethinking Journalism. Trust and Participation in a Transformed News Landscape*, edited by Chris Peters and Marcel Broersma, 1-12. New York: Routledge.

Castells, Manuel. 1996. *The Rise of Network Society*. Oxford: Blackwell.

Chalaby, Jean. 1996. "Journalism as an Anglo-American Invention: A Comparison of the Development of French and Anglo-American Journalism, 1830s-1920s." *European Journal of Communication* 11: 303–326.

Chalaby, Jean. 1998. *The Invention of Journalism*. Hampshire: Macmillan Press.

Conboy, Martin. 2008. "The Popular Press: Surviving Postmodernity." In *The Tabloid Culture Reader*, edited by Anita Biressi and Heather Nunn, 45–52. New York: Open University Press.

Davies, Nick. 2009. *Flat Earth News: An Award-Winning Reporter Exposes Falsehood, Distortion and Propaganda in the Global Media*. London: Vintage Books.

De Correspondent. 2013. "Crowdfunding Record for Quality Journalism." *Decorrespondent.Nl*. Accessed November 12 2015. http://blog.decorrespondent.nl/post/46365101498/crowd funding-record-for-quality-journalism

Deuze, Mark. 2008. "The Changing Context of News Work: Liquid Journalism and Monotorial Citizenship." *International Journal of Communication* 2: 848–865.

Deuze, Mark, and Jo Bardoel. 2001. "Network Journalism: Converging Competences of Old and New Media Professionals." *Australian Journalism Review* 23 (2): 91–103.

Ettema, James. 2009. "The Moment of Truthiness: The Right Time to Consider the Meaning of Truthfulness." In *The Changing Faces of Journalism. Tabloidization, Technology and Truthiness*, edited by Barbie Zelizer, 114–126. New York: Routledge.

Franklin, Bob. 2008. "Newzak: Entertainment versus News and Information." In *The Tabloid Culture Reader*, edited by Anita Biressi and Heather Nunn, 13–22. Berkshire: Open University Press.

Giddens, Anthony. 1994. "Living in a Post-Traditional Society." In *Reflexive Modernization. Politics, Tradition and Aesthetics in the Modern Social Order*, edited by Ulrich Beck, Anthony Giddens and Scott Lash, 56–109. Cambridge: Polity Press.

Greenberg, Susan. 2011. "Personal Experience, Turned Outward: Responses to Alienated Subjectivity." *Free Associations* 12 (2): 151–174.

Haas, Tanni, and Linda Steiner. 2006. "Public Journalism: A Reply to Critics." *Journalism* 7 (2): 238–254.

Hackett, Robert A., and Yuehzi Zhao. 1998. *Sustaining Democracy? Journalism and the Politics of Objectivity*. Toronto: University of Toronto Press.

Harbers, Frank. 2014. *Between Personal Experience and Detached Information. the Development of Reporting and the Reportage in Great Britain, the Netherlands and France,* 1880-2005. Groningen: s.i.

Hofmann, Lennart. 2014a. "Hoe De Strijd Tegen iS De Koerdische Vrouw Emancipeert." *De Correspondent*. December 17.

Hofmann, Lennart. 2014b. "In Deze Jungle Vinden Honderden Onopgemerkte Executies Van Papoea's Plaats." *De Correspondent*. May 28.

Jenkins, Henry. 2006. *Convergence Culture: Where Old and New Media Collide*. New York: New York University Press.

Karlsson, Michael. 2010. "Rituals of Transparency." *Journalism Studies* 11 (4): 535–545.

Kovach, Bill, and Tom Rosenstiel. 1999. *Warp Speed: American in the Age of Mixed Media*. New York: The Century Foundation.

Le Masurier, Megan. 2015. "What is Slow Journalism?" *Journalism Practice* 9 (2): 138–152.

Martijn, Maurits. 2014a. "Hoe ABN Amro Weet Dat Jij Een Buggy Nodiq Hebt." *De Correspondent*. June 20.

Martijn, Maurits. 2014b. "Het Adagium Van Obama Blijft: Yes We Scan." *De Correspondent*. January 22.

Martijn, Maurits. 2014c. "Dit Geef Je Allemaal Prijs Als Je Inlogt Op Een Openbaar Wifinetwerk." *De Correspondent*. March 20.

Martijn, Maurits. 2014d. "We Begrijpen Onze Technologie Niet (En Daar Kun Je Wat Aan Doen)." *De Corrrespondent*. July 10.

Martijn, Maurits. 2014e. "Hoe Wapenen We Ons Tegen De Machine Die Nooit Vergeet?" *De Correspondent*. January 6.

McNair, Brian. 2010. *Journalism and Democracy: An Evaluation of the Political Public Sphere*. London & New York: Routledge.

McNair, Brian. 2013. "Trust, Truth and Objectivity. Sustaining Quality Journalism in the Era of the Content-Generating User." In *Rethinking Journalism. Trust and Participation in a Transformed News Landscape*, edited by Chris Peters and Marcel Broersma, 75–88. New York: Routledge.

Muhlmann, Géraldine. 2008. *A Political History of Journalism*. Cambridge: Polity Press

Mulder, Vera. 2014a. "Een Opgewonden Juf is De Natte Droom Van Elke Puberjongen. Toch?" *De Correspondent*. January 20.

Mulder, Vera. 2014b. "De Cobra 6, Een Handgranaat Van Vijf Euro?" *De Correspondent*. August 13.

Njotea, Andrea. 2013. "News Distorts Our View of the World" *Journalismfund.Eu*. March 5. http://www.journalismfund.eu/news/"news-distorts-our-view-world"

Schudson, Michael. 2001. "The Objectivity Norm in American Journalism." *Journalism* 2 (2): 149–170.

Schudson, Michael. 2013. "Would Journalism Please Hold Still!" In *Rethinking Journalism. Trust and Participation in a Transformed News Landscape*, edited by Chris Peters & Marcel Broersma, 191–199. New York: Routledge.

Singer, Jane. 2003. "Who Are These Guys? The Online Challenge to the Notion of Journalistic Professionalism." *Journalism* 4 (2): 139–163.

Singer, Jane. 2010. "Journalism Ethics amid Structural Change." *Daedalus* 139 (2): 89–99.

Sparks, Colin. 2000. "Introduction. the Panic over Tabloid News." In *Tabloid Tales. Global Debates over Media Standards*, edited by Colin Sparks and John Tulloch, 1–40. New York: Rowman & Littlefield Publishers.

Van Casteren, Joris. 2014a. "Hier Schreef George Orwell Zijn Profetische Meesterwerk 1984." *De Correspondent*. July 18.

Van Casteren, Joris. 2014b. "De President Van Papoea Woont Al Veertig Jaar in Apeldoorn." *De Correspondent*. January 3.

Van der Valk, Leendert. 2015a. "In 8 Dagen 15 Duizend Abonnees Voor Een Medium Dat Nog Niet Bestaat." *Nieuwe Journalistiek*. March 3. http://nieuwejournalistiek.nl/startup-decorrespondent/2015/03/03/in-8-dagen-15-duizend-abonnees-voor-een-medium-dat-nog-niet-bestaat/.

Van der Valk, Leendert. 2015b. "De Correspondent Werd Bedacht Binnen De Muren Van NRC Media." *Nieuwe Journalistiek*, January 30. http://nieuwejournalistiek.nl/startup-decorrespondent/2015/01/30/de-correspondent-werd-bedacht-binnen-de-muren-van-nrc-media/.

Van Dijck, José. 2013. *The Culture of Connectivity. A Critical History of Social Media*. Oxford: Oxford University Press.

Van Zoonen, Liesbet. 2012. "*I*-Pistemology: Changing Truth Claims in Popular and Political Culture." *European Journal of Communication* 27 (1): 56–67.

Vermeulen, Maite. 2014. "Bijna Alle Noodhulp Ter Wereld Komt Uit Deze Woestijn." *De Correspondent*. June 18.

Wahl-Jorgensen, Karin. 2013. "The Strategic Ritual of Emotionality: A Case Study of Pulitzer Prize-Winning Articles." *Journalism* 14 (1): 129–145.

Ward, Stephen. 2004. *The Invention of Journalism Ethics: The Path to Objectivity and beyond*. Montreal & Kingston: McGill-Queen's University Press.

Welsch, Wolfgang. 2002. *Unsere Postmoderne Moderne*. Berlin: Akademie Verlag.

Wijnberg, Rob. 2013a. *De Nieuwsfabriek: Hoe De Media Ons Wereldbeeld Vervormen*. Amsterdam: De Bezige Bij.

Wijnberg, Rob. 2013b. "Waarom Een Verhaal Niet Zonder Verteller Kan." *De Correspondent*. April 13. [Consultable at: http://blog.decorrespondent.nl/post/47858813554/waarom-een-verhaal-niet-zonder-verteller-kan

Williams, Kevin. 2010. *Read All about It. A History of the British Newspaper*. New York: Routledge.

Zelizer, Barbie. 2004. "When Facts, Truth, and Reality Are God-Terms: On Journalism's Uneasy Place in Cultural Studies." *Communication and Critical/Cultural Studies* 1 (1): 100–119.

Zelizer, Barbie. 2007. "On "Having Been There": "Eyewitnessing" as a Journalistic Key Word." *Critical Studies in Media Communication* 24 (5): 408–428.

"MAKE EVERY FRAME COUNT"
The practice of slow photojournalism and the work of David Burnett

Andrew L. Mendelson and **Brian Creech**

This paper presents a case study of the possibilities of slow photojournalism. Over the past decade, award-winning photojournalist David Burnett has used a 60-year-old Speed Graphic film camera to document US political events, several Olympic Games, and the aftermath of Hurricane Katrina, among other projects. His photographs reveal a significantly different aesthetic from contemporary photojournalism and he is celebrated for the perspective his analog photographs offer. This analysis is based on two points of examination: first, a textual analysis of articles and videos discussing the work; and second, a semiotic analysis of the imagery. The examination suggests Burnett's photo aesthetic signifies a longing for an imagined analog, journalistic utopia of yore, where individual journalists had the time and freedom to put care and attention into their work.

Introduction

Journalism is at a time of incredible technological and economic disruption, leaving individual journalists with a great deal of professional uncertainty due to declining revenues, circulation, and public trust. While many journalists have lost their jobs over the past decade, those who remain are expected to do more with less, more quickly, on more platforms, with less oversight. Photojournalists have been especially hard hit, as the use of digital cameras by all journalists is expected (Anderson 2013; Associated Press 2013).

It is not surprising that many journalists wax nostalgically for the analog days of journalism, a perceived golden age when money, jobs, and time were plentiful. Photographers often lament the loss of the film as a symbol of more than just technological change. It symbolizes lost craftsmanship, thoughtfulness, and control in photojournalism, and ultimately, an essential journalistic perspective produced by skilled professionals.

Slow journalism offers one answer to the current era of journalistic hyper-speed. Inspired by the slow food movement, the term connotes a conscious rejection of mindless journalism (Le Masurier 2015). This paper presents a case study of the possibilities of slow *photo*journalism. Over the past decade, award-winning photojournalist David

Burnett has used a 60-year-old Speed Graphic film camera to document US political events, several Olympic Games, and the aftermath of Hurricane Katrina, among other projects. His photographs reveal a significantly different aesthetic from contemporary photojournalism and he is celebrated for the perspective his analog photographs offer. This analysis is based on two points of examination: first, a textual analysis of articles and videos discussing the work; and second, a semiotic analysis of the imagery. The examination suggests Burnett's photo aesthetic signifies a longing for an imagined analog, journalistic utopia of yore, where individual journalists had the time and freedom to put care and attention into their work.

Burnett has been a professional photographer for more than five decades, getting his start on his high school yearbook. Soon after, he began covering high school sports for local papers. He has never been a wire service or newspaper staff photographer, shooting mostly for magazines. He has photographed all over the world and, during the 1970s, made his name making photographs in places such as Vietnam, Chile, Pakistan, and Iran, mostly for *Time-Life* ("Shooting Film in the Digital Age and Other Conundrums" 2013). He has been known as a photographer who enjoys experimenting with a variety of cameras in order to get different views of situations. This has included standard 35 mm single lens reflex (SLR) cameras, both film and digital, plastic, fixed-lens Holgas, medium-format Mamiyas, and the larger format Speed Graphic.

The Possibilities of Slow Photojournalism

Digitization has meant the speeding of all aspects of journalism: faster reporting, faster production, and faster distribution. Many embrace the technological changes as a part of a new journalistic golden age, while others decry these changes as the end of many of the normative ideals of journalism (Creech and Mendelson 2015; McChesney 2013). The pressure to be first leads to inevitable errors, increased sensationalism, and increased reliance on sources for information and framing (Le Masurier 2015). As early as 1999, Kovach and Rosenstiel (1999, 5) argued that the practice of journalism was "being displaced by the continuous news cycle, the growing power of sources over reporters, varying standards of journalism, and a fascination with inexpensive, polarizing argument" (see also Mitchell 2015; Vehkoo 2009/10).

Slow journalism is part of a larger movement that calls for a conscious re-examination of the role of speed and technology in our lives. Many commentators see similarities between the slow food movement and a slow journalism movement. Gess (2012, 56) states: "As with food, much journalism has become an anonymous, homogenized, reliable product that can be accessed across the globe via television, print media, the Internet and, increasingly, mobile platforms." The same characteristics that make McDonald's uninteresting, and un-nourishing as food, make journalism uninteresting and un-nourishing for democracy (Franklin 2005).

Slow journalism implicates the commodification of news and the fetishization of digital technologies, reacting to the perceived decline in standards for contemporary journalism. As Rob Orchard, the editor of the slow journalism magazine *Delayed Gratification* states: "It's an antidote to the hyper, hyper speed of today's digital news production" (Orchard 2014, 15:48). While definitions of slow journalism vary, most emphasize quality journalistic content, produced through quality processes. Thus, slow journalism can be seen as the antithesis of and reaction to contemporary digital journalism, both in process and form, as its proponents seek to "disentangl[e] our association of news and journalism with speed and instantaneity" (Le Masurier 2015, 139).

Slow journalism consciously emphasizes the reporting and production process ("What is This Thing Called the Slow Journalism Movement?" 2010), arguing for a sense of craftsmanship that places individual journalistic voices over institutional ones. For instance, Le Masurier (2015) argues that journalists need to immerse themselves in places for extended periods of time to produce work that contains the subtleties of ethnography. A number of writers point to the work of Pulitzer Prize-winning journalist Paul Salopek, who, for *National Geographic*, is spending seven years walking out of Africa, retracing the path of human migration (Allen 2012; Osnos 2013; Smith 2013). As Howard (2015) quotes Paul Salopek, "Slow journalism allows me to make hidden connections that you miss when you travel too fast."

Ultimately, it could be said that slow journalism is a philosophy and a form of boundary maintenance. As Carlson (2015) notes, shifting technological conditions within the industry have led to a widespread sense of disruption around what it means to be a journalist and to do journalism. Movements and professional philosophies, such as slow journalism, emphasize certain values by defining and celebrating practices and identities that embody these values. As such, they create a definitional waypoint for understanding what good journalism looks like despite rapidly changing audiences, financial arrangements, and technological pressures. Photography, then, offers one place where the fight over these boundaries and values plays out.

Slow Photography

Digital photography has turned everyone into photographers through widespread diffusion of networked camera phones, allowing people with little training to produce and distribute photographs quickly (Gye 2007; Mendelson 2013; Vincent 2006). This has challenged the nature and practices of all forms of professional photography, including wedding photography, art photography, and photojournalism.

Not surprisingly, a parallel slow photography movement has formed, with proponents decrying the increasing emphasis on photographic quantity over quality (Budliger 2012; "What is the Slow Photography Movement" 2011; Wu 2011). Many see the rise of digital as the decline of thoughtfulness in photography. Wu (2011) expresses concern over the way tourists produce photographs: "Men and women would approach, say, Jesus' tomb, quickly turn their gaze to the back of their cameras, take a few flash photos, and move on." In essence, people are no longer experiencing subjects; they are merely checking off photographic boxes.

The slow photography approach often means looking back to older processes and equipment that by their nature require the photographer to be more intentional in what and how photographs are made (Kaplan 2013; Pullan, n.d.).[1] Austin (2012) sees slow photography as a rebellion, calling for a "mindful photography process," overthrowing the pressure to rapidly shoot and post photographs. Film, and the cameras that rely on it, is a large part of slow photography because it requires more attention and allows photographers to better demonstrate their skill. The use of film is more than just an aesthetic or technological choice; it is a philosophical one as well, as its permanence, scarcity, and finitude place more pressure on the photographer to think about every frame and make it count.

Slow photography is part of a larger critique of digital photography, which casts a skeptical eye toward overtly progressive notions of technological advancement. Some see digital images pushing toward a kind of postmodern inevitability, obscuring forever the relationship between the image and the reality it recorded (Coleman 1998; Lipkin 2005; Winston 1996). The proliferation of digital images has created the possibility for an infinite number of perspectives around an object, leading to what McKenzie (2014, 104) has identified as a void surrounding the authoritative representation of reality: "The digital era evolves from a larger history of photomedia but has maintained its own specific characteristics such as heightened fragmentation of image-spaces, and the instantaneous speed of light-time and its antithetical expression in slowness." For these critics, digital photography's storage capacity and the ability to quickly snap a botched shot dilutes the care that goes into each moment of photographic composition.

It is important to remember that digital and analog photography embody a continuity of similar practices. As Henning (2007, 53) argues, "Analog photography was not being outpaced or becoming obsolescent, it had to be *made* obsolescent." Digital photography grew out of a manufacturing process that derived profit from producing cameras that were mass-market consumables, thus leading to a broadly conceived notion of the digital image as being as disposable and easily reproduced as a Polaroid image. While the time-conscious demands of professional journalism would benefit from a digital workflow that reduced the number of steps between a photographer's initial perception of an image and the final product, the fidelity of early digital cameras did not meet the reproducibility standards of traditional publications. Only when digital cameras began to offer the same image control options available in high-end analog cameras did digital technology "appear just as a new, improved means for the practice of photography" (59). Yet, as a remnant and obsolescent technology, analog photography contains an alternative aesthetic and epistemological authority of representation once suppressed by dominant market forces, Henning argues. It is this alternative and possibility that Burnett's use of the Speed Graphic typifies, his images gaining part of their meaning and significance counter-posed to an idiom of image production dominated by the ways of seeing the digital camera embodies.

Conventions of Photojournalism

News photography, like all forms of journalism, is highly conventional and predictable, both in terms of content and form (Mendelson 1999, 2001; Rosenblum 1978). News photographers rely on a limited set of choices when making photographs, due to the equipment, definitions of news, professional standards, and time pressures. These ways of seeing are internalized through education and training, implicitly and explicitly dictating the nature of "good" photographs (Hall 1973; Lutz and Collins 1993; Newton 2001). For instance, news conventions can be seen in political photographs, which focus on a limited set of moments, such as speeches, campaign stops, and enthusiastic supporters with signs (Gleason 2005; Hall 1973). Similarly, sports photographs, emphasizing peak action, and moments of triumph and defeat, reflect a different set of narrow conventions (Hagaman 1993). Even feature photographs, those images of everyday life regularly found in newspapers, are structured around a limited set of visual tropes (Mendelson 2004). Additionally, the conventions of news photography, especially for newspapers, dictate a certain look that includes little evidence of the presence of the photographer (Mendelson 2013; Schwartz 1999). These conventions often extend from a production routine that privileges standardization, and as such, acts of slow photojournalism offer a critique of production routines via photographic aesthetics. As former Farm Security Administration photographer Arthur Rothstein argued:

> There is a definite relationship between the equipment used by the photojournalist and the style of his picture. This stems not only from the physical nature of the camera, lens and film used, but also from the manner of working which the equipment imposes. (Rothstein 1965, 173)

There have always been divides between various forms of photography: art versus photojournalism; newspaper versus magazine photography. Each area has different professional, stylistic, and technological norms (Rosenblum 1978). Traditionally, magazine photographers have had greater aesthetic latitude, often blurring the lines with art photography (Weinberg 1986), allowing more room for individual expression, over the more standardized look of newspaper photography. They embraced (or were allowed to embrace) such inventions as 35 mm cameras and color photography earlier than newspaper photographers. Moreover, due to the reproduction quality of magazines, greater subtlety was possible, both in terms of tonality and subject matter.

The multiple aesthetic traditions within photojournalism can grossly be divided into two areas: newspaper versus magazine, or alternatively, American versus European approaches. These traditions really become distinct in the 1930s and 1940s, as the use of the Speed Graphic became institutionalized in newspaper photography, especially in the United States, and the lighter 35 mm cameras were picked up by magazine photographers, beginning in Germany and France. Chapnick (1994, 233) differentiates between the American and European styles of photojournalism, with the latter being more personal, less reliant on norms of objectivity: "Most photographic staffs on American newspapers are interchangeable, endorsing the same photographic and journalistic aesthetic."

Weinberg (1986), in his catalog to an exhibit on "new color photojournalism," which included works by David Burnett, argues that such photographers are really hybrid, bridging boundaries between multiple aesthetic traditions. "The photographers in the exhibition successfully play art against journalism, trying to reap the most from each, honing their perceptual and observational powers in the process" (23). Moreover, this form of photojournalism, like the earlier new journalism movement, should be "seen as a critique of the traditional photojournalistic mode and as a personalizing and humanizing of the mass media" (30).

As digital changes affect work routines, this changes the way photographs are produced as news products. As Zavoina and Reichert (2000) found in the early days of newsrooms' digital transition, print-centric routines dominated as publishers and news executives were slow to treat digital news as fundamentally different from the printed product. Robinson (2011) chronicles the changes in several newsrooms in the latter part of the decade, finding that for many news workers, digital changes required an attention to relationship between organizational culture and work routines, including the skills that individuals were expected to know. Photography often gets overlooked in this mix, but digital cameras and digital workflows necessitated changes in the ways photographers and photo editors approached their work. As photographers navigated these changes individually and collectively, they created production standards that separated digital photojournalism from its analog predecessors, both aesthetically and logistically. Photojournalists continue to accommodate new tools and techniques into their practice, even when those tools are something as seemingly simple as a consumer image-filtering app (Alper 2014).

Perhaps most important for the purposes of this essay, scholars have found that digital cameras have had the most impact on the ways individual photographers work while in the field. Dunleavy (2004) notes that digital screens and viewfinders allow photographers to evaluate their work immediately and produce a comparatively unlimited number of images while shooting on assignment. This material arrangement condenses, and often collapses, "the transitional rite of exposing, developing and printing" (4). Digital tools allow for more reshoots and afforded photographers more opportunities to bring images closer to their individual perception. By way of contrast, as is apparent in Burnett's case, the analog Speed Graphic camera reasserts itself in the process, demanding that the photographer comport himself to its limits, with the mastery and understanding of the mercurial device becoming part of the individual's craft (Hauptman 1998).

Burnett first started using a Speed Graphic for journalistic purposes in 2003, covering hearings at the start of the Iraq war ("David Burnett Speaks at Luminance 2012" 2012; "In the Bag with David Burnett" 2011). The Speed Graphic was the mainstay camera for newspaper photographers for nearly 50 years from the mid-teens to the mid-sixties (Cookman 2009; Fulton 1988). This is the camera used by Joe Rosenthal on Iwo Jima, and the one used by Weegee to document the seedier side of New York City. As Weegee wrote:

> If you are puzzled about the kind of camera to buy, get a Speed Graphic … for two reasons … it is a good camera and moreover, it is standard equipment for all press photographers … with a camera like that the cops will assume that you belong on the scene and will let you get beyond the police lines. (Weegee [1945] 1973, 240)

The Speed Graphic afforded a certain way of seeing, one that intersected perfectly with professional norms of the time (Szarkowski 1973). The photos are most often straight shots with deep focus, mostly from a distance suggesting an onlooker's point of view, what Millet (2004, 1) calls "direct, unfussy". Cookman (2009, 97) describes the Speed Graphic aesthetic: "What seemed normal during the era is easily recognizable now as the Speed Graphic aesthetic–static, posed situations, illuminated by artificial lighting." Apart from the work of Weegee, the photographs of the Speed Graphic era appear interchangeable, with little in the way of individual expression.

These cameras are large when compared to 35 mm cameras, producing a 4 inch by 5 inch negative. Unlike the 35 mm roll film, the Speed Graphic used film holders, each holding two pieces of sheet film, which had to be loaded in advance in a darkroom (Collins 1990; Kobre 2008). Because each film holder only held two pieces of film, photographers were very frugal in how and what they shot, looking to capture an image that encapsulated an entire event. As Fulton states:

Each negative had to count because the time it took to pull out one holder and replace it with a second, plus the limited number of holders any one photographer could carry, meant that the photographer might have only one chance to capture an event. (Fulton 1988), 122)

The nature of the Speed Graphic required intentionality. There were a number of steps one had to go through to make a single image, from focusing, composing, removing the protective card over the film, releasing the shutter and replacing the card. Burnett uses a Speed Graphic Pacemaker from the late 1940s, along with a fast lens originally designed for reconnaissance flights during World War II ("David Burnett Speaks at Luminance 2012" 2012). This lens allows him to produce photographs with less depth of field than the standard lenses used by news photographers of the 1930s and 1940s.

Methodology

The following analysis approaches the case of Burnett from two angles: looking at the discourses that surround his work and semiotically analyzing his Speed Graphic photographs to learn what makes them aesthetically and rhetorically distinct from their digital counterparts. This approach allows us to account for the meanings embodied in the photos and the social meanings that surround them.

In order to analyze Burnett's images we relied on semiotics, treating the individual images and the body of work as a set of signs in dialogue with other forms of older and contemporary forms of news photography, as well as trends in digital photography, in general. Such an analysis requires "taking an image apart and tracing how it works in relation to broader systems of meaning" (Rose 2012, 105). This requires looking for, according to Hall (1975, 15), "recurring patterns [that] are taken as pointers to latent meaning." We are guided by Rose's (2012) and Barthes' (1977) structure for semiotic analysis, examining both denotative and connotative levels of meaning by interrogating subject matter and the inflections placed upon subjects through compositional choices.

In order to investigate these choices, we look at the vantage point of Burnett's images: from where do we see the subjects. Such choices include camera angle, distance to subject and subject placement within the frame, in addition to the use of graphical elements, such as repetition, leading lines, and lighting. It is the sum of the choices that constitute his individual perspective, the aesthetic imprint enabled by the technical choices the photographer makes.

To understand the social meanings around Burnett's images, we conducted a textual analysis of news coverage about and commentary on his process. To interrogate the field of discourse that makes sense of Burnett's work, we gathered articles and profiles that emphasize his process, searching for statements that articulate the value of his work and placing those within the larger context of conditions within the journalism industry. We located 12 articles from popular and trade publications, as well as blog posts, which discussed or interviewed Burnett about his use of the Speed Graphic. Additionally, we located 11 videos featuring Burnett discussing his use of this camera. The following themes recurred throughout the texts, articulating the significance of the alternative visual journalism embodied by Burnett's work: nostalgia and loss in the digital age; the Speed Graphic and the slowing of the image production process.

As Fursich (2009) argues, textual analysis allows scholars to attend to modes of meaning-making, treating journalistic texts as the sites where the reality and significance of an issue, event, or person adheres to clearly delineated structures of meaning. This means attending to the practices that bring texts into being and explicating the contexts that allow these texts to cohere and make sense. To trace the construction of social meaning across texts, Hall (1975) encourages researchers to attend to the conditions under which the statements and articulations found in media texts make sense, looking for patterns that coalesce into the broader articulation of a worldview. Articles about Burnett constitute what is known as "metajournalistic discourse," meaning that disparate texts can be read to understand the context that renders his work a significant example within the practice of journalism (Carlson 2013).

Analysis

Nostalgia and Loss in the Digital Age

Burnett sees himself as constantly looking for new ways to see events in order to challenge prevailing journalistic conventions by changing the technical aspects of his process ("David Burnett—On Conflicts, Olympics, Politics, & More—Photo Brigade Podcast #55" 2014). As he states: "The thing is, I've always liked new kinds of hardware because they give me another way to look at something. They help me see something in a little different way" (Estrin 2012). While he recognizes the value of digital cameras, he also states the mark of the artist gets lost in the process, partly due to the ease of operation of digital cameras:

> The new cameras let us make pictures that were never even imaginable a dozen years ago. But in all of that, in the rush to bestow the crown of technical achievement upon the head of digital photography, I think we risk losing a piece of the soul of all our work. (Burnett 2012)

Burnett often conflates the aesthetics of older, analog photographs with lost artistry:

> I look back at the pictures from the '20s and '30s and wonder how they got any pictures at all with the super-slow film and lenses. And they did a great job. I want to come up with something as timeless and classic. (Estrin 2012)

Such statements indicate an overarching nostalgia that Burnett is attempting to recapture and evoke via his own photographs, an act made possible only through the camera itself: "I get a lot of inspiration out of just trying to match what some great cigar chomping sports photographer did with an old Speed Graphic" (NBC News 2014).

Nostalgia in this sense is just as much about aesthetics as it is a strategy for claiming legitimacy. By consciously echoing an idealized bygone era, he claims the authority of history for his photos and offers a means by which they can be understood as valuable. For example, of some of his London 2012 Olympics photos, he states:

> The stuff I shot today, which is pretty much all in black & white although I shot in color too, the black & white has become a more timeless look. I was looking at one today, where the coach was lifting up the player and I thought this kind of looks like what the 1948 games might have looked like. (Jarecke 2014)

The Speed Graphic camera remains the key to the process, offering a technical means for transporting his photographic perspective into an era where the photographer's lens contained greater authority and value.

Speed Graphic and Slowed Process

Much of the praise for the Speed Graphic in a digital era centers on the fact that it requires photographers to slow down, to be mindful and intentional while shooting. This is not a camera that can be rushed. Burnett is only able to make one or two photographs, while colleagues utilizing digital cameras can fire off many more ("David Burnett Speaks at Luminance 2012" 2012). The camera itself demands that the individuals comport themselves to its workings:

> It forced me to start looking for pictures in a different way … In the era of digital, we are used to instant gratification. The Speed Graphic slows you down. You have to become a master of anticipation. (Rykoff and Newman 2015)

In a number of videos and articles about Burnett, there is an emphasis on the hard work, both physical and mental, required to use the Speed Graphic, especially compared to digital cameras. For example,

> Making pictures this way is, by the way, a huge pain in the ass. Those sheets of film need to be loaded in their holders in a darkroom—or, if you're a photojournalist on the road, a motel bathroom with a bathmat shoved against the light leaking under the door. (Magers and Burnett 2013)

As with artisanal processes in the slow food movement, the physical demands of the process necessitate a kind of attention often lost in more routinized, industrialized processes: "Shooting in the field requires its own deft dance: open the shutter, compose the photo, close the shutter, drop in the film holder, pull the darkslide, pop the shutter, return the darkslide, remove the film holder, repeat" (Magers and Burnett 2013); or, as Burnett states, "[The Speed Graphic] demands a lot. You have to do about eight things in the right order just to take a picture" ("David Burnett Speaks at Luminance 2012" 2012, 19:50). Therefore, it can be said that the camera asserts itself in the process. "It forces you to really figure out what you are trying to shoot. I am going to get one frame off, maybe a second" ("David Burnett Speaks at Luminance 2012" 2012, 23:32).

The resulting photographs are often described as something more than run-of-the-mill news photographs. As the *Washington Post*'s Van Riper states:

> The images Dave got—and still is getting—are gorgeous, with all of the wonderful tonal range and modeling that available light photography affords. In addition, the much shallower depth of focus of the 4 × 5 camera helps Burnett to isolate his subject dramatically. (Van Ripper 2004)

These photographs bear the evidence of their process in their compositional choices, for instance: "A tableau of field-hockey players looks like miniature dolls individually placed on a felt playmat. Beach volleyball players seem suspended by invisible string on a puppeteer's stage" (Schiesel 2005). These aesthetic distinctions, when celebrated by observers and critics, act as evidence of a photographic process that owes its value to the contrast it draws to a visual culture dominated by purely digital ways of seeing:

On the screen was a wide overhead picture of a John Kerry rally last fall in Madison, Wis., which Mr. Burnett shot with a Canon 20D digital camera, the same camera used by thousands of other professionals around the world. Not surprisingly, the picture looks like thousands of others that were shipped around the globe during the campaign … And then Mr. Burnett flipped to a photograph taken seconds later with the ancient Speed Graphic. Suddenly, the image took on a luminescent depth. The center of the image, with Mr. Kerry, was clear. Yet soon the crowd along the edges began to float into softer focus on translucent planes of color. (Schiesel 2005)

The aesthetics of individual photos become the evidence of a unique perspective behind the camera, of an artist who can and should be celebrated for his intentional technical intervention into the photographic process. In the highly technical field of photojournalism, Burnett's mastery over his process is often celebrated for its uniqueness. By turning to the photos themselves, we can begin to see how this uniqueness can be distilled as the interplay between the photographer and the device captured in the final object, as if these photos are consciously shot to bear the marks of their creation.

Speed Graphic Photographs and Broken Conventions

Celebrations of Burnett's Speed Graphic work often hinge upon the presence of a unique perspective captured in the photographs. To discern and interrogate the construction of this perspective, we examined nine different galleries on David Burnett's website (DavidBurnett.com 2015), featuring images produced using the Speed Graphic, organized around specific assignments, such as the aftermath of Hurricane Katrina or the London Olympics, or themes such as sport or Presidents. He also has a gallery, entitled "Big Camera," devoted to work with the Speed Graphic. In addition, we examined his Speed Graphic photographs in specific online publications, including *National Geographic* (Gaines and Burnett 2006), *Time* (Burnett 2007), Al Jazeera America (Lanpher 2015), Roads and Kingdoms (Thornburgh 2013), and *The Washington Post* (Tucker 2014). In total we examined 341 images.

In another gallery on his website, "Classics, Old and New," he presents a selection of his best-known photographs over the past five decades. Most of these represent conventional magazine photojournalism aesthetics, mostly shot from eye-level at a medium to close-up distance from the subject. These photographs emphasize specific newsworthy moments: Mary Decker at the Los Angeles Olympics in 1984 after being tripped, an Iranian protester holding up blood-soaked hands. Even in this collection, an individual point-of-view is evident, such as the photograph from above Juan Peron's open casket or Carl Lewis crossing the finish line to win, showing only his knees down and shadows.

Burnett mostly uses the Speed Graphic to produce images that stand in contrast to conventional news photographs, both in subject and aesthetics. The unique demands of Burnett's process, along with his celebrity as a photographer, afford him the freedom to turn his camera away from traditionally newsworthy moments and look elsewhere for images that transcend the news of the day. With the Speed Graphic, he positions himself further away from the "action" in order to take in a greater context, often at extreme high or low angles, views that are less common around newsworthy events.

A good example of the difference between more conventional news photographs and his work with the Speed Graphic can be seen in two photographs he made of John Kerry during a 2004 campaign stop in Madison, Wisconsin, discussed above by Schiesel (2005). Burnett photographed the speech from behind and above Kerry poised from the bucket of a cherry-picker, using both a digital SLR (DSLR) and the Speed Graphic. The DSLR image, because of the distance, renders Kerry and many of the crowd sharp enough to discern individual faces and signs. On the other hand, the Speed Graphic image has only a thin area in focus centered around Kerry, placing the viewer in a position as if looking into another world or peering through a microscope. This lack of sharpness renders most of the crowd unreadable as individuals, but, since it does not appear compressed there is a sense that the crowd goes on and on. The overall effect is a scene that looks like it is a diorama of a campaign. While both shots freeze Kerry in mid-gesture, the Speed Graphic image feels much less dynamic, as if this moment would go on forever, rather than quickly be over-written by Kerry's next gesture. This image, as a distillation of an event into a singular moment, demonstrates the aesthetics found throughout Burnett's Speed Graphic work.

Out of Time

Burnett's Speed Graphic photos convey the sense they exist outside time because they neither have the aesthetic style of 1930s Speed Graphic images, nor do they look like contemporary photojournalism. For instance, when Burnett photographed the back half of an Old Chevy in Havana, the use of the shallow/tilt focus and the washed-out colors enhanced an aesthetic frozenness to Cuba as a country and culture existing outside of normal geopolitical relations, even while a woman is caught in mid-action, climbing into the car.

In another gallery, Burnett photographed Lincoln re-enactors at a gathering in Illinois. Given evidence of contemporary life, the images read old, and not just due to the outfits of the re-enactors. They have the formality of portraits from the studio of Mathew Brady, the leading portrait, and later war, photographer of the US Civil War period. This aesthetic appears in many of his political portraits as well. They are classic, even Victorian, harkening back to daguerreotypes or wet plate portraits of politicians in their quietness and formality, where subjects had to hold themselves still due to the requirements of the cameras and photography process.

Burnett's photographs reveal an intentional echo to photographs from much earlier eras. A photograph from Bangladesh shows two people descending a gangplank with baskets of cement on their heads. They are the only two people in focus, as the rest of the image recedes in blur. A black and white image, it is toned to look like it could have been taken 150 years ago through wet process photography and a fixed aperture lens limiting the amount of focus, like a photograph out of the portfolio of Felice Beato, a mid-nineteenth-century photographer of India and China, whose images have a certain painterly look.

Many of his Olympic images likewise appear somehow out of time. In Sochi, Burnett photographed skiing events, isolating the athletes against dramatic skies or the slope. The tonality suggests another era, though not one associated with newspaper style. The look is closer to that of Leni Riefenstahl's stills from the 1936 Olympics, though she was just as likely to photograph close up, producing intense shots of people. Burnett's photographs are more likely to isolate lone athletes in a small portion of the frame. By stylistically placing his photographs out of time, Burnett separates subjects from their contemporary moment, distilling meaning into a moment that is not easily overwritten by other images due to its distinct look.

Dream-like and Psychologically Distant

Burnett's Speed Graphic photographs suggest a dream state into which viewers are peering at a removed distance. For example, in a photograph, titled "Baseball Returns to Washington, D.C.," a lone outfielder is viewed from behind looking toward the infield. In the distance, ghost-like players appear, barely readable, due to the tilt effect. Similarly, in a portfolio of D-Day veterans, the tilt effect echoes the fading, imperfect memories of both survivors and the larger culture. This can be seen in a number of other photographs he made of survivors of Pinochet's reign in Chile. In one image, a group of former political prisoners gather in the stadium where they were held. Only the center of the group is sharp and the photo blurs toward the periphery of the frame, an effect that renders many of the group increasingly ghost-like.

Limited focus, when used in sports photographs, suggests the zone top athletes enter, shutting out the world around them. In a rare victory shot, Burnett photographed the winner of the Men's Triathlon in London breaking the tape. Only the athlete is sharp. No other person is recognizable and therefore no other person matters; just the lone athlete lost in a world of intensity. In another photograph, Burnett freezes two synchronized divers soon after leaving the platform, unnamed, frozen in a moment of clarity surrounded by haze. Burnett often photographs quiet moments away from competition, as athletes prepare. These are not moments of interaction, but moments of intense focus, enhanced through aesthetic choices.

Burnett's images, rather than bringing viewers closer to a scene, often distance them. His images of Hurricane Katrina are vignetted, with washed-out color. The effect of both of these choices, in addition to shallow and tilted focus, creates dream-like, haunted looks. The photographs present what was left behind: dishes on a Formica counter, layered in sand and mud; a car covered in mud; a set of children's stained Sunday clothes hanging in a ruined house.

Each of Burnett's stylistic choices lends artistic and journalistic authority to a photographic aesthetic that bears the marks of a perspective closely tied to technical mastery. In a twenty-first-century update to Walter Benjamin's (1936) notion that important works of art lose the aura of their power in reproduction, pictures that bear the aesthetic marks of the photographer's process draw their value from the ways they distinguish themselves amid a field crowded with easily snapped and shared digital photographs. Such is the practice of creating contrasts: the photos are not easily replaced by anything else because they do not look like anything else

Conclusion

David Burnett's Speed Graphic work offers us a number of lessons about contemporary photojournalism and the larger slow journalism movement. His photographs differ from contemporary news photographs in how they were produced, what they show, and how they document news stories.

In terms of process, he literally and figuratively steps back and slows down, revealing moments before, between, or after the conventional or expected. His moments are more subtle, emphasizing, in narrative terms, moments on either side of the climax. This echoes Chapnick's (1994, 236) call: "There is more to the documentation of the human condition than the chronicling of dynamic events at decisive times." By using film and an antique, clunky camera, Burnett is forced to take his time, both in composing his photographs and making them. The camera does not allow quick alterations of setup, especially when using a tripod. Moreover, a limited number of film holders need to be prepared in advance. Finally, each frame takes about 30 seconds to make, requiring each push of the button to count. Paired with the complexity of the camera, Burnett also forces himself away from the more conventional moments and positions, looking for new scenes from new locations. He locates situations that are normally photographed in ways that emphasize dynamism as static and distant. This again means being mindful of what has come before and consciously not reproducing that. He attempts to create transcendent moments, using the capabilities of his Speed Graphic to do so.

Burnett's photographs are not just windows on the world, as conventional news photographs are expected to be, despite being shot with what was a conventional press camera. The resulting photographs are laden with symbolism, different from contemporary news photographs and even those that would have originally been produced with a Speed Graphic 60 years ago. The aesthetics force viewers to think about what is being shown and why it is being shown to us in that way. Burnett's photographs challenge the viewer to think about the reasons for the shallow depth-of-field, the miniature look to the figures, the washed-out color (Worth and Gross 1981). This is not the way news photographs are supposed to look. If conventional news photographs are declarative, stating definitively, "this is," Burnett's photographs force viewers to think beyond the "this is:" to wonder, question, and think about the subject. A slow and mindful approach to photography lends itself to a slow and mindful reception.

Conventional news images, those from 60 years ago and those from today's digital era, reflect a corporate, institutional voice. Though new photographs are initially shot by a photographer, the image that is published reflects a chain of implicit and explicit decision-making involving numerous people. The result of this gatekeeping, especially with today's time and economic pressures, is a rather homogenized product: standard ways of seeing standard subjects.

At a time when photojournalists face an insecure professional life, Burnett challenges the speed and generic nature of today's digital McJournalism (Franklin 2005). These Speed Graphic images demonstrate an alternative, though like much of the slow food movement, it would be anathema for this to scale to an industrial level. Limited to small-batch, yet highly prized, projects, Burnett's status over a 50-year career allows him the freedom to express himself away from the pack. The results are photographs that reflect not the traditional objective and institutional voice of journalism, but rather that of an individual artist. The camera does not just technologically determine his approach, as he combines the affordances of the Speed Graphic with his own contemporary sensibility. These images do not look like tabloid newspaper shots from the 1930 or 1940s. He uses the Speed Graphic to differentiate himself and demonstrate the value of an individual craftsman.

The nostalgia and sense of timelessness in the photos are not intrinsic to the moments that David Burnett captures, but are the intentional results of his process. They bear the imprimatur of a perspective that draws its value from being so different from everything else around it. Audiences can understand Burnett's use of the Speed Graphic as embodying a journalistic viewpoint capable of seeing things that contemporary, digitized processes foreclose precisely because they already consume from the crowded field of digital images from which Burnett's stand apart. While one can question the feasibility of returning to a time when every news image was shot on a large-format camera, it is perhaps more useful, we conclude, to focus on the possibility Burnett's photos contain: each act of journalism, digital or otherwise, may be rendered valuable and culturally significant if it embodies the care and thought of the person behind the tools.

DISCLOSURE STATEMENT

No potential conflict of interest was reported by the authors.

NOTE

1. While this paper focuses on analog forms of slow photography, there are forms of slow photography that are digital. *National Geographic* magazine, for example, provides photographers longer periods of time to produce photographic stories (Vanhanen 2015).

REFERENCES

Allen, Kate. 2012. "American Journalist Paul Salopek to Spend Next 7 Years Walking to Retrace Humankind's Origins." *Toronto Star*, December 22. http://www.thestar.com/news/world/2012/12/22/american_journalist_paul_sa
lopek_to_spend_next_7_years_walking_to_retrace_humankinds_origins.html

Alper, Meryl. 2014. "War on Instagram: Framing Conflict Photojournalism with Mobile Photography Apps." *New Media and Society* 16 (8): 1233–1248.

Anderson, Monica. 2013. "At Newspapers, Photographers Feel the Brunt of Job Cuts." *Pew Research Center*, November 11. http://www.pewresearch.org/fact-tank/2013/11/11/at-newspapers-photographers-feel-the-brunt-of-job-cuts/

Associated Press. 2013. "Chicago Sun-times Lays off All Its Full-Time Photographers." *New York times*, May 13. http://www.nytimes.com/2013/06/01/business/media/chicago-sun-times-lays-off-all-its-full-time-photographers.html?_r=1

Austin, Jim. 2012. "SPR: Slow Photography Rebellion! Film Photography Project." October 29. http://filmphotographyproject.com/content/features/2012/10/spr-slow-photography-re bellion

Barthes, Roland. 1977. *Image-Music-Text*. New York: Hill and Wang.

Benjamin, Walter. 1936 [1968]. "The Work of Art in the Age of Its Mechanical Reproduction." In *Illuminations: Essays and Reflections*, edited by Hannah Arendt, 217-252. New York: Harcourt Brace.

Budliger, Kurt. 2012. "Slow Photography Movement." *Kurt Budliger Photography*, June 12. http://kurtbudliger.com/slow-photography-movement/

Burnett, David. 2007. "The Boys Are All Right." *Time.Com*, July 26. http://con tent.time.com/time/photogallery/0,29307,1647411,00.html

Burnett, David. 2012. "2012 Summer Olympics - David Burnett." *SportsShooter.Com*, August 27. http://www.sportsshooter.com/news/2648

Carlson, Matt. 2013. "Gone but Not Forgotten: Memories of Journalistic Deviance as Meta-journalistic Discourse." *Journalism Studies* 15 (1): 33–47.

Carlson, Matt. 2015. "Introduction: The Many Boundaries of Journalism." In *The Boundaries of Journalism*, edited by Matt Carlson and Seth C. Lewis, 1–19. New York: Routledge.

Chapnick, Howard. 1994. *Truth Needs No Ally: Inside Photojournalism*. Columbia, MO: University of Missouri Press.

Coleman, Allan, D. 1998. *The Digital Evolution: Photography in the Electronic Age*. Portland, OR: Nazareli Press.

Collins, Douglas. 1990. *The Story of Kodak*. New York: Harry Abrams Inc.

Cookman, Claude. 2009. *American Photojournalism: Motivations and Meanings*. Evanston, Illinois: Northwestern University Press.

Creech, Brian, and Andrew L. Mendelson. 2015. "Imagining the Journalist of the Future: Technological Visions of Journalism Education and Newswork." *The Communication Review* 18 (2): 142–165.

"David Burnett - On Conflicts, Olympics, Politics, & More - Photo Brigade Podcast #55." 2014. YouTube video. Posted by "The Photo Brigade." December 24. https://www.youtube.com/watch?v=PZ6GT6MAZ28.

"David Burnett speaks at Luminance 2012." 2012. Vimeo video. Posted by "PhotoShelter.Com." October 17. https://vimeo.com/51632894.

DavidBurnett.com. 2015. "Galleries." http://www.davidburnett.com/portfolio.html?folio=Gal leries.

Dunleavy, Dennis. 2004. "In the Age of Instant: The Influence of the Digital Camera on the Photojournalistic Routines of Productivity, Empowerment, and Social Interaction between Subject and Photographer". PhD diss., University of Oregon.

Estrin, James. 2012. "An Olympic Photographer's Endurance." *NYTimes.Com*, June 19. http://lens.blogs.nytimes.com/2012/07/19/an-olympic-photographers-endurance/

Franklin, Bob. 2005. "McJournalism? The Local Press and the McDonaldization Thesis." In *Journalism: Critical Issues*, edited by Stuart Allan, 137–150. London: Open University Press.

Fulton, Marianne. 1988. *Eyes of Time: Photojournalism in America*. Boston, MA: Little, Brown and Company.

Fursich, Elfriede. 2009. "In Defense of Textual Analysis: Restoring a Challenged Method for Journalism and Media Studies." *Journalism Studies* 10 (2): 238–252.

Gaines, Ernest J., and David Burnett. 2006. "New Orleans Portfolio." *NationalGeographic.Com*, August. http://ngm.nationalgeographic.com/2006/08/hurricane-aftermath/gaines-text

Gess, Harold. 2012. "Climate Change and the Possibility of 'Slow Journalism'." *Ecquid Novi: African Journalism Studies* 33 (1): 54–65.

Gleason, Timothy. 2005. "The Candidate behind the Curtain: A Three-Step Program for Analyzing Campaign Images." *Simile* 5 (3): n.p.

Gye, Lisa. 2007. "Picture This: The Impact of Mobile Camera Phones on Personal Photographic Practices." *Continuum: Journal of Media & Cultural Studies* 21 (2): 279–288.

Hagaman, Diane. 1993. "The Joy of Victory, the Agony of Defeat: Stereotypes in Newspaper Sports Feature Photographs." *Visual Sociology* 8 (Fall): 48–66.

Hall, Stuart. 1973. "The Determinations of News Photographs." In *The Manufacture of News: Social Problems, Deviance, and the Mass Media*, edited by Stanley Cohen and Jock Young, 176–190. London: Constable.

Hall, Stuart. 1975. "Introduction." In *Paper Voices: The Popular Press and Social Change, 1935-1965*, edited by A.C.H. Smith, 11–24. Totowa, New Jersey: Rowan and Littlefield.

Hauptman, Jodi. 1998. "FLASH! the Speed Graphic Camera." *The Yale Journal of Criticism* 11 (1): 129–137.

Henning, Michelle. 2007. "New Lamps for Old: Photography, Obsolescence, and Social Change." In *Residual Media*, edited by Charles R. Acland, 48–65. Minneapolis, MN: University of Minnesota Press.

Howard, Brian Clark. 2015. "Seven-Year Walk Highlights Power of 'Slow Journalism." *NationalGeographic.Com*, January 16. http://news.nationalgeographic.com/news/2015/01/150114-slow-journalism-paul-salopek-eden-walk/

"In the Bag with David Burnett." 2011. YouTube video. Posted by "PhotoShelter". June 2. https://www.youtube.com/watch?v=UnL24q11oEU

Jarecke, Kenneth. 2014. "David Burnett - an Interview." Jarecke & Murnion Creative Group, February 21. http://www.jmgroupmt.com/blog/2/21/david-burnett-interview-sochi-olympics

Kaplan, Melanie D. G. 2013. "The 'Slow Photo' Movement, Developing a following." *The Washington Post*, August 25. http://www.melaniedgkaplan.com/IDEAS_articles_files/Slow%20Photo.pdf

Kobre, Kenneth. 2008. *Photojournalism: The Professionals' Approach*. Burlington, MA: Focal Press.

Kovach, Bill, and Tom Rosenstiel. 1999. *Warp Speed: America in the Age of Mixed Media*. New York: The Century Foundation.

Lanpher, Katherine. 2015. "Lincolnpalooza: At Their Annual Convention, Abe and Mary Todd Take over Small-Town Illinois." *Al Jazeera America*, May 1. http://projects.aljazeera.com/2015/05/lincoln-convention/

Le Masurier, Megan. 2015. "What is Slow Journalism?" *Journalism Practice* 9 (2): 138–152.

Lipkin, Jonathan. 2005. *Photography Reborn: Image Making in the Digital Era*. New York: Henry N. Abrams.

Lutz, Catherine A., and Jane L. Collins. 1993. *Reading National Geographic*. Chicago, IL: The University of Chicago Press.

Magers, Michael., and David Burnett. 2013. "The Speed Graphic Returns." *Roads & Kingdoms*. http://roadsandkingdoms.com/2013/the-speed-graphic-returns/

McChesney, Robert W. 2013. *Digital Disconnect: How Capitalism is Turning the Internet against Democracy*. New York: The New Press.

McKenzie, Jai. 2014. *Light + Photomedia: A New History and Future of the Photographic Image*. New York: I.B. Taurus and Co.

Mendelson, Andrew L. 1999. "What Makes a Winner? The Role of Novelty in the Pictures of the Year Competition." *Visual Communication Quarterly* 6 (4): 8–14.

Mendelson, Andrew L. 2001. "Effects of Novelty in News Photographs on Attention and Memory." *Media Psychology* 3 (2): 119–157.

Mendelson, Andrew L. 2004. "Slice-of-Life Moments as Visual 'Truth:' Norman Rockwell, Feature Photography, and American Values in Pictorial Journalism." *Journalism History* 29 (4): 166–178.

Mendelson, Andrew L. 2013. "The Indecisive Moment: Snapshot Aesthetics as Journalistic Truth." In *Assessing Evidence in a Postmodern World*, edited by Bonnie Brennen, 41–66. Milwaukee, WI: Marquette University Press.

Millet, Larry. 2004. *Strange Days Dangerous Nights: Photos from the Speed Graphic Era*. St. Paul, MN: Borealis.

Mitchell, Lincoln. 2015. "It's Time for a Slow Journalism Movement." *Observer,* January 1. http://observer.com/2015/01/the-media-embarrasses-itself-attacking-steve-scalise/

NBC News. 2014. "David Burnett: Capturing the New World in Old School Fashion." *KSL.Com*, February 21. http://www.ksl.com/?nid=335&sid=28802588

Newton, Julianne H. 2001. *The Burden of Visual Truth: The Role of Photojournalism in Mediating Reality*. Mahwah, NJ: Lawrence Erlbaum Associates.

Orchard, Rob. 2014. "The Slow Journalism Revolution." YouTube video. Posted by "TEDx Talks." Oct 13. https://www.youtube.com/watch?v=UGtFXtnWME4.

Osnos, Evan. 2013. "On Slow Journalism." *The New Yorker*, January 31. http://www.newyorker.com/news/daily-comment/on-slow-journalism

Pullan, Steven IV. n.d. "Slow Photography." http://ourcollective.org/slow-photography/.

Robinson, Sue. 2011. "News Work and News Space in the Digitally Transforming Newsroom." *Journal of Communication* 61 (6): 1122–1141.

Rose, Gillian. 2012. *Visual Methodologies: An Introduction to Researching with Visual Materials*. London: Sage Publications.

Rosenblum, Barbara. 1978. "Style as Social Process." *American Sociological Review* 43: 422–438.

Rothstein, Arthur. 1965. *Photojournalism: Pictures for Magazines and Newspapers*. New York: American Photographic Book Publishing Company Inc.

Rykoff, Mark, and Alex Newman 2015. "Master Photographer David Burnett Slows down with His Speed Graphic Camera." *Vantage*, May 5. https://medium.com/vantage/master-photographer-david-burnett-slows-down-with-his-speed-graphic-327ef7591368

Schiesel, Seth. 2005. "Which Camera Does This pro Use? It Depends on the Shot." *NYTimes.Com,* June 8. http://www.nytimes.com/2005/06/08/technology/circuits/which-camera-does-this-pro-use-it-depends-on-the-shot.html

Schwartz, Dona. 1999. "Objective Representation: Photographs as Facts." In *Picturing the past: Media, History, and Photography*, edited by Bonnie Brennen and Hanno Hardt, 158–181. Urbana, IL: University of Illinois Press.

"Shooting Film in the Digital Age and Other Conundrums." 2013. YouTube video. Posted by "B & H Photo." February 18. https://www.youtube.com/watch?v=9RRhDd8YWtk.'

Smith, Jenn. 2013. "National Geographic Journalists Follow Footsteps of Our Human Ancestors." *The Berkshire Eagle,* December 29. http://www.berkshireeagle.com/news/ci_24810405/trek-across-time-national-geographic-journalists-follow-footsteps

Szarkowski, John. 1973. *From the Picture Press*. New York: The Museum of Modern Art.

Thornburgh, Nathan. 2013. "David and Daniel." Roads and Kingdoms. http://roadsandking doms.com/2013/david-and-daniel/

Tucker, Neely. 2014. "No Ordinary Lives: A Tribute to Washington's WWII Veterans." *Washing-tonPost.Com*, November 7. https://www.washingtonpost.com/lifestyle/magazine/no-or dinary-lives-a-tribute-to-washingtons-wwii-veterans/2014/11/06/0bd95aee-5875-11e4-b812-38518ae74c67_story.html

Van Riper, Frank. 2004. "Burnett's 4x5: Covering Politics the Hard Way." WashingtonPost.Com, February 26. http://www.washingtonpost.com/wp-srv/photo/essays/vanRiper/040226. htm

Vanhanen, Hannu. 2015. "The Paradoxes of Quality Photographs: Slow Journalism in National Geographic." In *Integrated Media in Change*, edited by Riitta Brusila and Hannu Van-hanen, 85–104. Rovaniemi, Finland: Lapland University Press.

Vehkoo, Johanna. 2009/2010. "What is Quality Journalism and How It Can Be Saved." Reuters Institute Fellowship Paper. University of Oxford. https://reutersinstitute.politics.ox.ac. uk/sites/default/files/What%20is%20Quality%20Journalism%20and%20how%20can% 20it%20be%20saved'.pdf

Vincent, Jane. 2006. "Emotional Attachment and Mobile Phones." *Knowledge, Technology, & Policy* 19 (1): 39–44.

Weegee. [1945]1973. *The Naked City*. New York: Da Capo Press, Inc.

Weinberg, Adam D. 1986. *On the Line: The New Color Photojournalism*. Minneapolis, MN: Walker Art Center.

"What is the slow photography movement." 2011. *Jorg & Olif: The Slow Life Company*, Febru-ary 2. http://jorgandolif.com/think/slow-photography-movement/

"What is this Thing called the Slow Journalism Movement?" 2010. *YouTube Video from a Panel Discussion at USC. Posted by USCAnnenberg*, June 16. https://www.youtube.com/ watch?v=4WbP5H3AlW8

Winston, Brian. 1996. *Technologies of Seeing: Photography, Cinematography, and Television*. London: British Film Institute.

Worth, Sol, and Larry Gross. 1981. "Symbolic Strategies." In *Studying Visual Communication*, edited by Sol Worth and Sol Worth, 134–147. Philadelphia, PA: University of Pennsylva-nia Press.

Wu, Tim. 2011. "The Slow-Photography Movement." *Slate.Com*, January 18. http://www.slate. com/articles/life/obsessions/2011/01/the_slowphotography_movement.html

Zavonia, Susan, and Tom Reichert. 2000. "Media Convergence/Management Change: Evolving Workflow for Visual Journalists." *Journal of Media Economics* 13 (2): 143–151.

THE BUSINESS OF SLOW JOURNALISM
Deep storytelling's alternative economies

David Dowling

This study examines the commercial viability of Slow Journalism in light of its recent efforts to reinvent the business model in the news industry today that relies heavily or exclusively on display advertising for revenue. Some Slow Journalism companies, such as De Correspondent *and* Delayed Gratification, *have defiantly positioned themselves in opposition to advertising's prominent role in mitigating free online news production and consumption, which they argue is both philosophically and financially anathema to the intimate journalist–reader interface. Still others, such as* Narratively, *have also eliminated display advertisements, but openly embrace brand sponsorship through events, creative agency, and native advertising. Touting visually pleasing high-end production values for immersive reading environments free of distracting display advertisements, many publishers promote a relation in which supply meets demand without undisclosed, conflicting third-party or corporate interest. This research explores the methods by which several prominent Slow Journalism organizations have mobilized a critique of corporate media to strategically communicate their maverick missions. The case studies examine* Delayed Gratification, De Correspondent, Narratively, *and* The Big Roundtable *as expressions of Slow Journalism's experimental approaches to for-profit enterprise through alternative media business models.*

Introduction

> There's certainly a subversive pleasure in occupying yourself with something for an unreasonable length of time. (Peter Fischli, Experimental Artist)

The editorial policy of *De Correspondent*, the Dutch digital magazine, reads like a manifesto for a journalistic revolution. Boldly defying Big Media's escalating reliance on retailers and third-party corporate interests as vital sources of revenue, the editors pledge that "the ultimate goal" of the platform, like the larger Slow Journalism movement, "is to improve journalism, not to fill the pockets of shareholders" (Wijnberg 2013). For *Delayed Gratification*, the definition of Slow Journalism is also ostensibly viewed as an economic prospect. Under the heading "We Invest in Journalism," the editors assert that while "everyone else is sacking journalists, cutting editorial budgets, and using generic wire services to fill the gaps, we are going the other way." Their against-the-grain business model involves "putting every penny from every subscription to *Delayed Gratification* back into tracking down and publishing amazing stories from the journalists on the ground" (Orchard 2015). Slow, in this sense, means more accurate stories. Rather than entering the Twitter-driven race to dispatch summaries and flashy headlines "that fly around the high-speed high-tech world in an instant," the editors stake their claim on accuracy at the expense of speed (Bishop 2015). Hence, they reason that the added value of "slow" journalism's deep reporting and storytelling should command a price commensurate with its painstaking process of production. In a news ecosystem increasingly dominated by advertisers who entice media organizations to provide free content, most Slow Journalism publishers instead believe readers would be willing to pay for stories—in some cases as voluntary donations—written according to this higher journalistic standard.

This article examines Slow Journalism's experimental alternatives to mainstream media's reliance on traditional advertising as the main source for revenue. Most print and digital Slow Journalism publishers have either eliminated or severely restricted display, banner, and pop-up advertisements that compete with editorial content for readers' attention. Instead, they deploy a diverse array of revenue packages. The Spanish Slow Journalism magazine *Jot Down*, for example, augments its print subscription profits by selling 10 percent of the space in their main product to sponsors (Breiner 2015). The American publication *Narratively* draws income by functioning as a creative agency that brokers lists of its contributors to companies in need of content production, while earning supplemental financial support through brand sponsorships and native advertising (Fennell 2015; Rosenberg 2015). In these and other Slow Journalism companies, a limited use of advertising is just one part of an eclectic revenue mix that aims to immerse rather than distract reader attention, an approach well suited to the new digital market premium of time on page that has eclipsed the old metric of page views.

Case studies representing a wide range of publishing formats focus on the business models of the print-only *Delayed Gratification* and the digital-based *De Correspondent*, *Narratively*, and *The Big Roundtable*. With the exception of *Narratively*, which runs on a partnership model to support its longform journalism, the other three business models leverage various forms of subscription, micro-payment models for parts of the digital product or single purchase, including different forms of donation, social payment, and crowdfunding. In contrast to Slow Journalism's innovative and varied approaches to paid content, with most publications exploring business models that do not rely exclusively on advertising, the majority of mainstream news organizations that install paywalls do not take advantage of this full range of options (Breunig 2005; Casero-Ripolles and Izquierdo-Castillo 2015).

In detailing the business models of these four Slow Journalism publications, this research explores each company's attempt to reconcile its inevitable engagement in market competition with its renunciation of the conventional business ethics and practices of the publishing industry. *De Correspondent*'s editorial team operates a "for-profit enterprise," for example, while asserting their autonomy from corporate third-party financial interests. Thus, their capitalist interest is frankly disclosed, according to the ethic of transparency espoused by Slow Journalism (Greenberg 2013, 382; Le Masurier 2015, 142), in the company's "business model focused on selling content to readers, rather than selling readers to advertisers" (Wijnberg 2013). How can this renunciation of resources traditionally used for competitive advantage function as a viable business model? What appears a well-intended yet quixotic journalistic experiment has nonetheless proven an attractive alternative in today's digital and print markets. While openly pursuing profit, the relative transparency and economic autonomy of these publications tout an almost artisanal creativity purifying journalism from large corporate interests. Slow Journalism has arisen in opposition to the worst effects of the commercialization of journalism, and yet cannot escape the need to market its own journalistic products. To remain true to their editorial missions, these publishers have adopted innovative business models directly reinforcing various combinations of Slow Journalism values.

Through methods consonant with *De Correspondent*'s dedication to being "fully transparent" about "the nature and terms" of its partnerships—in reader relations, financial interests, and sourcing of its stories—Slow Journalism's Spartan business ethic and practice in several key instances has won a loyal paying audience (Wijnberg 2013). The record journalistic crowdfunding of *De Correspondent*, for example, earned "more than 1 million Euros from 1500 donors in just eight days" (Wijnberg 2013). Many publishers have amassed a growing audience without the use of seemingly essential promotional tools such as "the major magazine retailers of the Internet" including intermediaries like Jellyfish Publishing, who specialize in marketing subscriptions to periodicals "from the top sellers to the niche" (Stam 2014, 182) . The movement thus inverts the industry-wide assumption that "publishers and marketers desperately need each other to run their businesses" (DVorkin 2015). In doing so, it suggests that the value of slowly produced deep storytelling is not reducible to its salability to advertisers, a countercultural stance ironically not without its commercial appeal.

From 2013 through 2014, Slow Journalism publishers featuring little or no advertising in their products enjoyed the good fortune of competing in a market undergoing a backlash against traditional advertising. That period marked a dramatic 70 percent rise in the use of AdBlock Plus, the service that screens display advertisements for Web users (Blanchfield 2014). The skyrocketing use of AdBlock precipitated a crisis for online marketers who discovered that among their unblocked display advertisements 31 percent on average were not viewed. As little as 7 percent were seen by end users in the worst cases, explaining the alarmingly low 0.05 percent clickthrough rate for display advertisements (Lipsman 2012). The iOS 9, released by Apple in 2015, is the first to come standard with mobile adblocking enabled in Apple's default Safari browser. "The rise of adblocking has proved concerning for web publishers, many of whom rely largely or exclusively on display advertising for revenue," unlike most Slow Journalism publishers who tend not to rely largely or exclusively on display advertising for revenue (Hern 2015). The decline of banner and pop-up advertising online has elevated the importance of content (Cole and Greer 2013; Manjoo 2014; Pulizzi 2012). This shift played directly into the hands of Slow Journalism's investment in developing original premium editorial content. At the same time, tablet use expanded, and digital longform made its debut (Zickuhr 2013). *De Correspondent*, *Narratively*, and *The Big Roundtable* offer textured pieces ideal for tablet reading.

Given the immersive habits of tablet users, time on page, rather than clicks, thus represents "a clear departure from the dominant business model in online journalism, which has been driven by advertising revenue based on page views" (Ray 2013, 439). The new premium on content has now given rise to brand journalism, "custom content," and "custom publishing," marking an industry shift in which "companies hope to build trust using the relative power and credibility of editorial content, often seen as more 'pure' than advertising" (Cole and Greer 2013; 673–674). *Narratively*, for example, has entered into partnerships involving brand sponsorship through native advertising (Rosenberg 2015). Within this context of the importance of original editorial content, the four Slow Journalism publications analyzed in this article represent serious professional journalism competing for market share, only not through the conventional industry channels.

The following section considers Slow Journalism as a reaction to developments in the publishing industry that have threatened to erode the value of narrative and deep storytelling in journalistic culture. Then, case studies of Slow Journalism business models proceed with the print-only *Delayed Gratification*, a high-end publication that has invested in its Web presence to become a major standard bearer and proselytizer on behalf of Slow Journalism, as witnessed by its URL of "slow-journalism.com." The next section turns to a broader discussion of the reclamation of print culture for the digital age. Three case studies of digital magazines follow, beginning with *De Correspondent*, which also publishes print books penned by its contributors and designed by Momkai, the brand developer and talent amplifier whose clients include Red Bull and Nike (Momkai 2015). Digital-only platforms with minimal crossover into print are then considered in the final case studies of *Narratively* and *The Big Roundtable*. These Web publications specialize in longform "scrollytelling" with embedded multimedia illustrations, textboxes, and infographics. But their business models are extremely different, as *Narratively* is funded primarily through vetting its contributors to companies seeking freelancers, whereas *The Big Roundtable* relies primarily on the spreadability of its stories through social media as a means of generating social payment.

Slow Journalism in the Publishing Industry

Slow Journalism's simplified transparent business model could be imagined as a direct reaction against what Braverman (1974) calls "Taylorization." Frederick Winslow Taylor was a technologist who sought "to rationalize the labor process by dividing production into its smallest and most efficient units," eventuating in a reorganization of social institutions like those of the publishing industry "into more efficient systems which function according to an instrumental, or binary, means/ends logic," as Fredric Jameson (1981, 227) explains.

With the logos of advertising-dependent journalism accelerating toward this end, longform journalism has responded to a broader cultural pattern that Jameson (1981, 227) describes in another context as "the loss inherent in this process, the wholesale dissolution of traditional institutions and social relations," a process "fatal to the older social forms" such as storytelling and narrative. Reviving these functions of journalism attempts to restore nonfiction storytelling in a culture suffering from "narrative deprivation" (Helfand and Maeda 2001). In the first decade of the internet, technological development was designed to enhance advertisers' interests at the expense of narrative, threatening to eliminate the time-honored notion of the less distracting reading environment of print journalism where long feature stories and "grey text" flourished (Carr 2011, 95).

High standards of publishing and writing, as *Harper's* publisher John R. MacArthur (2013, 9) argued in his promotion of *XXI*, a print-only sophisticated French journal identifying with Slow Journalism approaches, are "guaranteed not by fickle marketers suffering from short attention spans but by faithful readers whose powers of concentration—whose appreciation of the elegant sentence and the hard-earned insight—have survived the onslaught of the Web's unedited mediocrity."

De Correspondent, *Narratively*, and *The Big Roundtable* have leveraged digital technology, and *Delayed Gratification* has leveraged print media, to concentrate audience attention rather than scattering it throughout the internet via a multitude of advertisers' links. Such meaningful, deep reading presents itself to readers willing to "turn off the 'speed up' world long enough to slow down and take personal inventory" of consumption patterns, observes Cooper (2011, 5). This awareness of "how and if each medium should be ingested or could be creatively employed" (5) calls into question the low standard of journalism in what Richard Lanham calls "the economy of attention." The concept describes how an overabundance of data dwarfs our limited supply of attention to make sense of it, which inclines journalistic enterprise toward quick-hitting superficial content desperate to attract notice (Lanham 2006; Briggs 2012, 14). The key to the process, especially "In a world of fast media where new technologies, programs, software and publications come at you faster than you can digest the old," is "to *slow down* … to the speed of comprehension and overview," a deep understanding, "where Emerson and Thoreau, among others, found transcendence" (Cooper 2011, 16).

Rapid production of superficial news has led to "a commodification of writing itself" (MacArthur 2013, 8). Free content "in the quest for more advertising" is a system in which publishers dishonor the journalist "by devaluing their work and by feeding it—with little or no remuneration—to search engines, which in turn feed information to advertising agencies," as MacArthur observes (8). "Internet advertising," Kovarik (2011, 188) explains, "is not aimed at mass markets, but rather at individuals and small groups of consumers" through micro-targeting. The proliferation of digital content marketers such as Quill has blurred editorial and advertising distinctions (Miller 2014; Pulizzi 2012, 118). Content marketing and brand journalism has arisen in place of traditional journalism, as the American Bureau of Labor Statistics 2014 report indicated: "over the last ten years, the number of reporters decreased from 52,550 to 43,630, a 17 percent loss" compared to "the growth of public relations specialists during this same period by 22 percent from 166,210 to 202,530" (Marron 2014, 347). Slow Journalism's focus on high-quality journalism thus sharply contrasts with non-media producers such as Purina and Coca-Cola, who produce features, profiles, and documentary shorts packaged as "news" from their company websites (Miller 2014). Because it is a media company specializing in painstakingly reported and compellingly written stories, *Narratively*'s use of native advertising as part of its revenue mix carries entirely different ramifications for journalistic standards than if practiced by companies whose main products are not journalistic. The business models of the following four case studies of Slow Journalism publishers distance themselves from the data mining of audiences to attract advertisers for online micro-targeting.

Print with a Web Presence: *Delayed Gratification*

The business model for *Delayed Gratification* operates from the premise that news consumers will gain greater satisfaction of deeper reporting and more carefully crafted writing and illustrations in print than hastily produced advertisement-laden stories on a Web template. Its challenge is to re-train news audiences into investing in the benefits of patience and anticipation over instant gratification. The editors have assumed that most readers will have a basic knowledge of daily news given its ubiquitous presence and redundancy due to overproduction on the internet. In each issue, *Delayed Gratification* revisits a selection of the top news stories from the past three months, treating each with greater context and analysis with infographics worthy of the Information is Beautiful Awards and graphic illustrations like those found in *The Believer* and *XXI* as well as literary graphic novels such as *Maus* and *Persepolis*. The selected stories receive in-depth reporting and researching in a print product of journalistic substance that reaches for the prestige and enduring quality of a hardcover book.

Delayed Gratification's website functions as a promotional platform for its print journal to showcase the Slow Journalism brand. In doing so, the website offers an array of Slow Journalism news under the categories of "Slow Posts" and "Slow Subjects," an important marketing strategy that enhances the organization's Web presence through spreadable media products. This is essential for a print-only publication that would otherwise suffer a lack of online exposure where current news companies thrive on discussion among readers via social media. "Slow Posts" consist of passages and excerpts from its own issues, and "Slow Subjects" also position the company as the defining leader and editorial tastemaker in the Slow Journalism movement. The company's signature long view appears in "Five Things We Learned Last Month," a list of penetrating insight and wit clearly inspired by *Harper's* "Index" yet intended for sharing on social media. *Delayed Gratification* began rolling its own online news as a blog called "The Slow Journal" in this manner—a mix of original infographics and stories from its print-only quarterly journal, along with aggregated pieces from Slow Journalism sources specializing in longform off the 24-hour news cycle. The website sells single issues as well as back issue sets with reduced rates for higher quantities. *Delayed Gratification*'s annual subscription rate is £36, which accounts for its main source of revenue. Subscribers save 25 percent off the online single-issue price, offering readers incentive to opt for an annual subscription.

Of the four case studies covered in this research, *Delayed Gratification* has been the most aggressive in branding itself as Slow Journalism. Indeed, the search terms "slow journalism" in Google yield the journal's website first on the list, along with its subsections. This is due in part to the journal's subtitle, "The Slow Journalism Magazine." As such, the editors have positioned themselves as the most accessible of the four case studies via online search. They have fashioned themselves as ambassadors of Slow Journalism by educating readers about the basic tenets of the movement as a means of promoting their brand. Thus, they address on the website "Why Slow Journalism Matters" as both a self-definition and a description that resonates with the broader movement. The website also functions, unlike that of *De Correspondent*, as a vigorous aggregator of headlines intended to amplify the significance of Slow Journalism. Perhaps most notable was the declaration that Jill Abramson, former *New York Times* editor-in-chief and self-described "Snow Faller in chief," had joined the Slow Journalism revolution in December of 2014.

Along with Steven Brill, Abramson's business plan shares *De Correspondent* and *Delayed Gratification*'s goal of eliminating third-party distractions and focusing exclusively on producing high-quality journalism to generate revenue primarily through subscriptions. Her news organization intends to revive the eroding quality of digital journalism by providing "one perfect whale of a story" each month based on extensive reporting. However, unlike the publicized business plans of those journals that do not mention raising journalists' wages, Abramson made a point that her venture would revolutionize journalist salaries, offering an average payment of $100,000 per contribution. This monetary investment in the value of quality journalistic writing is a bold statement against free digital news that in her view degrades the profession of journalism into mere "content production" for the sake of carrying paid advertising. Abramson's dedication to extensive reporting and protracted longform storytelling dates from the publication of the *New York Times'* 2012 milestone "Snow Fall" under her editorial watch. "I want to be a spokeswoman for the slow-writing movement," she proclaimed, since the industry's emphasis on speed has made her "seriously worried that the quality of [digital journalistic] writing has deteriorated" (Orchard 2014b).

A Print Ethic for a Digital Age

The focus on print only by *Delayed Gratification* and *XXI* has a strong backing from legacy media titan *Harper's Monthly*. As a monthly available in print or digital via subscription only, *Harper's* is one of the few holdouts among legacy media against pressure to make its content free online, an economy to which the *New Yorker* has succumbed in part by offering single stories free online and charging for entire digital issues. *Harper's* publisher John R. MacArthur (2014, 46) has argued that free online content instead leaves journalism "hostage to monopolistic practices controlled by huge, multi-national companies." MacArthur nonetheless also complains about the loss of advertisers to the Web, whom he wishes to attract to print. This is a decidedly opposite aim of the Slow Journalism venues he touts, such as *XXI* and *Delayed Gratification*. His closing anecdote is designed to illustrate how the now maverick status of print journalism can actually attract lucrative advertising deals despite most marketers "hav[ing] abandoned newspapers and magazines in droves for the promise of digital riches" (MacArthur 2014, 46). MacArthur's pen-and-paper note in 1998 to Steve Jobs urged that *Harper's* dedication to print ironically made it a kindred spirit of Apple's "Think Different" campaign, unlike the popular news journals such as *Time* and *Newsweek* featuring the advertisements at the time. MacArthur reports triumphantly that Jobs replied with an insertion order for the advertisements to run in the next *Harper's* issue, a sentiment that champions partnership with perhaps the largest of the "huge, multi-national companies" he demonizes (46). The contradiction is symptomatic of *Harper's* position at the crossroads of legacy media and Slow Journalism, one with clear leanings away from free content and the notion of digital speed as a necessity for quality journalism that nonetheless still views corporate sponsorship as its lifeblood. This dependence on corporate sponsorship is the authentic situation *Harper's* faces despite its publisher's staunch advocacy of paid rather than free content. This predicament, however, does not mean *Harper's* is somehow not reporting and writing according to a Slow Journalism model. Indeed, it, as well as the *New Yorker*, developed the reporting methods now commonly associated with the movement.

Built into David Simon's (2011) otherwise bold advocacy of paywalls is a similar assumption that journalism's solvency necessarily depends on corporate underwriting.

Paid digital subscriptions, he insists, work best not in establishing freedom and independence from commercial interests in the manner of *De Correspondent*, but in attracting more, and better paying, advertising. "Advertisers—considering a *paid* circulation base rather than meaningless Web hits—might be willing to once again to pay a meaningful rate," Simon argues (53). He thus backs paywalls as a means of increasing the value of readers in the eyes of marketers. *De Correspondent* instead regards the quality of its monetized product as the primary means of expanding its audience base rather than as a method of drawing sponsors with deep pockets. MacArthur's dedication to print reflected in his handwritten note to Steve Jobs was a quirky means of attracting Apple, the world's most coveted corporate sponsor. In the landscape of Slow Journalism, *Jot Down*, a Spanish digital "contemporary culture mag," converges old and new media as well as print and digital business models. While *Jot Down* generates 70 percent of its revenue from sales of its 320-page print quarterly that contains only two to three pages of advertising, the other 30 percent comes from digital advertising (Breiner 2015). Unlike legacy outlets like *Harper's*, *Jot Down*'s print product is virtually advertisement free; its use of the Web to sell advertising is a novel innovation among Slow Journalism titles. Despite using a business model that relies on advertising, *Harper's* has emerged as legacy media's most vocal supporter of Slow Journalism. The publication's advocacy of paywalls and print is consonant with the respective business models of *De Correspondent* and *Delayed Gratification*. As MacArthur (2014, 45) has noted, many born-digital platforms—*Pitchfork*, *Politico*, *Pando*, and *The Los Angeles Review of Books*—have established print editions, and still others have built new pay walls. This reversal of the common migration of print to digital is a sign of growth for these online platforms. Indeed, *Narratively*'s first print publication announced in September 2015 after three years exclusively online, marks such growth (Fennell 2015).

The advocacy of print is rooted in several studies on reading that build on older research touted by Web dystopian Nicholas Carr (2011), who argued that online reading discourages comprehension and reflective depth through its overwhelming emphasis on speed and superficiality. One Norwegian study found performance on tests was significantly superior for subjects reading print compared to digital (Mangen et al. 2013). The cause was due to how screen reading perpetuates a culture of shallow reading, a point confirming Carr's argument. The lower cognitive test scores associated with digital reading derived from how "the common perception of screen presentation as an information source intended for shallow messages may reduce the mobilization of cognitive resources that is needed for effective self-regulation" (Mangen et al. 2013). In a similar study, researchers found that readers of print news could recall significantly more news stories than readers of online news (Santana et al. 2013). The reason lies in how "the scattershot nature of the online news story coupled with its fleeting nature make the online news consumer's experience quite different than that of a print reader," as another study on the topic concluded (as quoted in MacArthur 2014).

Highly commercialized online news layouts are designed to optimize exposure to sponsors as the main priority over providing a pleasurable reading experience that aids comprehension. According to this template, news stories appear on unnecessary multiple pages to increase the reader's exposure to advertisements. The tactic is known as "juicing page views" (Manjoo 2014). But with the tablet and its growing market on the rise, journalism has found a digital alternative that has all but eliminated the scattershot fleeting nature of the Web news template. The tablet provides a reading experience favoring stories that read as if on an app rather than the open Web. "Snow Fall" was the innovator of this model that then inspired *Narratively* and *The Big Roundtable*, and more recently *Faction* (factual stories that read like fiction in the narrative nonfiction longform genre), an emergent genre of digital Slow Journalism that radically qualifies the above-mentioned research findings arguing for the cognitive advantages of print. Digital longform on the tablet renders an experience arguably more immersive than print due to its interactivity, yet one free from "the overcrowded, overstuffed, slow-loading web" with its "carnival of pop-ups and interstitials—interim ad pages served up before or after your desired content—and scammy come-ons daring you to click," as Farhad Manjoo (2014) describes the traditional internet news ecosystem.

Alternative Business Economics: *De Correspondent*

In his slow news manifesto, Peter Laufer (2011) exhorts readers to "buy some of your news" and to "evade news-like assaults that merely convey commercials." In his assessment of the digital news industry, he laments how "answering to shareholders trumps the sense of public service" making it "easy to rationalize the search for methods to save money and still generate content that appears to be news" (Laufer 2011, 68). Free news bears this liability. Slow news businesses have eschewed angel investors and private sponsors traditionally providing start-up capital for digital ventures, primarily because of the loss of financial independence these deals demand. Angel investors, as Briggs (2012) explains, launch companies with one investment, with revenue sharing in the long run typically breaching 50 percent. Angel investing, the fastest growing area of investment startup in 2012, has become the dominant model for online entrepreneurial journalism. Angel investors typically require yielding "30 to 40 percent of the company in return for a round of investment of $100,000 to $500,000" (Briggs 2012, 186). The advantage of tapping into private capitalists' rich resources diminishes rapidly in light of the requirement of such a high return of ownership to the investor. This arrangement is the antithesis of economic autonomy prominent in *De Correspondent* and *Delayed Gratification*'s business models. These Slow Journalism publishers have not established their businesses with the long-term financial goal of "selling the business to a bigger company" upon the establishment of a viable profit margin (Briggs 2012, 186).

De Correspondent's success began with its record-breaking accumulation of crowd-sourced funding, consisting of donations with no corporate strings attached. After a five-month wait, investors received a Web app with a responsive design and high-quality advertising-free journalism covering a range of topics not typically considered news (Pfauth 2013). Although the company produces stories daily, each piece is the result of a long-term project that delves into broad trends in the news over time. Free to cater to its readers as the primary stakeholders, *De Correspondent*'s business model offers a free mailing list that includes individual stories in Dutch or English for purchase. Its main source of revenue comes from annual subscriptions charged at 60 per year. The core principle is "Partners not Advertisers" that invites "entering into partnerships with third parties, like universities or research institutes, but these partners will have no stake in the profitability of *De Correspondent*, and *De Correspondent* will be transparent about the nature and terms of such partnerships" (Pfauth 2013). The company's journalistic brand is one that is perennially salable by virtue of renouncing the economic domination of the conventional free market—namely sponsorship as a means of imposing the sponsor's will on the recipient—that erodes journalistic standards. Economic autonomy drives creative freedom through what Pierre Bourdieu (1992) calls charismatic or "symbolic capital." Bourdieu describes this type of cultural value as an alternative to financial profit—aligning precisely with *De Correspondent*'s "Journalism Before Profit" credo—"a kind of 'economic' capital denied but recognized, and hence legitimate" (142). It functions as prestige, a "veritable credit, and capable of assuring, under certain conditions and in the long term, 'economic' profits" (142). Economic autonomy and executive transparency thus drive *De Correspondent*'s business plan as a means of generating both real and symbolic capital.

Narratively *and* The Big Roundtable*: Marketing Digital Longform*

MacArthur's (2014) stand against the commercialized internet bears Slow Journalism's commitment to the clean text that honors content as sacred space for an immersive, rich reading experience. In 2013, *XXI* editors called for a return not only to textured narrative nonfiction, but also to a streamlined business model. Eschewing both computer and tablets for enticing readers into distraction, they describe the typical reader of online news as "faithless and unpredictable—this transgressive freedom is what he appreciates most" (Beccaria and Saint-Exupery 2013, 22). Distilling and focusing reader attention, however, is the effect of *Narratively*'s tablet-inspired design. Embedded multimedia add-ons automatically play; hyperlinks to sources do not send the reader onto the open Web, but to the actual document consulted. Readers on *Narratively* are presented with stories on one long page with engaging vibrant visuals, background design, and clips. Publisher and editor-in-chief Noah Rosenberg established a layout analogous to *XXI*'s reaction against readers as "information consumers" which in turn transforms journalists and design engineers into "information technicians" (Beccaria and Saint-Exupery 2013, 22). Rosenberg has cultivated an intimate relationship with Marquee, *Narratively*'s design engineering team forged on a shared vision of digital publishing rooted in Slow Journalism's liberation from conventional Web news templates that feature banner and marginal advertisements. The central aim is to allow the narrative rather than the medium to dictate the presentation of the story. Both small close-knit companies who aim "to take the necessary time to produce good work," Marquee and *Narratively*'s mutually shared philosophy toward digital journalism is to build powerful narratives by allowing the story to be its natural length and the reporting to take its natural time (Hiatt 2014).

Although this model of slow production suggests a capricious indifference to the exigencies of the capitalist digital market for journalism, Slow Journalism's online venues have been hardly so naïve. Carefully constructed to respond to all the demands of competition for journalistic talent as a means of attracting and maintaining a wide audience, Slow Journalism's digital outlets do not all replicate *De Correspondent*'s business model. Instead, they show an imaginative and resourceful array of revenue sources from services and training workshops (*Atavist*) to outsourcing of contributors (*Narratively*) to solicitation of reader donations for contributors (*The Big Roundtable*). Whereas some Slow Journalism organizations have eschewed digital altogether, such as *XXI* and *Delayed Gratification*, opting instead for an even more aggressive return to reader intimacy by keeping their publications in print only, digital outlets have engaged the challenge of reinventing the online marketplace for journalism. *De Correspondent*'s capacity to maintain the challenge of operating exclusively on reader subscriptions is not an option universally available to other Slow Journalism venues. The Dutch digital magazine has that capacity primarily because it generated such a massive base of supporters in its initial campaign to crowd source its start-up capital. That critical mass converted into an instant readership broad enough to support the organization. Others, like *Narratively*, were forced to seek revenue from other sources.

Narratively, unlike *De Correspondent*, offers its born-digital content without charge. A paywall would deter readers in their case, given the less loyal and more modest reader support it commands. Editor Brandon Spiegel of the Brooklyn -based company instead recruits authors drawn from his regional editors to contribute. They earn a nominal fee for stories ranging from 2000 to 5000 words that are embedded with multimedia graphics, pictures, and video clips. Contributors' salaries are not the real incentive, since the company brokers their names on lists to large corporations such as General Electric seeking public relations strategic communicators. *Narratively* functions as a talent agency, successfully leveraging corporate capital to enrich its contributors. This process begins when the editors of *Narratively* send the names of their best contributors, with their consent, to companies who select among them for potential hiring, mostly for freelance assignments. The company then invites selected candidates for interviews. *Narratively* therefore provides a service to the industry in placing needy journalists in paid positions, while also creating income for itself in the form of payment from their partner companies (Hiatt 2014). Sponsorships with brands on their website, as mentioned earlier, is also in their growing revenue channel, that includes sponsored, ticketed live events, native advertising, and plans for an NPR-inspired membership opportunity for readers based on pledge donations. In an attempt to create a "membership mentality," Rosenberg seeks "an audience that supports us, feels special in doing so, and gets something special in return" (Fennell 2015).

The Big Roundtable has taken a different approach to paying its contributors and generating revenue. Like *Narratively*, it has no paywall, but the similarities end there. Its method of compensating authors is entirely unique in the Slow Journalism world, as it offers opportunities throughout each story for reader donations. *The Big Roundtable*'s gratuity model of voluntary contributions functions as expressions of reader satisfaction. Gratuity prompts are embedded in the template of *The Big Roundtable*'s stories, appearing in yellow tabs reading "Support this Writer's Work" and in a window at the end explaining that 10 percent of all donations go to *The Big Roundtable* along with an undisclosed amount to Paypal. The Tip Jar Model initiated by investigative foreign reporter Chris Albritton a decade earlier operated differently. It provided the means for soliciting funds based on past projects to underwrite his travel to Iraq and other Middle Eastern locations to carry out future assignments (Gillmor 2006, 155). Albritton's donations anticipated Kickstarter's public donation campaign platform through its solicitation of funds for future projects.

Social payment can also combine with paid subscription as a voluntary tip to the author. Thomas Frank's *The Baffler*, whose stories *Delayed Gratification* aggregates on its promotional website in a gesture of solidarity with Slow Journalism, published the widely acclaimed "The Worst Industrial Disaster in the World." The story appears online in "scrollytelling" format. As with *The Big Roundtable*, donation prompts beckon from the margin of the advertising-free layout. But unlike *The Big Roundtable*, *The Baffler*'s revenue draws from subscriptions for either digital only at US$27 or print plus digital at US$30 annually.

Conclusion

The case studies above represent an array of imaginative approaches to funding Slow Journalism, all of which reinforce the importance of quality journalistic content. These four publishers make explicit in their revolutionary editorial policies—*De Correspondent* calls theirs a "Manifesto"—their uncompromising dedication to maintaining a high standard of reporting and writing that strives for accuracy and excellence over speed. The ubiquity of speed is in part due to the short supply of user attention which traditional news companies have attempted to capture through headlines, lists, and briefs. The deterioration of quality in news content is epitomized in companies such as Journatic, which have emerged precisely to process and systematize the production of the news with rigid assembly-line precision. This "Taylorization" of journalism that relies on "software [that] continuously scans its database and the flow of news from its sources to produce articles that a battery of editors, English speakers who often reside in developing countries, rewrite for a few dollars" (MacArthur 2013). The founder of Journatic has logically eliminated the need for rigorous well-compensated journalism for this cheap alternative. His conclusion hauntingly sounds a death knell for the integrity of the profession: "If we reprocess a press release, why would anyone pay reporter-type wages to do that?" (as quoted in MacArthur 2013). Such "churnalism", or rewriting of press releases, accounts for 54 percent of online journalism in the United Kingdom (Orchard 2014a). In Journatic we find the antithesis of Jill Abramson's vision for her new "slow writing" venture to publish one thoroughly researched and reported piece per month by a vetted journalist, whose product would command $100,000 on average. At bottom, the editors of *XXI* attest, "what has to be restored is the exchange value between news publications and their readers," one that "isn't an abstraction reducible to what he buys, his level of education, or his professional status," but a unique individual with whom news organizations must re-establish "reciprocal ties" (Beccaria and Saint-Exupery 2013, 23).

The experimental business models represented in the four case studies suggest a desire among the leading Slow Journalism publishers not only "to reinvent the press's economic model," but to win the reader's trust and interest. These organizations' larger purpose is to transform readers from a collective commodity "delivered" to advertisers to a humanized audience honored for their capacity to delve deeply into longform stories. To this end, "Everything must be done to convey news more intensely," rather than briefly and hastily, "to concentrate on lasting substance" (Beccaria and Saint-Exupery 2013, 24). The renunciation of conventional news business models has been good business for Slow Journalism, whose most salable and recognizable brand is really an anti-brand, one profoundly resistant to the homogenizing standardization of mass-produced online news according to the Journatic model. Slow Journalism's alternative media brand has created an alternative to conventional online commercialized journalism "which is a bazaar where everything's for sale and contradictory promises are the order of the day" (Beccaria and Saint-Exupery 2013, 22). *Narratively*'s alternative editorial outlook, for example, is dedicated to "human stories, boldly told" and avoids "the breaking news and the next big headline" to "focus instead on slow storytelling" delivering "the characters and narratives that mainstream media aren't finding" (Rosenberg 2015).

The economic transparency and autonomy at the foundation of Slow Journalism echoes nineteenth-century socialist reformer Edward Bellamy's ([1888] 2009, 97) utopic vision of newspaper management with "no counting-room to obey, or interests of private capital as against the public good to defend", evoking the purity of supply meeting demand imagined by Adam Smith. A seemingly socialistic business model bears the markings of a surprisingly agile and lean return to original ideals for free market competition.

Like cable TV, premium digital longform journalism also began modestly. "First someone had to dream it," as David Simon (2011) observed of the rise of commercial-free pay TV. Industry veterans like *Atavist* spearheaded the embedded multimedia storytelling movement online in 2011 with few titles, but increased revenue led to a vast expansion of the product, as with cable (Simon 2011, 47). *Faction* is the latest independent platform seeking this result with rich reporting and compelling narration enhanced by document-based visuals such as scanned-in artifacts and primary sources.

Just as *Atavist* and *Faction* have prevented third-party interests from influencing their stories, *XXI*'s manifesto similarly shields the sacred relationship between journalist, editor, and reader from commercial intermediaries. In it, the editors denounce "pompous phrases about the need 'to reinvent the press's economic model'" while backing instead a more deliberate, almost Thoreauvean, approach: "To be useful, desirable, and necessary—that's the only economic model worth considering," because it is "as old as the world, as old as commerce" (Beccaria and Saint-Exupery 2013, 23). David Monod (1996, 66) demonstrates that ideals of smallness, independence, community, and fair competition represented an anti-monopoly "folklore of retailing" prevalent in the last decades of the nineteenth century. Like the movement to save independent bookstores from corporate chain retailers at the turn of the twenty-first century, Slow Journalism positions itself as a noble alternative to advertising-dependent formats. The lack of substantial journalism on heavily commercialized sites straining for page views instead of prioritizing enduring storytelling is evidenced by *BuzzFeed*'s decision in 2013 to "delete more than four thousand of its staff writers' early posts, apparently because, as time passed, they looked stupider and stupider" (Lepore 2014, 34). The deletion was consonant with *BuzzFeed*'s larger campaign to win a more sophisticated audience through recent longform pieces such as "Atari Teenage Riot," a story about the origins of the video game industry. Thus aggressively commercial news organizations like *BuzzFeed* have engaged in slower reporting and writing for deeper storytelling. Several Slow Journalism platforms have reached to advertising as a supplemental revenue stream, a gesture that points to the diverse, experimental nature of the movement. Indeed, the new start-ups under the Slow Journalism banner are seeking creative ways to survive financially. Those that include advertising in the mix should not be considered ideological heretics, but instead as innovators harnessing market forces to fund deep storytelling. The small-scale presence of advertising in Slow Journalism content does not necessarily negate or profane the journalistic integrity so many of its editors allude to in their mission statements.

Slow Journalism's artisanal small business ethic is particularly attractive to readers seeking virtually advertising-free carefully crafted boutique journalism, as in the four journals that comprise the case studies of this article. The countercultural appeal of most of these transparent brands thrives on *à la carte* and subscription revenue streams. The industry standard has discouraged paywalled online news given the abundance of free content elsewhere (Simon 2011). The values of the Slow Journalism (anti) brand authentically portray through storytelling and platform design an approach toward the digital news market that privileges deeper rather than faster reporting and writing. Those principles function to justify payment for relatively expensive journalistic products in a digital ecosystem dominated by free news.

Despite risking appearing anachronistic, Slow Journalism has boldly reclaimed the civic value of reporting and writing as "the incommensurable sacred" that stands in opposition to "the marketable profane" (Miller 2007, 19). Rather than representing a liability, however, elevating journalism to a "sacred product" transforms service to readers into the genre's most marketable feature. Slow Journalism similarly seeks to humanize and reclaim journalism through the branding of its unique genre.

To achieve intimacy with their audiences, Slow Journalism publishers have aimed at eliminating what Henry James identified as the bane of the publishing industry: gross "meddling between the supply and demand of a commodity" (as quoted in Edel 1984, 220). This is not a renunciation of competition and advertising altogether, but one pursued according to a Smithean ideal evocative of the self-made entrepreneur (Smith 1776). "Capitalism fits well with large bureaucratic organizations," especially since bureaucracy is such "an efficient means to centralize power, control labor, and create profit," as Laura Miller (2007, 193) observes. But many Slow Journalism editors' rejection of the capitalist methods associated with large corporate media has offered them a distinct advantage in the race for the tablet market and the recovery of print audiences through immersive longform journalism. These educated affluent audiences, Robert Boynton (2013, 129) describes as "the envy of advertisers." Evan Osnos (2013) observed that despite how readers are becoming more "wary than they used to be of nanosecond-interpretations of Supreme Court decisions," the reality remains that "the economics of the business have not suddenly improved" throughout the industry. But Slow Journalism's major publications have made clear inroads toward such improvement with alternative business models that have replaced content providers with authors, and the algorithms of automatic wire services with deep reporting and vibrant writing.

DISCLOSURE STATEMENT

No potential conflict of interest was reported by the author.

REFERENCES

Beccaria, Laurent, and Patrick Saint-Exupery. 2013. "Content and Its Discontents." *XXI*. Winter, 4–7.

Bellamy, Edward. [1888] 2009. *Looking Backward, 2000–1887*. Oxford: Oxford University Press.

Bishop, Colby. 2015. "Slow Journalism: Deep Storytelling in the Digital Age." *National Geographic*, Janurary 7. http://voices.nationalgeographic.com/2015/01/07/slow-journalism-deep-storytelling-in-the-digital-age/

Blanchfield, Sean. 2014. "2014 Report: Adblocking Goes Mainstream." *Pagefair*, September 9. http://blog.pagefair.com/2014/adblocking-report/

Bourdieu, Pierre. 1992. *The Rules of Art: Genesis and Structure of the Literary Field*. Edited by Werner Hamacher and David E. Wellbery. Stanford: Stanford University Press.

Boynton, Robert. 2013. "Notes toward a Supreme Nonfiction: Teaching Literary Reportage in the Twenty-first Century." *Literary Journalism Studies* 5.2 (Fall): 125–131.

Braverman, Harry. 1974. *Labor and Monopoly Capital*. New York: Monthly Review.

Breiner, James. 2015. "Cultural Publication Flirts with the 'Dark Side' in Spain." *News Entrepreneurs*. July 28. http://newsentrepreneurs.blogspot.com/2015/07/digital-publication-flirts-with-dark.html

Breunig, Christian. 2005. "Paid Content on the Internet: A Successful Business Model? Market Opportunities for Paid Online Content." *Media Perspektiven* (8): 407–418.

Briggs, Mark. 2012. *Entrepreneurial Journalism*. New York: CQ Press.

Carr, Nicholas. 2011. *The Shallows: What the Internet is Doing to Our Brains*. New York: Norton.

Casero-Ripolles, Andreu, and Jessica Izquierdo-Castillo. 2015. "Between Decline and a New Online Business Model: The Case of the Spanish Newspaper Industry." *Journal of Media Business Studies* 10 (1): 63–78.

Cole, James T., and Jennifer D. Greer. 2013. "Audience Response to Brand Journalism: The Effect of Frame, Source and Involvement." *Journalism & Mass Communication Quarterly* 90 (4): 673–690.

Cooper, Thomas. 2011. *Fast Media/Media Fast: Life in an Age of Media Overload*. Boulder, CO: Gaeta Press.

DVorkin, Lewis. 2015. "Inside Forbes: What Journalists Must Know—And Can Do—About New Upheavals in the Ad World." *Forbes*. January 21. http://www.forbes.com/sites/lewisdvorkin/2015/01/21/inside-forbes-what-journalists-must-know-and-can-do-about-new-upheavals-in-the-ad-world/

Edel, Leon. 1984. *Literary Criticism: Essays on Literature, American Writers, and English Writers*. New York: Library of America.

Fennell, Marc. 2015. "Facebook Dislike? Narrative.Ly & Twitch Vs YouTube." *Download This Show, ABC.Net*, September 19. http://www.abc.net.au/radionational/programs/downloadthisshow/dst1909/6784272

Gillmor, Dan. 2006. *We the Media: Journalism by the People, for the People*. Sebastopol, CA: O'Reilly Media.

Greenberg, Susan. 2013. "Slow Journalism in the Digital Fast Lane." In *Global Literary Journalism: Exploring the Journalistic Imagination*, edited by Richard Lance Keeble and John Tulloch, 381–393. New York: Peter Lang.

Helfand, Jessica, and John Maeda. 2001. *Screen: Essays on Graphic Design, New Media and Visual Culture*. Princeton, NJ: Princeton Architectural Press.

Hern, Alex. 2015. "IOS9 Ad Blocker Apps Shoot to Top of Charts on Day One." *The Guardian*, September 17.

Hiatt, Anna. 2014. "The Future of Digital Longform: All the Space in the World." *Tow Center for Digital Journalism*. http://longform.towcenter.org/report/case-studies/

Jameson, Fredric. 1981. *The Political Unconscious: Narrative as a Socially Symbolic Act*. Ithaca, New York: Cornell University Press.

Kovarik, Bill. 2011. *Revolutions in Communication: Media History from Gutenberg to the Digital Age*. New York: Bloomsbury.

Lanham, Richard. 2006. *The Economics of Attention: Style and Substance in the Age of Information*. Chicago, IL: University of Chicago Press.

Laufer, Peter. 2011. *Slow News: A Manifesto for the Critical News Consumer*. Corvallis: University of Oregon Press.

Le Masurier, Megan. 2015. "What is Slow Journalism?" *Journalism Practice* 9 (2): 138–152.

Lepore, Jill. 2014. "The Cobweb: Can the Internet Be Archived?" *The New Yorker*, January 26. 34–41.

Lipsman, Andrew. 2012. "ComScore Introduces Validated Campaign Essentials." *ComScore*, January 19. http://www.comscore.com/Insights/Press-Releases/2012/1/comScore-Introduces-Validated-Campaign-Essentials

MacArthur, John. 2013. "Publisher's Letter." *Harper's*, October. 7–9.

MacArthur, John. 2014, July/August. "False Idol: The Scourge of 'Digital Correctness'." *Columbia Journalism Review* 44–46.

Mangen, Anne, Bente R. Walgermo, and Kolbjorn Bronnick. 2013. "Reading Linear Texts on Paper versus Computer Screen: Effects on Reading Comprehension." *International Journal of Educational Research* 58: 61–68.

Manjoo, Farhad. 2014. "Fall of the Banner Ad: The Monster That Swallowed the Web." *New York times*, November 5. http://www.nytimes.com/2014/11/06/technology/personaltech/banner-ads-the-monsters-that-swallowed-the-web.html?rref=collection%2Fcolumn%2Fstate-of-the-art&_r=0

Marron, Maria. 2014. "Content Creation Spans All Aspects of J-Programs." *Journalism & Mass Communication Educator* 69 (4): 347–348.

Miller, Laura. 2007. *Reluctant Capitalists: Bookselling and the Culture of Consumption*. Chicago, IL: University of Chicago Press.

Miller, Charles.2014. "Call that a story? No, It's Content Marketing." *British Broadcast Company*, November 21. http://www.bbc.co.uk/blogs/collegeofjournalism/entries/e8dd00d2-51f8-3d96-811196f87735183e

Momkai. 2015. "De Correspondent: Brand Identity and Books." *Momkai—A Digital Creative Agency*. http://www.momkai.com/#/cases/de_correspondent_branding

Monod, David. 1996. *Store Wars: Shopkeepers and the Culture of Mass Marketing*. Toronto: University of Toronto Press.

Orchard, Rob. 2014a. "The Slow Journalism Revolution." *TEDxMadrid*, October 30. Video. http://www.slow-journalism.com/slow-journalism

Orchard, Rob. 2014b. "Jill Abramson Joins the Slow Journalism Revolution." *Delayed Gratification*, December 5. http://www.slow-journalism.com/jill-abramson-joins-the-slow-journalism-revolution#more-3715

Orchard, Rob. 2015. "Why Slow Journalism Matters." *Delayed Gratification*. [nd] http://www.slow-journalism.com/slow-journalism

Osnos, Evan. 2013. "On Slow Journalism." *New Yorker*, January 31. http://www.newyorker.com/news/daily-comment/on-slow-journalism

Pfauth, Ernst-Jan. 2013. "How We Turned a World Record in Journalism Crowd-funding into an Actual Publication" *Medium*, November 27. https://medium com/de-correspondent/

how-we-turned-a-world-record-in-journalism-crowd-funding-into-an-actual-publication-2a06e298afe1

Pulizzi, Joe. 2012. "The Rise of Storytelling as the New Marketing." *Publishing Research Quarterly* 28: 116–123.

Ray, Vin. 2013. "News Storytelling in a Digital Landscape." In *Journalism: New Challenges*, edited by Karen Fowler-Watt and Stuart Allen, 435–443. UK: Bournemouth University Press.

Rosenberg, Noah. 2015. "Advertising and Sponsorships." *Narratively*, September 19. http://narrative.ly/advertising-sponsorships/.

Santana, Arthur D., Randall M. Livingstone, and Yoon Y. Cho. 2013. "Print Readers Recall More than Do Online Readers." *Newspaper Research Journal* 34: 2.

Simon, David. 2011. "Build the Wall." In *Will the Last Reporter Please Turn out the Lights: The Collapse of Journalism and What Can Be Done to Fix It*, edited by Robert W. McChesney and Victor Pickard, 45–53. New York: The New Press.

Smith, Adam. 1776. *The Wealth of Nations*. Edited by Robert Reich. New York: Modern Library.

Stam, David. 2014. "Magazine Distribution, Sales and Marketing." In *Inside Magazine Publishing*, edited by David Stam and Andrew Scott, 166–195. London: Routledge.

Wijnberg, Rob. 2013. "Our Manifesto." *De Correspondent*, March. https://decorrespondent.nl/en.

Zickuhr, Kathryn. 2013. "Tablet Ownership 2013." *Pew Research Internet Project*, June 10. http://www.pewinternet.org/2013/06/10/tablet-ownership-2013/.

SLOW JOURNALISM AND THE OUT OF EDEN WALK

Don Belt and Jeff South

Journalism does not get much slower than National Geographic's Out of Eden Walk, *a seven-year, around-the-world journey being undertaken by two-time Pulitzer Prize winner Paul Salopek. This article explains how Salopek's Walk is a particularly useful and beautiful example of slow journalism that renders the oldest story in human history using innovative digital tools of the twenty-first century. It also offers university educators ideas on using the Out of Eden Walk as a teaching tool, by exposing classrooms to the literary and visual delights of the project while having students design and implement a narrative walk of their own.*

Introduction: The Enduring Power of Slow

"We swim in a sea of information," writes Susan Greenberg (2007), who first used the term "slow journalism" in an article for *Prospect*, the British magazine of ideas. In retrospect, "swim" may be the wrong word. Today journalists, like everyone else, are struggling against a tidal wave of electronic information that grows faster and more superficial by the day, threatening to engulf modern descendants of the clever primate, *Homo sapiens*, who walked out of Africa's Rift Valley some 60,000 years ago during a period of particularly low sea levels.

In an average minute, we modern humans send more than 200 million emails, perform 4 million searches on Google, "like" more than 4 million posts on Facebook, upload 300 hours of video to YouTube, and tap out almost 350,000 tweets (James 2015). For many of us, "swimming" feels more like drowning. Long form reading, once a principal mode of learning and leisure, is becoming the exception rather than the rule, as electronic media, including journalism, become more ubiquitous, more cryptic, and more superficial. The proliferation of free information on the internet has forced publishers and broadcasters to abandon traditional business models that invested in quality over quantity of information.

To keep up, news organizations reduce staff, cut field expenses, and adopt less-expensive business practices; some are even tempted to engage in what Nick Davies (2009, 59) calls "churnalism," the practice of publishing press releases, with few if any changes, as news articles. The pressure to publish quickly, cheaply, and sensationally has stripped away context and left media consumers in a state of confusion—"informed bewilderment," in the words of Manuel Castells (1998, 358). As Le Masurier (2015, 140) writes, "In the flurry of speed and immediacy, the possibility of considered reflection, of narrative, of contextualized information, disappears, for both producers and consumers of journalism."

Over the past decade, however, an alternative vision of journalism has emerged, partly inspired by the Slow Food movement, a collection of European chefs and activists, led by Carlo Petrini, whose protest at a McDonald's in Rome grew to oppose the industrial approach to food. "Speed became our shackles," reads the movement's 1989 manifesto (Slow Food 2010). It describes fast food as a "virus," symptomatic of "the 'fast life' that fractures our customs and assails us even in our own homes … Homo sapiens must regain wisdom and liberate itself from the 'velocity' that is propelling it on the road to extinction." Today there are similarly inspired movements for slow science, slow travel, slow parenting, slow exercise, slow manufacturing, slow sex, and even slow television. More than 1.4 million people have viewed a TED talk, "In Praise of Slowness," by Canadian author Carl Honoré (2005). There is even a World Institute of Slowness, founded in 1999 by Norwegian physicist Geir Bethelsen, who said that "the best thinking often comes from a walk in the 'slow lane'" (World Institute of Slowness, n.d.). According to Honoré (2015), Slow

> is a cultural revolution against the notion that faster is always better. The Slow philosophy is not about doing everything at a snail's pace. It's about seeking to do everything at the right speed … It's about quality over quantity in everything from work to food to parenting.

Like these movements, which advocate a return to traditional values of quality, slow journalism embraces time-honored principles of long-form reportage. It incorporates aspects of New Journalism, creative nonfiction, explanatory journalism, immersive journalism, "gonzo" journalism, ethnographic journalism, and literary journalism. Slow journalism favors in-depth reporting, accuracy, style, and context over being fast and first. It relies on the power of narrative and the telling detail, and it takes time to find things out. Launching the British quarterly *Delayed Gratification* in 2010, editors Marcus Webb and Rob Orchard described their magazine as an "antidote to throwaway media" which "measures news in months not minutes, returning to stories after the dust has settled" (Oliver 2010). "We're trying to give a definitive analysis of the past three months, and pick up on a lot of the stories that the other media miss," says Orchard. "You can look at *Delayed Gratification* as either a slow magazine—or a fast history book." *Delayed Gratification* is not alone, of course. Publications such as *The New Yorker* in the United States, *Granta* in the United Kingdom, and *XXI* in France have managed to maintain a strong narrative tradition despite the increasing pressures of time and finances. Other magazines, including *GQ*, *Vanity Fair*, *National Geographic*, *The New York Times Magazine*, and London's *Sunday Times Magazine* also invest in giving writers the time and resources to produce in-depth articles with a long shelf-life.

Currently, one of the most ambitious projects in the genre is *National Geographic*'s Out of Eden Walk, being undertaken by Paul Salopek, a two-time Pulitzer Prize-winning author who has dedicated his life and career to exploring the frontiers of slow journalism. Salopek has embarked on a seven-year, 22,000-mile reporting trip—on foot along the path of 60,000 years of human migration, from the oldest *Homo sapiens* site in Ethiopia to land's end at Tierra del Fuego, Chile. It is an epic journey that aims to create a unique record of life in the twenty-first century. It is also a textbook study in slow journalism that has inspired a university course in this emerging form of reportage.

The History of Slow Journalism

Although the term slow journalism is relatively new, its defining characteristics have roots that date to ancient storytellers. From the days of caves and campfires, riveting stories have been based on a synthesis of facts and observations emanating from an individual's lived experiences. Such stories define civilization. As Ursula Le Guin (1979, 31) noted, "There have been great societies that did not use the wheel, but there have been no societies that did not tell stories."

Even before the printing press, handwritten books contained the seeds of slow journalism. Medieval adventurers, for example, chronicled their exploits in epic travelogues. Around 1300, Rustichello da Pisa and Marco Polo wrote *Livres des Merveilles du Monde* (commonly titled *The Travels of Marco Polo*), describing Polo's trips through Asia and his interactions with Kublai Khan. Similarly, in 1355, the Moroccan scholar Abu Abdullah Muhammad Ibn Battuta detailed his journeys through the known Islamic world and beyond in *The Travels of Ibn Battuta*.

Qualities of slow journalism can be seen in what has been called "the first substantial work of modern journalism" (Miller 2011): *The Storm*, by Daniel Defoe. It was published in 1704, subtitled *A Collection of the Most Remarkable Casualties and Disasters Which Happen'd in the Late Dreadful Tempest, Both by Sea and Land*. The book described a weeklong storm that ravaged England the previous year, demolishing hundreds of homes and killing thousands of people. Not only did Defoe recount what he saw, but he also solicited personal accounts from fellow Londoners, blending his information with an eye for drama and human interest. Defoe went on to write *Robinson Crusoe* and achieve fame as a novelist, but he may have been the first slow journalist. Charles Dickens was another British journalist-novelist whose news reporting reflected features of slow journalism, including descriptive detail, realistic dialogue, and dramatic literary techniques. Dickens captured everyday life in London in *Sketches by Boz* in 1836 and *The Pickwick Papers* in 1836–1837 and turned his attention to the United States with *American Notes for General Circulation* in 1842. His societal portraits are often cited as literary journalism (Zdovc 2008, 10), a forerunner of slow journalism.

Literary journalists of the nineteenth century were versatile writers who could glide easily among genres. They provided "a challenge to or resistance against mainstream 'factual' or 'objective' news," according to John Hartsock (2000, 41–42). These writers developed a reporting style "designed to narrow the distance between the alienated subjectivity and the indeterminate object in a narrative strategy opposite that of objectified versions of journalism." This style was adopted by Mark Twain in *The Innocents Abroad, or The New Pilgrims' Progress*, which in 1869 described his travels through Europe and the Holy Land with a group of Americans. Another practitioner was Lafcadio Hearn, who employed the techniques as a newspaper reporter covering crime and other subjects in Cincinnati (1872–1877) and New Orleans (1877–1887) and then while writing magazine articles and books in Martinique and Japan. Hearn embedded himself in a community to write such accounts as *The Story of a West-Indian Slave*, published in 1890.

Slow journalists take a deep dive, and in that regard, Nellie Bly qualifies for *Ten Days in a Mad-House*, which ran as a series of articles in *The New York World* and then was published as a book in 1887. Feigning insanity, Bly was committed to the Women's Lunatic Asylum on Blackwell's Island and documented horrific conditions there. In the

1890s, champions of literary journalism included Lincoln Steffens, who as city editor of the *New York Commercial Advertiser* refused to hire old-school reporters in favor of writers who "openly or secretly, hoped to be a poet, a novelist, or an essayist" (Steffens 1931, 314); and Stephen Crane, whose keen critiques of everyday life informed his news reporting (the *New-York Tribune*) and novels (*The Red Badge of Courage*).

In the late nineteenth century, the muckraker Jacob Riis applied the new medium of the day—photography—to immersive journalism. He used his camera to document life in the slums in *How the Other Half Lives*, published in *Scribner's Magazine* in 1889 and then as a book, subtitled *Studies Among the Tenements of New York*, the following year. Riis may have inspired Jack London, who took a live-it-to-write-it approach to his journalism and novels. After living for several months and sometimes sleeping on the streets in London's East End, London published *The People of the Abyss* in 1903, a first-hand account of poverty there. London employed similar techniques in reporting on the Klondike Gold Rush and on the earthquake and fire that devastated San Francisco in 1906.

George Orwell used first-person reporting and other techniques of literary journalism in several works, including *Down and Out in Paris and London*, published in 1933, and *Homage to Catalonia*, his 1938 account of fighting in the Spanish Civil War. War provided the backdrop for other predecessors of slow journalism, including Alan McCrae Moorehead, who chronicled his experiences with Allied troops in North Africa in the early 1940s, and John Hersey, who reconstructed the dropping of the atomic bomb on Hiroshima from the residents' perspective. Hersey's *Hiroshima* was published first in *The New Yorker* and then as a book in 1946. Hersey's novelistic structure and evocative descriptions set the stage for a reporting style that came to be known as New Journalism—and it, too, laid the foundation for slow journalism. In 1966, examples included *In Cold Blood*, Truman Capote's book of a heinous murder and its aftermath, and *Hell's Angels: The Strange and Terrible Saga of the Outlaw Motorcycle Gangs*, by "gonzo journalist" Hunter S. Thompson. Two years later, Norman Mailer published *The Armies of the Night*, a "nonfiction novel" about an anti-war protest; Joan Didion published *Slouching Towards Bethlehem*, about California counterculture; and Tom Wolfe published *The Electric Kool-Aid Acid Test*, which invited readers to follow the author Ken Kesey and his Merry Pranksters through their LSD-driven bus trips across America. Such writing joined the intimacy and mood of fiction with the authority and accuracy of journalism. In *The New Journalism*, Wolfe and Johnson (1973, 31–32) issued a manifesto supporting this stylistic shift. New Journalism, he said, emphasized multiple viewpoints, strong scenes and dialogue, and rich characters and details. It often put the author at the center of the story, channeling a character's thoughts.

Wolfe was followed by writers who espoused more grit than gonzo, who favored the "literature of the everyday" over outlandish scenes and outsized characters, says Robert Boynton (2005, xv). He calls them *The New New Journalism*—the title of his 2005 anthology. Boynton says these writers "emphasize the importance of rigorous reporting on the events and characters of everyday life over turns of bravura in writing style. Reporting on the minutiae of the ordinary—often over a period of years—has become their signature method" (xv). The New New Journalists owed more to writers like John McPhee than to Wolfe. In tackling subjects ranging from nuclear weapons to fishing, McPhee has shunned putting himself at the center of the story and kept the focus on characters and narrative. A prime example is McPhee's 1976 book *Coming into the*

Country, about his travels through Alaska with bush pilots, prospectors, and others. Boynton's New New Journalists included Leon Dash, who used ethnographic research—living in impoverished neighborhoods and interviewing families over years—to produce a *Washington Post* series and a 1996 book, *Rosa Lee: A Mother and Her Family in Urban America*; Jon Krakauer, who joined a team climbing Mount Everest in 1996, witnessed the ensuing disaster, and then wrote an article for *Outside* magazine and a book, *Into Thin Air*; and Ted Conover, who lived as a hobo for his 1984 book *Rolling Nowhere* and worked as a prison guard for *Newjack: Guarding Sing Sing*, published in 2000. Conover is one kind of slow journalist: a participant in the story. He follows in a tradition of such reporters as John Howard Griffin, a white man who spent five weeks disguised as an African American in the South and then published *Black Like Me* in 1961. A more recent participant journalist is Barbara Ehrenreich, who worked undercover as a waitress and a maid and in other low-wage jobs for her 2001 book *Nickel and Dimed: On (Not) Getting By in America*.

Another type of slow journalist is more of an embedded observer. The late Richard Ben Cramer exemplified this fly-on-the-wall approach in his 1049-page chronicle of the 1988 presidential campaign, *What It Takes: The Way to the White House*. The book, published in 1992, is "widely considered the greatest modern presidential campaign book" (Smith 2010). Political campaigns, which are largely reported in a torrent of quick-hit articles, lend themselves to this long-view retelling. So do military campaigns, as Michael Herr demonstrated in 1977 with *Dispatches*, about the Vietnam War, and Ryszard Kapuściński showed in 1992 in *The Soccer War*, his reflections on covering conflicts in Africa, Latin America, and the Middle East for the Polish Press Agency.

Slow journalists imbue their work with a sense of place and prodigious research, amplifying otherwise-unheard voices. Katherine Boo spent three years interviewing residents and poring over documents for her 2012 book *Behind the Beautiful Forevers: Life, Death, and Hope in a Mumbai Undercity*. Les Zaitz spent nine months investigating the drug trade in the Pacific Northwest, interviewing narco-traffickers and drug users, as well as law enforcement officers, health officials and other experts, to produce a 2013 series for *The Oregonian* newspaper. Also Diana Marcum of *The Los Angeles Times* won a Pulitzer Prize in Feature Writing for her 2014 articles about the impact of drought on Californians—lyrical portraits that evoked John Steinbeck and Dorothea Lange.

Slow journalism and its antecedents traditionally have found a welcome in magazines, from *The Saturday Evening Post* to *Rolling Stone*. In recent years, numerous magazines have emerged with a focus on slow and long-form journalism. They include *The Atavist*, *Byliner*, *Compass Cultura*, *Epic*, *Latterly Magazine*, and *Narratively*, as well as *Long Play*, *Monocle*, and the aggregator *Longreads*. Those startups publish primarily if not exclusively online—and that represents another trend in slow journalism: the use of multimedia. Text is complemented by photo galleries, videos, maps, timelines, graphics, and other interactive elements. "Snow Fall: The Avalanche at Tunnel Creek," published online by *The New York Times* in 2012, epitomized how digital tools can create a dramatic and immersive environment for readers and viewers.

Just as Hartsock (2000, 3–6) cited disagreements over what constitutes literary journalism, there is no unanimous definition of slow journalism. To a large extent, it can be defined by what it is not: fast journalism. Slow journalism is a reaction against reportage that, to many media critics and consumers, seems rushed, superficial, and poorly informed. As Paul Salopek chronicles the Out of Eden Walk, he is following in the footsteps of centuries of journalistic traditions and innovations, including literary journalism, creative nonfiction, narrative journalism, immersive journalism, New (and newer) Journalism, ethnographic journalism, and multimedia journalism. Still, Salopek shares a goal with kindred writers from Ibn Battuta to Mark Twain to Tom Wolfe: to tell stories that reveal the human experience.

The Out of Eden Walk

When Salopek describes the Out of Eden Walk as slow journalism, he means it literally: he is purposely traveling in the manner that early humans used to explore their world—on foot, one step at a time. After planning the Out of Eden Walk for nearly two years, including in-depth research conducted during a Nieman Fellowship at Harvard, Salopek set out in January 2013 to trace the pathways of human migration out of Africa. He started from Herto Bouri, Ethiopia, where the earliest *Homo sapiens* site in Africa is being investigated by paleoanthropologist Tim White of the University of California, Berkeley. His final destination, Tierra del Fuego, Chile, lies at the southernmost tip of South America, where our ancestors finally arrived at land's end about 11,000 years ago.

A long-time practitioner of slow journalism for *National Geographic* and the *Chicago Tribune*, Salopek is reporting from the field using the latest in digital technology and communications, thus combining both ancient and ultra-modern methods of reportage. In an email, Salopek explained:

> This isn't just a walk about the past—the world as we first discovered it in the Pleistocene. It is a walk through what we've made of that world, a walk into the Anthropocene. I'm hoping to highlight that contrast as I move, noting the changes at ground level. But hopefully, by using the hi-tech tools of communication available today, the sat-phone, a small laptop, I can connect thinkers who see these changes from orbit, as it were—the big picture—with the lives of ordinary people grappling with the new uncertainties and challenges of surviving in a human-made world—whether beleaguered farmers, swelling ranks of urbanites, or innovators at the local level. (personal communication, March 11, 2013)

In addition to occasional long-form magazine pieces for *National Geographic*, Salopek is filing hundreds of dispatches, videos, photographs, sound files, interviews, social media posts, and map materials as he walks, providing followers with a wealth of fact-rich documentation about the geography, history, cultures, and current events along his route. The deliberate pace of Salopek's reportage, and its depth, allows the reader to linger over any detail, and, if interested, delve deeper into the subject to understand its context and meaning in relation to the broader trends Salopek is finding as he walks.

His approach is both prolific and systematic. Equipped with a GPS that enables him to map his exact route, Salopek pauses every 100 miles to record the editorial equivalent of a geologist's core sample, called a Milestone. Besides collecting basic data such as elevation and longitude and latitude, Salopek records audio and video of the location, documents it in photographs, samples the Twittersphere within a 50-mile radius (non-English tweets are later translated), and interviews the nearest human being, asking the same three questions: Who are you? Where do you come from? Where are you going?

Milestones are embedded on the project's interactive map, which serves to aggregate and make accessible all of Salopek's reporting. By the end of the Walk, these Milestones will number several thousand—and will be left as an open-source legacy for researchers and readers alike, an extraordinary cross-section of the places and people Salopek encountered as he walked around the world. Also available on the project's website are a number of interactive portals: Dispatches (translations of Salopek's blog posts for *National Geographic*, in 13 languages), Lab Talk (innovation for fellow journalists), Classroom (for educators), Map Room (featuring special map stories such as "Police Stops" and "Walking Jerusalem"), and other resources either created for or inspired by the slow approach to journalism at the core of the project.

Seen as a ground-breaking enterprise, the Out of Eden project has won support from *National Geographic*; the Knight Foundation; Harvard's Nieman Foundation, Graduate School of Education, and Center for Geographic Analysis; the Pulitzer Center on Crisis Reporting; and other organizations dedicated to journalism and education. The Walk was the focus of a program titled "Slow Journalism: Deep Storytelling in a Digital Age" that was held in January 2015 at the Newseum in Washington, DC. Frank Sesno, director of the School of Media and Public Affairs at George Washington University, moderated a panel of journalists and educators as they discussed the project. Salopek joined the program via Skype from Tblisi in the Republic of Georgia, where he had paused after walking along Turkey's perilous border with Syria. During the forum, Salopek pointed out that walking is our species' natural pace for encountering the world. On foot, there is time for the human brain to process new information and impressions and extract meaning from the ephemera of existence. Putting those impressions into words has always been the essence of a journalist's craft, from the grunts of the earliest campfire storytellers to the keyword-searchable narratives and tweets of today. Poetry is where you find it, as Evan Osnos of *The New Yorker*, one of the Newseum panelists, pointed out in his essay, "On Slow Journalism" (Osnos 2013). One night in Ethiopia, shortly after Salopek started his journey, he thumbed out this tweet: "No wells. Bummed murky water off nomads in this enormity. Electric blue moonlight the color of pure thought."

What Makes the Walk Slow Journalism

Salopek's chronicles of his odyssey exemplify slow journalism in several respects. He clearly reflects the characteristics of slow journalism articulated by journalism professor Mark Berkey-Gerard (2009). Berkey-Gerard wrote that slow journalism:

Gives up the fetish of beating the competition.

Values accuracy, quality, and context, not just being fast and first.

Avoids celebrity, sensation, and events covered by a herd of reporters.

Takes time to find things out.

Seeks out untold stories.

Relies on the power of narrative.

Sees the audience as collaborators.

Salopek is certainly taking his time to find things out: the Walk will take at least seven years. Along the way, he has demonstrated a commitment to conveying the stories of "real people"—stories that otherwise would go untold. As *National Geographic* described the project,

> Moving at the slow beat of his footsteps, Paul is engaging with the major stories of our time—from climate change to technological innovation, from mass migration to cultural survival—by walking alongside the people who inhabit them every day. As he traverses the globe from Africa to South America, he is revealing the texture of the lives of people he encounters: the nomads, villagers, traders, farmers, and fishermen who never make the news. (*National Geographic* 2013)

Salopek said he has embarked on this project for many reasons:

> to relearn the contours of our planet at the human pace of three miles an hour. To slow down. To think. To write. To render current events as a form of pilgrimage. I hope to repair certain important connections burned through by artificial speed, by inattentiveness. I walk, as everyone does, to see what lies ahead. I walk to remember. (Salopek 2013d)

Salopek infuses his dispatches with narrative; he truly tells stories, not just the news. Consider, for example, his report in December 2013 as he emerged from the Ethiopian desert to a paved road and industrial development: a sugar plantation that will create jobs and might help break the country's dependence on foreign aid.

> But the benefits of economic progress are rarely shared equally with all involved. There are winners and losers in every improvement scheme. Here, one of the losers is a bright young Afar woman—a girl, really, though her poise makes her seem old beyond her years. She is wrapped in a red dress. She stands by a new levee. She is collecting water from what used to be the Awash River.

> "The company moved us off our land," she tells us, waving her arm at the sheets of cane. "We get a little work, we Afars, but it is always the lowest work. Watchmen. Shovel work."

> A typical sugar plantation salary: $20 a month. The girl says police came to expel the Afar diehards who refused to move. Shots were exchanged. Blood flowed on both sides. (Salopek 2013d)

Salopek then relates the Afars' ordeal to the plights of Native Americans, Irish farmers, Mexican ranchers, and others who have been forced off their land. This context—thoughtful connections and historical background—is another feature of slow journalism. "Slow journalism allows me to make hidden connections that you miss when you travel too fast," Salopek told the audience at the Newseum. "The world is complicated, and we require more than just short bits of information" (Goldberg et al. 2015).

Salopek has described his approach to reporting as "immersive" and "an anthropological way of doing journalism" (Seminara 2015). "I'm interested in narrative, I'm interested in storytelling," he told National Public Radio (2013):

> After jetting around the world as a foreign correspondent, after flying into stories, after driving into them, helicoptering in, even, I thought about what it would be like to walk between stories. Not just to see the stories we were missing by flying over them, but to understand the connective tissue of all the major stories of our day.

Those compelling stories, recounted by everyday people and framed by historical background and on-the-ground insights, are emblematic of slow journalism. It is the kind of reporting Salopek has been doing throughout the Out of Eden Walk.

Teaching the Out of Eden Walk

If you want to walk fast, walk alone. If you want to walk far, walk together. (African proverb)

"Slow Journalism in a Fast World: The Out of Eden Experiment" is an intensive special topics seminar first offered by Virginia Commonwealth University's Robertson School of Media and Culture. Taught by Don Belt, longtime editor and chief foreign correspondent for *National Geographic*, students developed their multimedia storytelling skills—and their slow journalism skills—by using the Out of Eden Walk as a model. Belt's students applied the principles of slow journalism to semester-long narrative projects of their own, which were built upon in-depth field reporting they accumulated on foot in and around historic Richmond, Virginia. Along the way, students practiced all aspects of digital storytelling: research, story development, pitching, reporting, writing, photography, cartography, videography, social media, Web design, and platform building. Also because this was slow journalism, they created a uniquely perceptive record of their community, weaving in details that "fast" journalism would miss.

In the seminar, upper-level journalism students developed their multimedia narrative skills by studying and applying the lessons offered by Salopek's reporting project. The curriculum, like The Walk, was designed to explore the creative frontiers of slow journalism—a movement away from the hyperventilated, superficial coverage that dominates modern news media and toward a more in-depth, deliberate, mindful approach to narrative journalism using the latest tools of digital technology. Salopek and his Walk partners have set out to change the way digital journalists cover the world, and students were invited to become pioneers in that effort, applying the lessons of slow journalism to their class projects, their work, and their lives. Over the course of a 15-week semester, students read and analyzed the literature of the Walk, including the more than 150,000 words Salopek had published to date, along with a large and growing body of multimedia reporting. Students also were required to develop and execute a walk of their own, either individually or in small teams. They published their work online, both incrementally (via social media) and as a complete, multimedia project on the class website.

Interviewing Salopek and members of his creative team via Skype, students learned to build compelling narratives and practiced a range of reportorial skills. Course objectives were twofold:

1. To build students' global cultural literacy through engagement with the themes, literary style, and factual content (culture, history, geography, anthropology, geopolitics) of the Out of Eden Walk, based on the materials generated during the project's first year and a half.
2. To explore the horizons of slow journalism in a workshop and field setting, as students conceive, design, and implement a multimedia narrative project of their own design, based on the concepts and example of the Out of Eden Walk.

The main text for the course was the extensive and expanding body of written and multimedia work posted by Salopek, all available online. Students also read selected chapters from *The Storytelling Animal: How Stories Make Us Human*, by Jonathan Gottschall (2012), and *On Looking: A Walker's Guide to the Art of Observation*, by Alexandra Horowitz (2014).

Equipment. Although students conducted their fieldwork at a walking pace, they used the technology and tools of a working journalist—including notebooks, pens, a camera and video/audio recorder (or smartphone equivalent), computer, sneakers or walking shoes, and granola bars.

Online accounts. Students used their Facebook and/or Twitter account (Instagram optional), along with a class WordPress account or other blogging platform.

Key links. The primary bookmark was the Out of Eden Walk site, designed and maintained by Patrick Wellever at the MIT Science Journalism program. Students explored the site and signed up for project email alerts. Belt also created a closed Facebook group for the class to post announcements, assignments, and special readings. We also had students "like" the project's Facebook page and follow @paulsalopek and @outofedenwalk on Twitter. They also followed the Walk's Instagram feed.

Online resources

Project website: www.outofedenwalk.com.

NationalGeographic Dispatches: http://outofedenwalk.nationalgeographic.com.

Salopek's Twitter feed: https://twitter.com/PaulSalopek.

Out of Eden Walk's Twitter feed: https://twitter.com/outofedenwalk.

Out of Eden Walk's Instagram feed: http://instagram.com/outofedenwalk.

Out of Eden Walk's Facebook page: www.facebook.com/OutOfEdenWalk.

Weeks 1–5: Introduction, Orientation, Reading in Depth

During the first third of the course, the class studied the Out of Eden Walk as a modern digital manifestation of an ancient narrative tradition that has long been a foundational skill for a great reporter—one who deals not just in information, but in storytelling and meaning. The class discussed strategies for slowing down, taking time, and engaging in close, focused observation in contrast to the frenetic, the superficial, the "fast." We looked at Salopek's original project memo to understand his conceptual framework and think through the practicalities of such an audacious undertaking. Belt wanted students to get their heads around the project's daunting logistics and opportunities.

During the course, students were required to read all of Salopek's dispatches, engage with multimedia elements, and study his long-form articles about the Walk in *National Geographic*. For their written assignments, students did a combination of analytic and creative writing, along with multimedia assignments of increasing complexity, including mapping, photography, videography, sound recording, and Web design. We selected a number of Salopek's dispatches for in-class analysis. They helped students learn on several levels—about science (geography, geology, anthropology, climate change); about reporting (how to slow down, settle in, observe, and ask questions); and about telling the story (through the finely tuned use of first person, by offering key details, by connecting to meta ideas, and by adding value through links and multimedia). Students also learned how to render the drama, as Salopek did in his report on "The Things They Leave Behind":

> "Paul?" Alema hisses urgently in the dark. "Hey, Paul."

> But I have heard it already: a disturbance in the night air. A faint rumbling, growing almost imperceptibly louder, like the approach of herd [sic] of wild animals. But can there be animals in this place? The nearest blade of grass, the nearest well, is miles away. I sit up.

> And then they come, in the pale beam of Alema' s flashlight, a column of figures.

> They are men and women in a bas relief, as if carved in greys and blacks from the branches of the night. Five, six. A dozen. Then scores. They file past our camp in single file. I attempt to count them, but give up after reaching 90. Their shuffling feet raise a veil of dust. They don't look up. They carry no lights. They leave little behind. We exchange not a single word. My tongue is immobilized. (Salopek 2013a)

Weeks 6–10: Students Create a Walk of Their Own. This module was devoted to launching students on their own narrative walk projects. Because of the urban setting of the Virginia Commonwealth University campus and the time of year (winter and spring, much of it before daylight savings time), we assigned teams of two or three reporters to work together for security's sake. We sought to assemble teams with a diversity of viewpoints and professional strengths. Each reporting group was assigned to generate at least three ideas for a walk project and to reach a consensus on the order of preference. Students were required to present their ideas as "elevator pitches" to the class at large, with the group of 15 students encouraged to give constructive feedback. Belt provided guidance to help each group decide on its ultimate direction. The groups then developed their projects to a full proposal (one or two pages) that included both strategic and practical considerations. Each proposal detailed a narrative arc, a specific route, coverage plan, reporting strategies, the reporters' roles, social and multimedia strategies, and ways in which the principles of slow journalism would be applied. Students then presented their final story proposals to the entire class. Belt, in the role of editor-in-chief, ran this session as a formal story meeting, encouraging critical comments from other students before weighing in himself.

While continuing to study Salopek's dispatches, the class Skyped with Salopek (then in the West Bank) and Wellever, designer for the Out of Eden Walk website. We also met with a Richmond historian and archivist and interviewed a filmmaker with expertise on crowdfunding and on making broadcast-quality videos with smartphones. The class also continued to study dispatches, such as "Goodbye to Banounah" (Salopek 2013c), from which students learned about the use of memorable phrases, humor, and a sense of place, as well as how to add depth via self-awareness and how to engage readers. That article begins:

Banounah walks no farther. He has laid aside his walking stick. He has hung up his boonie cap.

He will not walk with us to the Jordanian frontier. He will not follow the old Haj trail from Sham or see the ruined Ottoman forts that crumble like rotting brown teeth atop the burning hills—how they guard nothing now except for the passage of the hot winds. Winds that send out flying columns of dust devils that spin atop the blistering plains. Whirlwinds that some call djinn. He will not cross the wadis where the tombs of Nabateans are cut into stone cliffs that glow the hue of fire-red clouds at sunset. He will not walk where Moses walked, dry-shod, onto the beaches of Arabia after parting the Red Sea.

Banounah is an ex-soldier. He is trained to keep pain stoppered, this time to his detriment. (When is it not?) And this trek, this strange journey, this forever walk begins to circle a familiar, melancholy topography, the rolling basin and range of new friends made and left behind: beloved people waving, one hand up in a parting salute, on the horizons. "We were a great team," Banounah, gripping my hand in his hospital bed, says hoarsely. "Weren't we?" (Salopek 2013c)

Weeks 10–15: Out of Eden, into Richmond. During the final phase of the course, students concentrated on publishing their walk-inspired reporting projects, devoted to subjects such as the proliferation of urban street murals, the local microbrew movement, cultural remnants of the Civil War (including monuments to the Confederacy), the human impact of a controversial development project, and a distinct urban subculture around the railways of Richmond. Every class meeting was a combination of reality check and progress report that included a tutorial on an aspect of reporting and preparing the stories for publication. Students collaborated on photos, multimedia, text, and mapping, seeking to post online content in the most compelling way. They revised their story drafts based on feedback from Belt. Also we introduced new open-source storytelling tools developed by the Knight Lab, such as StoryMap JS and Timeline JS, with tutorials contributed by Jeff South, an associate professor in Virginia Commonwealth University's Robertson School. As part of their final grade, students presented TED-style talks on their narrative projects, including a review of the strategy, editorial purpose, and execution of the final story. They also discussed what they learned from the Out of Eden Walk model. Final grades were based on quiz performance, interim assignments, final paper, posted reportage, triangular peer review, class participation, attitude, and leadership.

What Students Learn from the Walk

What students learn from the Walk depends, of course, on how they engage with it. Schoolchildren following Salopek's journey learn about geography, history, and different countries, cultures and religions. Project Zero, a research center at the Harvard Graduate School of Education, has launched an initiative called Out of Eden Learn. It is an online community of teachers and students across the world. "They explore their own neighborhoods, investigate contemporary global issues, and reflect on how they as individuals fit into a broader geographical and historical context," the project's website says (Out of Eden Learn n.d.). "The goal is to ignite students' interest in the wider world and support them to become more informed, thoughtful, and engaged 'global citizens.'"

"We have thousands of school kids around the world following this project using the Walk's journalism as a teaching tool," Salopek told the BBC (Seminara 2015). He said the Walk is "about reminding young people that the world is not a dangerous place. Thrill seekers who go on TV to do extreme things, by the very nature of what they do, they're implying that the world is a dangerous place. My philosophy is 180 degrees the opposite. The world is yours. Whether you realise it or not, you own it. You can walk through it as if you own it or you can fear it and be afraid to go out and claim it." Salopek added that the Walk is inspiring young people to explore their own environs with a critical eye. "You don't have to go to Patagonia. You don't have to go to Chechnya. Go out in your own neighbourhood and walk around. Take a notebook or an iPhone with you. Slow down and have a look around your own backyard, and you get to rediscover the world."

In May 2015, the Pulitzer Center convened a dozen university professors to discuss how the Walk could be used in college programs, with Belt's Virginia Commonwealth University curriculum as a practical guide and template. Afterward, Ann Peters (2015), the center's director of development and outreach, wrote, "The walk offers a unique window into early migration routes and modern-day issues—a terrific resource for educators in wide-ranging fields: anthropology, geography, environmental science, religion, journalism and more." For journalism students especially, the Walk offers an opportunity to learn a range of traditional and new skills. Salopek's journey has inspired young journalists to embark on local walks with a similar intent: to tell the stories of everyday people. In doing so, students learn how to:

- Do background research on the area they plan to explore.
- Pitch their idea to their professor and the class.
- Interview people along the route they have selected.
- Write engaging, narrative-driven stories.
- Take and edit photos of people and sights on their walk.
- Produce videos, and audio and slide shows about the walk.
- Use social media—such as blogs, Facebook, Twitter, Instagram, Flickr, and YouTube—to publish and promote their work.
- Design a website and use a content management system.
- Create an online map (e.g., using Google Maps or StoryMap JS) to offer a visualization of their walk.
- Curate the social media stream for content relevant to their focus.

In addition, students discuss crowdfunding and other ways to support such journalistic ventures. Above all, in narrating their own walks, students develop a sense of curiosity, strategies for learning new technologies and skills, and an appreciation for the virtues of slow reporting.

The Out of Eden Walk and the Future of Journalism

Speaking at the Newseum's slow journalism forum, *National Geographic* editor Susan Goldberg summarized the genre this way: "Fast journalism is mostly about information. Slow journalism is mostly about meaning" (Goldberg et al. 2015). Clearly, journalism is under immense pressure to adapt to a tumultuous media environment while preserving its vital role in a free society—seeking out and sharing information, speaking truth to power, and illuminating, through narrative, the verities of the human experience. As long as people walk the planet, we will need both factual news of the day and stories grounded in the realities of life to help us understand our world. As Paul Salopek and other journalists are demonstrating, slow reporting can open doors of understanding for modern readers and help them sift the torrent of bytes and sound bites to find the deeper meaning at ground level, present in the real lives of ordinary people whom journalists tend to overlook. Such accounts, well told, are rooted in the earliest forms of human storytelling, which can deliver not only goose bumps but empathy.

There is an extraordinary reporter walking the world right now who writes deeply, and sublimely, about the people he meets along the way. So it requires a certain humility to remind us how fleeting his reporting might be, as Salopek does in a sound clip embedded in "Goodbye to Alema" (Salopek 2013b). In that dispatch, the consummate slow journalist writes that the stories told by his departing cameleers about their shared journey through Ethiopia are more likely than the reporter's dispatches to stand the test of time:

> My stories fossilize the moment I put pen to paper, but in societies that are pre-literate, that tell the stories about who they are orally, the story changes all the time. Will it be as "accurate" as mine? Who's to say? But odds are it'll be truer. Because stories told verbally, through the years, what Muhammad and Khader will remember of these days, will be like river stones—smoothed by the tongue, rounded by repetition, improved upon by memory, so that only a core of truth remains that's important to the teller. Already, I think, in that sense, our paths have diverged. (Salopek 2013b)

DISCLOSURE STATEMENT

No potential conflict of interest was reported by the authors.

REFERENCES

Berkey-Gerard, Mark. 2009. "Tracking the 'Slow Journalism' Movement." *Campfire Journalism Blog*, July 29. http://markberkeygerard.com/2009/07/.

Boynton, Robert. 2005. *The New New Journalism*. New York: Vintage Books.

Castells, Manuel. 1998. *End of Millennium. The Information Age: Economy, Society and Culture, Volume III*. Malden, MA: Blackwell Publishers.

Davies, Nick. 2009. *Flat Earth News: An Award-winning Reporter Exposes Falsehood, Distortion and Propaganda in the Global Media*. London: Vintage.

Goldberg, Susan, Ann Marie Lipinksi, Evan Osnos, and Paul Salopek. 2015, January 13. "Slow Journalism: Deep Storytelling in a Digital Age." Panel discussion at the Newseum, Washington, DC.

Gottschall, Jonathan. 2012. *The Storytelling Animal: How Stories Make Us Human*. New York: Houghton Mifflin Harcourt.

Greenberg, Susan. 2007. "Slow Journalism." *Prospect*, February 26. http://www.prospect magazine.co.uk/magazine/slowjournalism/#.UiahWuDtKfR.

Hartsock, John. 2000. *A History of American Literary Journalism: The Emergence of a Modern Narrative Form*. Amherst, MA: University of Massachusetts Press.

Honoré, Carl. 2015. "In Praise of Slow." http://www.carlhonore.com/books/in-praise-of-slow ness/.

Honoré, Carl. 2005, July. "In Praise of Slowness." *Filmed*. TED video, 19:14. Posted February 2007. http://www.ted.com/talks/carl_honore_praises_slowness.

Horowitz, Alexandra. 2014. *On Looking: A Walker's Guide to the Art of Observation*. New York: Scribner.

James, Josh. 2015. "Data Never Sleeps 3.0." *Domosphere Blog*, August 13. https://www.domo.com/blog/2015/08/data-never-sleeps-3-0/.

Le Guin, Ursula. 1979. *The Language of the Night: Essays on Fantasy and Science Fiction*. New York: Ultramarine Publishing.

Le Masurier, Megan. 2015. "What is Slow Journalism?" *Journalism Practice* 9 (2):138-152. doi:10.1080/17512786.2014.916471.

Miller, John. 2011. "Writing up a Storm." *The Wall Street Journal*, August 13. http://www.wsj.com/articles/SB10001424053111904800304576476142821212156.

National Geographic. 2013. "About the Journey: A Walk through Time." *Out of Eden Walk*, January 22. http://outofedenwalk.nationalgeographic.com/about/.

National Public Radio. 2013. "What Do You Pack for a Seven-year Trip?" *NPR*, January 10. http://www.npr.org/2013/01/10/168961210/what-do-you-pack-for-a-seven-year-trip.

Oliver, Laura. 2010. "Delayed Gratification: New Magazine Launches Dedicated to 'Slow Journalism." *Journalism.Co.Uk*, December 13. https://www.journalism.co.uk/news/delayed-gratification-new-magazine-launches-dedicated-to-slow-journalism-/s2/a541963/.

Osnos, Evan. 2013. "On Slow Journalism." *The New Yorker*, January 31. http://www.newyorker.com/news/daily-comment/on-slow-journalism/.

Out of Eden Learn. n.d. "About Us." Project Zero at the Harvard Graduate School of Education. Accessed July 11, 2015. http://learn.outofedenwalk.com/about/.

Peters, Ann. 2015. "Out of Eden Walk Workshop for University Professors with Don Belt." *Pulitzer Center Blog*, May 18. http://pulitzercenter.org/blog/out-eden-walk-workshop-university-professors-paul-salopek-slow-journalism.

Salopek, Paul. 2013a. "The Things They Leave behind." *National Geographic out of Eden Walk*, March 10. http://outofedenwalk.nationalgeographic.com/2013/03/10/the-things-they-leave-behind.

Salopek, Paul. 2013b. "Goodbye to Alema." *National Geographic out of Eden Walk*, March 15. http://outofedenwalk.nationalgeographic.com/2013/03/15/goodbye-to-alema/.

Salopek, Paul. 2013c. "Goodbye to Banounah." *National Geographic out of Eden Walk*, September 18. http://outofedenwalk.nationalgeographic.com/2013/09/18/goodbye-to-banounah.

Salopek, Paul. 2013d. "To Walk the World." *National Geographic*, December. http://ngm.nationalgeographic.com/2013/12/out-of-eden/salopek-text.

Seminara, Dave. 2015. "Paul Salopek." *BBC Travel*, March. http://www.bbc.com/travel/bespoke/story/20150326-travel-pioneers/paul-salopek/.

Slow Food. 2010. *Slow Food Manifesto*. http://www.slowfood.com/_2010_pagine/com/popup_pagina.lasso?-id_pg=121.

Smith, Ben. 2010. "The Book That Defined Modern Campaign Reporting." *Politico*, December 30. http://www.politico.com/news/stories/1210/46906.html.

Steffens, Lincoln. 1931. *The Autobiography of Lincoln Steffens*. vol. 1. Berkeley, CA: Heyday.

Wolfe, Tom, and E. W. Johnson. 1973. *The New Journalism*. New York: Harper and Row.

World Institute of Slowness. n.d. "Home Page." Accessed July 11, 2015. http://www.theworldinstituteofslowness.com/.

Zdovc, Sonja Merljak. 2008. *Literary Journalism in the United States of America and Slovenia*. Lanham, Maryland: University Press of America.

Index

For Product Safety Concerns and Information please contact our EU
representative GPSR@taylorandfrancis.com
Taylor & Francis Verlag GmbH, Kaufingerstraße 24, 80331 München, Germany

www.ingramcontent.com/pod-product-compliance
Ingram Content Group UK Ltd.
Pitfield, Milton Keynes, MK11 3LW, UK
UKHW051832180425
457613UK00022B/1222